شرح

الأصول الثلاثة

The Explanation of

THE THREE FUNDAMENTAL PRINCIPLES

Shaykh Ṣāliḥ al-Fawzān

ISBN: 978-1-7923-0837-6 (softback)
978-1-7923-0955-7 (hardback)

First Edition: Sha'bān 1440 AH / April 2019 CE

Cover Design: Usul Design
Email: info@usuldesign.com

Translator: Raha Batts

Editing & Formatting: Danielle Lebenson al-Amrikiyyah
www.amrikiyyahdesign.com

Publisher's Information:
Authentic Statements Publishing
P.O. Box 15536
Philadelphia, PA 19131
215.382.3382
215.382.3782 – Fax

Store:
5000 Locust St.(Side Entrance)
Philadelphia, PA 19139

Website: www.authenticstatements.com
E-mail: info@authenticstatements.com

Transliteration Table

Consonants

ء	'	د	d	ض	ḍ	ك	k
ب	b	ذ	dh	ط	ṭ	ل	l
ت	t	ر	r	ظ	ẓ	م	m
ث	th	ز	z	ع	ʿ	ن	n
ج	j	س	s	غ	gh	ه	h
ح	ḥ	ش	sh	ف	f	و	w
خ	kh	ص	ṣ	ق	q	ي	y

Vowels

Short	ـَ	a	ـِ	i	ـُ	u
Long	ـَا	ā	ـِي	ī	ـُو	ū
Diphthongs	ـَيْ	ay	ـَوْ	aw		

Glyphs

ﷺ *Ṣallāllāhu ʿalayhi wa sallam* (May Allāh's praise & salutations be upon him)

عليه السلام *ʿAlayhis-salām* (Peace be upon him) / عليهم السلام *ʿAlayhim as-salām* (Peace be upon them)

رضي الله عنه *Raḍiyallāhu ʿanhu* (May Allāh be pleased with him)

رضي الله عنهما *Raḍiyallāhu ʿanhumā* (May Allāh be pleased with them both)

رضي الله عنها *Raḍiyallāhu ʿanhā* (May Allāh be pleased with her)

رحمه الله *Raḥimahullāh* (May Allāh have mercy on him)

تبارك وتعالى *Tabāraka wa Taʿālā* (Blessed and Exalted be He)

سبحانه وتعالى *Subḥānahu wa Taʿālā* (Glorified and Exalted be He)

عز وجل *ʿAzza wa Jall* (The Mighty and Majestic)

جل وعلا *Jalla wa ʿAlā* (The Majestic and High)

CONTENTS

01

Translator's Foreword

All praise is due to Allāh, the Lord of all that exists. May the prayers and peace from Allāh be upon our Prophet Muhammad, his family members, and his Companions, altogether.

To proceed: Indeed, it pleases me to have a hand in presenting to the English-speaking Muslims another magnificent explanation of this great work: *The Three Fundamental Principles*, this explanation being by Shaykh Ṣāliḥ bin Fawzān al-Fawzān, may Allāh preserve him.

Previously, our brothers at Authentic Statements published the first portion of the book under the title *The Three Treatises*, which was an explanation of the introduction only. In this version, we have the complete explanation of the book itself, along with the introduction, and all praise is due to Allāh with whose aid the good deeds are completed.

As an added benefit, the Arabic text of the book has been placed in the beginning to assist in the memorization of this great work, for those who wish to do so. Thanks are due to brother Abu Rumaysah Mujahid for facilitating the production of this work; to Abu Qaylah Rasheed Barbee for his checking of the translation; to sister Umm Yaasir for her transcription of the manuscript; and to all else who played a role in the production of this work.

I pray that Allāh makes it a benefit for the Muslims, and that He rewards the author, the explainer, the translator, and all involved in its production with the best reward; indeed, He is Ever-Near and Responsive.

And the last of our supplications is:

الحمد لله رب العالمين.

All praise is due to Allāh, the Lord of all that exists.

Aboo Moosaa Raha bin Donald Batts, Durham, NC
April 23, 2013 CE / 13 Jumādā ath-Thānī 1434 AH

02

Arabic Text of The Three Fundamental Principles

بِسْمِ ٱللَّهِ ٱلرَّحْمَٰنِ ٱلرَّحِيمِ

اِعْلَمْ - رَحِمَكَ اللهُ – أَنَّهُ يَجِبُ عَلَيْنَا تَعَلُّمُ أَرْبَعِ مَسَائِلَ, اَلْأُولَى: اَلْعِلْمُ وَ هُوَ مَعْرِفَةُ اللهِ, وَ مَعْرِفَةُ نَبِيِّهِ, وَ مَعْرِفَةُ دِينِ الْإِسْلَامِ بِالْأَدِلَّةِ. اَلثَّانِيَةُ: اَلْعَمَلُ بِهِ اَلثَالِثَةُ: الدَّعْوَةُ إِلَيْهِ. اَلرَّابِعَةُ: اَلصَّبْرُ عَلَى الْأَذَى فِيهِ. وَ الدَّلِيلُ قَوْلُهُ تَعَالَى: ﴿ وَالْعَصْرِ ۝١ إِنَّ الْإِنسَانَ لَفِي خُسْرٍ ۝٢ إِلَّا الَّذِينَ آمَنُوا وَعَمِلُوا الصَّالِحَاتِ وَتَوَاصَوْا بِالْحَقِّ وَتَوَاصَوْا بِالصَّبْرِ ۝٣ ﴾ [العصر: ٣-١]. قَالَ الشَّافِعِي - رَحِمَهُ اللهُ -: لَوْ مَا أَنْزَلَ اللهُ حُجَّةً عَلَى خَلْقِهِ إِلَّا هَذِهِ السُّورَةَ لَكَفَتْهُمْ وَ قَالَ الْبُخَارِي – رَحِمَهُ اللهُ تَعَالَى -: بَابُ الْعِلْمِ قَبْلَ الْقَوْلِ وَ الْعَمَلِ. وَ الدَّلِيلُ: ﴿فَاعْلَمْ أَنَّهُ لَا إِلَهَ إِلَّا اللَّهُ وَاسْتَغْفِرْ لِذَنبِكَ﴾ [محمد:٩١]. فَبَدَأَ بِالْعِلْمِ قَبْلَ الْقَوْلِ وَ الْعَمَلِ. اِعْلَمْ - رَحِمَكَ اللهُ – أَنَّهُ يَجِبُ عَلَى كُلِّ مُسْلِمٍ وَ مُسْلِمَةٍ تَعَلُّمُ ثَلَاثِ هَذِهِ الْمَسَائِلِ وَ الْعَمَلُ بِهِنَّ.

اَلْأُولَى: أَنَّ اللهَ خَلَقَنَا وَ رَزَقَنَا, وَ لَمْ يَتْرُكْنَا هَمَلاً. بَلْ أَرْسَلَ إِلَيْنَا رَسُولاً. فَمَنْ أَطَاعَهُ دَخَلَ الْجَنَّةَ, وَ مَنْ عَصَاهُ دَخَلَ النَّارَ. وَ الدَّلِيلُ قَوْلُهُ تَعَالَى: ﴿ إِنَّا أَرْسَلْنَا إِلَيْكُمْ رَسُولًا شَاهِدًا عَلَيْكُمْ كَمَا أَرْسَلْنَا إِلَىٰ فِرْعَوْنَ رَسُولًا ﴿١٥﴾ فَعَصَىٰ فِرْعَوْنُ الرَّسُولَ فَأَخَذْنَاهُ أَخْذًا وَبِيلًا ﴿١٦﴾﴾ [المزمل: ١٦ – ١٥].

اَلثَّانِيَةُ: أَنَّ اللهَ لَا يَرْضَى أَنْ يُشْرَكَ مَعَهُ أَحَدٌ غَيْرُهُ فِي عِبَادَتِهِ, لَا مَلَكٌ مُقَرَّبٌ وَ لَا نَبِيٌّ مُرْسَلٌ. وَ الدَّلِيلُ قَوْلُهُ تَعَالَى: ﴿وَأَنَّ الْمَسَاجِدَ لِلَّهِ فَلَا تَدْعُوا مَعَ اللَّهِ أَحَدًا﴾ [الجن: ١٨].

اَلثَّالِثَةُ: أَنَّ مَنْ أَطَاعَ الرَّسُولَ, وَ وَحَّدَ اللهَ, لَا يَجُوزُ لَهُ مُوَالَاةُ مَنْ حَادَّ اللهَ وَ رَسُولَهُ وَ لَوْ كَانَ أَقْرَبَ قَرِيبٍ وَ الدَّلِيلُ قَوْلُهُ تَعَالَى: ﴿ لَّا تَجِدُ قَوْمًا يُؤْمِنُونَ بِاللَّهِ وَالْيَوْمِ الْآخِرِ يُوَادُّونَ مَنْ حَادَّ اللَّهَ وَرَسُولَهُ وَلَوْ كَانُوا آبَاءَهُمْ أَوْ أَبْنَاءَهُمْ أَوْ إِخْوَانَهُمْ أَوْ عَشِيرَتَهُمْ ۚ أُولَٰئِكَ كَتَبَ فِي قُلُوبِهِمُ الْإِيمَانَ وَأَيَّدَهُم بِرُوحٍ مِّنْهُ ۖ وَيُدْخِلُهُمْ جَنَّاتٍ تَجْرِي مِن تَحْتِهَا الْأَنْهَارُ خَالِدِينَ فِيهَا ۚ رَضِيَ اللَّهُ عَنْهُمْ وَرَضُوا عَنْهُ ۚ أُولَٰئِكَ حِزْبُ اللَّهِ ۚ أَلَا إِنَّ حِزْبَ اللَّهِ هُمُ الْمُفْلِحُونَ ﴾ [المجادلة: ٢٢].

اِعْلَمْ أَرْشَدَكَ اللهُ لِطَاعَتِهِ, أَنَّ الْحَنِيفِيَّةَ مِلَّةَ إِبْرَاهِيمَ أَنْ تَعْبُدَ اللهَ مُخْلِصًا لَهُ الدِّينَ. وَ بِذَلِكَ أَمَرَ اللهُ جَمِيعَ النَّاسِ, وَ خَلَقَهُمْ لَهَا كَمَا قَالَ تَعَالَى: ﴿وَمَا خَلَقْتُ الْجِنَّ وَالْإِنسَ إِلَّا لِيَعْبُدُونِ﴾ [الذاريات: ٦٥]. وَ مَعْنَى (يَعْبُدُونِ): يُوَحِّدُونِ. وَ أَعْظَمُ مَا أَمَرَ اللهُ بِهِ التَّوْحِيدُ, وَ هُوَ إِفْرَادُ اللهِ بِالْعِبَادَةِ, وَ أَعْظَمُ مَا نَهَى عَنْهُ الشِّرْكُ, وَ هُوَ دَعْوَةُ غَيْرِهِ مَعَهُ وَ الدَّلِيلُ قَوْلُهُ تَعَالَى: ﴿وَاعْبُدُوا اللَّهَ وَلَا تُشْرِكُوا بِهِ شَيْئًا﴾ [النساء: ٣٦].

فَإِذَا قِيلَ لَكَ: مَا الْأُصُولُ الثَّلَاثَةُ الَّتِي يَجِبُ عَلَى الْإِنْسَانِ مَعْرِفَتُهَا؟ فَقُلْ: مَعْرِفَةُ الْعَبْدِ رَبَّهُ، وَ دِينَهُ، وَ نَبِيَّهُ مُحَمَّدًا – صَلَّى اللهُ عَلَيْهِ وَ سَلَّمَ. فَإِذَا قِيلَ لَكَ: مَنْ رَبُّكَ؟ فَقُلْ: رَبِّي اللهُ الَّذِي رَبَّانِي وَ رَبَّى جَمِيعَ الْعَالَمِينَ بِنِعَمِهِ. وَ هُوَ مَعْبُودِي لَيْسَ لِي مَعْبُودٌ سِوَاهُ. وَ الدَّلِيلُ قَوْلُهُ تَعَالَى: ﴿الْحَمْدُ لِلَّهِ رَبِّ الْعَالَمِينَ﴾ [الفاتحة: ٢] وَ كُلُّ مَا سِوَى اللهِ عَالَمٌ وَ أَنَا وَاحِدٌ مِنْ ذَلِكَ الْعَالَمِ. فَإِذَا قِيلَ لَكَ: بِمَا عَرَفْتَ رَبَّكَ؟ فَقُلْ: بِآيَاتِهِ وَ مَخْلُوقَاتِهِ. وَ مِنْ آيَاتِهِ اللَّيْلُ وَ النَّهَارُ وَ الشَّمْسُ وَ الْقَمَرُ. وَ مِنْ مَخْلُوقَاتِهِ: السَّمَوَاتُ السَّبْعُ، وَ الْأَرَضُونَ السَّبْعُ وَ مَا فِيهِنَّ، وَ مَا بَيْنَهُمَا، وَ الدَّلِيلُ قَوْلُهُ تَعَالَى: ﴿وَمِنْ آيَاتِهِ اللَّيْلُ وَالنَّهَارُ وَالشَّمْسُ وَالْقَمَرُ ۚ لَا تَسْجُدُوا لِلشَّمْسِ وَلَا لِلْقَمَرِ وَاسْجُدُوا لِلَّهِ الَّذِي خَلَقَهُنَّ إِن كُنتُمْ إِيَّاهُ تَعْبُدُونَ﴾ [فصلت: ٣٧] وَ الدَّلِيلُ قَوْلُهُ تَعَالَى: ﴿إِنَّ رَبَّكُمُ اللَّهُ الَّذِي خَلَقَ السَّمَاوَاتِ وَالْأَرْضَ فِي سِتَّةِ أَيَّامٍ ثُمَّ اسْتَوَىٰ عَلَى الْعَرْشِ يُغْشِي اللَّيْلَ النَّهَارَ يَطْلُبُهُ حَثِيثًا وَالشَّمْسَ وَالْقَمَرَ وَالنُّجُومَ مُسَخَّرَاتٍ بِأَمْرِهِ ۗ أَلَا لَهُ الْخَلْقُ وَالْأَمْرُ ۗ تَبَارَكَ اللَّهُ رَبُّ الْعَالَمِينَ﴾ [الأعراف: ٥٤] وَ الرَّبُّ هُوَ الْمَعْبُودُ، وَ الدَّلِيلُ قَوْلُهُ: ﴿يَا أَيُّهَا النَّاسُ اعْبُدُوا رَبَّكُمُ الَّذِي خَلَقَكُمْ وَالَّذِينَ مِن قَبْلِكُمْ لَعَلَّكُمْ تَتَّقُونَ ﴿٢١﴾ الَّذِي جَعَلَ لَكُمُ الْأَرْضَ فِرَاشًا وَالسَّمَاءَ بِنَاءً وَأَنزَلَ مِنَ السَّمَاءِ مَاءً فَأَخْرَجَ بِهِ مِنَ الثَّمَرَاتِ رِزْقًا لَّكُمْ ۖ فَلَا تَجْعَلُوا لِلَّهِ أَندَادًا وَأَنتُمْ تَعْلَمُونَ ﴿٢٢﴾﴾ [البقرة: ٢٢-٢١]. قَالَ ابْنُ كَثِيرٍ: الْخَالِقُ لِهَذِهِ الْأَشْيَاءِ هُوَ الْمُسْتَحِقُّ لِلْعِبَادَةِ.

وَ أَنْوَاعُ الْعِبَادَةِ الَّتِي أَمَرَ اللهُ بِهَا مِثْلَ الْإِسْلَامِ وَ الْإِيمَانِ وَ الْإِحْسَانِ، وَ مِنْهُ الدُّعَاءُ، وَ الْخَوْفُ، وَ الرَّجَاءُ، وَ التَّوَكُّلُ، وَ الرَّغْبَةُ، وَ الرَّهْبَةُ، وَ الْخُشُوعُ، وَ الْخَشْيَةُ، وَ الْإِنَابَةُ، وَ الْإِسْتِعَانَةُ،

وَ الْإِسْتِعَاذَةُ, وَ الْإِسْتِغَاثَةُ, وَ الذَّبْحُ, وَ النَّذْرُ, وَ غَيْرُ ذَلِكَ مِنْ أَنْوَاعِ الْعِبَادَةِ الَّتِي أَمَرَ اللهُ بِهَا, كُلُّهَا للهِ تَعَالَى.

وَ الدَّلِيلُ قَوْلُهُ تَعَالَى: ﴿وَأَنَّ الْمَسَاجِدَ لِلَّهِ فَلَا تَدْعُوا مَعَ اللَّهِ أَحَدًا﴾ [الجن: ١٨]. فَمَنْ صَرَفَ مِنْهَا شَيْئًا لِغَيْرِ اللهِ, فَهُوَ مُشْرِكٌ كَافِرٌ وَ الدَّلِيلُ قَوْلُهُ تَعَالَى: ﴿وَمَن يَدْعُ مَعَ اللَّهِ إِلَـٰهًا آخَرَ لَا بُرْهَانَ لَهُ بِهِ فَإِنَّمَا حِسَابُهُ عِندَ رَبِّهِ ۚ إِنَّهُ لَا يُفْلِحُ الْكَافِرُونَ﴾ [المؤمنون: ١١٧]. وَ فِي الْحَدِيثِ: ((الدُّعَاءُ مُخُّ الْعِبَادَةِ)). وَ الدَّلِيلُ: قَوْلُهُ تَعَالَى: ﴿وَقَالَ رَبُّكُمُ ادْعُونِي أَسْتَجِبْ لَكُمْ ۚ إِنَّ الَّذِينَ يَسْتَكْبِرُونَ عَنْ عِبَادَتِي سَيَدْخُلُونَ جَهَنَّمَ دَاخِرِينَ﴾ [غافر: ٦٠].

وَ دَلِيلُ الْخَوْفِ قَوْلُهُ تَعَالَى: ﴿فَلَا تَخَافُوهُمْ وَخَافُونِ إِن كُنتُم مُّؤْمِنِينَ﴾ [آل عمران: ١٧٥]. وَ دَلِيلُ الرَّجَاءِ قَوْلُهُ تَعَالَى: ﴿فَمَن كَانَ يَرْجُو لِقَاءَ رَبِّهِ فَلْيَعْمَلْ عَمَلًا صَالِحًا وَلَا يُشْرِكْ بِعِبَادَةِ رَبِّهِ أَحَدًا﴾ [الكهف: ١١٠]. وَ دَلِيلُ التَّوَكُّلِ قَوْلُهُ تَعَالَى: ﴿وَعَلَى اللَّهِ فَتَوَكَّلُوا إِن كُنتُم مُّؤْمِنِينَ﴾ [المائدة: ٢٣]. وَ قَوْلُهُ تَعَالَى: ﴿وَمَن يَتَوَكَّلْ عَلَى اللَّهِ فَهُوَ حَسْبُهُ﴾ [الطلاق: ٣]. وَ دَلِيلُ الرَّغْبَةِ وَ الرَّهْبَةِ وَ الْخُشُوعِ قَوْلُهُ تَعَالَى: ﴿إِنَّهُمْ كَانُوا يُسَارِعُونَ فِي الْخَيْرَاتِ وَيَدْعُونَنَا رَغَبًا وَرَهَبًا ۖ وَكَانُوا لَنَا خَاشِعِينَ﴾ [الأنبياء: ٩٠]. وَ دَلِيلُ الْخَشْيَةِ قَوْلُهُ تَعَالَى: ﴿فَلَا تَخْشَوْهُمْ وَاخْشَوْنِي﴾ [البقرة: ١٥٠]. وَ دَلِيلُ الْإِنَابَةِ قَوْلُهُ: ﴿وَأَنِيبُوا إِلَىٰ رَبِّكُمْ وَأَسْلِمُوا لَهُ﴾ [الزمر: ٥٤]. وَ دَلِيلُ الْإِسْتِعَانَةِ قَوْلُهُ تَعَالَى: ﴿إِيَّاكَ نَعْبُدُ وَإِيَّاكَ نَسْتَعِينُ﴾ [الفاتحة: ٥]. وَ فِي الْحَدِيثِ: ((إِذَا اسْتَعَنْتَ فَاسْتَعِنْ بِاللهِ)) وَ دَلِيلُ الْإِسْتِعَاذَةِ قَوْلُهُ تَعَالَى: ﴿قُلْ أَعُوذُ بِرَبِّ الْفَلَقِ﴾ [الفلق: ١]. وَ قَوْلُهُ تَعَالَى:

بِالطَّاغُوتِ, وَ الإِيْمَانُ بِاللهِ. قَالَ ابْنُ الْقَيِّمِ - رَحِمَهُ اللهُ تَعَالَى -: (مَعْنَى (الطَّاغُوتِ): مَا تَجَاوَزَ بِهِ الْعَبْدُ حَدَّهُ مِنْ مَعْبُودٍ أَوْ مَتْبُوعٍ أَوْ مُطَاعٍ)).

وَ الطَّوَاغِيتُ كَثِيرٌ رُؤُوسُهُمْ خَمْسَةٌ: إِبْلِيسُ لَعَنَهُ اللهُ, وَ مَنْ حَكَمَ بِغَيْرِ مَا أَنْزَلَ اللهُ, وَ الدَّلِيلُ قَوْلُهُ تَعَالَى: ﴿لَا إِكْرَاهَ فِي الدِّينِ ۖ قَد تَّبَيَّنَ الرُّشْدُ مِنَ الْغَيِّ ۚ فَمَن يَكْفُرْ بِالطَّاغُوتِ وَيُؤْمِن بِاللَّهِ فَقَدِ اسْتَمْسَكَ بِالْعُرْوَةِ الْوُثْقَىٰ لَا انفِصَامَ لَهَا ۗ وَاللَّهُ سَمِيعٌ عَلِيمٌ﴾[البقرة: ٢٥٦],وَ هَذَا مَعْنَى لَا إِلَهَ إِلَّا اللهُ. وَ فِي الْحَدِيثِ: ((رَأْسُ الْأَمْرِ الْإِسْلَامِ, وَ عَمُودُهُ الصَّلَاةُ, وَ ذِرْوَةُ سَنَامِهِ الْجِهَادُ فِي سَبِيلِ اللهِ)), وَ اللهُ أَعْلَمُ. وَ صَلَّى اللهُ عَلَى نَبِيِّنَا مُحَمَّدٍ, وَ عَلَى آلِهِ وَ صَحْبِهِ وَ سَلَّمَ.

03

Author's Introduction

ORIGINAL TEXT

قال رحمه الله: بسم الله الرحمن الرحيم.

The author, may Allāh have mercy upon him, said:

In the name of Allāh, the Most Merciful, the Bestower of Mercy.

EXPLANATION

He ﷺ began with the *basmalah,*[1] following the example of the Book of Allāh ﷻ. The first thing your vision lands upon in the *muṣ'ḥaf* and before every chapter in it is the *basmalah*; hence, one is to begin with it in letters, books, and writings, following the example of the Book of Allāh. Likewise, the Prophet ﷺ would write it at the beginning of his letters which he wrote to the rulers and leaders and to the various places of the earth calling them to Islām; he would begin his writing with the *basmalah*.

Likewise, he would begin his addresses and speeches with the *basmalah*, and this indicates that beginning with the *basmalah* is

1 **Translator's Note:** The *basmalah* is the statement "In the name of Allāh, the Most Merciful, the Bestower of Mercy" (بسم الله الرحمن الرحيم). This is different from the *tasmiyah* (the mentioning of Allāh's name), which is the phrase "In the name of Allāh" (بسم الله).

the Sunnah of the Messenger ﷺ; just as with Sulaymān عليه السلام when he wrote to Bilqīs, the Queen of Saba'—he began his letter with the *basmalah*.

﴿ قَالَتْ يَا أَيُّهَا الْمَلَأُ إِنِّي أُلْقِيَ إِلَيَّ كِتَابٌ كَرِيمٌ ﴿٢٩﴾ إِنَّهُ مِن سُلَيْمَانَ وَإِنَّهُ بِسْمِ اللَّهِ الرَّحْمَٰنِ الرَّحِيمِ ﴿٣٠﴾ أَلَّا تَعْلُوا عَلَيَّ وَأْتُونِي مُسْلِمِينَ ﴿٣١﴾ ﴾

She said, "O chiefs! Verily! Here is delivered to me a noble letter; verily! It is from Sulaymān, and verily! It (reads): 'In the name of Allāh, the Most Beneficent, the Most Merciful; be you not exalted against me, but come to me as Muslims (true believers who submit to Allāh with full submission).'"

[Sūrah an-Naml 27:29-31]

Hence, it is proper to begin with the *basmalah* in every important affair, every important writing, and every letter.

Based upon this, those who do not begin their writings and letters with the *basmalah* have abandoned the Prophetic Sunnah and following the example of the Book of Allāh. And perhaps due to this, these books and writings of theirs contain no blessing. They are of no benefit. This is because they are devoid of the *basmalah*, so the benefit has been snatched away from them. Why would they abandon the *basmalah*? They have only abandoned it because it is the Sunnah and they flee from the Sunnah, or they blindly follow someone who flees from the Sunnah. Therefore, one must beware of the likes of this.

The meaning of the *basmalah* is: seeking help, in the name of Allāh. The statement "In the name of Allāh" (بسم الله) is a genitive phrase connected to a latent phrase (i.e., implied but not written), which is: "I seek help, in the name of Allāh, the Most Merciful, the Bestower of Mercy," or: "I begin with the name of Allāh, the Most Merciful, the Bestower of Mercy, seeking blessings and the aid of Allāh by way of it."

Therefore, it is a tremendous preface to speech, books, and letters, for the person is seeking help with Allāh in the (very) beginning and seeking blessing in His name.

04

The First Treatise: The Four Affairs Contained in Sūrah al-ʿAṣr

ORIGINAL TEXT

اعلمْ—رحمكَ اللهُ...

Know, may Allāh have mercy upon you...

EXPLANATION

His statement "*know*" is a word that indicates the importance of the subject matter. When he said "know," it means that the affair which shall be presented to you is an important affair. Therefore, this statement indicates the importance of the subject matter he will explain. The meaning of "know" is that it is a command that is extracted from the word *ʿilm* (knowledge), meaning "learn." And knowledge is being cognizant of a thing based upon its reality; or understanding the affair in accordance with its reality. And having knowledge of a thing in opposition to its reality, or to interpret a thing based upon other than its reality, is ignorance, and this is the opposite of knowledge.

His statement, "*may Allāh have mercy upon you,*" is a supplication for the student of knowledge. Therefore, the Shaykh is supplicating for Allāh to have mercy upon the students of knowledge and for Him to administer mercy to them. This is kindness from the teacher to the student, and it is a means of beginning with mild or goodly speech and a righteous supplication in order for this to have an effect and make the student focus on his teacher. As for if the teacher were to begin with harsh speech and speech that is inappropriate, then this would chase the people away. What is obligatory upon the teacher—as well as upon the one that calls to Allāh and upon the one who commands what is good and prohibits what is evil—is that he be kind to the one he addresses and that he supplicates for him and commends him, speaking goodly words and using mild speech. This increases the chances of one's speech being accepted. As for the one who is obstinate and arrogant, then he should be addressed in another way.

Allāh the Exalted has said:

﴿ وَلَا تُجَادِلُوا أَهْلَ الْكِتَابِ إِلَّا بِالَّتِي هِيَ أَحْسَنُ إِلَّا الَّذِينَ ظَلَمُوا مِنْهُمْ ۖ وَقُولُوا آمَنَّا بِالَّذِي أُنزِلَ إِلَيْنَا وَأُنزِلَ إِلَيْكُمْ وَإِلَٰهُنَا وَإِلَٰهُكُمْ وَاحِدٌ وَنَحْنُ لَهُ مُسْلِمُونَ ﴾

And argue not with the People of the Scripture (Jews and Christians), unless it be in (a way) that is better (with good words and in a good manner, inviting them to Islamic monotheism with His verses), except with such of them as do wrong, and say (to them): "We believe in that which has been revealed to us and revealed to you; our *Ilāh* (God) and your *Ilāh* (God) is one (i.e., Allāh), and to Him we have submitted (as Muslims)."

[Sūrah al-'Ankabūt 29:46]

Therefore, those who acted oppressively from the People of the Book and were obstinate and arrogant are not to be addressed with that which is best. Rather, they are to be addressed with that which will rebut them. Allāh the Exalted has said:

﴿ يَا أَيُّهَا النَّبِيُّ جَاهِدِ الْكُفَّارَ وَالْمُنَافِقِينَ وَاغْلُظْ عَلَيْهِمْ ۚ وَمَأْوَاهُمْ جَهَنَّمُ ۖ وَبِئْسَ الْمَصِيرُ ﴾

O Prophet (Muḥammad ﷺ)! Strive hard against the disbelievers and the hypocrites, and be harsh against them; their abode is Hell, and worst indeed is that destination.

[Sūrah at-Tawbah 9:73]

The hypocrites are not to be struggled against with weaponry. Rather, one is to struggle against them by way of proofs and speech, and they are to be refuted with sternness and a means of repudiation for them so that the people will beware of them. Allāh the Exalted has said regarding them:

﴿ وَقُل لَّهُمْ فِي أَنفُسِهِمْ قَوْلًا بَلِيغًا ﴾

And speak to them an effective word (i.e., to believe in Allāh, worship Him, obey Him, and be afraid of Him) to reach their inner selves.

[Sūrah an-Nisā' 4:63]

Therefore, these people are to be addressed in a specific way because they are people of obstinance and arrogance, and they do not want the truth. Rather, they want to lead the people astray. Hence, they are to be addressed with that which is befitting for them. As for the student who is seeking guidance, then he is to be addressed with gentleness, mercy, and kindness, because he wants the truth and he desires knowledge and benefit.

Knowledge

ORIGINAL TEXT

...أَنَّهُ يجبُ علينا تَعَلُّمُ أربعِ مسائلَ؛ الأُولى: العِلْمُ...

...it is obligatory upon us to learn four affairs. The first: knowledge...

EXPLANATION

His statement "*it is obligatory*": This means that which is an obligation; and it is that which a person shall be rewarded for if he does it and punished for if he abandons it. That which is *mustaḥabb* (highly recommended) is that which the person is rewarded for doing, but he is not punished if he abandons it. And that which is *mubāḥ* (permissible) is that which is not rewarded if he does it, nor is he punished if he abandons it.

The author said "*it is obligatory*," meaning: this affair is not recommended nor is it merely permissible. Rather, it is obligatory upon every individual. Therefore, if we were to abandon learning these issues, we would be sinning, because this is the status of something that is obligatory. He did not say that it is recommended for us or that it is good for us; rather, he said it is obligatory upon us. Meaning, [it is] an obligation, and the obligation is that which is binding. Therefore, whoever abandons it is sinning, because knowledge is not attained except by way of learning, and learning requires consideration, work, and time. It requires understanding and presence of heart. This is learning.

His statement "*four affairs*": This means [four] fields of study. They are called "affairs" (مسائل) because it is obligatory to ask about them and to give them due consideration.

His statement "*knowledge*": What is intended by "knowledge" here is legislative knowledge, because it is that which is obligatory to learn. These issues are such that they are obligatory upon every Muslim, male or female, free person or slave, rich or poor, king or subject; every Muslim must learn these four affairs. This is what the scholars call *al-wājib al-'aynī* (the individual obligation), and it is that which is obligatory upon each individual among the Muslims. Therefore, five prayers upon every male and female—as well as the Jumu'ah prayer or the congregational prayer in the mosques for the men—are an obligation upon every individual among the Muslims. Thus, he must learn them. Due to this, he said "*it is obligatory upon us*." He did not say, "It is obligatory upon some of us." Rather, he said "*it is obligatory upon us*"; "us" meaning "the assembly of

Muslims," and this is from the knowledge that each individual must learn because knowledge is divided into two categories:

The First: That which is obligatory upon each individual. Therefore, none is excused for being ignorant of it and it is that without which the religion cannot be established, such as the pillars of Islām, which are five. They are: the two testimonies, the establishment of the *ṣalāh*, the payment of the *zakāh*, fasting during Ramaḍān, and pilgrimage to the Sacred House of Allāh. It is not permissible for the Muslim to be ignorant of them. Rather, it is a must that he learns them because learning the meaning of the two testimonies is learning the correct belief system. The Muslim must learn the correct belief system so that he may act upon it, and he must learn its opposite so that he may avoid it. This is what is contained in the two testimonies.

Likewise, he must learn the pillars of prayer, the conditions of prayer, and the prayer's obligatory elements, as well as the *sunan* of the prayer. It is a must that one learns the details of these affairs, not simply that he prays while not knowing the rulings of prayer. How can a person do an action while not knowing the reality of this action that he is performing? How can he perform the prayer while he is ignorant of its ruling? Therefore, it is a must that one learns the ruling of prayers as well as the invalidators of prayer. He must learn these things.

Likewise, he must learn the rulings of *zakāh,* and he must learn the rulings of fasting and the rulings of Ḥajj. If he wants to perform Ḥajj, then he must learn the rulings of Ḥajj and the rulings of 'Umrah so that he may perform these acts of worship in the legislated manner. No one is excused for being ignorant of this category of knowledge; it is that which is called the "individual obligation" upon every Muslim.

The Second: That which is a supplement to the legislated rulings, which the *ummah* is in need of on a communal level, yet perhaps not every individual specifically is in need of it. For example: the rulings of buying and selling, the rulings of social interactions, the rulings of religious endowments, inheritance, and wills, the rulings of marriage, and the rulings of criminal justice. It is a must that the *ummah* has these things in place. However, it is not obligatory that each individual from the *ummah* learns them. Rather, if someone were to learn them from the scholars by way of which the desired result could be established, then this is sufficient, so that they may establish what the Muslims are in need of from judgments, issuing religious verdicts, teaching, and other than this. This is what is called *wājib al-kifāyah* (communal obligation): if some of the people establish it in a manner that is sufficient, then the sin is removed from everyone else; and if everyone abandons it, then everyone would be considered sinful.

It is a must that some of the people learn this category of knowledge for the *ummah* because they are in need of it. However, it is not said to every individual, "It is obligatory upon you to have knowledge of these issues," because these issues may not affect everyone. Rather, this is relegated to those who have the ability and those who are capable from the *ummah*. This is because, if some of the *ummah* learns this branch of knowledge, then they have established that which is obligatory.

This is in opposition to the first category—every person is responsible for [the first category] within himself because it is not possible to act upon these affairs except by way of knowledge. Due to this, the author رحمه الله said "*it is obligatory upon us*." He did not say, "It is obligatory upon the Muslims," or, "It is obligatory upon some of them." Rather, he said, "It is obligatory upon us." Meaning, upon every individual among us.

Therefore, let us also know before discussing the issues that what is intended by "knowledge which is obligatory upon the *ummah*"—either on an individual level or a communal level—is legislative knowledge that the Messenger ﷺ came with. As for worldly knowledge, such as knowledge of manufacturing, agriculture, accounting, mathematics, and engineering—this knowledge is permissible. It is permissible to learn it, and perhaps the *ummah* may need it. Hence, it is obligatory upon the one who has it. However, it is not the knowledge that is intended in the Qur'ān and Sunnah, and whose people Allāh praises and commends, or the knowledge concerning which the Prophet ﷺ said:

العلماء ورثة الأنبياء.

The scholars are the inheritors of the prophets.[1]

What is intended by this is legislated knowledge. As for worldly knowledge, the one who is ignorant of it is not sinning, and it is permissible for the one who learns it; and if he benefits the *ummah* by way of it, then he will be rewarded for it. If a person were to die while being ignorant of this knowledge, he would not be taken to account for it on the Day of Judgment. However, the one who dies while being ignorant of legislative knowledge—specifically, the necessary knowledge—he will be asked about it on the Day of Judgment: "Why did you not learn it? Why did you not ask about it?"

The one who says, when he is placed inside his grave, "My Lord is Allāh, Islām is my religion, and my Prophet is Muḥammad ﷺ," shall be saved, and it will be said to him, "How did you come to know this?" He will say, "I read the Book of Allāh and I learned it." As for the one who turns away from that, then he shall be questioned in his grave, but he will say: "Ha, I don't know. I heard the people saying something, so I said it." This person will have his grave engulfed in flames, and refuge is sought with Allāh. It will be made tight upon him to the point that his ribs interlace, and it will become a pit from the pits of Fire, because he did not know nor did he read. Hence, it will be said to him, "You did not know nor did you recite (i.e., the Book of Allāh)."[2]

He did not learn, nor did he take the example of the people of

---

[1] Reported by al-Bukhārī in "The Book of Knowledge, Chapter: Knowledge Before Speech and Action" (#67), and by Abū Dāwūd (#3641), Ibn Mājah (#223), and at-Tirmidhī (#2682) from the *ḥadīth* of Abud-Dardā' رضي الله عنه.

[2] Reported by al-Bukhārī, summarized from the *ḥadīth* of Anas (#1338). Muslim reported it as well, summarized from the *ḥadīth* of Anas رضي الله عنه (#2870). Also, it was reported by Abū Dāwūd from the *ḥadīth* of al-Barā' bin 'Āzib رضي الله عنه (#4753).

knowledge. Rather, he squandered his life. This person will be thrown into misery, and refuge is sought with Allāh. Therefore, the statement *"knowledge"* refers to legislative knowledge that is required upon us individually and as a community; and it is the knowledge of Allāh, His names and attributes, and knowledge of His right upon us, which is to worship Him alone without associating partners with Him. Therefore, the first of that which is obligatory upon the servant is to have knowledge of his Lord and how to worship Him.

ORIGINAL TEXT

...وهوَ معرفةُ اللهِ، ومعرفةُ نبيِّهِ...

...and it is knowledge of Allāh and knowledge of His Prophet...

EXPLANATION

His statement "*and it is knowledge of Allāh*": How does a servant know his Lord? He knows him by way of His signs and His creation. From His signs are the night and the day, and from His creations are the sun and the moon, as shall come, if Allāh wills. Allāh is known by way of His universal signs as well as His Quranic signs. If one reads the Qur'ān, he will know Allāh ﷻ, and he will know that He is the one who has created the heavens and the earth, He is the one who has subjugated what is in the heavens and the earth, He is the one who gives life and causes death, He has the ability to do all things, and He is the Most Merciful, the Bestower of Mercy.

Therefore, the Qur'ān gives one knowledge of Allāh ﷻ and the fact that He is the one that bestows favors upon us by way of all of His blessings, and that He is the one who has created us and provided for us. If you read the Qur'ān, you will know your Lord by way of His names, attributes, and actions. And when you look within the universe, you will know your Lord ﷻ and that He is the one who has created His creation and has subjugated this universe; and He has made it run on its course by way of His wisdom and knowledge. This is knowledge of Allāh.

Concerning his statement *"knowledge of His Prophet"*: He is Muḥammad ﷺ. This is because he is the one who has conveyed the message from Allāh ﷻ, and he is the medium between us and Allāh in terms of conveyance of the message. It is a must that you know him. Do you know who he is? And do you know his lineage, his land, and that which he came with? Do you know how the revelation started coming to him and how he established the call to Allāh in Makkah and Madīnah? Do you know his *sīrah*, even in a summarized way?

The Messenger ﷺ is Muḥammad bin 'Abdillāh bin 'Abdul-Muṭṭalib bin Hāshim bin 'Abd-Manāf, to the end of the prophetic lineage which ends at Ibrāhīm عليه السلام. So, you must know how he lived before he was commissioned as a Prophet and how the revelation came to him from Allāh عز وجل, and what he did after he was commissioned as a Prophet. You will come to know this by studying his *sīrah*. It is not proper for the Muslim to be ignorant of the Messenger ﷺ. How can you follow someone you do not know? This is impossible.

ORIGINAL TEXT

...ومعرفةُ دينِ الإسلامِ بالأدلةِ.

...and knowledge of the religion of Islām with the evidences.

EXPLANATION

His statement "*knowledge of the religion of Islām*": This is the religion of this Messenger ﷺ. Rather, it is the religion of Allāh عز وجل which He has commanded His servants to follow. And it is what He has commanded you to follow and has required of you. It is required that you know this religion. Islām is the religion of all the messengers, for every messenger was such that his religion was Islām, in the general sense. So, whoever followed amMessenger from amongst the messengers was a Muslim for the sake of Allāh عز وجل, having yielded and submitted to Him as a monotheist. This is Islām in the general sense. It is the religion of all the messengers.

Islām is to submit to Allāh in *tawḥīd* and to yield obediently to Him, and to free oneself from polytheism and its people. As for Islām in a specific sense, it is that which Allāh sent his Prophet ﷺ with. This is because, after the sending of the Messenger ﷺ, there is no religion other than his religion, and Islām is restricted to his followers. Therefore, it is not possible for a Jew to say, "I am Muslim," or for a Christian to say, "I am Muslim," after the sending of the Prophet ﷺ while he does not follow him. Therefore, Islām after the sending of the Prophet ﷺ means following him ﷺ. Allāh the Exalted has said:

﴿ قُلْ إِن كُنتُمْ تُحِبُّونَ اللَّهَ فَاتَّبِعُونِي يُحْبِبْكُمُ اللَّهُ ﴾

Say (O Muḥammad ﷺ to mankind): "If you (really) love Allāh, then follow me; Allāh will love you."

[Sūrah Āli 'Imrān 3:31]

This is Islām in the general sense and the specific sense. As for his statement *"with the evidences,"* this means "not by way of blind following." It is only by way of the evidences from the Qur'ān and the Sunnah. This is knowledge.

Ibn al-Qayyim said in *Al-Kāfiyah ash-Shāfiyah*:

العلم قال الله قال رسوله

قال الصحابة هم أولو العرفان

ما العلم نصبك للخلاف سفاهة

بين الرسول وبين رأي فلان

Knowledge is "Allāh said and his Messenger said"

And "the Ṣaḥābah said," for they are the people of cognizance.

Therefore, knowledge is not foolishly opposing the Messenger by way of the opinions of so-and-so.

This is knowledge. It is knowledge of the Book and the Sunnah. As for the statements of the scholars, then they only explain and clarify, explaining the speech of Allāh and His Messenger ﷺ; and perhaps the speech or some of the statements of the scholars can be incorrect. "The evidences" does not mean the speech of the scholars. The evidences are only the Quranic verses and Prophetic narrations. As for the speech of the scholars, then it explains and clarifies them, and it is not an evidence by itself.

This is the first issue, and it is the foundation. The author رحمه الله began with it because it is the foundation, and one must begin with the *'aqīdah* and with the foundation in teaching and learning, as well as calling to Allāh عز وجل because it is the basis and it is the foundation.

Acting Upon Knowledge

Original Text

الثانيةُ: العملُ بهِ.

The second: Acting upon it.

Explanation

His statement *"Acting upon it"*: Meaning, acting upon knowledge. This is because it is not sufficient that a person teaches and learns. Rather, it is required that he acts upon this knowledge. Knowledge without action is a proof against the person. Hence, knowledge is not beneficial except by way of action. As for he who has knowledge but does not act, Allāh is angry with him because he knows the truth but has abandoned it while having knowledge. The poet said:

عالم بعلمه لم يعملن

معذب من قبل عباد الوثن

The one who has knowledge but does not act upon it will be punished before the worshipers of an idol.

And this is mentioned in a noble *ḥadīth*, wherein the Prophet ﷺ said:

إن من أول من تسعر بهم النار يوم القيامة عالم لم يعمل بعلمه.

Indeed, from the first for whom the Fire is kindled on the Day of Judgment will be the scholar who does not act upon his knowledge.[3]

Knowledge must be accompanied by action. Action is the fruit of knowledge; therefore, knowledge without action is like a tree without fruits: it contains no benefit. And knowledge was only sent down for the purpose of action, just as action without knowledge is a means of misery and deviation for its companion. If a person acts without knowledge, then his action will be a means of misery and thus burden its companion. The Prophet ﷺ said:

من عمل عملا ليس عليه أمرنا فهو رد.

He who does an action which is not from this affair of ours, it shall be rejected.[4]

Due to this, we recite within al-Fātiḥah in every *rak'ah*:

﴿ اهْدِنَا الصِّرَاطَ الْمُسْتَقِيمَ ۝٦ صِرَاطَ الَّذِينَ أَنْعَمْتَ عَلَيْهِمْ غَيْرِ الْمَغْضُوبِ عَلَيْهِمْ وَلَا الضَّالِّينَ ۝٧ ﴾

Guide us to the Straight Way. The way of those on whom You have bestowed Your grace, not (the way) of those who earned Your anger (such as the

---

[3] Reported by at-Tirmidhī (#2382), and in it is mentioned the first three for whom Allāh will kindle the Fire on the Day of Judgment, from the *ḥadīth* of Abū Hurayrah ﷺ.

[4] Reported by al-Bukhārī (#7350) and Muslim (#18, #1718), from the *ḥadīth* of 'Ā'ishah ﷺ. Al-Bukhārī likewise reported from the Prophet ﷺ on the authority of 'Ā'ishah that he said:

من أحدث في أمرنا هذا ما ليس منه فهو رد.

He who innovates into this affair of ours that which is not from it, it shall be rejected.

Reported by al-Bukhārī (#2697) and Muslim (#17, #1718), on the authority of 'Ā'ishah ﷺ.

Jews), nor of those who went astray (such as the Christians).

[Sūrah al-Fātiḥah 1:6-7]

Allāh has referred to those who act without knowledge as astray, and those who have knowledge but do not act upon it as being those who have earned His wrath. Therefore, let us pay attention to this, as it is very important.

Calling to Knowledge

ORIGINAL TEXT

الثالثةُ: الدعوةُ إليهِ.

The third: Calling to it.

EXPLANATION

His statement *"Calling to it"*: This means it is not sufficient that the individual learns and acts for himself but does not call to Allāh ﷻ. Rather, it is required that one call others so that he may benefit himself and benefit others. This is because this knowledge is a trust; it is not a possession which you own and store, thus depriving the people of it while the people are in need of it. It is obligatory upon you to convey, clarify, and call the people to good. This knowledge which Allāh has guided you to does not end with you; rather, it is for you and for others. Therefore, do not hoard it for yourself and prevent the people from benefiting from it. Rather, it is required that you convey it. It is required that you clarify it to the people. Allāh the Exalted has said:

﴿ وَإِذْ أَخَذَ اللَّهُ مِيثَاقَ الَّذِينَ أُوتُوا الْكِتَابَ لَتُبَيِّنُنَّهُ لِلنَّاسِ وَلَا تَكْتُمُونَهُ ﴾

(And remember) when Allāh took a covenant from those who were given the scripture (Jews and Christians) to make it known and clear to mankind,

and not to hide it.

[Sūrah Āli 'Imrān 3:187]

This is a covenant which Allāh has taken upon the scholars—that they convey to the people what Allāh has taught them so that they can spread goodness and so they can take the people from darkness to light. This is the action of the messengers ﷺ as well as those who follow them. Allāh the Exalted has said:

﴿ قُلْ هَٰذِهِ سَبِيلِي أَدْعُو إِلَى اللَّهِ ۚ عَلَىٰ بَصِيرَةٍ أَنَا وَمَنِ اتَّبَعَنِي ۖ وَسُبْحَانَ اللَّهِ وَمَا أَنَا مِنَ الْمُشْرِكِينَ ﴾

Say (O Muḥammad ﷺ): "This is my way; I invite unto Allāh with sure knowledge, I and whosoever follows me. And Glorified and Exalted be Allāh (above all that they associate as partners with Him). And I am not of the polytheists."

[Sūrah Yūsuf 12:108]

This is the path of the Messenger ﷺ and those who follow him. Knowledge, action, and calling to Allāh عزوجل. Therefore, he who does not call while having the ability to and having knowledge, and who conceals that knowledge, will be bridled with a bridle of fire on the Day of Judgment, as has come in the narration.[5]

---

[5] It is reported on the authority of Abū Dāwūd (#3658) as well as at-Tirmidhī (#2649) and Ibn Mājah (#261, #266) from the *ḥadīth* of Abū Hurayrah رضي الله عنه who said, "The Messenger of Allāh ﷺ said:

من سئل عن علم يعلمه فكتمه، ألجم يوم القيامة بلجام من نار.

"'Whoever is asked regarding knowledge which he knows and he conceals it, Allāh will bridle him with a bridle of fire of the Day of Judgment.'"

Ibn Mājah reported from the *ḥadīth* of Abū Sa'īd al-Khudrī رضي الله عنه who said: "The Messenger of Allāh ﷺ said:

من كتم علما مما ينفع الله به في أمر الناس، أمر الدين، ألجمه الله يوم القيامة بلجام من نار.

"'He who conceals knowledge that Allāh has benefited him with regarding the affairs of the people and the affairs of the religion, Allāh will bridle him on the Day of Judgment with a bridle of fire.'"

Patience in Bearing Harm Encountered Upon It

ORIGINAL TEXT

الرابعةُ: الصبرُ علَى الأَذى فيهِ.

The fourth: Patience in encountering harm upon it.

EXPLANATION

The statement "*Patience in encountering harm upon it*": It is known that whoever calls the people or commands what is good and prohibits what is evil will be exposed to harm from the evil people, because many of the people do not want good. Rather, they want to follow their desires and they want the impermissible and false caprices. So when one comes who calls to Allāh and rebuts their desires, it is inevitable that there shall be from amongst them one who rejects him in statement and action. What is obligatory upon the one who calls to Allāh and desires the Face of Allāh is that he be patient upon that harm and continue calling to Allāh.

His example in this is the messengers عليهم السلام. The best of them and the seal of them was Muḥammad ﷺ. What did he encounter from the people and how much harm in statement and action did he encounter from them? They said that he was a magician and a liar, and they said that he was insane. They said about him that which Allāh عز وجل has mentioned in the Qur'ān, and they visited him with harm. Due to what he called them to (calling them to Allāh), they slandered him and pelted him with stones until blood flowed to his ankles. They tossed camel intestines upon his back while he was prostrating at the Ka'bah. They threatened him with murder, and they terrorized him. In the Battle of Uḥud, they afflicted him and his Companions with that which they afflicted them with. They broke his tooth and hit his head. He fell into a pit, while he is the Prophet of Allāh. All of this harm was due to calling to Allāh عز وجل. However, he was patient and he bore this while being the best of creation ﷺ.

Reported by Ibn Mājah (#265).

Therefore, it is inevitable that the one who establishes this call will be exposed to harm in proportion to his faith and his call. However, it is upon him to be patient. As long as he is upon the truth, he is to be patient and bear this harm, for it is in the path of Allāh. And that which he encounters from harm will be on his scale of good deeds and he shall attain a reward from Allāh ﷻ.

ORIGINAL TEXT

والدليلُ قولُه تعالَى: بسم الله الرحمٰن الرحيم: ﴿ وَالْعَصْرِ ① إِنَّ الإِنسَانَ لَفِي خُسْرٍ ② إِلاَّ الَّذِينَ آمَنُوا وَعَمِلُوا الصَّالِحَاتِ وَتَوَاصَوْا بِالْحَقِّ وَتَوَاصَوْا بِالصَّبْرِ ③ ﴾ [العصر].

The evidence is the statement of Allāh the Exalted:

By [the phenomenon of] time. Indeed, [all of] mankind is in loss. Except those who believe and work righteous deeds and mutually advise each other [in calling to] the truth and mutually advise each other with patience.

[Sūrah al-'Aṣr 103:1-3]

EXPLANATION

It is obligatory upon you to learn these four issues in detail. Is there proof for what the author has mentioned? Indeed, it is obligatory upon us to learn these four affairs, and we know that he does not say anything except with evidence. Therefore, what is the evidence? He said that the evidence for this is the statement of Allāh the Exalted:

﴿ وَالْعَصْرِ ① إِنَّ الْإِنسَانَ لَفِي خُسْرٍ ② إِلَّا الَّذِينَ آمَنُوا وَعَمِلُوا الصَّالِحَاتِ وَتَوَاصَوْا بِالْحَقِّ وَتَوَاصَوْا بِالصَّبْرِ ③ ﴾

By [the phenomenon of] time. Indeed, [all of] mankind is in loss. Except those who believe and

work righteous deeds and mutually advise each other [in calling to] the truth and mutually advise each other with patience.

[Sūrah al-'Aṣr 103:1-3]

He mentioned: **"Except those who believe."** This is the first issue, which is knowledge, because *īmān* is based upon knowledge. It is the awareness of Allāh, the awareness of His Prophet, and the awareness of the religion of Islām with the evidences.

The Second Issue: Righteous actions; and this is acting upon knowledge.

The Third Issue: Enjoining one another with truth; this is calling to knowledge and action.

The Fourth Issue: Enjoining one another with patience; this is in encountering harm in the path of calling to knowledge and action.

His statement in which he said:

﴿ وَالْعَصْرِ ﴾

By [the phenomenon of] time.

[Sūrah al-'Aṣr 103:1]

The letter *wāw* (و) is the *wāw* of oath. *Al-'aṣr* is a name of that which has been sworn by, and it is in the genitive case. The sign of it being genitive is the *kasrah*. What is intended by it is "time" or a time frame. Allāh the Exalted is swearing by time or a time frame, and this is a created thing. Allāh ﷻ swears by whatever He wills to swear by from the creation, and the creation is not to swear by anything other than Allāh. Allāh does not swear except by something which has importance, and in it is a sign from amongst His signs. Therefore, time contains lessons and it has importance. Due to this, Allāh swears by the time and by the night as it covers, and He swears by the forenoon. As for the creation, they are not to swear by anything other than Allāh, and it is not permissible for us to swear by anything other than Allāh. The Prophet ﷺ said:

من حلف بغير الله فقد كفر أو أشرك.

Whoever swears by other than Allāh has disbelieved or committed *shirk*.[6]

He likewise said:

من كان حالفا فليحلف بالله أو ليصمت.

Whoever swears, then let him swear by Allāh or be silent.[7]

Therefore, Allāh swears by whatever He wills, and He does not swear by anything unless it contains importance and benefit. So what is the benefit in swearing by time? The lessons within it are tremendous. The night and the day follow one another in succession and they take from one another. So the night takes from the day and the day takes from the night. Thus, this one may be long while the other is short, or vice versa. And they follow one another in succession with this amazing structure, and it does not change and it is not altered. This is evidence for the power of Allāh ﷻ.

Moreover, whatever occurs within this time from incidents and disasters and calamities, as well as blessings and goodness, is included amongst these lessons. Similarly, the night and the day are a time for righteous actions. Allāh the Exalted has said:

﴿ وَهُوَ الَّذِي جَعَلَ اللَّيْلَ وَالنَّهَارَ خِلْفَةً لِّمَنْ أَرَادَ أَن يَذَّكَّرَ أَوْ أَرَادَ شُكُورًا ﴾

And He it is who has put the night and the day in succession, for such who desires to remember or desires to show his gratitude.

[Sūrah al-Furqān 25:62]

---

[6] Reported by Abū Dāwūd (#3251) and at-Tirmidhī (#1535) from the *ḥadīth* of Ibn 'Umar ﷺ.

[7] Reported by al-Bukhārī (#6108) and Muslim (#1646) from the *ḥadīth* of Ibn 'Umar ﷺ.

Meaning: He has made them follow one another in succession, and in some of the wordings it is recited: "For the one who wishes to reflect."

Therefore, the night and the day are a tremendous means of earning for the one who utilizes them in the obedience of Allāh ﷻ, and the time frame of action is both the night and the day. You do not have anything other than the night and the day; they are the time for doing actions and (acquiring) goodly earnings in this life as well as the Hereafter. Within the night and the day, there are various lessons and benefits. Due to this, Allāh swears by the time.

What is being sworn to? It is the statement of Allāh:

﴿ إِنَّ الْإِنسَانَ لَفِي خُسْرٍ ﴾

Indeed, [all of] mankind is in loss.

[Sūrah al-'Aṣr 103:2]

The word ***"al-insān"*** (mankind) refers to all of the children of Ādam, and none have been exempted—not a king or a leader, the rich or the poor, the free person or the slave, male or female. The definite article *"al"* (ال) on the word *"al-insān"* (الإنسان) is to denote full inclusion of all the children of Ādam, (for they all) are in loss. Meaning, they are in a state of loss and destruction, for they have squandered this valuable time and utilized it in the disobedience of Allāh and in that which harms them.

This time—which is considered cheap, according to many of the people—seems long to them. They become bored and they say, "We want to kill time." Therefore, they engage in various types of entertainment, or they travel to do away with being idle and to waste time, or they laugh and joke in order to pass time. These are those who have wasted their time and squandered it, so they are in a state of loss and it will be a means of regret for them on the Day of Judgment. It would have been the source of their happiness had they preserved it. Therefore, all the children of Ādam are in loss and destruction with the exception of those who are described with four characteristics, and they are:

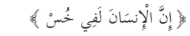

1) Knowledge

2) Action

3) Calling to Allāh

4) Patience in bearing the harm

Whoever is described with these four characteristics will be saved from this loss. It is not possible to have *īmān* in Allāh except by knowledge, which is awareness of Allāh. He mentioned:

﴿ وَعَمِلُوا الصَّالِحَاتِ ﴾

...and work righteous deeds...

[Sūrah al-'Aṣr 103:3]

Meaning: they do righteous actions from that which is obligatory and that which is recommended. Therefore, they utilize their time in righteous actions, in what is beneficial to them in their religion and in their worldly life. Even actions for the *dunyā* contain goodness. It contains reward if the individual intends by it to utilize it in the obedience of Allāh. So how much more reward do actions that are done for the Hereafter contain? It is important that you do not waste time. Rather, utilize it in something which benefits you and is useful for you.

He went on to say:

﴿ وَتَوَاصَوْا بِالْحَقِّ ﴾

...and mutually advise each other [in calling to] the truth...

[Sūrah al-'Aṣr 103:3]

Meaning: they command with good and they prohibit evil, and they call to Allāh ﷻ. They teach beneficial knowledge, and they spread knowledge and goodness amongst the people. They have become callers to Allāh ﷻ.

He said:

﴿ وَتَوَاصَوْا بِالصَّبْرِ ﴾

...and mutually advise each other with patience.

[Sūrah al-ʿAṣr 103:3]

They are patient with what they encounter. And "patience" in the Arabic language means "restraint." What is intended by **"patience"** here is restraining the soul upon the obedience of Allāh, and it is of three types:

1) Patience upon the obedience of Allāh.

2) Patience in staying away from what Allāh has prohibited.

3) Patience upon the decree of Allāh.

The first is patience upon the obedience of Allāh. This is because the soul is inclined towards laziness and it desires relaxation. Therefore, it is incumbent that one forces it to be patient upon the obedience of Allāh, and upon prayer, fasting, and *jihād* in the path of Allāh even though it detests these things. One must compel it to be patient and restrain it upon the obedience of Allāh.

The second is patience in staying away from what Allāh has prohibited; this is because the soul desires those impermissible and desirable things. It inclines towards them and is pulled towards them. Therefore, one must bridle and restrain it from that which is impermissible, and this requires patience. It is not easy to restrain the soul from impermissible desires. Whoever does not have patience, his soul shall overpower and compel him towards that which is impermissible.

The third is patience upon the painful decree of Allāh and calamities which afflict a person, from the death of a relative, the loss of wealth, or sickness which afflicts the person. It is a must that one be patient upon the divine decree and the preordainment of Allāh. One must not become disgruntled or displeased. Rather, he is to restrain his tongue from displaying displeasure or discontent. He must restrain himself from disgruntlement and he must restrain his limbs from slapping his cheeks and tearing his clothing. This is patience upon calamities.

As for one's own shortcomings or flaws, one is not to become patient with them. Rather, he is to repent to Allāh and flee from them. However, regarding calamities which afflict you against your will: they come from Allāh ﷻ; He has decreed them for you as a test and trial or as a punishment for you due to sins you have committed. As Allāh has said:

﴿ وَمَا أَصَابَكُم مِّن مُّصِيبَةٍ فَبِمَا كَسَبَتْ أَيْدِيكُمْ وَيَعْفُو عَن كَثِيرٍ ﴾

And whatever of misfortune befalls you, it is because of what your hands have earned. And He pardons much.

[Sūrah ash-Shūrā 42:30]

Hence, if a calamity befalls a Muslim in his person, his wealth, his child, his relative, or one of his Muslim brothers, it is upon him to be patient and anticipate the reward of Allāh. Allāh the Exalted has said:

﴿ الَّذِينَ إِذَا أَصَابَتْهُم مُّصِيبَةٌ قَالُوا إِنَّا لِلَّهِ وَإِنَّا إِلَيْهِ رَاجِعُونَ ﴿١٥٦﴾ أُولَٰئِكَ عَلَيْهِمْ صَلَوَاتٌ مِّن رَّبِّهِمْ وَرَحْمَةٌ ۖ وَأُولَٰئِكَ هُمُ الْمُهْتَدُونَ ﴿١٥٧﴾ ﴾

Who, when afflicted with calamity, say, "Truly! To Allāh we belong and truly, to Him we shall return." They are those on whom are the *ṣalawāt* (i.e., blessings, etc.) from their Lord, and (they are those who) receive His mercy, and it is they who are the guided ones.

[Sūrah al-Baqarah 2:156-157]

This is patience. And from that is patience in encountering harm while calling to Allāh ﷻ, for indeed this is from the calamities. Hence, it is upon you to be patient in bearing that which you encounter from harm in the path of goodness. And do not slacken in doing goodness. Some people want to do good, but when they are faced with something they dislike, they say, "It is not obligatory upon me to enter into these affairs." Then, he abandons learning if he is a student or he abandons calling to Allāh, or he abandons delivering sermons if he is the *khaṭīb* of the *masjid*, or he abandons being the *imām* of the *masjid*. He abandons commanding the good and prohibiting the evil. This person is not patient upon what afflicted him from harm.

And if you err, it is upon you to return to the truth and to that which is correct. As for if you are upon the truth and you are not errant, it is upon you to be patient and anticipate the reward of Allāh, and to bear in mind that this is in the path of Allāh ﷻ and that you shall be rewarded for it. You should bear in mind that which afflicted the prophets ﷺ from harm, and how they were patient and struggled in the path of Allāh until Allāh gave them victory.

ORIGINAL TEXT

قَالَ الشافعيُّ رحمَهُ اللهُ تعالَى: لَوْ مَا أَنْزَلَ اللهُ حُجَّةً عَلَى خَلْقِهِ إلاَّ هٰذه السُّورَةَ لَكَفَتْهُمْ.

Ash-Shāfi'ī رحمه الله said: "Had Allāh not sent down any proof against His creation except this *sūrah*, it would have sufficed them."

EXPLANATION

His statement *"Ash-Shāfi'ī"* refers to Imām Muḥammad bin Idrīs ash-Shāfi'ī. The ascription was to his fourth grandfather, Shāfi', who was from the Quraysh by way of al-Muṭṭalib. Ash-Shāfi'ī died in 204 AH; he is one of the four Imāms. He said this statement because Allāh clarified in this *sūrah* the reasons for misery and the reasons for happiness. Therefore, the reasons for happiness are that the person is described with these four characteristics: knowledge, action, *da'wah*, and patience in bearing the harms in the path of Allāh the Exalted. Therefore, Allāh established the proof against the creation by way of this *sūrah*. Allāh the Exalted is saying to them: "Indeed, I have clarified to you the means of happiness in this short and concise *sūrah*."

The entirety of the Qur'ān and Sunnah contains details regarding these four issues. However, this *sūrah* clarifies the means of happiness, in general. Therefore, the proof is established by way of it against the creation, and the rest of the text of the Qur'ān and Sunnah contaisn details and a clarification of these four affairs. The meaning of ash-Shāfi'ī's speech is not that this *sūrah* would have sufficed the people had Allāh not sent down anything other than it. However, it establishes the proof against them because Allāh clarified within it the reasons for happiness and the reasons for misery. Therefore, none on the Day of Judgment will be able to say, "I did not know the reasons for happiness, nor did I know the means for misery," while he read this concise and short chapter.

ORIGINAL TEXT

وقال البخاريُّ رحمَهُ اللهُ تعالى : بابُ العلمُ قبلَ القولِ والعملِ، والدليلُ قولُه تعالى : ﴿ فَاعْلَمْ أَنَّهُ لَا إِلَهَ إِلَّا اللَّهُ وَاسْتَغْفِرْ لِذَنبِكَ ﴾ [محمد:١٩] . فبدأ بالعلمِ قبلَ القولِ والعملِ .

Al-Bukhārī said, "Chapter: Knowledge precedes speech and action." And the proof is the statement of Allāh:

So know (O Muḥammad 🙵) that none has the right to be worshiped but Allāh, and ask forgiveness for your sin.

[Sūrah Muḥammad 47:19]

Therefore, he began with knowledge before speech and action.

EXPLANATION

Al-Bukhārī is the Imām, Muḥammad bin Ismā'īl bin Ibrāhīm al-Bukhārī. His name is an ascription to Bukhara, which was from the lands of the East. He is the Imām of the people of *ḥadīth* and a mountain of preservation. He is the author of the *Ṣaḥīḥ,* which is the most authentic book after the Book of Allāh. He said, "Knowledge precedes speech and action." This is because action is not beneficial unless it is predicated upon knowledge.

As for action, if it is predicated upon ignorance, it will not benefit the one who does it. Rather, it will be a means of misery and misguidance on the Day of Judgment. Therefore, it is a must that learning knowledge precedes action. His statement *"And the proof"* means that the proof for this statement is the saying of Allāh the Exalted:

﴿ فَاعْلَمْ أَنَّهُ لَا إِلَٰهَ إِلَّا اللَّهُ وَاسْتَغْفِرْ لِذَنبِكَ ﴾

So know (O Muḥammad ﷺ) that none has the right to be worshiped but Allāh, and ask forgiveness for your sin.

[Sūrah Muḥammad 47:19]

For Allāh began with knowledge. His statement in which He said:

﴿ وَاسْتَغْفِرْ ﴾

...and ask forgiveness...

[Sūrah Muḥammad 47:19]

This is the action. Therefore, Allāh began with knowledge before action, because if action is based upon ignorance, it will not benefit anyone. Hence, a person must begin with knowledge first, then action upon what he has learned; and this is the foundation.

05

The Second Treatise: Three Issues Which are Incumbent Upon the Muslim to Learn & Act Upon

ORIGINAL TEXT

اعلمْ رحِمكَ اللهُ: أنَّهُ يجبُ على كلِّ مسلم ومسلمة تَعَلُّمُ هٰذه الثلاث مسائل والعملُ بهنَّ.

Know, may Allāh have mercy upon you, that it is obligatory upon every Muslim, male and female, to learn these three issues and to act in accordance with them.

EXPLANATION

His statement *"Know"*: This statement, as has preceded, is a statement which is made to indicate the importance of what comes after it, and the meaning of it is "learn, understand, and have certainty."

His statement *"may Allāh have mercy upon you"*: This is a supplication for you to receive mercy. This, as has preceded, is the teacher—as is proper for him—having kindness for the student and supplicating for him and encouraging him. Indeed, this is from the greatest means of learning. It is not proper for him to display hardness, sternness, and rigidness towards his student, because this will chase the student away from knowledge. Moreover, it indicates sincere advice from the author رحمه الله and the fact that he wants benefit and correct guidance as well as sincere advice for others.

His statement *"that it is obligatory"*: Obligation is well-known according to the scholars of *uṣūl*. That which is *wājib* is the thing that is binding. The scholars of *uṣūl* have defined it as being that for which the one who does it is rewarded, and for which the one who abandons it is punished.

The origin of "obligation" in the Arabic language is that which is affirmed from what has been decided. It is said, "Such-and-such is obligatory." Meaning, it has been affirmed and decided. Allāh the Exalted said regarding cattle:

﴿ فَإِذَا وَجَبَتْ جُنُوبُهَا فَكُلُوا مِنْهَا وَأَطْعِمُوا ﴾

Then, when they are down on their sides (after slaughter), eat thereof, and feed (others)...

[Sūrah al-Ḥajj 22:36]

Meaning, it has dropped to the earth and become *maytah* (dead) after having been sacrificed. The statement in which he said *"it is obligatory"* indicates that the affair is not one of recommendation, such that whoever wants to do it may do it and whoever does not want to do it may abandon it. Rather, the affair is one that Allāh made binding, and this obligation did not come from the author himself. Rather, it came from Allāh تعالى in that which He has sent down in the Book and the Sunnah from making these affairs obligatory upon his servants.

He said *"it is obligatory upon every Muslim, male and female"*: Meaning, it is obligatory upon every male and female from the Muslims, whether they are free people or slaves, male or female. This is because the woman is the counterpart of the man in many of the obligations, unless the evidence explicitly indicates that the affair is specific to the men, in which case it is specific to them. For example: the obligation of congregational prayer in the *masjid* and the Jumu'ah prayer. Likewise, visiting the graves. These things are specific to the men, as well as *jihād* in the path of Allāh, for it is specific to the men. Therefore, that which the evidence indicates is specific to men is specific to them; otherwise, the origin is that men and women are the same in their obligations and in avoiding the prohibited matters, as well as the rest of the responsibilities, and from that is learning knowledge. This is obligatory upon men and women because it is not possible to worship Allāh ﷻ—for which He has created us—except by way of learning knowledge which will enable us to worship our Lord. This obligation upon the men and women is that they learn the affairs of their religion, especially the affairs of *'aqīdah*.

His statement *"three issues"*: Learning here means taking knowledge from the scholars, as well as memorization, understanding, and comprehension. This is learning. The intent is not that one simply reads or does "free reading," as it is called. This is not learning. Learning is taking knowledge from the people of knowledge along with memorization of that, understanding it, and comprehending it completely. This is correct learning.

As for merely reading or reviewing, then it is not sufficient in terms of learning. It is something that is required and contains benefit, but it is not sufficient, and one should not suffice with it. It is not permissible to be a student of books, as is the reality in this time. This is because being a student of books is very dangerous, and corruption results from it; and one feigning knowledge is more harmful than ignorance, because the ignorant person knows he is ignorant and he will stop at his level. However, the one who feigns knowledge deems himself to be a scholar, so he will make permissible that which Allāh has made impermissible and make impermissible that which Allāh has made permissible, and he will say things regarding Allāh without knowledge. Therefore, the affair is very dangerous. Knowledge is not taken from books alone. Books are only a means. As for the reality of knowledge, it is taken from the scholars, generation after generation, and the books are a means for seeking knowledge.

Believing that Allāh Created Us, Provided for Us, & Did Not Leave Us Without Purpose

ORIGINAL TEXT

الأولى: أنَّ الله خَلَقنا ورَزَقَنا ولم يترُكْنا هملاً.

The first [issue]: That Allāh created us, provided for us, and did not leave us without purpose.

EXPLANATION

His statement *"The first: That Allāh has created us"*: Meaning, He has brought us into existence from nothingness. Before Allāh created us, we were not anything, as Allāh has said:

﴿ هَلْ أَتَىٰ عَلَى الْإِنسَانِ حِينٌ مِّنَ الدَّهْرِ لَمْ يَكُن شَيْئًا مَّذْكُورًا ﴾

Has there not been over man a period of time when he was nothing to be mentioned?

[Sūrah al-Insān 76:1]

Likewise, Allāh has said:

﴿ قَالَ كَذَٰلِكَ قَالَ رَبُّكَ هُوَ عَلَيَّ هَيِّنٌ وَقَدْ خَلَقْتُكَ مِن قَبْلُ وَلَمْ تَكُ شَيْئًا ﴾

He said, "So (it will be). Your Lord says, 'It is easy for Me.' Certainly I have created you before, when you had been nothing!"

[Sūrah Maryam 19:9]

Before the human being was created, he was nothing, and the one who brought him into existence and created him is Allāh. Allāh has said:

﴿ أَمْ خُلِقُوا مِنْ غَيْرِ شَيْءٍ أَمْ هُمُ الْخَالِقُونَ ﴾

Were they created by nothing, or were they

themselves the creators?

[Sūrah aṭ-Ṭūr 52:35]

His statement *"provided for us"*: Since we were in need of provision for food, drink, clothing, dwelling, modes of transportation, and other beneficial affairs, Allāh knew our need. Therefore, He made that which is in the heavens and the earth subservient to us in its entirety for our benefit, so that we may remain living, and so that we may seek help with those things to do what Allāh has created us for, which is worshiping Allāh.

His statement *"and did not leave us without purpose"*: The word *al-hamal* (الهمل) means that thing which is neglected and abandoned, not being cared for. Allāh has cared for us and provided for us due to a wisdom. He has not created us in folly, nor did He create us in vain without purpose. Allāh has said:

﴿ أَفَحَسِبْتُمْ أَنَّمَا خَلَقْنَاكُمْ عَبَثًا وَأَنَّكُمْ إِلَيْنَا لَا تُرْجَعُونَ ﴾

Did you think that We had created you in play (without any purpose), and that you would not be brought back to Us?

[Sūrah al-Mu'minūn 23:115]

Likewise, Allāh has said:

﴿ أَيَحْسَبُ الْإِنسَانُ أَن يُتْرَكَ سُدًى ﴿٣٦﴾ أَلَمْ يَكُ نُطْفَةً
مِّن مَّنِيٍّ يُمْنَىٰ ﴿٣٧﴾ ثُمَّ كَانَ عَلَقَةً فَخَلَقَ فَسَوَّىٰ ﴿٣٨﴾ ﴾

Does man think that he will be left neglected? Was he not a *nuṭfah* (mixed male and female discharge of semen) poured forth? Then he became a clot; then (Allāh) shaped and fashioned (him) in due proportion.

[Sūrah al-Qiyāmah 75:36-38]

Allāh has likewise said:

﴿ وَمَا خَلَقْنَا السَّمَاءَ وَالْأَرْضَ وَمَا بَيْنَهُمَا بَاطِلًا ۚ ذَٰلِكَ ظَنُّ الَّذِينَ كَفَرُوا ۚ فَوَيْلٌ لِّلَّذِينَ كَفَرُوا مِنَ النَّارِ ﴾

And We created not the heaven and the earth and all that is between them without purpose! That is the consideration of those who disbelieve! Then woe to those who disbelieve, from the Fire!

[Sūrah Ṣād 38:27]

Allāh has created us, and He created for us these provisions and means due to a tremendous wisdom and a lofty objective, which is that we worship Him ﷻ. He did not create us to be like the animals whom He created for the benefit of His worshipers, who then die and depart, because they are not responsible nor are they commanded or prohibited. Rather, He has created us for His worship. As Allāh has said:

﴿ وَمَا خَلَقْتُ الْجِنَّ وَالْإِنسَ إِلَّا لِيَعْبُدُونِ ﴿٥٦﴾ مَا أُرِيدُ مِنْهُم مِّن رِّزْقٍ وَمَا أُرِيدُ أَن يُطْعِمُونِ ﴿٥٧﴾ ﴾

And I (Allāh) created not the *jinn* and humans except that they should worship Me (alone). I seek not any provision from them (i.e., provision for themselves or for My creatures) nor do I ask that they should feed Me (i.e., feed themselves or My creatures).

[Sūrah adh-Dhāriyāt 51:56-57]

And He has not created us for the life of this world only. Thus, we live within it, we rest, and we depart. We eat, we drink, and we seek to amass (wealth) within it, and there's nothing to come after it. This life is only a farm and a marketplace for the abode of the Hereafter. We take our provisions in it by way of righteous actions, then we die and we will depart from it. Then we shall be resurrected, called to account, and rewarded for our actions.

This is the objective behind the creation of the *jinn* and mankind.

The evidence for this is contained in many verses proving the resurrection and the next life, as well as the reward and the recompense. The intellect establishes this as well, for it is not befitting of the wisdom of Allāh ﷻ that He creates this amazing creation, subjugating this universe to the children of Ādam, just to abandon them so they die and depart without any end result. This is folly. It is a must that the end results of the actions be seen in the abode of the Hereafter.

Due to this, there may be from amongst the people he who spends the entirety of his life worshiping Allāh and in the obedience of Allāh, while he is poor and in need. Perhaps he is oppressed and downtrodden and had straitened circumstances. He does not attain any recompense in this life. On the opposite end, perhaps, a person may be a disbeliever, religious deviant, and evil, and he lives a comfortable life in this world. He has ease and is given whatever he desires, yet he embarks upon that which Allāh has made prohibited. He oppresses the slaves of Allāh, transgressing against them. He usurps their wealth, and he kills without right. He seizes authority and wields power over them; then he dies in this condition, and no type of recompense ever comes to him. Does it fit the justice of Allāh ﷻ and His wisdom that He leaves this obedient person without reward and that He leaves this disbeliever without recompense? This does not befit the justice of Allāh ﷻ.

Due to this, He has made the next abode to be the abode wherein the one who does good shall be recompensed for his good and the one who does evil shall be recompensed for his evil. Thus, the fruits of one's actions shall be made manifest. The *dunyā* is the abode of action; as for the Hereafter, it is the abode of recompense—either Paradise or the Hellfire. He did not leave us without purpose, as some of the atheists and secularists think. Allāh has said:

﴿وَقَالُوا مَا هِيَ إِلَّا حَيَاتُنَا الدُّنْيَا نَمُوتُ وَنَحْيَا وَمَا يُهْلِكُنَا إِلَّا الدَّهْرُ ۚ وَمَا لَهُم بِذَٰلِكَ مِنْ عِلْمٍ ۖ إِنْ هُمْ إِلَّا يَظُنُّونَ﴾

And they say, "There is nothing but our life of this world; we die and we live and nothing destroys

us except *ad-dahr* (the time)." And they have no knowledge of it, they only conjecture.

[Sūrah al-Jāthiyah 45:24]

This is the statement of the atheists who do not believe in the resurrection and the next life. Allāh ﷿ censured them wherein He said:

﴿ أَفَنَجْعَلُ الْمُسْلِمِينَ كَالْمُجْرِمِينَ ﴿٣٥﴾ مَا لَكُمْ كَيْفَ تَحْكُمُونَ ﴿٣٦﴾ ﴾

Shall We then treat the (submitting) Muslims like the criminals? What is the matter with you? How judge you?

[Sūrah al-Qalam 68:35-36]

Likewise, Allāh has said:

﴿ أَمْ حَسِبَ الَّذِينَ اجْتَرَحُوا السَّيِّئَاتِ أَن نَّجْعَلَهُمْ كَالَّذِينَ آمَنُوا وَعَمِلُوا الصَّالِحَاتِ سَوَاءً مَّحْيَاهُمْ وَمَمَاتُهُمْ ۚ سَاءَ مَا يَحْكُمُونَ ﴾

Or do those who earn evil deeds think that We shall hold them equal with those who believe and do righteous good deeds, in their present life and after their death? Worst is the judgment that they make.

[Sūrah al-Jāthiyah 45:21]

Allāh has also said:

﴿ أَمْ نَجْعَلُ الَّذِينَ آمَنُوا وَعَمِلُوا الصَّالِحَاتِ كَالْمُفْسِدِينَ فِي الْأَرْضِ أَمْ نَجْعَلُ الْمُتَّقِينَ كَالْفُجَّارِ ﴾

Shall We treat those who believe and do righteous good deeds, as corrupters within the earth? Or shall We treat the pious as criminals?

[Sūrah Ṣād 38:28]

Therefore, this is impossible, and it can never be.

ORIGINAL TEXT

بل أرسلَ إلينا رسولاً...

Rather, He has sent a messenger to us...

EXPLANATION

Since it is not permissible for us to take worship from our whims or to blindly follow so-and-so from the people, Allāh sent a messenger to us to clarify how to worship Him. This is because acts of worship are *tawqīfiyyah*.[1] It is not permissible for us to worship Allāh with anything other than that which He has legislated. Therefore, acts of worship are *tawqīfiyyah* and they are based upon that which the messengers came with ﷺ. The wisdom in sending the messengers is that they clarify to the people how to worship their Lord and they prohibit them from polytheism and disbelief in Allāh ﷻ. This is the focus of the messengers ﷺ. Due to this, the Prophet ﷺ said:

من عمل عملا ليس عليه أمرنا فهو رد.

He who does an action which is not from this affair of ours, it shall be rejected.[2]

Hence, worship is *tawqīfiyyah* and innovation is rejected. Likewise, superstition is rejected, and bigoted blind following is rejected. Acts of worship are not taken except from the legislation which the Messenger ﷺ has come with.

---

[1] **Translator's Note:** This means that they are not subjected to intellectual free thinking; they can only be extracted from the texts.

[2] Reported by al-Bukhārī (#7350) and Muslim (#18, #1718) from the *ḥadīth* of 'Ā'ishah ﷺ. Al-Bukhārī likewise reported from the Prophet ﷺ on the authority of 'Ā'ishah that he said:

من أحدث في أمرنا هذا ما ليس منه فهو رد.

He who innovates into this affair of ours that which is not from it, it shall be rejected.

Reported by al-Bukhārī (#2697) and Muslim (#17, #1718) on the authority of 'Ā'ishah ﷺ.

His statement, *"Rather, He has sent a messenger to us"*: This is in reference to Muḥammad ﷺ, the seal of the prophets. He sent him in order to clarify to us the reason we were created, to clarify that we should worship Allāh عزوجل, and to prohibit us from polytheism, disbelief, and sins. This is the focus of the Messenger ﷺ, and he conveyed the message with a clear conveyance, he discharged the trust, and he advised the *ummah*. He clarified and explained, and he left us upon a clear and radiant path. Its night is like its day, and none deviates from it except one who is destroyed. As Allāh the Exalted has said:

﴿ الْيَوْمَ أَكْمَلْتُ لَكُمْ دِينَكُمْ وَأَتْمَمْتُ عَلَيْكُمْ نِعْمَتِي وَرَضِيتُ لَكُمُ الْإِسْلَامَ دِينًا ﴾

This day, I have perfected your religion for you, completed My favor upon you, and have chosen for you Islām as your religion.

[Sūrah al-Mā'idah 5:3]

ORIGINAL TEXT

...فمنْ أطاعَهُ دخلَ الجنَّةَ ومنْ عصاهُ دخلَ النّارَ.

...so he who obeys him will enter Paradise and he who disobeys him will enter the Fire.

EXPLANATION

His statement *"he who obeys him"*: Meaning, [he who obeys him] in that which he has commanded will enter Paradise.

His statement *"he who disobeys him"*: Meaning, [he who disobeys him] in that which he has prohibited will enter the Fire. That which attests to the truthfulness of this statement is abundant in the Qur'ān. Allāh the Exalted has said:

﴿ مَّن يُطِعِ الرَّسُولَ فَقَدْ أَطَاعَ اللَّهَ ﴾

He who obeys the Messenger (Muḥammad ﷺ) has

indeed obeyed Allāh.

[Sūrah an-Nisā' 4:80]

Likewise, Allāh has said:

﴿ وَمَا أَرْسَلْنَا مِن رَّسُولٍ إِلَّا لِيُطَاعَ بِإِذْنِ اللَّهِ ﴾

We sent no messenger but to be obeyed by Allāh's leave.

[Sūrah an-Nisā' 4:64]

Allāh has likewise said:

﴿ وَإِن تُطِيعُوهُ تَهْتَدُوا ﴾

If you obey him, you shall be on the right guidance.

[Sūrah an-Nūr 24:54]

Allāh has likewise said:

﴿ وَأَطِيعُوا الرَّسُولَ لَعَلَّكُمْ تُرْحَمُونَ ﴾

And obey the Messenger (Muḥammad ﷺ) so that you may receive mercy (from Allāh).

[Sūrah an-Nūr 24:56]

Therefore, he who obeys him is guided and will enter Paradise. He who disobeys him has gone astray and will enter the Fire. The Prophet ﷺ said:

كلكم يدخل الجنة إلا من أبى.

All of you will enter Paradise except those who refuse.

They said, "O Messenger of Allāh, who would refuse?" He said:

من أطاعني دخل الجنة ومن عصاني فقد أبى.

He who obeys me will enter Paradise, and he who disobeys me has refused.[3]

---

[3] Reported by al-Bukhārī (#7280) from the *ḥadīth* of Abū Hurayrah ﷺ.

His ﷺ statement **"has refused"**: Meaning, he has refused to enter Paradise.

He ﷺ said:

لا يسمع بي يهودي ولا نصراني ثم لا يؤمن بالذي جئت به إلا دخل النار.

No Jew or Christian hears about me and doesn't believe in what I come with except that he will enter the Fire.[4]

Therefore, he who obeys him will enter Paradise and he who disobeys him will enter the Fire. And this is the distinguishing line between a believer and a disbeliever.

ORIGINAL TEXT

والدليلُ قولُهُ تعالى: ﴿ إِنَّا أَرْسَلْنَا إِلَيْكُمْ رَسُولاً شَاهِدًا عَلَيْكُمْ كَمَا أَرْسَلْنَا إِلَى فِرْعَوْنَ رَسُولاً ﴿١٥﴾ فَعَصَى فِرْعَوْنُ الرَّسُولَ فَأَخَذْنَاهُ أَخْذًا وَبِيلاً ﴾ [المزمل: ١٦-١٥].

And the evidence is the statement of Allāh the Exalted:

> **Verily, We have sent to you a messenger (Muḥammad ﷺ) to be a witness over you, as We did send a messenger to Fir'awn. But Fir'awn disobeyed the messenger, so We seized him with a severe punishment.**
>
> *[Sūrah al-Muzammil 73:15-16]*

EXPLANATION

His statement *"And the evidence"*: Meaning, [the evidence] for the sending of the Messenger is the statement of Allāh the Exalted:

﴿ إِنَّا أَرْسَلْنَا إِلَيْكُمْ رَسُولًا شَاهِدًا عَلَيْكُمْ كَمَا أَرْسَلْنَا إِلَىٰ

[4] Reported by Muslim (#153) from the *ḥadīth* of Abū Hurayrah ﷺ.

فِرْعَوْنَ رَسُولًا ﴿١٥﴾ فَعَصَىٰ فِرْعَوْنُ الرَّسُولَ فَأَخَذْنَاهُ أَخْذًا
وَبِيلًا ﴿١٦﴾ ﴾

Verily, We have sent to you a messenger (Muḥammad ﷺ) to be a witness over you, as We did send a messenger to Fir'awn. But Fir'awn disobeyed the messenger, so We seized him with a severe punishment.

[Sūrah al-Muzammil 73:15-16]

His statement, **"Verily, We"**: The pronoun refers to Allāh ﷻ. And this is the pronoun which is utilized to denote the grandeur of Himself, because He is tremendous ﷻ.

He said, **"We have sent"**: Similarly, the pronoun is used to denote grandeur. And the meaning of "We have sent" is "We have inspired and revealed to."

He said, **"to you"**: Meaning, "O assembly of *jinn* and mankind." The address is to all people. The message of this messenger is general for all of mankind until the Hour is established.

He said, **"a messenger"**: This is in reference to Muḥammad ﷺ.

He said, **"to be a witness"**: Meaning, before Allāh ﷻ on the Day of Judgment; [a witness] that he has conveyed to you the message of Allāh and established the proof against you. As Allāh the Exalted has said:

﴿ رُّسُلًا مُّبَشِّرِينَ وَمُنذِرِينَ لِئَلَّا يَكُونَ لِلنَّاسِ عَلَى اللَّهِ
حُجَّةٌ بَعْدَ الرُّسُلِ ﴾

Messengers as bearers of good news as well as of warning, in order that mankind should have no plea against Allāh after the messengers.

[Sūrah an-Nisā' 4:165]

Therefore, none on the Day of Judgment will say, "I did not know

I was created to worship Allāh. I did not know what was obligatory upon me nor did I know what was prohibited from me." No one will be able to say this. This is because the messengers ﷺ have conveyed [the message] to them. This *ummah* of Muḥammad ﷺ will testify against them. Allāh the Exalted has said:

﴿ وَكَذَٰلِكَ جَعَلْنَاكُمْ أُمَّةً وَسَطًا لِّتَكُونُوا شُهَدَاءَ عَلَى النَّاسِ وَيَكُونَ الرَّسُولُ عَلَيْكُمْ شَهِيدًا ﴾

Thus We have made you a just nation, that you be witnesses over mankind and the Messenger (Muḥammad) be a witness over you.

[Sūrah al-Baqarah 2:143]

Therefore, on the Day of Judgment, this *ummah* will testify against the previous nations that the messages of Allāh have reached them by the ways they find in the Book of Allāh ﷻ, because Allāh has narrated to us the information of the previous nations, the messengers, and that which they said to their nations. All of this we know from the Book of Allāh ﷻ, which falsehood cannot approach, from before it or from behind it. It is a revelation from one who is Wise and Praiseworthy.

Allāh has likewise said, **"and [that] the Messenger (Muḥammad) [may] be"**: This is in reference to Muḥammad ﷺ being a witness against you, O *ummah* of Muḥammad. He will testify against you before Allāh that he established the proof against you, he conveyed to you the message, and he advised you for the sake of Allāh. Therefore, there remains no argument for anyone on the Day of Judgment. None will be able to say, "Nothing has reached me," or "No warner has come to me." Even the disbelievers will acknowledge [the reality] when they are tossed into the Fire, for Allāh has said:

﴿ كُلَّمَا أُلْقِيَ فِيهَا فَوْجٌ سَأَلَهُمْ خَزَنَتُهَا أَلَمْ يَأْتِكُمْ نَذِيرٌ ۝٨ قَالُوا بَلَىٰ قَدْ جَاءَنَا نَذِيرٌ فَكَذَّبْنَا وَقُلْنَا مَا نَزَّلَ اللَّهُ مِن شَيْءٍ إِنْ أَنتُمْ إِلَّا فِي ضَلَالٍ كَبِيرٍ ۝٩ ﴾

Every time a group is cast therein, its keeper will ask, "Did no warner come to you?" They will say, "Yes, indeed; a warner did come to us, but we belied him and said, 'Allāh never sent down anything (of revelation); you are only in great error.'"

[Sūrah al-Mulk 67:8-9]

They said to their messengers, "You are only in great error." They bely the messengers and consider them to be misguided. This is the wisdom of sending the messengers to establish the proof against the slaves of Allāh and to guide those for whom Allāh wills guidance. Allāh guides by way of the messengers whomever He wills, and He establishes the proof against whoever is an obstinate rejecter and disbelieves.

Allāh said, **"as We did send a messenger to Fir'awn."** This Messenger was Mūsā عليه السلام. Fir'awn was a tyrannical ruler in Egypt who claimed lordship for himself. "Fir'awn" was the title of every sovereign of Egypt; he would be called Fir'awn. What is intended by "Fir'awn" here is the Fir'awn who claimed lordship.

﴿ فَقَالَ أَنَا رَبُّكُمُ الْأَعْلَىٰ ﴾

Saying: "I am your lord, most high."

[Sūrah an-Nāzi'āt 79:24]

Allāh went on to say, **"But Fir'awn disobeyed the messenger"**: Meaning, Mūsā. Fir'awn disbelieved in him, as Allāh has narrated the story in His Book regarding what occurred between Mūsā and Fir'awn, and the end result of Fir'awn and his people.

Allāh said, **"so We seized him"**: Meaning, "We seized Fir'awn with a punishment"; and this was that Allāh drowned him and his people and then He entered them into the Fire. Allāh has said:

﴿ مِّمَّا خَطِيئَاتِهِمْ أُغْرِقُوا فَأُدْخِلُوا نَارًا ﴾

Because of their sins they were drowned, then were

made to enter the Fire.

[Sūrah Nūḥ 71:25]

Therefore, they are in a Fire in the Barzakh. Allāh has said:

﴿ النَّارُ يُعْرَضُونَ عَلَيْهَا غُدُوًّا وَعَشِيًّا ﴾

The Fire; they are exposed to it, morning and afternoon.

[Sūrah Ghāfir 40:46]

So this is taking place in the Barzakh before the Hereafter. They are exposed to the Fire every morning and every evening until the Hour is established. This is evidence for the punishment of the grave, and refuge is sought with Allāh. Allāh said:

﴿ وَيَوْمَ تَقُومُ السَّاعَةُ أَدْخِلُوا آلَ فِرْعَوْنَ أَشَدَّ الْعَذَابِ ﴾

And on the Day when the Hour will be established (it will be said to the angels): "Cause Fir'awn's (Pharaoh's) people to enter the severest torment!"

[Sūrah Ghāfir 40:46]

So, these are their three punishments:

1) Allāh drowned them and wiped them out in one instance.

2) They are punished in the Barzakh until the Hour is established.

3) When they are resurrected on the Day of Judgment, they will enter a punishment that is more severe; refuge is sought with Allāh. Likewise for those who disobey Muḥammad ﷺ; that which awaits them is more severe than the punishment of the people of Fir'awn, because Muḥammad ﷺ is the best of the messengers. Therefore, he who disobeys him will have a more severe punishment.

He said, **"with a severe punishment"**: Meaning, it was severe and there was no lightness in it. Allāh said:

﴿وَكَذَٰلِكَ أَخْذُ رَبِّكَ إِذَا أَخَذَ الْقُرَىٰ وَهِيَ ظَالِمَةٌ ۚ إِنَّ أَخْذَهُ أَلِيمٌ شَدِيدٌ﴾

Such is the seizure of your Lord when He seizes the (population of) towns while they are doing wrong. Verily, His seizure is painful and severe.

[Sūrah Hūd 11:102]

This verse is a proof of the favor Allāh had upon us by sending the Messenger Muḥammad ﷺ to us, and that the objective for sending him was to clarify the path of worship to us. He who obeys him will enter Paradise, and he who disobeys him will enter the Fire, just like Fir'awn when he disobeyed their messenger Mūsā عليه السلام. Likewise, the enemies of the Messenger are all upon the same way, and this was their path.

Allāh is Not Pleased That Partners Should Be Set Up With Him in His Worship

ORIGINAL TEXT

الثانية: أنَّ اللهَ لا يرضى أن يُشْرِك معهُ أحدٌ في عبادتِه...

The second [issue]: That Allāh is not pleased that partners should be set up with Him in His worship...

EXPLANATION

This issue is connected to the first issue because the first is a clarification of the obligation of worshiping Allāh and following the Messenger ﷺ; and this is the meaning of the two testimonies. It is the meaning of the testimony that none has the right to be worshiped except Allāh and the testimony that Muḥammad is the Messenger of Allāh.

The second issue is that worship is such that if polytheism is mixed with it, then it will not be accepted, because it is required that worship be pure for the Face of Allāh ﷻ. Therefore, he who worships Allāh and also worships other than Him along with Him, his worship is invalid and its existence is the same as if it didn't exist, because worship will not benefit unless it contains sincerity and *tawḥīd*. If polytheism mixes with it, then it is corrupted. As Allāh the Exalted has said:

﴿ وَلَقَدْ أُوحِيَ إِلَيْكَ وَإِلَى الَّذِينَ مِن قَبْلِكَ لَئِنْ أَشْرَكْتَ لَيَحْبَطَنَّ عَمَلُكَ وَلَتَكُونَنَّ مِنَ الْخَاسِرِينَ ﴾

And it was already revealed to you and to those before you that if you should associate [anything] with Allāh, your work would surely become worthless, and you would surely be among the losers.

[Sūrah az-Zumar 39:65]

Likewise, Allāh the Glorified has said:

﴿ وَلَوْ أَشْرَكُوا لَحَبِطَ عَنْهُم مَّا كَانُوا يَعْمَلُونَ ﴾

But if they had joined in worship others with Allāh, all that they used to do would have been of no benefit to them.

[Sūrah al-An'ām 6:88]

Therefore, worship is not referred to as "worship" unless it is accompanied by *tawḥīd*, just as prayer is not referred to as "prayer" unless it is accompanied by purification. Hence, if polytheism mixes with worship, it corrupts it, just like a nullifier of *wuḍū'* corrupts and invalidates one's purification if it is mixed with it. Due to this, Allāh has combined the command of worshiping Him with the prohibition of polytheism. Allāh the Exalted has said:

﴿ وَاعْبُدُوا اللَّهَ وَلَا تُشْرِكُوا بِهِ شَيْئًا ﴾

Worship Allāh and join none with Him in worship...

[Sūrah an-Nisā' 4:36]

Likewise, Allāh has said:

﴿ وَمَا أُمِرُوا إِلَّا لِيَعْبُدُوا اللَّهَ مُخْلِصِينَ لَهُ الدِّينَ حُنَفَاءَ ﴾

And they were commanded not but that they should worship Allāh, and worship none but Him alone...

[Sūrah al-Bayyinah 98:5]

Allāh ﷻ has also said:

﴿ وَمَا أَرْسَلْنَا مِن قَبْلِكَ مِن رَّسُولٍ إِلَّا نُوحِي إِلَيْهِ أَنَّهُ لَا إِلَٰهَ إِلَّا أَنَا فَاعْبُدُونِ ﴾

And We did not send any messenger before you (O Muḥammad ﷺ) but We inspired him (saying): None has the right to be worshiped but I (Allāh), so worship Me.

[Sūrah al-Anbiyā' 21:25]

Therefore, the statement of Allāh in which He said, **"None has the right to be worshiped but I,"** contains two affairs. It contains the negation of polytheism and the affirmation of worship for Allāh the Exalted.

Likewise, Allāh has said:

﴿ وَقَضَىٰ رَبُّكَ أَلَّا تَعْبُدُوا إِلَّا إِيَّاهُ ﴾

And your Lord has decreed that you worship none but Him.

[Sūrah al-Isrā' 17:23]

Allāh has also said:

﴿ وَلَقَدْ بَعَثْنَا فِي كُلِّ أُمَّةٍ رَّسُولًا أَنِ اعْبُدُوا اللَّهَ وَاجْتَنِبُوا الطَّاغُوتَ ﴾

And verily, We have sent among every *ummah* (community, nation) a messenger (proclaiming):

"Worship Allāh (alone), and avoid the false deities."

[Sūrah an-Naḥl 16:36]

So, He combined worship of Allāh along with the avoidance of the false deities because the worship of Allāh is not considered worship unless it is accompanied by the avoidance of false deities, which is polytheism. Allāh the Exalted has said:

﴿ فَمَن يَكْفُرْ بِالطَّاغُوتِ وَيُؤْمِن بِاللَّهِ فَقَدِ اسْتَمْسَكَ بِالْعُرْوَةِ الْوُثْقَىٰ لَا انفِصَامَ لَهَا ﴾

Whoever disbelieves in the false deities and believes in Allāh, then he has grasped the most trustworthy handhold that will never break.

[Sūrah al-Baqarah 2:256]

Therefore, *īmān* in Allāh is not sufficient unless it is accompanied by disbelief in the false deities. Otherwise, the polytheists would be considered those who believe in Allāh, but they associate partners with him [so they actually disbelieve in Allāh]. Allāh has said:

﴿ وَمَا يُؤْمِنُ أَكْثَرُهُم بِاللَّهِ إِلَّا وَهُم مُّشْرِكُونَ ﴾

And most of them believe not in Allāh except that they attribute partners unto Him.

[Sūrah Yūsuf 12:106]

Allāh, Exalted be He, has clarified that they had *īmān* in Allāh. However, they corrupted it with polytheism, and refuge is sought with Allāh. This is the meaning of the statement of the author: whoever worships Allāh and obeys the Messenger is not to associate anything as a partner with Allāh, because Allāh is not pleased that anyone should be made to share with Him in His worship. The Prophet ﷺ said in what he has narrated from his Lord:

قال الله تبارك وتعالى أنا أغنى الشركاء عن الشرك من عمل عملا أشرك فيه معي غيري تركته وشركه.

Allāh ﷻ has said, "I am the least in need of polytheism. Therefore, he who does an action in which he associates other than Me with Me, then I will leave his action to the one he associated as a partner with Me."[5]

There are a people who pray and testify that none has the right to be worshiped except Allāh and that Muḥammad is the Messenger of Allāh, doing so in abundance; they fast and they perform pilgrimage. However, they supplicate to mausoleums and they worship al-Ḥasan, al-Ḥusayn, al-Badawī, so-and-so, and such-and-such. They seek salvation from the deceased. These people are such that their worship is invalid because they are associating partners with Allāh ﷻ. Their worship is mixed with polytheism; hence, their actions are invalid and will be so until they single out Allāh ﷻ, make their worship pure for Him, and abandon worshiping anything beside Him. They are not upon anything unless they do this.

So, one must pay attention to this because Allāh is not pleased that anyone be made a sharer in His worship along with Him, no matter who they are. He, Glorified be He, is not pleased that anything should be made a sharer along with him. None can say, "I take intercession from the *awliyā'*, the righteous people, and the goodly people, and I do not worship idols or altars as was done in the Pre-Islamic Days of Ignorance. I simply take them as intercessors and I do not worship them."

We say to him that this is a statement of the Pre-Islamic Days of Ignorance, wherein they took these people as intercessors with Allāh because they are righteous and from the *awliyā'* of Allāh, yet Allāh is not pleased with this.

ORIGINAL TEXT

...لا مَلَكٌ مُقَرَّب ولا نبيٌّ مُرْسَل.

...neither an angel brought near, nor a prophet sent as a messenger.

[5] Reported by Muslim (#2985) from the *ḥadīth* of Abū Hurayrah ﷺ.

EXPLANATION

His statement *"neither an angel brought near, nor a prophet sent as a messenger"*: An angel that is near to Allāh is the best of the angels, such as Jibrīl عليه السلام, as well as the carriers of the Throne and those who are around it. The angels who are near to Allāh have a lofty station with Allāh. Despite their closeness in proximity to Allāh and their nearness by way of their worship and status with Allāh, if one were to associate them as partners with Allāh in worship, then Allāh is not pleased that an angel who is near to Him be associated with Him as a partner in worship, nor any prophet that was sent as a messenger, such as Muḥammad ﷺ, 'Īsā, Nūḥ, or Ibrāhīm, who are the Messengers of Strong Will. Allāh is not pleased that anyone should be set up as a partner along with Him, even if they are from the best of the angels and even if they are from the best of mankind.

He is not pleased that anyone from the angels or from the messengers be associated with Him in worship, so how about other than them from the *awliyā'* and the righteous people? Therefore, other than the angels and messengers are such that He would be even more displeased with them being associated with Him in worship. This is a refutation against the people who claim that they are taking the righteous people and the *awliyā'* as intercessors with Allāh so that they may bring them nearer to Allāh in position, just as the people of the Pre-Islamic Days of Ignorance would say, as Allāh has said concerning them:

﴿ مَا نَعْبُدُهُمْ إِلَّا لِيُقَرِّبُونَا إِلَى اللَّهِ زُلْفَى ﴾

"We worship them only that they may bring us near to Allāh."

[Sūrah az-Zumar 39:3]

Besides this, they believe that these deities did not create anything, nor did they provide, nor did they control death, life, or resurrection. Their only objective is utilizing them as intermediaries with Allāh عزّ وجلّ. Due to this, they have devoted to them some acts of worship, seeking the means of nearness to them. So they slaughter for the graves and they make vows for the graves; they seek salvation from and call upon the dead.

ORIGINAL TEXT

والدليلُ قولُهُ تعالى: ﴿ وَأَنَّ الْمَسَاجِدَ لِلَّهِ فَلَا تَدْعُوا مَعَ اللَّهِ أَحَدًا ﴾ [الجن:١٨].

The evidence is the statement of Allāh the Exalted:

And the mosques are for Allāh (alone), so invoke not anyone along with Allāh.

[Sūrah al-Jinn 72:18]

EXPLANATION

Allāh is not pleased that anyone should be made a sharer along with Him in worship, whoever that may be. This is explicitly stated in the Qur'ān and the Sunnah. However, it is also clear for those who have intellect, who ponder and abandon bigoted blind following and false justifications, and who pay attention to themselves. The proof that Allāh is not pleased that anyone should be made a partner with Him in worship, no matter who it may be, is the statement of Allāh the Exalted:

﴿ وَأَنَّ الْمَسَاجِدَ لِلَّهِ فَلَا تَدْعُوا مَعَ اللَّهِ أَحَدًا ﴾

And the mosques are for Allāh (alone), so invoke not anyone along with Allāh.

[Sūrah al-Jinn 72:18]

The *masājid* are the houses of Allāh. They are also the places that are prepared for prayer, and they are the most beloved of places to Allāh. They are the houses that Allāh has allowed to be constructed so that His name may be remembered within them. It is obligatory that these *masājid* are places reserved for the worship of Allāh alone, and nothing (no form of worship) should occur within them for other than Allāh. Graves are not to be built within them, nor edifices. This is because the Prophet ﷺ cursed those who do this and informed us that this is the action of the Jews and Christians, and he prohibited us from this at the end of his life while he was in the throes of death ﷺ. He said:

ألا إن من كان قبلكم كانوا يتخذون القبور مساجد.

Indeed, those who were before you used to take the graves as places of worship.

He said this while he was on the verge of death. He went on to say:

ألا فلا تتخذوا القبور مساجد، إني أنهاكم عن ذلك.

Do not take the graves as places of worship, for indeed I prohibit you from this.[6]

He likewise said:

لعنة الله على اليهود والنصارى، اتخذوا قبور أنبيائهم مساجد.

May Allāh curse the Jews and Christians, for they took the graves of their prophets as places of worship.[7]

Therefore, it is a must that the *masājid* be purified from the traces of polytheism and idolatry, and that they should not be erected upon graves nor should the dead be buried in them after they are built. Rather, they should be places for the worship of Allāh alone. Within them, prayer is to be established, the name of Allāh is to be remembered, the Qur'ān should be recited, beneficial lessons should be established, and one should perform *al-i'tikāf* for the worship of Allāh. This is the function of the *masājid.*

As for establishing idolatry within them and worshiping other than Allāh, then these places (in which this is done) are not *masājid*; rather, they are places of polytheism, even though the people refer to them as *masājid.* This is because Allāh says:

---

[6] Reported by Muslim (#532) from the *ḥadīth* of Jundub bin 'Abdillāh al-Bajalī.

[7] Reported by al-Bukhārī (#43, #436) as well as Muslim (#531) from the *ḥadīth* of 'Ā'ishah and Ibn 'Abbās ﷺ.

﴿ وَأَنَّ الْمَسَاجِدَ لِلَّهِ ﴾

And the mosques are for Allāh (alone)...

[Sūrah al-Jinn 72:18]

Meaning, they are not for other than Him, because the *masājid* are the gathering places of the people wherein they meet. Therefore, it is obligatory that they be purified from polytheism, innovation, and superstition, because the people seek knowledge within them and they perform acts of worship. If they find any polytheism or superstition in the *masājid*, they will be affected by this and they will spread it upon the earth. So it is obligatory that the *masājid* be purified from polytheism. The greatest of them is al-Masjid al-Ḥarām, as Allāh has commanded that it be purified, wherein He said:

﴿ وَإِذْ بَوَّأْنَا لِإِبْرَاهِيمَ مَكَانَ الْبَيْتِ أَن لَّا تُشْرِكْ بِي شَيْئًا
وَطَهِّرْ بَيْتِيَ لِلطَّائِفِينَ وَالْقَائِمِينَ وَالرُّكَّعِ السُّجُودِ ﴾

And [mention, O Muḥammad], when We designated for Ibrāhīm the site of the House, [saying], "Do not associate anything with Me and purify My House for those who perform *ṭawāf* and those who stand [in prayer] and those who bow and prostrate."

[Sūrah al-Ḥajj 22:26]

He said to purify it; from what? Purify it from polytheism, innovation, and superstition, as well as from impurities and filth. The statement of Allāh in which He said:

﴿ فَلَا تَدْعُوا مَعَ اللَّهِ أَحَدًا ﴾

...so invoke not anyone along with Allāh.

[Sūrah al-Jinn 72:18]

This *lā* (لا) is known as "the *lā* of prohibition"; and His statement **"invoke"** is a present-tense verb that is *majzūm* due to the *lā* of prohibition. Therefore, do not invoke, O people, anyone along with Allāh. Do not seek salvation with anyone along with Allāh, such as saying, "O Allāh, O Muḥammad; O Allāh, O 'Abdul-Qadīr." Or saying, "O 'Abdul-Qadīr, O Muḥammad," or whatever resembles this. Allāh is not pleased with this nor will He accept it. The statement of Allāh in which He said:

﴿ أَحَدًا ﴾

...anyone...

[Sūrah al-Jinn 72:18]

This statement is indefinite in the context of the prohibition. Therefore, it is general for all things, and nothing is an exception—not an angel that is near nor a prophet that is sent as a messenger, nor an altar, an idol, a grave, a *shaykh*, or a *walī*, nor one who is alive or one who is dead, whoever it may be. Therefore, it is general for all things which are called upon other than Allāh. He said:

﴿ فَلَا تَدْعُوا مَعَ اللَّهِ أَحَدًا ﴾

...so invoke not anyone along with Allāh.

[Sūrah al-Jinn 72:18]

This verse proves that worship will not benefit unless it is accompanied by *tawḥīd*, and that if polytheism mixes with it, it is invalidated and it will be a means of destruction for its proponent.

Allāh said:

﴿ وَأَنَّ الْمَسَاجِدَ لِلَّهِ ﴾

And the mosques are for Allāh (alone)...

[Sūrah al-Jinn 72:18]

It is obligatory that they be built with a pure intention, and the intent behind building them is not ostentation, seeking reputation, or seeking that you will be mentioned among the people—as some say—in order that one may see the Islamic effects upon that land. All of this is invalid. The *masājid* are built for the worship of Allāh, with the intention of worship. The intention in that must be pure, for Allāh alone. Also, they must be built from lawful earnings; they must not be built from impermissible earnings. This is because it is for Allāh 🟦. The Prophet said:

إِنَّ اللهَ طيب ولا يقبل إلا طيبا.

Indeed, Allāh is pure, and He does not accept anything except what is pure.[8]

Therefore, the *masājid* are built from lawful earnings, and the intention in building them must be pure, seeking the noble Face of Allāh 🟦. One should not desire praise from the people for building them, nor perpetual mention, ostentation, or seeking reputation. The building of the *masājid* is an act of worship, and worship must be pure for the sake of Allāh 🟦.

AL-WALĀ' WAL-BARĀ' (ALLEGIANCE & DISASSOCIATION)

ORIGINAL TEXT ──────────────────────────

الثالثة: أَنَّ مَنْ أَطَاعَ الرسولَ ووَحَّدَ اللهَ لا يجوزُ لهُ مُوالاةُ مَنْ حادَّ اللهَ ورسولَهُ ولو كان أَقْرَبَ قريبٍ.

The third [issue]: Whoever is obedient to the Messenger and singles out Allāh in *tawḥīd*, it is not permissible for him to have allegiance to those who oppose Allāh and His Messenger, even if they are those who are most closely related to him.

────────────── EXPLANATION ──────────────

It is not permissible for one who does this to have allegiance to those who oppose Allāh and His Messenger, even if they are the most closely related to him. This is the issue of *al-walā' wal-barā'*, and it is a subsidiary of *tawḥīd*. From the rights of *tawḥīd* is *al-walā'* (allegiance) to the friends of Allāh and *al-barā'* (disassociation) from the enemies of Allāh. And *al-muwālāh* (الموالاة) and *al-walā'* (الولاء) bear the same meaning. What is intended by *al-walā'* is: love within

───────────────────

[8] Reported by Muslim (#1015) from the *ḥadīth* of Abū Hurayrah 🟦.

the heart, cooperation, and assistance. What is also intended by it is: inheritance and connection in blood money.

Hence, the Muslim has allegiance to the friends of Allāh, meaning his love is restricted to the friends of Allāh and he aids them. The Muslim is with the Muslims, as Allāh the Exalted has said:

﴿ وَأُولُو الْأَرْحَامِ بَعْضُهُمْ أَوْلَىٰ بِبَعْضٍ فِي كِتَابِ اللَّهِ ﴾

But kindred by blood are nearer to one another regarding inheritance in the decree ordained by Allāh.

[Sūrah al-Anfāl 8:75]

Therefore, paying blood money in the case of accidental death is something which is done between the Muslims, and it is called *at-takāful.* All of this falls under *al-walā'*. Therefore, *al-walā'* is not between the Muslim and the disbeliever. Love, aid, inheritance, paying blood money, guardianship in marriage, and guardianship in terms of judgments and other than it—these do not take place between the Muslim and the disbeliever. They are only between the Muslims, due to the statement of Allāh the Exalted:

﴿ وَلَن يَجْعَلَ اللَّهُ لِلْكَافِرِينَ عَلَى الْمُؤْمِنِينَ سَبِيلًا ﴾

And never will Allāh grant to the disbelievers a way (to triumph) over the believers.

[Sūrah an-Nisā' 4:141]

Thus, it is obligatory that the believers be distinguished from the disbelievers. Hence, it is not permissible for one who singles out Allāh in *tawḥīd* and obeys the Messenger ﷺ to have allegiance with those who oppose Allāh; and the meaning of "opposition" is that the person is on one side while Allāh, His Messenger, and the believers are on the opposing side. The one who is in opposition to them is on the side of the disbelievers; this is opposition.

His statement *"even if they are those who are most closely related to him"*: Meaning, in lineage. If your relative is in opposition to Allāh and His Messenger, then it is obligatory upon you to oppose him and cut him off. It is obligatory upon you to love the one who is a friend to Allāh and his Messenger, and to have allegiance to him even if he is distant from you in terms of blood relation. Even if he is a foreigner or he is black or white or red, it is obligatory upon you to have allegiance with him and to love him, whether he is from your land or from the furthest lands of the east or the furthest lands of the west. Allāh the Exalted said:

﴿ وَالْمُؤْمِنُونَ وَالْمُؤْمِنَاتُ بَعْضُهُمْ أَوْلِيَاءُ بَعْضٍ ﴾

The believers, men and women, are supporters of one another.

[Sūrah at-Tawbah 9:71]

Meaning: Between them there is love, mutual assistance of one another, cooperation, and friendship. This is between the believers.

ORIGINAL TEXT

والدليلُ قوله تَعَالى: ﴿ لاَ تَجِدُ قَوْمًا يُؤْمِنُونَ بِاللَّهِ وَالْيَوْمِ الآخِرِ يُوَادُّونَ مَنْ حَادَّ اللَّهَ وَرَسُولَهُ وَلَوْ كَانُوا آبَاءَهُمْ أَوْ أَبْنَاءَهُمْ أَوْ إِخْوَانَهُمْ أَوْ عَشِيرَتَهُمْ أُوْلَئِكَ كَتَبَ فِي قُلُوبِهِمُ الإِيمَانَ وَأَيَّدَهُمْ بِرُوحٍ مِنْهُ وَيُدْخِلُهُمْ جَنَّاتٍ تَجْرِي مِنْ تَحْتِهَا الأَنْهَارُ خَالِدِينَ فِيهَا رَضِيَ اللَّهُ عَنْهُمْ وَرَضُوا عَنْهُ أُوْلَئِكَ حِزْبُ اللَّهِ أَلاَ إِنَّ حِزْبَ اللَّهِ هُمُ الْمُفْلِحُونَ ﴾ [المجادلة: ٢٢].

The proof is the statement of Allāh the Exalted:

You will not find any people who believe in Allāh and the Last Day making friendship with those who oppose Allāh and His Messenger (Muḥammad ﷺ), even if they were their fathers, their sons, their brothers, or their kindred (people). For such He has written faith in their hearts, and strengthened them with *rūḥ* from Himself. And We will admit them to Gardens (Paradise) under which rivers flow, to

dwell therein (forever). Allāh is pleased with them, and they with Him. They are the party of Allāh. Verily, it is the party of Allāh that will be successful.

[Sūrah al-Mujādilah 58:22]

EXPLANATION

His statement, **"You will not find"**: This address is to the Prophet ﷺ, meaning: this will not occur and it will never exist, that one who is a (true) believer in Allāh and His Messenger would love the disbelievers. If he loves them, he is not a believer, even though he may claim to be one.

Ibn al-Qayyim رحمه الله mentioned in *Al-Kāfiyah ash-Shāfiyah*:

أتحب أعداء الحبيب وتدعى

حبا له ما ذاك في إمكان

وكذا تعادي جاهدا أحبابه

أين المحبة يا أخا الشيطان

Do you love the enemies of the one whom you love, while claiming to have love for him? This is not possible.

Likewise, to transgress against and fight those whom He loves; then where, in reality, is this love, O brother of Shayṭān?

It is not at all possible for one to love the disbelievers and also say, "I love Allāh and His Messenger." This is due to the statement of Allāh, the Exalted:

﴿ يَا أَيُّهَا الَّذِينَ آمَنُوا لَا تَتَّخِذُوا عَدُوِّي وَعَدُوَّكُمْ أَوْلِيَاءَ تُلْقُونَ إِلَيْهِم بِالْمَوَدَّةِ وَقَدْ كَفَرُوا بِمَا جَاءَكُم مِّنَ الْحَقِّ يُخْرِجُونَ الرَّسُولَ وَإِيَّاكُمْ ۙ أَن تُؤْمِنُوا بِاللَّهِ رَبِّكُمْ إِن كُنتُمْ خَرَجْتُمْ جِهَادًا فِي سَبِيلِي وَابْتِغَاءَ مَرْضَاتِي ۚ تُسِرُّونَ إِلَيْهِم بِالْمَوَدَّةِ وَأَنَا أَعْلَمُ بِمَا أَخْفَيْتُمْ وَمَا أَعْلَنتُمْ ۚ وَمَن

يَفْعَلْهُ مِنكُمْ فَقَدْ ضَلَّ سَوَاءَ السَّبِيلِ ﴿١﴾ إِن يَثْقَفُوكُمْ
يَكُونُوا لَكُمْ أَعْدَاءً وَيَبْسُطُوا إِلَيْكُمْ أَيْدِيَهُمْ وَأَلْسِنَتَهُم
بِالسُّوءِ وَوَدُّوا لَوْ تَكْفُرُونَ ﴿٢﴾ لَن تَنفَعَكُمْ أَرْحَامُكُمْ وَلَا
أَوْلَادُكُمْ ۚ يَوْمَ الْقِيَامَةِ يَفْصِلُ بَيْنَكُمْ ۚ وَاللَّهُ بِمَا تَعْمَلُونَ
بَصِيرٌ ﴿٣﴾ قَدْ كَانَتْ لَكُمْ أُسْوَةٌ حَسَنَةٌ فِي إِبْرَاهِيمَ وَالَّذِينَ
مَعَهُ إِذْ قَالُوا لِقَوْمِهِمْ إِنَّا بُرَآءُ مِنكُمْ وَمِمَّا تَعْبُدُونَ مِن
دُونِ اللَّهِ كَفَرْنَا بِكُمْ وَبَدَا بَيْنَنَا وَبَيْنَكُمُ الْعَدَاوَةُ وَالْبَغْضَاءُ
أَبَدًا حَتَّىٰ تُؤْمِنُوا بِاللَّهِ وَحْدَهُ ﴾

O you who have believed, do not take My enemies and your enemies as allies, extending to them affection while they have disbelieved in what came to you of the truth, having driven out the Prophet and yourselves [only] because you believe in Allāh, your Lord. If you have come out for *jihād* in My cause and seeking means to My approval, [take them not as friends]. You confide to them affection, but I am most knowing of what you have concealed and what you have declared. And whoever does it among you has certainly strayed from the soundness of the Way. If they gain dominance over you, they would be to you as enemies and extend against you their hands and their tongues with evil, and they wish that you would disbelieve. Never will your relatives or your children benefit you on the Day of Resurrection; He will judge between you. And Allāh is the All-Seer of what you do. There has already been for you an excellent example in Ibrāhīm and those with him, when they said to their people, "Indeed, we are disassociated from you and from whatever you worship other than Allāh. We have denied you, and there has appeared between us and you animosity and hatred forever, until you believe

in Allāh alone."

[*Sūrah al-Mumtaḥinah* 60:1-4]

He said:

$$ ﴿ وَمَا كَانَ اسْتِغْفَارُ إِبْرَاهِيمَ لِأَبِيهِ إِلَّا عَن مَّوْعِدَةٍ وَعَدَهَا إِيَّاهُ فَلَمَّا تَبَيَّنَ لَهُ أَنَّهُ عَدُوٌّ لِّلَّهِ تَبَرَّأَ مِنْهُ ۚ إِنَّ إِبْرَاهِيمَ لَأَوَّاهٌ حَلِيمٌ ﴾ $$

And the request of forgiveness of Ibrāhīm for his father was only because of a promise he had made to him. But when it became apparent to Ibrāhīm that his father was an enemy to Allāh, he disassociated himself from him. Indeed, Ibrāhīm was compassionate and patient.

[*Sūrah at-Tawbah* 9:114]

This is the religion of Ibrāhīm. He freed himself from his father, who was the closest of people in relation to him, due to what he displayed of being an enemy to Allāh. This verse also proves that loving the disbeliever contradicts *īmān* in Allāh and the Last Day, either at its root or its completion. However, if the love is accompanied by assisting their way and their disbelief, this expels one from the religion. As for if it is merely love without aiding them, this is considered something which weakens *īmān*; it is sinful, and it is something that diminishes one's *īmān*.

It has been said that this verse was revealed regarding Abū 'Ubaydah bin al-Jarrāḥ 🙵 when he killed his father on the day of Badr, because his father was upon disbelief and wanted to kill his son, Abū 'Ubaydah. Therefore, Abū 'Ubaydah killed him because he was an enemy of Allāh. And the fact that he was his father did not prevent him from killing him out of anger for the sake of Allāh.

His statement, **"They"**: Meaning, those who stay away from love and affection for those who oppose Allāh and his Messenger. He went on to say, **"He has written faith in their hearts"**: Meaning, Allāh has made it firm in their hearts and has made *īmān* firmly embedded in their hearts.

He went on to say, **"and strengthened them with *rūḥ* from Himself. And We will admit them to Gardens (Paradise) under which rivers flow."** The meaning of *at-ta'yīd* (التأييد) (support) is "to strengthen." So Allāh strengthened them with a *rūḥ* from himself; and the *rūḥ* has a number of applications in the Qur'ān. From them is the *rūḥ* which refers to the soul by way of which the person lives. From them is *al-waḥī* (revelation), as Allāh has said:

$$ \text{﴿ وَكَذَٰلِكَ أَوْحَيْنَا إِلَيْكَ رُوحًا مِّنْ أَمْرِنَا ﴾} $$

And thus We have sent to you (O Muḥammad) a *rūḥ* (an inspiration) of Our command.

[Sūrah ash-Shūrā 42:52]

And from them is Jibrīl عليه السلام; he is ar-Rūḥ al-Quddus, and he is ar-Rūḥ al-Amīn (the Trustworthy Spirit). Allāh the Exalted has said:

$$ \text{﴿ قُلْ نَزَّلَهُ رُوحُ الْقُدُسِ مِن رَّبِّكَ بِالْحَقِّ لِيُثَبِّتَ الَّذِينَ} $$
$$ \text{آمَنُوا وَهُدًى وَبُشْرَىٰ لِلْمُسْلِمِينَ ﴾} $$

Say (O Muḥammad ﷺ): Ar-Rūḥ al-Quddus [Jibrīl] has brought it (the Qur'ān) down from your Lord with truth, that it may make firm and strengthen (the faith of) those who believe, and as a guidance and glad tidings to those who have submitted.

[Sūrah an-Naḥl 16:102]

Allāh the Exalted likewise said:

$$ \text{﴿ نَزَلَ بِهِ الرُّوحُ الْأَمِينُ ﴾} $$

Which the Rūḥ [Jibrīl] has brought down.

[Sūrah ash-Shūrā 26:193]

From these meanings is that which is in this verse, which is "strength." So Allāh supported them with strength from Himself, meaning support from Him ﷻ; the strength of *īmān* in this life as well as the Hereafter.

He went on to say, **"And We will admit them to Gardens"**: "Gardens" is the plural of "garden," and *al-jannah* in the Arabic language refers to pastures. It is called "Jannah" because it is filled with trees, meaning it is covered by them. And the trees overlap one another because al-Jannah is shaded and it contains trees, rivers, and castles. The highest of it and its ceiling is the throne of ar-Raḥmān.

He went on to say, **"And We will admit them to Gardens (Paradise) under which rivers flow, to dwell therein (forever)"**: Meaning, they are going to remain within it and they are never going to leave it. Allāh the Exalted has said:

﴿ خَالِدِينَ فِيهَا لَا يَبْغُونَ عَنْهَا حِوَلًا ﴾

Wherein they shall dwell (forever). No desire will they have to be removed therefrom.

[Sūrah al-Kahf 18:108]

They will not fear death, nor will they fear that anyone will expel them or remove them, as occurs in the *dunyā*. Perhaps a person in the *dunyā* may be in a castle, but he is not safe from death which would remove him from it. And he is not safe from enemies taking control of him and expelling him from his castle. The person is always in a state of fear in the *dunyā*.

He went on to say, **"Allāh is pleased with them, and they with Him"**: Since they had enmity with their relatives from amongst the disbelievers and they took them as enemies, Allāh allowed them to have pleasure from Him as a recompense for them. Therefore, their enmity for their relatives was recompensed by way of the pleasure of Allāh. Allāh is pleased with them and they are pleased with Him.

He went on to say, **"They are the party of Allāh"**: Meaning, the group of Allāh. As for the disbelievers, they are the party of Shayṭān, as Allāh the Exalted has said regarding them:

﴿ إِنَّ حِزْبَ الشَّيْطَانِ ﴾

They are the party of Shayṭān (Satan).

[Sūrah al-Mujādilah 58:19]

Meaning, they are the group of Shayṭān and the supporters of Shayṭān.

As for this group, then they are a party of the Lord. Therefore, this issue is connected to enmity for the disbelievers and not having allegiance for them. And this does not necessitate that we cut off the disbelievers in worldly affairs. Rather, certain affairs are the exception to this. From them: while we hate them and have enmity for them, we must call them to Allāh ﷻ. It is obligatory that we call them to Allāh, and that we do not leave them and say, "These are the enemies of Allāh and our enemies." We must call them to Allāh. Perhaps Allāh will guide them. And if they do not respond, then we fight against them if we have the ability to do so. Therefore, either they will enter Islām or they will pay the *jizyah* if they are from the Jews, Christians, or Magians and they are subjugated and subjected to the ruling of Islām. Thus, they are to be left upon what they are upon with the condition that they pay the *jizyah*, and thus feel themselves subdued to the ruling of Islām. As for if they are other than the People of the Book and the Magians, then there is a difference of opinion between the scholars in taking the *jizyah* from them.

The second exception: There is no harm in entering truces with the disbelievers if there is a need to do so, and if the Muslims need to enter a treaty with them due to the fact that the Muslims do not have the ability to fight against them, and due to fear from the Muslims of their evil. There is no harm in entering a treaty with them until the Muslims are strong enough to fight against them, or if they seek a treaty from the Muslims. Allāh has said:

﴿ وَإِن جَنَحُوا لِلسَّلْمِ فَاجْنَحْ لَهَا ﴾

But if they incline to peace, you also incline to it.

[Sūrah al-Anfāl 8:61]

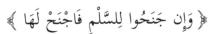

Therefore, the Muslims can make treaties with them. However, it is not ongoing. It is only for a specific amount of time determined by the ruler of the Muslims, due to what it contains of benefit.

The third exception: There is no harm in repaying the good which they do if they do good for the Muslims. There is no harm in recompensing them for their goodness. Allāh has said:

﴿ لَّا يَنْهَاكُمُ اللَّهُ عَنِ الَّذِينَ لَمْ يُقَاتِلُوكُمْ فِي الدِّينِ وَلَمْ يُخْرِجُوكُم مِّن دِيَارِكُمْ أَن تَبَرُّوهُمْ وَتُقْسِطُوا إِلَيْهِمْ ۚ إِنَّ اللَّهَ يُحِبُّ الْمُقْسِطِينَ ﴾

Allāh does not forbid you to deal justly and kindly with those who fought not against you on account of religion and did not drive you out of your homes. Verily, Allāh loves those who deal with equity.

[Sūrah al-Mumtaḥinah 60:8]

The fourth exception: It is obligatory for the Muslim child to be kind to his Muslim or non-Muslim father. However, he does not obey him in his disbelief. This is due to the statement of Allāh the Exalted:

﴿ وَوَصَّيْنَا الْإِنسَانَ بِوَالِدَيْهِ حَمَلَتْهُ أُمُّهُ وَهْنًا عَلَىٰ وَهْنٍ وَفِصَالُهُ فِي عَامَيْنِ أَنِ اشْكُرْ لِي وَلِوَالِدَيْكَ إِلَيَّ الْمَصِيرُ ﴿١٤﴾ وَإِن جَاهَدَاكَ عَلَىٰ أَن تُشْرِكَ بِي مَا لَيْسَ لَكَ بِهِ عِلْمٌ فَلَا تُطِعْهُمَا ۖ وَصَاحِبْهُمَا فِي الدُّنْيَا مَعْرُوفًا ۖ وَاتَّبِعْ سَبِيلَ مَنْ أَنَابَ إِلَيَّ ۚ ثُمَّ إِلَيَّ مَرْجِعُكُمْ فَأُنَبِّئُكُم بِمَا كُنتُمْ تَعْمَلُونَ ﴿١٥﴾ ﴾

And We have enjoined on man (to be dutiful and good) to his parents. His mother bore him in weakness and hardship upon weakness and hardship, and his weaning is in two years. Give thanks to Me and to your parents; unto Me is the final destination. But if they endeavor to make you

associate with Me that of which you have no knowledge, do not obey them, but accompany them in [this] world with appropriate kindness and follow the way of those who turn back to Me [in repentance]. Then to Me will be your return, and I will inform you about what you used to do.

[Sūrah Luqmān 31:14-15]

Therefore, the father has a right even if he is a disbeliever. However, one is not to love him with the entirety of one's heart. Rather, you are to recompense him for his cultivation of you and the fact that he is your father so he has a right. You are to recompense him due to that.

The fifth exception: One is allowed to do business with them and to purchase from them, purchasing one's needs from them, importing goods from them, and buying weaponry at a cost. There is no harm in this. The Prophet ﷺ used to deal with the disbelievers. He likewise dealt with the people of Khaybar, who were Jews; they made an agreement for them to cultivate the land with a portion of that which was removed from it. This is not allegiance or love; it is mutually benefiting one another. And it is obligatory to know these affairs and to know that they do not fall under having allegiance [with the disbelievers], nor are they prohibited.

Likewise, we may take loans from them. The Prophet ﷺ took a loan of some food from a Jew and mortgaged his armor with him to do so. He ﷺ died while his armor was mortgaged with a Jew for some food that he had purchased for his family. There is no harm in this because these are worldly affairs and beneficial matters. It does not denote love or affection from the heart.

It is a must that we distinguish between this and that, because some of the people are such that when they hear the texts regarding enmity for the disbelievers and not loving them, perhaps they understand that they are not able to deal with them and that they are to have no connection with them whatsoever, and that they must have an absolute disconnection from them. This is not the case. This is restricted to the legislative rulings in the realms of the legislation, and with conditions that are known to the people of knowledge, extracted from the Book of Allāh and the Sunnah of the Messenger of Allāh ﷺ.

The sixth exception: Allāh has allowed marriage to women from the People of the Book with the condition that they are chaste in their honor. Allāh has allowed us, likewise, to eat their slaughtered meat.

The seventh exception: There is no harm in accepting their invitations and eating their permissible foods, as the Prophet ﷺ would do this.

The eighth exception: Being kind to one's neighbors who are disbelievers, because they have the rights of the neighbor.

The ninth exception: It is not permissible to oppress them. Allāh the Exalted has said:

﴿ وَلَا يَجْرِمَنَّكُمْ شَنَآنُ قَوْمٍ عَلَىٰٓ أَلَّا تَعْدِلُوا ۚ اعْدِلُوا هُوَ أَقْرَبُ لِلتَّقْوَىٰ ﴾

And let not the enmity and hatred of others make you avoid justice. Be just; that is nearer to piety.

[Sūrah al-Mā'idah 5:8]

ORIGINAL TEXT

اعلَمْ—أرشدَكَ اللهُ لطاعتِه...

Know, may Allāh direct you to His obedience...

EXPLANATION

His statement, *"Know, may Allāh direct you to His obedience"*: It is as if he is beginning the third treatise, because the first two treatises have passed. The first treatise is the four issues which are contained in Sūrah al-'Aṣr. The second treatise is the three preceding affairs. The third treatise is this; and the fourth treatise shall come, which is the three fundamental principles.

So, his statement, *"Know"*: Speech has preceded regarding this term and a clarification of its meaning, and what is intended by its mention.

His statement *"may Allāh direct you"*: This is a supplication from the author رحمه الله for everyone who reads this treatise—understanding it and seeking to act in accordance with it—for Allāh to direct him. The meaning of *al-irshād* (direction) is guidance to that which is correct and the *tawfīq* (success) to have beneficial knowledge and righteous actions. *Ar-rushd* (right guidance) is the opposite of misguidance. Allāh the Exalted has said:

﴿ قَد تَّبَيَّنَ الرُّشْدُ مِنَ الْغَيِّ ﴾

Verily, right guidance has become distinct from the wrong path.

[Sūrah al-Baqarah 2:256]

Likewise, Allāh has said:

﴿ وَإِن يَرَوْا سَبِيلَ الرُّشْدِ لَا يَتَّخِذُوهُ سَبِيلًا وَإِن يَرَوْا سَبِيلَ الْغَيِّ يَتَّخِذُوهُ سَبِيلً ﴾

And if they see the right guidance, they will not adopt it as the Way, but if they see the way of error (polytheism, crimes, and evil deeds), they will adopt that way.

[Sūrah al-A'rāf 7:146]

Ar-rushd is the religion of Islām, whereas misguidance is the religion of Abū Jahl and his likes.

His statement *"may Allāh direct you to His obedience"*: This is a tremendous supplication. If Allāh guides the Muslim to His obedience, then he will be successful in this life as well as the Hereafter. The meaning of *aṭ-ṭā'ah* (obedience) is adherence to what Allāh has commanded and the avoidance of what Allāh has prohibited. This is obedience: that you obey Allāh in what He has commanded, thus enacting His commands; and you avoid His prohibitions, adhering to the command of Allāh and seeking the Face of Allāh ﷻ, hoping for His reward and fearing His punishment. He who is given success in obeying Allāh has been guided to the obedience of Allāh, so he will be successful in this life as well as the Hereafter.

06

The Third Treatise: Monotheism is the Religion of Ibrāhīm

ORIGINAL TEXT

...أنَّ الحنيفيةَ: مِلَّةَ إبراهيمَ.

...indeed, al-Ḥanīfiyyah is the religion of Ibrāhīm.

EXPLANATION

His statement *"indeed, al-Ḥanīfiyyah is the religion of Ibrāhīm"*: Meaning, that which is obligatory upon you to learn and to know is that al-Ḥanīfiyyah is the religion of Ibrāhīm. And the term *al-ḥanaf* in the Arabic language means "inclination". Therefore, the meaning of al-Ḥanīfiyyah is the religion that inclines away from polytheism and towards *tawḥīd*. Ibrāhīm عليه السلام was a *ḥanīf* (monotheist) and a Muslim. He was a *ḥanīf*, meaning, he inclined away from polytheism towards *tawḥīd* and sincerity for Allāh عز وجل. Allāh the Exalted has said:

﴿ إِنَّ إِبْرَاهِيمَ كَانَ أُمَّةً قَانِتًا لِّلَّهِ حَنِيفًا وَلَمْ يَكُ مِنَ الْمُشْرِكِينَ ﴾

Verily, Ibrāhīm was a nation, obedient to Allāh, a

ḥanīf **(monotheist), and he was not one of those who were polytheists.**

[Sūrah an-Naḥl 16:120]

Therefore, *al-ḥanīf* is a description of Ibrāhīm عليه السلام. Meaning, he was one who turned away from *shirk* and inclined away from it totally, towards at *tawḥīd*; directing all of his worship and turning in sincerity to Allāh. Allāh the Exalted has said:

﴿ ثُمَّ أَوْحَيْنَا إِلَيْكَ أَنِ اتَّبِعْ مِلَّةَ إِبْرَاهِيمَ حَنِيفًا ۖ وَمَا كَانَ مِنَ الْمُشْرِكِينَ ﴾

Then, We have inspired you (O Muḥammad ﷺ, saying): "Follow the religion of Ibrāhīm, *ḥanīfa* (monotheism)." And he was not from the polytheists.

[Sūrah an-Naḥl 16:123]

Allāh has likewise said:

﴿ مَا كَانَ إِبْرَاهِيمُ يَهُودِيًّا وَلَا نَصْرَانِيًّا وَلَٰكِن كَانَ حَنِيفًا مُّسْلِمًا وَمَا كَانَ مِنَ الْمُشْرِكِينَ ﴾

Ibrāhīm (Abraham) was neither a Jew nor a Christian, but he was a true Muslim monotheist, and he was not from the polytheists.

[Sūrah Āli 'Imrān 3:67]

These are the descriptions of Ibrāhīm عليه السلام. From them is that he was a *ḥanīf* (monotheist) and that his religion was al-Ḥanīfiyyah, and it is the religion that is pure for Allāh عزوجل, which contains no polytheism. Allāh has ordered His Prophet ﷺ to follow this religion. He said:

﴿ ثُمَّ أَوْحَيْنَا إِلَيْكَ أَنِ اتَّبِعْ مِلَّةَ إِبْرَاهِيمَ حَنِيفًا ۖ وَمَا كَانَ مِنَ الْمُشْرِكِينَ ﴾

Then, We have inspired you (O Muḥammad ﷺ,

saying): "Follow the religion of Ibrāhīm, *ḥanīfa* (monotheism)." And he was not from the polytheists.

[Sūrah an-Naḥl 16:123]

We have been commanded, likewise, to follow the religion of Ibrāhīm. Allāh the Exalted has said:

﴿ هُوَ اجْتَبَاكُمْ وَمَا جَعَلَ عَلَيْكُمْ فِي الدِّينِ مِنْ حَرَجٍ ۚ مِّلَّةَ أَبِيكُمْ إِبْرَاهِيمَ ۚ هُوَ سَمَّاكُمُ الْمُسْلِمِينَ ﴾

He has chosen you and has not laid upon you in religion any hardship. It is the religion of your father Ibrāhīm (Abraham). It is He (Allāh) Who has named you Muslims.

[Sūrah al-Ḥajj 22:78]

It is likewise the religion of all the messengers. However, [this religion is attached to him] because Ibrāhīm is the best of the prophets after our Prophet Muḥammad ﷺ, and he encountered in the path of calling to *tawḥīd* torment and trials the likes of which none besides him had encountered. Yet he was patient upon this. And [it is attached to him] because he was the father of the prophets, for the prophets that came after him were all from his lineage. Hence, al-Ḥanīfiyyah is the religion of all the prophets, and it is the call to *tawḥīd* and the prohibition of polytheism. This is the religion of all the messengers; however, due to Ibrāhīm's specific rank, this religion is attached to him, as well as to those who came after him. And the prophets after him were all upon the religion of Ibrāhīm, and it is the religion of *tawḥīd* and sincerity for Allāh.

What is this religion which we and our Prophet ﷺ were commanded to follow? It is obligatory upon us to know it because it is obligatory upon the Muslim to know what Allāh has made obligatory upon him, so that he may adhere to it and not lapse regarding it. It is not sufficient to ascribe to it without knowledge. It is likewise not sufficient to ascribe to Islām without knowing it or without knowing what the nullifiers of Islām are, and what the legislations and rulings of Islām are. It is not sufficient to ascribe to the religion of Ibrāhīm while you do not know what it is, such that if you are asked regarding it, you would say, "I don't know." This is not permissible. It is obligatory upon you to know it in an excellent manner so that you may traverse upon it with clear insight and not lapse in anything from it.

ORIGINAL TEXT

أنْ تعبدَ اللهَ وحدَهُ مخلصًا له الدِّين.

It is that you worship Allāh alone, making the religion purely for Him.

EXPLANATION

His statement, *"It is that you worship Allāh alone, making the religion purely for Him"*: This is the religion of Ibrāhīm: that you worship Allāh, making the religion purely for Him. So you must combine between two affairs: the first is sincerity, and the second is worship.

The one who worships Allāh but does not make his religion pure for Him—his worship does not amount to anything. He who worships Allāh, fasts, performs Ḥajj, prays, performs 'Umrah, gives charity, pays *zakāh*, and does an abundance of acts of obedience, but he does not do them with sincerity for Allāh عزَّوجلَّ—either because he has done all of these things in order to show off or gain reputation, or he has mixed his actions with something from polytheism (such as making *du'ā'* to other than Allāh, seeking salvation from other than Allāh, or slaughtering for other than Allāh)—then this person is not pure in his worship. Rather, he is a polytheist and he is not upon the religion of Ibrāhīm عليه السلام.

Many of those who ascribe to Islām today fall into major polytheism: from supplicating to other than Allāh, and worshiping graves and edifices, slaughtering for them, making vows for them, performing *ṭawāf* around them, and rubbing them to seek blessings and salvation with the dead, and other than this. Yet they say that they are Muslims. These people do not know the religion of Ibrāhīm عليه السلام, which our Prophet ﷺ was upon. They do not know it, or they knew it but they opposed it upon knowledge; and refuge is sought with Allāh. This [second one] would be worse.

Therefore, the religion of Ibrāhīm does not accept polytheism in any form, and he who mixes his actions with polytheism is not upon the religion of Ibrāhīm even if he ascribes to it and claims that he is Muslim. So it is obligatory to know the religion of Ibrāhīm, and to act upon it and to hold fast to it by worshiping Allāh, making the religion purely for Him; and there should not be any polytheism, minor or major, within your worship. This is the religion of Ibrāhīm, al-Ḥanīfiyyah, which completely disavows polytheism and completely devotes one to *tawḥīd*, meaning that you worship Allāh while making the religion purely for Him.

ORIGINAL TEXT

وبذلك أَمَرَ اللهُ جميعَ الناس وخلَقهم لها.

With this, Allāh has commanded all of mankind and He has created them for it.

EXPLANATION

The statement, *"With this, Allāh has commanded"*: This is referring to the statement, *"That you worship Allāh while making the religion purely for him,"* meaning: He has commanded with the worship of Allāh, making the religion purely for Him. Allāh has commanded all of the creation; Allāh has commanded all of mankind, whether they are Arab on non-Arab, white or black—all of mankind from the time of Ādam to the end of humanity in this world. All of them have been commanded by Allāh to worship Him, making the religion purely for Him in worship. Allāh the Exalted has said:

﴿ أَيُّهَا النَّاسُ اعْبُدُوا رَبَّكُمُ الَّذِي خَلَقَكُمْ وَالَّذِينَ مِن
قَبْلِكُمْ لَعَلَّكُمْ تَتَّقُونَ ﴿٢١﴾ الَّذِي جَعَلَ لَكُمُ الْأَرْضَ فِرَاشًا

وَالسَّمَاءَ بِنَاءً وَأَنزَلَ مِنَ السَّمَاءِ مَاءً فَأَخْرَجَ بِهِ مِنَ الثَّمَرَاتِ رِزْقًا لَّكُمْ ۖ فَلَا تَجْعَلُوا لِلَّهِ أَندَادًا وَأَنتُمْ تَعْلَمُونَ ﴿٢٢﴾

O mankind! Worship your Lord (Allāh), who created you and those who were before you so that you may become people of *taqwā*. He who has made the earth a resting place for you, and the sky as a canopy, and sent down water (rain) from the sky and brought forth therewith fruits as a provision for you. Then do not set up rivals unto Allāh (in worship) while you know (that He alone has the right to be worshiped).

[Sūrah al-Baqarah 2:21-22]

He has no rivals, likenesses, or partners, nor is there any equal to Him. This makes major *shirk* and minor *shirk* prohibited. Allāh has commanded all of mankind with this, from the first of them to the last of them.

His statement *"and He has created them for it"*: Meaning, for them to worship Him alone, not associating any partner with Him. They were created for this purpose, as Allāh has said:

﴿ وَمَا خَلَقْتُ الْجِنَّ وَالْإِنسَ إِلَّا لِيَعْبُدُونِ ﴾

And I (Allāh) created not the *jinn* and humans except that they should worship Me (alone).

[Sūrah adh-Dhāriyāt 51:56]

They were likewise commanded with that in the statement of Allāh the Exalted:

﴿ يَا أَيُّهَا النَّاسُ اعْبُدُوا رَبَّكُمُ الَّذِي خَلَقَكُمْ ﴾

O mankind! Worship your Lord (Allāh), who created you.

[Sūrah al-Baqarah 2:21]

This is the meaning of the statement of the author; He has created them for it and commanded them with it. He combined the two affairs in his statement: *"With this, Allāh has commanded all of mankind and He has created them for it."*

As Allāh the Exalted has said:

﴿ وَمَا خَلَقْتُ الْجِنَّ وَالْإِنسَ إِلَّا لِيَعْبُدُونِ ﴾

And I (Allāh) created not the *jinn* and humans except that they should worship Me (alone).

[Sūrah adh-Dhāriyāt 51:56]

His statement, **"And I (Allāh) created not the *jinn* and humans"**: Allāh is the Creator. He is the one who creates all things; and from that which He has created are the *jinn* and mankind, and He has given them intellect and made them responsible for worshiping Him alone, not associating anything as a partner with Him. He specified them with the command to worship Him because Allāh has given them intellects, and He has given them that by which they are able to distinguish between what is harmful and what is beneficial, between truth and falsehood. And He has created all things for their use and benefit. Allāh the Exalted has said:

﴿ وَسَخَّرَ لَكُم مَّا فِي السَّمَاوَاتِ وَمَا فِي الْأَرْضِ ﴾

And He has subjected to you all that is in the heavens and all that is in the earth...

[Sūrah al-Jāthiyah 45:13]

All things were made subservient to the prophet Ādam so that he could utilize them to do what he had been created for, which is worship Allāh ﷻ, as Allāh has said:

﴿ وَمَا خَلَقْتُ الْجِنَّ وَالْإِنسَ إِلَّا لِيَعْبُدُونِ ﴾

And I (Allāh) created not the *jinn* and humans except that they should worship Me (alone).

[Sūrah adh-Dhāriyāt 51:56]

The *jinn* are a creation from the realm of the unseen. We do not see them. But they are required to worship Allāh, and they are prohibited from polytheism and from disobedience just as the children of Ādam are. However, they are different in their makeup from the children of Ādam. From the perspective of commands and prohibitions, they are similar to the children of Ādam; they are commanded and they are prohibited. The *jinn* are a creation from the creation of the unseen; we do not see them, but they exist.

Al-ins (mankind, الإنس) are the children of Ādam. They are called *al-ins* because some of them associate with others, and they gather and they intermingle. The *jinn* are referred to as *jinn* from the word *al-ijtinān* (الإجتنان), which means "something that is hidden." From this word, as well, is the word *al-janīn* (the fetus, الجنين) because it is hidden inside the womb. There is, likewise, the phrase "جنه الليل" ("the night has covered him"), as well as the word *al-mijann* (المجن), which is a shield, which is taken as protection from arrows and the likes during times of war; therefore, it covers the one who carries it.

Hence, *al-ijtinān* and *al-janīn* both refer to something that is hidden and covered; and the *jinn* are hidden from us, so we do not see them. They are a creation that exists, and whoever denies their existence is a disbeliever because he has belied Allāh and His Messenger, as well as all of the Muslims.

Allāh has clarified that He did not create the *jinn* and mankind except to worship Him—not for anything else. Therefore, He did not create them in order to benefit Him, to harm Him, to be honored by them, or due to Him being in a humiliating circumstance, or so that He may have a large group after having only a few along with Him. He is not in need of the creation. He did not create them due to a need for them, and He did not create them so that they could provide for Him or earn wealth for Him. Allāh has said:

﴿ مَا أُرِيدُ مِنْهُم مِّن رِّزْقٍ وَمَا أُرِيدُ أَن يُطْعِمُونِ ﴿٥٧﴾ إِنَّ
اللَّهَ هُوَ الرَّزَّاقُ ذُو الْقُوَّةِ الْمَتِينُ ﴿٥٨﴾ ﴾

I seek not any provision from them (i.e., provision for themselves or for My creatures) nor do I ask that they should feed Me (i.e., feed themselves or My creatures). Verily, Allāh is the All-Provider, Owner of Power, the Most-Strong.

[Sūrah adh-Dhāriyāt 51:57-58]

Therefore, Allāh is not in need of the creation. Rather, He has created the *jinn* and mankind for one thing only: to worship Him. He is not in need of their worship of Him; rather, they are in need of it. This is because Allāh will ennoble them and enter them into Paradise if they worship Allāh. Therefore, the benefit of worship goes back to them, and the harm of sins likewise will come back upon them. As for Allāh ﷻ, the obedience of the one who is obedient, or the sin of the one who is disobedient, does not harm Him. Allāh has said:

﴿وَقَالَ مُوسَىٰ إِن تَكْفُرُوا أَنتُمْ وَمَن فِي الْأَرْضِ جَمِيعًا فَإِنَّ اللَّهَ لَغَنِيٌّ حَمِيدٌ﴾

And Mūsā (Moses) said, "If you disbelieve, you and all on earth together, then verily! Allāh is Rich (free of all wants), Owner of All Praise."

[Sūrah Ibrāhīm 14:8]

Therefore, Allāh is not harmed by the disobedience of the sinner nor is He benefited by the obedience of the obedient one. This harm or benefit returns to the creation themselves. If they obey Him, then they are benefiting, and if they disobey Him, they are caused harm by disobeying Him.

ORIGINAL TEXT

ومعنى ﴿يَعْبُدُونِ﴾ يوحِّدونِ.

The meaning of "to worship Him" is to single Him out in *tawḥīd*.

EXPLANATION

His statement, *"The meaning of 'to worship Him' is to single Him out in tawḥīd"*: Meaning, to single Him out in worship, for worship and *tawḥīd* bear the same meaning. *Tawḥīd* has been explained to mean worship, and worship has been explained to mean *tawḥīd*. So they bear the same meaning. In this lies a refutation against those who explain *tawḥīd* as affirming that Allāh is the Creator, the Provider, the One who gives life and causes death, and the One who controls the affairs; this is not the *tawḥīd* for which the creation has been created. Rather, the creation has been created in order to implement *tawḥīd* in worship, which is Tawḥīd al-Ulūhiyyah. As for affirming the *tawḥīd* of Allāh's Lordship only, the one who does so is not a *muwaḥḥid* (monotheist), and he is not from the people of Paradise. Rather, he is from the people of the Fire because he has not implemented the *tawḥīd* for which he was created, which is worship.

The Greatest of That Which Allāh Has Commanded with is Tawḥīd

ORIGINAL TEXT

وأعظمُ ما أَمرَ اللهُ به التوحيدَ وهو: إفرادُ اللهِ بالعبادة.

The greatest of that which Allāh has commanded with is *tawḥīd*, which is to single out Allāh in worship.

EXPLANATION

His statement, *"The greatest of that which Allāh has commanded with is tawḥīd"*: This is very important. Indeed, *tawḥīd* is the greatest of that which Allāh has commanded with, and every other command which Allāh has commanded with comes after *tawḥīd*. The evidence that the greatest of that which Allāh has commanded with is *tawḥīd* is the statement of Allāh:

﴿ وَاعْبُدُوا اللَّهَ وَلَا تُشْرِكُوا بِهِ شَيْئًا ۖ وَبِالْوَالِدَيْنِ إِحْسَانًا

وَبِذِي الْقُرْبَىٰ وَالْيَتَامَىٰ وَالْمَسَاكِينِ وَالْجَارِ ذِي الْقُرْبَىٰ
وَالْجَارِ الْجُنُبِ وَالصَّاحِبِ بِالْجَنبِ وَابْنِ السَّبِيلِ وَمَا
مَلَكَتْ أَيْمَانُكُمْ ۗ إِنَّ اللَّهَ لَا يُحِبُّ مَن كَانَ مُخْتَالًا
فَخُورًا ﴾

Worship Allāh and join none with Him in worship, and do good to parents, kinsfolk, orphans, the poor, the neighbor who is near of kin, the neighbor who is a stranger, the companion by your side, the wayfarer (you meet), and those (slaves) whom your right hands possess. Verily, Allāh does not like such as are proud and boastful.

[Sūrah an-Nisā' 4:36]

This verse contains ten rights. Due to this, it is referred to as "the verse of the ten rights." The first of these rights is the right of Allāh, the Glorified. Allāh has said, **"Worship Allāh and join none with Him in worship."**

Then He said **"and do good to parents."** This is the second right.

He mentioned **"kinsfolk"**; this is the third right. [This means] those who are near kindred, those who you are connected to by way of lineage from the mother or father, such as one's forefathers and grandfathers as well as paternal uncles and paternal aunts, maternal uncles and maternal aunts, brothers and sisters, nieces and nephews, or the children of the paternal aunts and uncles. They are those who are near kindred and have the right of kinship.

He went on to say **"the orphans"**; this refers to the orphans amongst the Muslims, and they are those whose father died while they were children who had not yet reached puberty. Thus, they are in need of someone to secure for them their father's wealth and to cultivate them, spending upon them and doing what is beneficial for them, as well as removing what is harmful. This is because they do not have a father to protect them, spend upon them, or defend them. Therefore, they need one who will aid them because they have lost their father and family, and they have a right in Islām.

What is important is that Allāh began this verse by mentioning His right, wherein He said: **"Worship Allāh and join none with Him in worship."** He did not stop short at saying "worship Allāh." This is because worship is not correct when paired with polytheism, nor will it benefit, and it is not called worship unless it is purely for the sake of Allāh ﷻ. If it is mixed with polytheism, it is not called worship, no matter how much the person tires himself out in doing so. He connected the command to worship with the prohibition of polytheism. Therefore, worship is not correct with the existence of polytheism.

This is a proof of the author's statement, *"The greatest of that with which Allāh has commanded is tawḥīd,"* for Allāh began with it in many verses. From them is this verse, and from them is the statement of Allāh:

﴿ وَقَضَىٰ رَبُّكَ أَلَّا تَعْبُدُوا إِلَّا إِيَّاهُ ﴾

And your Lord has decreed that you worship none but Him.

[Sūrah al-Isrā' 17:23]

Therefore, Allāh began with *tawḥīd*. This proves that it is the greatest of that which Allāh has commanded with. Allāh has likewise said:

﴿ قُلْ تَعَالَوْا أَتْلُ مَا حَرَّمَ رَبُّكُمْ عَلَيْكُمْ ۖ أَلَّا تُشْرِكُوا بِهِ شَيْئًا ۖ وَبِالْوَالِدَيْنِ إِحْسَانًا ۖ وَلَا تَقْتُلُوا أَوْلَادَكُم مِّنْ إِمْلَاقٍ ﴾

Say (O Muḥammad): "Come, I will recite what your Lord has prohibited you from: join not anything in worship with Him; be good and dutiful to your parents; kill not your children because of poverty."

[Sūrah al-An'ām 6:151]

This is a proof for that which shall come, which is the fact that the greatest of what Allāh has prohibited is polytheism. If the greatest of that which Allāh has commanded with is *tawḥīd,* it is obligatory that the person begin with learning *'aqīdah* before anything else. *'Aqīdah* is the foundation, so it is obligatory that a person begin with it in learning and teaching, and that one is perpetually teaching it and clarifying it to the people. This is because it is the greatest of that which Allāh has commanded with. It is not appropriate to make it the last thing or to not give concern to it at all, because today there are callers who abstain from teaching *tawḥīd* and *'aqīdah*. There are people who are tried with this, because lapsing regarding it means lapsing in the entirety of the religion. Therefore, it is obligatory to give due importance to it.

And what is *tawḥīd*? Is it that you affirm that Allāh is the Creator, the Provider, the One who gives life and causes death? No; *tawḥīd* is to single out Allāh in worship, because Allāh has said:

﴿ وَمَا خَلَقْتُ الْجِنَّ وَالْإِنسَ إِلَّا لِيَعْبُدُونِ ﴾

And I (Allāh) created not the *jinn* and humans except that they should worship Me (alone).

[Sūrah adh-Dhāriyāt 51:56]

The scholars of *tafsīr* said that the meaning of **"they should worship Me"** is to single out Allāh. Therefore, they explained *tawḥīd* to mean "worship." Hence, *tawḥīd* is to single out Allāh in worship, and it is not merely to affirm that Allāh is the Creator, the Provider, the One who gives life, the One who causes death, and the One who controls, because this is present in our natural disposition. It is present in the minds of the intelligent, and there does not exist an intelligent person on earth who believes that someone other than Allāh has created the heavens and the earth. There does not exist anyone in the entire world, from the disbelievers and the atheists, who believes that the human being created another human being. Allāh has said:

﴿ وَلَئِن سَأَلْتَهُم مَّنْ خَلَقَهُمْ لَيَقُولُنَّ اللَّهُ ﴾

And if you ask them who created them, they will surely say, "Allāh."

[Sūrah az-Zukhruf 43:87]

There does not exist an intelligent person in the world who believes that a human being created another human being who walks upon the earth, speaks, eats, and drinks. Does there exist any intelligent being who believes this? Allāh has said:

﴿أَمْ خُلِقُوا مِنْ غَيْرِ شَيْءٍ أَمْ هُمُ الْخَالِقُونَ ﴿٣٥﴾ أَمْ خَلَقُوا السَّمَاوَاتِ وَالْأَرْضَ ۚ بَل لَّا يُوقِنُونَ ﴿٣٦﴾﴾

Were they created by nothing, or were they themselves the creators? Or did they create the heavens and the earth? Nay, but they have no firm belief.

[Sūrah aṭ-Ṭūr 52:35-36]

Tawḥīd ar-Rubūbiyyah exists in the natural dispositions of the people and (is firmly embedded) in their minds. However, it is not sufficient without Tawḥīd of Worship, which is to single out Allāh in worship.

Due to this, the Shaykh said, *"...tawḥīd, which is to single out Allāh in worship."* He did not say, "It is to single out Allāh in creation, provision, giving life, and causing death," for these things are known. Tawḥīd of Lordship (alone) is not sufficient in defining *tawḥīd*.

The Greatest of That Which Allāh Has Prohibited is Polytheism

ORIGINAL TEXT

وأعظمُ ما نهى عنه الشركُ...

The greatest of that which Allāh has prohibited is polytheism...

EXPLANATION

The statement of the author, *"The greatest of that which Allāh has prohibited is polytheism"*: This is a tremendous benefit, because some people believe that there are things which are greater crimes and that there are more heinous things which Allāh has prohibited. So one may say that *ribā* (usury) is the greatest of affairs, or that fornication is the greatest of the prohibited affairs. Due to this, they focus on the prohibition of *ribā* and the prohibition of fornication, or the prohibition of the corruption of one's character. However, they have no concern for the affair of polytheism, and they do not warn against it while they see the people falling into it. This is from a tremendous ignorance regarding the legislation of Allāh.

Therefore, the greatest of that which Allāh has prohibited is polytheism, and it is greater in severity than *ribā* and greater than the consumption of intoxicants, and greater than theft, eating the wealth of the people unjustly, and gambling; it is the greatest of the prohibited affairs. The proof is the statement of Allāh the Exalted:

﴿ قُلْ تَعَالَوْا أَتْلُ مَا حَرَّمَ رَبُّكُمْ عَلَيْكُمْ ۖ أَلَّا تُشْرِكُوا بِهِ
شَيْئًا ۖ وَبِالْوَالِدَيْنِ إِحْسَانًا ۖ وَلَا تَقْتُلُوا أَوْلَادَكُم مِّنْ إِمْلَاقٍ ۖ
نَّحْنُ نَرْزُقُكُمْ وَإِيَّاهُمْ ۖ وَلَا تَقْرَبُوا الْفَوَاحِشَ مَا ظَهَرَ مِنْهَا
وَمَا بَطَنَ ۖ وَلَا تَقْتُلُوا النَّفْسَ الَّتِي حَرَّمَ اللَّهُ إِلَّا بِالْحَقِّ ۚ
ذَٰلِكُمْ وَصَّاكُم بِهِ لَعَلَّكُمْ تَعْقِلُونَ ﴿١٥١﴾ وَلَا تَقْرَبُوا مَالَ
الْيَتِيمِ إِلَّا بِالَّتِي هِيَ أَحْسَنُ حَتَّىٰ يَبْلُغَ أَشُدَّهُ ۖ وَأَوْفُوا
الْكَيْلَ وَالْمِيزَانَ بِالْقِسْطِ ۖ لَا نُكَلِّفُ نَفْسًا إِلَّا وُسْعَهَا ۖ
وَإِذَا قُلْتُمْ فَاعْدِلُوا وَلَوْ كَانَ ذَا قُرْبَىٰ ۖ وَبِعَهْدِ اللَّهِ أَوْفُوا ۚ
ذَٰلِكُمْ وَصَّاكُم بِهِ لَعَلَّكُمْ تَذَكَّرُونَ ﴿١٥٢﴾ ﴾

Say (O Muḥammad ﷺ): "Come, I will recite what your Lord has prohibited you from: join not anything in worship with Him; be good and dutiful to your parents; kill not your children because of

poverty—We provide sustenance for you and for them; come not near to shameful sins, whether committed openly or secretly; and kill not anyone whom Allāh has forbidden, except for a just cause. This He has commanded you that you may understand. And come not near to the orphan's property, except to improve it, until he (or she) attains the age of full strength; and give full measure and full weight with justice. We burden not any person but with that which he can bear. And whenever you give your word (i.e., judge between men or give evidence, etc.), say the truth even if a near relative is concerned, and fulfill the covenant of Allāh. This He commands you, that you may remember.

[Sūrah al-An'ām 6:151-152]

These verses are referred to as "the ten advices." Allāh began these prohibited matters with the statement, **"Join not anything in worship with Him"**; this indicates that polytheism is the greatest of that which Allāh has prohibited. In Sūrah al-Isrā', Allāh the Exalted has said:

﴿ لَّا تَجْعَلْ مَعَ اللَّهِ إِلَـٰهًا آخَرَ فَتَقْعُدَ مَذْمُومًا مَّخْذُولًا ﴾

Do not set up with Allāh any other deity (god), or you will sit down reproved, forsaken (in the Hellfire).

[Sūrah al-Isrā' 17:22]

Therefore, He began by prohibiting polytheism, and He concluded with the prohibition of polytheism. Allāh has said:

﴿ ذَٰلِكَ مِمَّا أَوْحَىٰ إِلَيْكَ رَبُّكَ مِنَ الْحِكْمَةِ ۗ وَلَا تَجْعَلْ مَعَ اللَّهِ إِلَـٰهًا آخَرَ فَتُلْقَىٰ فِي جَهَنَّمَ مَلُومًا مَّدْحُورًا ﴾

And do not set up with Allāh any other deity lest you should be thrown into Hell, blameworthy and

rejected (from Allāh's mercy).

[Sūrah al-Isrā' 17:39]

This proves that the greatest of that which Allāh has prohibited is polytheism, thus proving the statement of the author: *"The greatest of that which Allāh has prohibited is polytheism."*

In an authentic narration, the Prophet ﷺ was asked, "Which is the greatest sin? He said:

أن تجعل لله ندا وهو خلقك.

That you should make a rival unto Allāh while He has created you.

It was said, "And then what?" He said:

أن تقتل ولدك خشية أن يطع معك.

That you should kill your child out of fear that he would eat with you.

It was said, "And then what?" He said:

أن تزاني حليلة جارك.

That you should fornicate with the woman of your neighbor.[1]

Allāh has revealed that which confirms this in His statement:

﴿ وَالَّذِينَ لَا يَدْعُونَ مَعَ اللَّهِ إِلَـٰهًا آخَرَ وَلَا يَقْتُلُونَ النَّفْسَ الَّتِي حَرَّمَ اللَّهُ إِلَّا بِالْحَقِّ وَلَا يَزْنُونَ ۚ وَمَن يَفْعَلْ ذَٰلِكَ يَلْقَ أَثَامًا ﴾

And those who invoke not any other deity (god) along with Allāh, nor kill such life as Allāh has forbidden except for just cause, nor commit illegal sexual intercourse; and whoever does this shall

[1] Reported by al-Bukhārī (#6861) and Muslim (#86) from the *ḥadīth* of 'Abdullāh bin Mas'ūd ﷺ.

receive the punishment.

[Sūrah al-Furqān 25:68]

He began with polytheism wherein he said:

أن تجعل لله ندا وهو خلقك.

That you should make a rival unto Allāh while He has created you.

And he said that this is the greatest of sins because he was asked, "Which sin is the greatest?" He began with polytheism.

The Prophet ﷺ said:

اجتنبوا السبع الموبقات.

Avoid the seven deadly destructive sins.

It was said, "And what are they, O Messenger of Allāh?" He said:

الشرك بالله، والسحر، وقتل النفس التي حرم الله إلا بالحق...

The association of partners with Allāh, magic, killing a soul that Allāh has prohibited except in due right...[2]

Hence, he began by mentioning polytheism. This proves that polytheism is the greatest of sins. Due to this, the polytheist will never enter Paradise. Allāh the Exalted has said:

﴿ لَقَدْ كَفَرَ الَّذِينَ قَالُوا إِنَّ اللَّهَ هُوَ الْمَسِيحُ ابْنُ مَرْيَمَ ۖ وَقَالَ الْمَسِيحُ يَا بَنِي إِسْرَائِيلَ اعْبُدُوا اللَّهَ رَبِّي وَرَبَّكُمْ ۖ إِنَّهُ مَن يُشْرِكْ بِاللَّهِ فَقَدْ حَرَّمَ اللَّهُ عَلَيْهِ الْجَنَّةَ وَمَأْوَاهُ النَّارُ ۖ وَمَا لِلظَّالِمِينَ مِنْ أَنصَارٍ ﴾

Verily, whosoever sets up partners in worship with Allāh, then Allāh has forbidden Paradise for him, and the Fire will be his abode. And for the wrong-

[2] Reported by al-Bukhārī (#2766) and Muslim (#89) from the *ḥadīth* of Abū Hurayrah ﷺ.

doers there are no helpers.

[Sūrah al-Mā'idah 5:72]

And the polytheist is such that Allāh will not forgive him; thus, He said:

﴿ إِنَّ اللَّهَ لَا يَغْفِرُ أَن يُشْرَكَ بِهِ وَيَغْفِرُ مَا دُونَ ذَٰلِكَ لِمَن يَشَاءُ ﴾

Verily, Allāh forgives not that partners should be set up with him in worship, but He forgives except that (anything else) to whom He pleases.

[Sūrah an-Nisā' 4:48]

This proves that the polytheist is prohibited from entering Paradise and that Allāh will not forgive him, and this indicates that polytheism is the greatest sin because sins which are less than *shirk* are subject to Allāh's forgiveness. As Allāh has said:

﴿ إِنَّ اللَّهَ لَا يَغْفِرُ أَن يُشْرَكَ بِهِ وَيَغْفِرُ مَا دُونَ ذَٰلِكَ لِمَن يَشَاءُ ﴾

Verily, Allāh forgives not that partners should be set up with him in worship, but He forgives except that (anything else) to whom He pleases.

[Sūrah an-Nisā' 4:48]

Therefore, fornication, theft, consumption of intoxicants, and *ribā* all fall under the will of Allāh. If Allāh wills, He will forgive the one who commits them, and if He wills, He will punish him. As for polytheism, it will not be forgiven; the ruling of Allāh regarding it is that He will not forgive it.

Likewise, the sinner is such that if he has major sins which are less than polytheism, he is not prohibited from entering Paradise. His end result will be Paradise—either Allāh will forgive him at the beginning of this affair and enter him into Paradise, or he will come out of the Fire after having been punished and then enter Paradise.

No matter what the believer has from wrongdoings and iniquities which are less than polytheism, he is not to despair from the mercy of Allāh nor will he be prohibited from entering Paradise. He is subject to be forgiven by way of the will of Allāh.

As for the polytheist, he will be deprived of all of that, and refuge is sought with Allāh. This proves that polytheism is the greatest sin. Allāh the Exalted has said:

﴿ إِنَّ الشِّرْكَ لَظُلْمٌ عَظِيمٌ ﴾

Verily! Joining others in worship with Allāh is a great *ẓulm* (wrong) indeed.

[Sūrah Luqmān 31:13]

Likewise, Allāh has said:

﴿ وَمَن يُشْرِكْ بِاللَّهِ فَقَدِ افْتَرَىٰ إِثْمًا عَظِيمًا ﴾

And he who associates others with Allāh has indeed fabricated a tremendous sin.

[Sūrah an-Nisā' 4:48]

And Allāh has said:

﴿ وَمَن يُشْرِكْ بِاللَّهِ فَقَدْ ضَلَّ ضَلَالًا بَعِيدًا ﴾

Whoever sets up partners in worship with Allāh, has indeed strayed far away.

[Sūrah an-Nisā' 4:116]

All of this indicates that polytheism is the greatest sin. And since polytheism is the greatest sin, it is obligatory upon the scholars and the students of knowledge to prohibit it, to warn against it, and to not be silent regarding warning against polytheism. It is obligatory to establish *jihād* against polytheism when one is able to do so, just as the Messenger of Allāh ﷺ fought *jihād* against it. Allāh has said:

﴿ فَاقْتُلُوا الْمُشْرِكِينَ حَيْثُ وَجَدتُّمُوهُمْ وَخُذُوهُمْ

﴿ وَاحْصُرُوهُمْ وَاقْعُدُوا لَهُمْ كُلَّ مَرْصَدٍ ﴾

...then kill the polytheists wherever you find them, and capture them and besiege them, and prepare for them each and every ambush.

[Sūrah at-Tawbah 9:5]

Therefore, it is obligatory to warn against polytheism and to clarify it to the people so that they may avoid it. This is what is obligatory. As for remaining silent regarding polytheism, and leaving the people to fall headlong into the worship of other than Allāh while claiming Islām, with no one prohibiting and no one warning—this affair is very dangerous.

There are people who focus on the prohibition of *ribā*, fornication, and the corruption of manners. These affairs are prohibited and in them lies corruption; however, polytheism is greater. So why do they not give importance to prohibiting polytheism and warning against polytheism, clarifying the major polytheism people fall into while claiming Islām? Why do they have this level of laxity in the affair of polytheism? Why are they heedless regarding it? Why leave the people in that which they are falling into while the scholars are present? They live alongside these people, but they are silent regarding them.

What is obligatory is that one firstly focuses on the prohibition of this great danger which has destroyed the *ummah* bit by bit; every sin besides it is less significant than it. It is obligatory to begin with the most important and then move on to that which is next in importance.

ORIGINAL TEXT

...وهو دعوةُ غيرِهِ معهُ.

...and it is to call upon other than Allāh along with Him.

EXPLANATION

This is the definition of polytheism. It is to call upon other than Allāh along with Him, meaning that one gives something of worship to other than Allāh, (whether it may be) an angel, a prophet, a righteous person, something which is erected, or other than this from any created being. Whoever devotes any form of worship to other than Allāh [has committed] the greatest of that which Allāh has prohibited. This is polytheism.

Therefore, know the explanation of *tawḥīd* and the explanation of polytheism, because there are people who explain *tawḥīd* with other than its proper explanation, and they explain polytheism with other than its proper explanation. From amongst the people is he who says that polytheism is to associate partners in rulership; and unfortunately, this is prevalent today. Ruling with other than what Allāh has sent down is one of the types of polytheism. It is referred to as *shirk aṭ-ṭā'ah* (polytheism in obedience, شرك الطاعة). Without a doubt, obedience to the creation in making permissible that which Allāh has made impermissible, or making impermissible that which Allāh has made permissible, is a type of polytheism. However, there is that which is greater than this, which is worshiping other than Allāh by slaughtering for them, making vows, performing *ṭawāf*, and seeking salvation from them. So what is obligatory is that one beware of all forms of polytheism, and that he does not embark upon any of them, and that he abandons the greatest and most dangerous of them.

Therefore, polytheism should not be explained as being polytheism in rulership only, or polytheism in politics. Thus, they say polytheism at the graves is an insignificant form of polytheism. This is a crime against Allāh ﷻ. Polytheism is the greatest of that which Allāh has prohibited, and it is to call upon other than Allāh along with Him. This is polytheism.

From them, there is he who says polytheism is love of the *dunyā*, love of wealth. Wealth is such that Allāh has made it to be beloved with a natural love, as Allāh has said:

﴿ وَتُحِبُّونَ الْمَالَ حُبًّا جَمًّا ﴾

And you love wealth with much love!

[Sūrah al-Fajr 89:20]

Likewise, Allāh has said:

﴿ وَإِنَّهُ لِحُبِّ الْخَيْرِ لَشَدِيدٌ ﴾

And verily, he is intense in the love of wealth.

[Sūrah al-'Ādiyāt 100:8]

Meaning, in your love of wealth. Likewise, Allāh has said:

﴿ قُلْ إِن كَانَ آبَاؤُكُمْ وَأَبْنَاؤُكُمْ وَإِخْوَانُكُمْ وَأَزْوَاجُكُمْ وَعَشِيرَتُكُمْ وَأَمْوَالٌ اقْتَرَفْتُمُوهَا وَتِجَارَةٌ تَخْشَوْنَ كَسَادَهَا وَمَسَاكِنُ تَرْضَوْنَهَا أَحَبَّ إِلَيْكُم ﴾

Say: "If your fathers, your sons, your brothers, your wives, your kindred, the wealth that you have gained, the commerce in which you fear a decline, and the dwellings in which you delight are more beloved to you than…"

[Sūrah at-Tawbah 9:24]

Allāh said, **"(If they) are more beloved to you"**; He did not repudiate them for loving them. However, He repudiated them for giving it precedence in love over the love of Allāh. The love of wealth is not polytheism because this is a natural love. People need wealth and they love it. The love of wealth is not polytheism because it is from the love of that which is beneficial to the person. However, those who say this statement are either ignorant and have not learned *tawḥīd* or polytheism; or they are rejecters, seeking to divert the people from these realities towards what they want and to the objectives they desire, and Allāh knows best their objectives.

What is important is that this is not polytheism. Polytheism is to call on other than Allāh along with Him or to give any type of worship to other than Allāh, such as slaughtering, making vows, supplicating, seeking salvation, seeking aid, seeking refuge, or having fear, hope, and other than this. This is a polytheism which is the greatest sin: calling upon other than Allāh along with Him. This is because *du'ā'* is the greatest type of worship. Allāh the Exalted has said:

﴿ لَهُ دَعْوَةُ الْحَقِّ ۖ وَالَّذِينَ يَدْعُونَ مِن دُونِهِ لَا يَسْتَجِيبُونَ لَهُم بِشَيْءٍ ﴾

For Him (alone) is the Word of Truth. And those whom they call upon, answer them not...

[Sūrah ar-Ra'd 13:14]

Likewise, Allāh has said:

﴿ فَادْعُوا اللَّهَ مُخْلِصِينَ لَهُ الدِّينَ وَلَوْ كَرِهَ الْكَافِرُونَ ﴾

So, call you (O Muḥammad ﷺ and the believers) upon Allāh, making (your) worship pure for Him (alone) even if the disbelievers may hate (it).

[Sūrah Ghāfir 40:14]

Therefore, *du'ā'* (supplicating) to other than Allāh is polytheism which Allāh and His Messenger have prohibited. As for these crimes which they deem to be polytheism, then it is not like this. However, it is said that some of them are a type of polytheism, although there is that which is more dangerous than it and more important than it. Polytheism varies, and some of its types are more severe than others; and refuge is sought with Allāh.

ORIGINAL TEXT

والدليل قوله تعالى: ﴿ وَاعْبُدُوا اللَّهَ وَلَا تُشْرِكُوا بِهِ شَيْئًا ﴾ [النساء:٣٦].

The proof is the statement of Allāh the Exalted:

Worship Allāh and join none with Him in worship.

[Sūrah an-Nisā' 4:36]

EXPLANATION

His statement, "*The proof is the statement of Allāh the Exalted: 'Worship Allāh and join none with Him in worship'*": We say that the proof that the greatest of what Allāh has commanded with is *tawḥīd* is the statement of Allāh the Exalted:

﴿ وَاعْبُدُوا اللَّهَ وَلَا تُشْرِكُوا بِهِ شَيْئًا ﴾

Worship Allāh and join none with Him in worship.

[Sūrah an-Nisā' 4:36]

Then, He mentioned thereafter the remaining rights. Since He began with *tawḥīd* and the prohibition of polytheism, this is a proof that the greatest of that which Allāh has commanded with is *tawḥīd*, because Allāh has said, **"Worship Allāh,"** and He followed this by stating, **"and join none with Him in worship."**

This is a prohibition. Therefore, He began by commanding with *tawḥīd* and prohibiting polytheism. This proves that the greatest of that which Allāh has commanded with is *tawḥīd*, and the greatest of that which He has prohibited is polytheism, because Allāh began with this, and He does not begin except with that which is the most important, and then that which is next in terms of importance. This is how this verse is utilized as a proof.

07

The First Principle: Knowledge of Allāh

The Three Principles Which are Obligatory to Know

ORIGINAL TEXT

الْأَصْلُ الْأَوَّلُ: مَعْرِفَةُ اللهِ عَزَّ وَ جَلَّ:

فَإِذَا قِيلَ لَكَ: مَا هِيَ الْأُصُولُ الثَّلَاثَةُ الَّتِي تَجِبُ مَعْرِفَتُهَا؟ فَقُلْ: مَعْرِفَةُ الْعَبْدِ رَبَّهُ، وَ دِينَهُ، وَ نَبِيَّهُ مُحَمَّداً صَلَّى اللهُ عَلَيْهِ وَ سَلَّمَ.

The First Principle: Knowledge of Allāh ﷻ

So, if it is said to you, "What are the three principles which are obligatory to know?" Then say:

1) The servant knowing his Lord

2) [Knowing] his religion

3) [Knowing] his Prophet Muḥammad ﷺ

EXPLANATION

Regarding his statement *"principles"*: *Al-uṣūl* (الأصول) is the plural of *al-aṣl* (principle, الأصل). The *aṣl* is that which other than it is built upon. The branch is that which is built upon other than it. These are called *uṣūl* because other than it, from the affairs of the religion, are built upon them. Due to this, they are called *uṣūl*, because the matter of the religion is built upon them and all of the religion revolves around these three principles.

His statement *"The servant knowing his Lord"*: (The word) "his Lord" is in the accusative case because it is the object of (the word) "knowing" (معرفة). This is because the verbal noun (معرفة, knowing) is attached to the doer of the action (العبد, the servant). When the verbal noun is attached, it (takes the role) of enacting the action of the verb, according to the grammarians. The verbal noun here is attached (to the servant), so it does the action of the verb.

His statement *"[knowing] his religion, and [knowing] his Prophet"*: This is mentioned in conjunction with it (i.e., in being in the accusative case). These are the principles of the religion in general. Details regarding this shall come in the speech of the Shaykh رحمه الله, if Allāh wills.

Why did he specify these three principles? He did so because they are foundations of the religion of al-Islām; also, because they are the affairs the slave will be asked about when he is placed in his grave. When the servant is placed in his grave and the dirt is cast upon him, and the people depart from him returning to their families, the two angels will come to him in his grave. His soul will be returned to his body, and he will be made to live the life of the Barzakh. It is not like the life of the *dunyā*; it is a life whose details Allāh is the most knowledgeable about.

They will make him sit up in his grave and they will say to him, "Who is your Lord? What is your religion? Who is your Prophet?" The believer will say, "My Lord is Allāh; my religion is al-Islām; and Muḥammad ﷺ is my Prophet." So it will be said to him, "How do you know this?" He will say, "I read Allāh's Book, so I knew and recognized (the truth)." Then a caller will proclaim, "My slave has spoken truthfully. So spread a bed for him from Paradise and open a door for him into Paradise."

His grave will be expanded for him as far as the eye can see, and the scent and aroma of Paradise will come to him; and he will look at his place in Paradise, so he will say, "O my Lord, establish the Hour so that I may return to my family and possessions."

As for the doubter who lived in doubt and skepticism without certainty—even if he claimed Islām—such as the hypocrite, he will stutter because he had doubt and skepticism about the religion of Allāh. When they say to him, "Who is your Lord?" He will say, "I don't know." When they say, "What is your religion?" He will say,"I don't know." When it is said, "Who is your Prophet?" He will say, "Ah, ah, I don't know. I heard the people saying something, so I said it."

Meaning: In the *dunyā*, he said what the people said without having *īmān*; and refuge is sought with Allāh. This is the hypocrite who outwardly displays Islām but does not believe in his heart. He only outwardly displays it for some worldly benefit. So he says in the *dunyā*, "Allāh is my Lord," yet he does not believe it. His heart rejects it, and refuge is sought with Allāh.

He says, "My religion is al-Islām," yet he does not believe in al-Islām. His heart rejects it. He says, "My Prophet is Muhammad ﷺ," yet he does not believe in the messengership of Muḥammad in his heart; he only says it with his tongue. This is the hypocrite. It will be said to him, "You did not know, nor did you follow the path of those who knew."

So he will be struck with a large iron hammer, from which he will scream in such a manner that if the two classes (*jinn* and mankind) were to hear him, they would pass out. Everything except mankind will hear it, and if mankind heard it, they would pass out; meaning, they would die from terror.

His grave will become constricted until his ribs cave in upon each other. A door to the Fire will be opened for him, and its hot wind and heat will come to him, and he will say, "O my Lord, do not establish the Hour." This is his life and state in the grave, and refuge is sought with Allāh. This is because he did not respond with the upright answer. Due to this, a caller will proclaim, "My servant has lied. So spread for him a bed from the Fire and open for him a door from the Fire." Refuge is sought with Allāh.

Since these questions have such importance, it is obligatory upon us to learn them and believe in them, and not to suffice with simply learning them. Rather, we learn them, we believe in them, we have *īmān* in them, and we act upon them our whole lives in hopes that Allāh will make us firm when being questioned in the grave. Allāh the Exalted says:

﴿ يُثَبِّتُ اللَّهُ الَّذِينَ آمَنُوا بِالْقَوْلِ الثَّابِتِ فِي الْحَيَاةِ الدُّنْيَا وَفِي الْآخِرَةِ ۖ وَيُضِلُّ اللَّهُ الظَّالِمِينَ ۚ وَيَفْعَلُ اللَّهُ مَا يَشَاءُ ﴾

Allāh will keep firm those who believe, with the word that stands firm in this world (i.e., they will keep on worshiping Allāh alone and none else), and in the Hereafter. And Allāh will cause to go astray those who are *ẓālimūn* (polytheists and wrongdoers, etc.), and Allāh does what He wills.

[Sūrah Ibrāhīm 14:27]

So, these three principles have great importance. Due to this, the Shaykh has based this treatise upon them and clarified them so that we may study them, examine them carefully, believe in them, and act upon them in hopes that Allāh will make us and you firm with the firm statement in the life of the *dunyā* and the Hereafter.

ORIGINAL TEXT

فَإِذَا قِيلَ لَكَ: مَنْ رَبُّكَ؟ فَقُلْ: رَبِّي اللهُ الَّذِي رَبَّانِي وَ رَبَّى

So if it is said to you, "Who is your Lord?" Then say, "My Lord is Allāh, who has nurtured me and has nurtured all of the creation with His favors."

———————————— EXPLANATION ————————————

After the Shaykh clarified the three principles in a general manner, he wanted to (thereafter) clarify them individually, one by one, with their evidences from the Book and the Sunnah, with the signs of Allāh in the universe, and with their intellectual evidences. Thus, it is obligatory that the creed be predicated upon proofs from the Book and the Sunnah, and upon investigating the universal signs of Allāh, so that you may become grounded and firm at heart and have all doubts removed.

As for the creed which is predicated upon ambiguities, doubts, the statements of the people, and blind following, then it is a transient creed and it is not firm. It is exposed to deficiency and falsehood. The *'aqīdah* and the rest of the legislative rulings are not established except with evidence from the Book and the Sunnah, and with sound intellectual evidences.

Due to this, the Shaykh cited many evidences for these three principles. There does not come a principle therein except that it is supported by sure proofs and evidences which repel doubts and desires, and firmly embed the *'aqīdah* in the heart.

His statement, *"So, if it is said to you"* (i.e., you are asked) *"who is your Lord?"*: This question will be asked in the *dunyā* and the Hereafter. So it is a must that you know your Lord and that you respond with a correct answer predicated upon certainty and proofs. So say, "My Lord is Allāh"; this is the answer. "...the one who has nurtured me and has nurtured all of the creation with His favors"; this is the intellectual derivation (of proofs).

The Lord is the one who nurtures all of His servants with His favors. He nourishes them with His provisions. He creates them after they were a thing not even worth mentioning; in their mother's womb, a creation after another creation in three stages of darkness. He makes the provision reach them even in their mother's womb. Due to that, the body grows within his mother's womb and becomes bigger, because the provisions and nourishment reach him from Allāh ﷻ.

Then the soul is breathed into him and he moves and comes alive, by the permission of Allāh; this is the nurturing within the womb. Then, when he comes out, Allāh the Glorified nurtures him by His favor of health and wellbeing, and He causes the milk of his mother to flow for him so that he is nourished until he can eat food and no longer needs milk. Then, bit by bit, his intellect, hearing, and sight grow. They grow, bit by bit, until he reaches maturity. Then they continue to grow, bit by bit, until he reaches his prime, and he reaches 40 years old and he is at his full strength.

So, who is the one who nourishes him from the day that He created him in his mother's womb until he dies? Who is He that nourishes him? And then, who is He that makes this food and drink accessible for him within his body so that it reaches every cell and muscle and every place in his body? Who is He that gives him food and drink? Who is He that removes from him and takes from him that which is harmful? Who is He who does that and nurtures the individual? Is it not Allāh ﷻ? This is the Lord ﷻ, the one who nurtures. He is the one who nurtures me and all of the creation with His favors.

Everything on the face of the earth—from the human beings and the animals, the creation on land and in the sea, from the greatest of the creation and the smallest, on land and in the ocean—all of them are nourished with the favors of Allāh and His provision. The Most High has said:

﴿ أَمَّنْ هَٰذَا الَّذِي يَرْزُقُكُمْ إِنْ أَمْسَكَ رِزْقَهُ ﴾

Who is he that can provide for you if He should withhold His provision?

[Sūrah al-Mulk 67:21]

He said:

﴿ وَمَا مِن دَابَّةٍ فِي الْأَرْضِ إِلَّا عَلَى اللَّهِ رِزْقُهَا وَيَعْلَمُ مُسْتَقَرَّهَا وَمُسْتَوْدَعَهَا ﴾

And no (moving) living creature is there on earth but its provision is due from Allāh. And He knows its dwelling place and its deposit (in the uterus, grave, etc.).

[Sūrah Hūd 11:6]

And He said:

﴿ وَكَأَيِّن مِّن دَابَّةٍ لَّا تَحْمِلُ رِزْقَهَا اللَّهُ يَرْزُقُهَا وَإِيَّاكُمْ ۚ وَهُوَ السَّمِيعُ الْعَلِيمُ ﴾

And so, many a moving (living) creature there is, that carries not its own provision! Allāh provides for it and for you. And He is the All-Hearer, the All-Knower.

[Sūrah al-'Ankabūt 29:60]

This is the Lord, Glorified be He.

﴿ ذَٰلِكُمُ اللَّهُ رَبُّكُمْ فَاعْبُدُوهُ ﴾

That is Allāh, your Lord; so worship Him (alone).

[Sūrah Yūnus 10:3]

As for other than Allāh ﷻ, they do not own any of that whatsoever; not the idols nor other than them. No one owns any of the provision; they are only provided for, and they are created beings just like you.

ORIGINAL TEXT

وَ هُوَ مَعْبُودِي لَيْسَ لِي مَعْبُودٌ سِوَاهُ.

"He is my object of worship and I have no object of worship besides

Him."

EXPLANATION

His statement, *"He is my object of worship"*: The Lord is the one who has this status. He is the one who has the right to be worshiped by me and other than me. Then the Shaykh ﷺ drew attention to the fact that it is not sufficient to only affirm Lordship. It is not sufficient that you say, "My Lord is Allāh who has nurtured me with His favors." This is not sufficient. You must acknowledge servitude to Him as well, and (you must) make your worship purely for Him.

This is the difference between the *muwaḥḥid* and the *mushrik*. The *muwaḥḥid* affirms the Lordship of Allāh ﷻ and [he also affirms] servitude to Him alone, without any partners. The *mushrik* affirms the Lordship of Allāh, but he associates partners with Him in worship; he associates other than Him along with Him in worship; he associates with Him one who does not create, provide, or own anything. This is the difference between the *muwaḥḥid* and the *mushrik*.

The *muwaḥḥid* says, "My Lord is Allāh, and He (alone) is my object of worship. I do not have any object of worship besides Him." As for the *mushrik*, he says, "My Lord is Allāh." However, according to him, worship is not due exclusively to Allāh. So he worships trees, stones, the *awliyā'*, the righteous people, and the graves along with Allāh. Due to this, he is a *mushrik*, and his affirmation of the Lordship will not benefit him, nor has he entered Islām by way of it.

His statement, *"He is my object of worship"*: Meaning, He is the deity whom I worship.

His statement, *"I have no object of worship besides Him"*: Meaning, not from the angels, the messengers, the righteous, the trees, stones, or anything; I have no object of worship besides Him ﷻ.

This is affirmation of *at-tawḥīd* by way of the evidence, and this is intellectual evidence; and he mentioned textual evidence from the

Qur'ān. The evidence is His statement:

﴿ الْحَمْدُ لِلَّهِ رَبِّ الْعَالَمِينَ ﴾

All praises and thanks be to Allāh, the Lord of the *'ālamīn* (mankind, *jinn*, and all that exists).

[Sūrah al-Fātiḥah 1:2]

This verse is the first of the Qur'ān in the *muṣ'ḥaf.* There is nothing before it except:

﴿ بِسْمِ اللَّهِ الرَّحْمَٰنِ الرَّحِيمِ ﴾

In the name of Allāh, the Most Merciful, the Bestower of Mercy.

[Sūrah al-Fātiḥah 1:1]

It is also the last of the speech of the people of Paradise. The Most High has said:

﴿ دَعْوَاهُمْ فِيهَا سُبْحَانَكَ اللَّهُمَّ وَتَحِيَّتُهُمْ فِيهَا سَلَامٌ ۚ وَآخِرُ دَعْوَاهُمْ أَنِ الْحَمْدُ لِلَّهِ رَبِّ الْعَالَمِينَ ﴾

And the close of their request will be, "*Al-ḥamdu lillāhi Rabbil-'ālamīn*" [All praises and thanks are to Allāh, the Lord of the *'ālamīn* (mankind, *jinn*, and all that exists)].

[Sūrah Yūnus 10:10]

Allāh ﷻ also commenced the creation with it. The Most High has said:

﴿ الْحَمْدُ لِلَّهِ الَّذِي خَلَقَ السَّمَاوَاتِ وَالْأَرْضَ وَجَعَلَ الظُّلُمَاتِ وَالنُّورَ ﴾

All praises and thanks be to Allāh, who (alone) created the heavens and the earth, and originated the darkness and the light.

[Sūrah al-An'ām 6:1]

Likewise, He will conclude the creation with it. He, the Most High, said:

﴿ وَقُضِيَ بَيْنَهُم بِالْحَقِّ وَقِيلَ الْحَمْدُ لِلَّهِ رَبِّ الْعَالَمِينَ ﴾

And they (all the creatures) will be judged with truth, and it will be said: "All praises and thanks be to Allāh, the Lord of the *'ālamīn* (mankind, *jinn*, and all that exists)."

[Sūrah az-Zumar 39:75]

The creation began with it and it will end with it, so it is a great statement.

His statement, Exalted be He, ***"al-ḥamd"*** (الْحَمْدُ), means: laudation of the one who is praised along with love and veneration of Him. The definite article (*al*) in *al-ḥamd* is for all-inclusiveness; i.e., all forms of praise are for Allāh, with this being solely His right. He has absolute right to the *ḥamd.*

As for other than Him, they are praised in accordance with what they have done from virtuous actions and good. As for the absolute and complete form of *ḥamd*, it is for Allāh ﷻ because all favors are from Him. Even if the creation were to extend to you some form of good treatment, then it is also from Allāh ﷻ. He is the one who has subjected this created being to you, and He is the one who has made it possible for him to treat you well. So the praise goes back to Allāh ﷻ.

His statement ***"lillāh"*** (for Allāh, لله) contains a preposition and an object of the preposition (*jār wa majrūr*) in connection with a predicate that has been left off of the subject; i.e., the *ḥamd* is dedicated or affirmed for Allāh ﷻ.

The meaning of Allāh is: the one who possesses divinity and servitude over all of His creation; and none besides Him, Glorified be He, has this name. No one can be called Allāh. Even Fir'awn did not say, "I am Allāh." Rather, he said, "I am your lord." So this name is exclusively for Allāh. No one can ever be named with it and none should dare to say, "I am Allāh."

Rabb (lord, رَبِّ) is an adjective for the noun of majesty (i.e., Allāh); it is in the genitive case and it is *muḍāf* (i.e., connected to another noun).

Al-'ālamīn (mankind, the *jinn*, and all that exists; الْعَالَمِين) is *muḍaf ilayhi* (i.e., that which the aforementioned noun is connected to), hence it is in the genitive case. The sign of it being in the genitive case is the (letter) *yā'*, because it comes within the sound masculine plural. So it is clear that all forms of *ḥamd* are for Allāh, the Lord of all that exists.

The creation of the angels, the creation of inanimate beings and birds, the creation of beasts of prey, the creation of animals, the creation of insects and atoms, creatures of the land and sea which none knows except Allāh and none can enumerate except Allāh—Allāh is the Lord of them all.

Rabbil-'ālamīn (Lord of all that exists, رَبِّ الْعَالَمِين): This term is not applicable except to Allāh, the Glorified, Mighty, and Majestic. It is not to be said regarding anyone that he is the lord of the *'ālamīn*.

So, if it is said "*ar-Rabb*" (the Lord), then this is not applicable to anything or anyone except Allāh ﷻ; and it is not to be given except to Him. As for the creation, then it is to be restricted, such that it is said "*rabbud-dār*" (lord of the home) or "*rabbul-bahīmah*" (lord of the animals), i.e., their owner and custodian.

ORIGINAL TEXT

وَ كُلُّ مَا سِوَى اللهِ عَالَمٌ، وَ أَنَا وَاحِدٌ مِنْ ذَلِكَ الْعَالَمِ.

"Everything besides Allāh is *'ālam* (a created being) and I am one of that (genus of) *'ālam*."

EXPLANATION

Then the Shaykh ﷺ clarified the point of derivation (of evidence) with this verse (i.e., al-Fātiḥah 1:2) So his statement, *"Everything besides Allāh is 'ālam (a created being) and I am one of that (genus of) 'ālam,"* is saying, "Allāh is my Lord because He is the Lord of everything that exists, and I am one of the *'ālamīn*."

No one can say, "I have a Lord other than Allāh," whether he be a *kāfir* or a Muslim; this is never possible. No one who has intellect would say it, and this is evidence for the Lordship of Allāh ﷻ. As long as He is the Lord of the *'ālamīn*, then He (alone) has the right to worship. This fact falsifies the worship of other than Allāh ﷻ. Due to this, He said thereafter:

﴿ إِيَّاكَ نَعْبُدُ وَإِيَّاكَ نَسْتَعِينُ ﴾

You (alone) we worship, and You (alone) we ask for help (for each and every thing).

[Sūrah al-Fātiḥah 1:5]

This denotes restriction. This is because mentioning the one to whom the action is done ("you alone," إِيَّاكَ) before the doer of the action ("we worship," نَعْبُدُ) indicates restriction. So, "you alone we worship" (إِيَّاكَ نَعْبُدُ) is different from "we worship You" (نعبدك). This is because "we worship You" (نعبدك) only contains an affirmation. However:

﴿ إِيَّاكَ نَعْبُدُ وَإِيَّاكَ نَسْتَعِينُ ﴾

You (alone) we worship, and You (alone) we ask for help (for each and every thing).

[Sūrah al-Fātiḥah 1:5]

This contains a negation and an affirmation. Meaning: We do not worship anyone or anything except You. Worship is not correct except with negation and affirmation, and this is the meaning of *lā ilāha ill-Allāh* (none has the right to be worshiped except Allāh). Within it is a negation and an affirmation: negation of divinity from any besides Allāh, and affirmation of divinity for Allāh alone

عَزَّوَجَلَّ.

ORIGINAL TEXT

فَإِذَا قِيلَ لَكَ: بِمَا عَرَفْتَ رَبَّكَ؟ فَقُلْ: بِآيَاتِهِ وَ مَخْلُوقَاتِهِ.

So, if it is said to you, "How did you come to know your Lord?" Then say, "By His signs and His creation."

EXPLANATION

You said, "Allāh is my Lord," or, "My Lord is Allāh, who has nurtured me with His favors." So what is the evidence that Allāh is your Lord who has nurtured you with His favors?

The Shaykh brought evidences from the revelation and he brought intellectual ones, as shall come. If it is said to you, "How did you come to know your Lord?"—this is because he who claims a thing must have evidence for his claim:

وَ الدَّعَاوَى إِذَا لَمْ يُقِيمُوا

عَلَيْهَا بَيِّنَاتٍ أَهْلُهَا أَدْعِيَاءُ

If they do not establish proofs for the claims,

then the people who make them are impostors.

It is a must that every claimant establishes evidence for his claim; otherwise, his claim is not correct. You say, "My Lord who has nurtured me and all of the creation with His favors." So what is the evidence? Say, "The evidence is His signs and His creation."

Al-āyāt (signs, الآيات) is plural for *āyah* (sign, آية). In the language, it means: a sign of something and that which indicates a thing. As the Prophet ﷺ said:

آيَةُ الْمُنَافِقِ ثَلَاثٌ...

The signs of the hypocrite are three…[1]

Meaning: His distinguishing marks.

His statement, *"By His signs"*: Meaning, the signs and indications which prove Him سُبْحَانَهُ وَتَعَالَىٰ (i.e., indicate that He is the Lord). All of these existent beings which you see were all nonexistent, then Allāh brought them into existence and created them by His power سُبْحَانَهُ وَتَعَالَىٰ.

From them are creations which reproduce, such as the plants, children, and other things which did not exist, and then they came into existence so now you see them. Who is He that created them? It is Allāh سُبْحَانَهُ وَتَعَالَىٰ. Did they create themselves? Did one of the human beings create them? No; no one would make such a claim nor is it possible for one to claim this. The Most High has said:

﴿أَمْ خُلِقُوا مِنْ غَيْرِ شَيْءٍ أَمْ هُمُ الْخَالِقُونَ ﴿٣٥﴾ أَمْ خَلَقُوا السَّمَاوَاتِ وَالْأَرْضَ ۚ بَل لَّا يُوقِنُونَ ﴿٣٦﴾﴾

Were they created by nothing, or were they themselves the creators? Or did they create the heavens and the earth? Nay, but they have no firm belief.

[Sūrah aṭ-Ṭūr 52:35-36]

These things did not bring themselves into existence, nor did other than them from the creation bring them into existence. No one will ever create a tree, a mosquito, or a fly.

﴿إِنَّ الَّذِينَ تَدْعُونَ مِن دُونِ اللَّهِ لَن يَخْلُقُوا ذُبَابًا وَلَوِ اجْتَمَعُوا لَهُ﴾

Verily! Those on whom you call besides Allāh, cannot create (even) a fly, even though they join together for the purpose.

[Sūrah al-Ḥajj 22:73]

---

[1] Al-Bukhārī reported it (#33), as did Muslim (#59) from the *ḥadīth* of Abū Hurayrah رَضِيَ اللَّهُ عَنْهُ.

This creation indicates the Creator ﷻ. Due to this, \
to the Bedouins in the remote desert, "By what do yc
Lord?" They say, "The camel droppings are proof for tl
of the camel; the footsteps are proof of the person wal...g, so does this universe not prove the Sublime and Well-Informed (Allāh)?"

When you see the footsteps imprinted on the ground, does this not indicate to you that someone has walked upon this ground? When you see the droppings of the camel, does this not indicate to you that there is a camel in this land or that a camel has passed through it? The droppings indicate the camel and the footsteps indicate the walker.

ORIGINAL TEXT

وَ مِنْ آيَاتِهِ: اللَّيْلُ وَ النَّهَارُ، وَ الشَّمْسُ وَ الْقَمَرُ، وَ مِنْ مَخْلُوقَاتِهِ: السَّمَوَاتُ السَّبْعُ وَ الْأَرَضُونَ السَّبْعُ، وَ مَا فِيهِنَّ وَ مَا بَيْنَهُمَا.

From His signs are the night and the day, and the sun and the moon. From His creation are the seven heavens and the seven earths; those who are within them and those who are between them.

EXPLANATION

His statement, *"From His signs are the night and the day, and the sun and the moon"*: *Āyāt* are of two types:

The First Type: Universal *āyāt* which you see, such as the heavens, the earth, the stars, the sun, the moon, the mountains, the trees, and the oceans; (these are all) called "signs," because by way of them one gets an indication of their Creator ﷻ. Due to this, Abul-'Atāhiyyah said:

فَيَا عَجَبًا كَيْفَ يُعْصَى الْإِلَٰهُ

أَمْ كَيْفَ يَجْحَدُهُ الْجَاحِدُ

وَ فِي كُلِّ شَيْءٍ لَهُ آيَةٌ

تَدُلُّ عَلَى أَنَّهُ وَاحِدٌ

وَ لِله فِي كُلِّ تَحْرِيكَةٍ

وَ تَسْكِينَةٍ فِي الْوَرَى شَاهِدٌ

How strange is it how the Ilāh (i.e., Allāh) is disobeyed,
Or the insolent one can be insolent towards Him.
In everything there is a sign of Him
Indicating that He is one.
For Allāh, within every moving and still being
from mankind, there is a witness.

How can one be insolent against Allāh ﷻ and say, "There is no Lord for this entire universe; these created beings came into existence without a creator"? And if they did come into existence with a creator, then who is this creator other than Allāh ﷻ? Inform me!! You will not find a creator other than Allāh ﷻ.

Or do they assign to Allāh partners who created the like of His creation, so that the creation [which they made and His creation] seemed alike to them.

﴿ أَمْ جَعَلُوا لِلَّهِ شُرَكَاءَ خَلَقُوا كَخَلْقِهِ فَتَشَابَهَ الْخَلْقُ عَلَيْهِمْ ۚ قُلِ اللَّهُ خَالِقُ كُلِّ شَيْءٍ وَهُوَ الْوَاحِدُ الْقَهَّارُ ﴾

"Or do they assign to Allāh partners who created the like of His creation, so that the creation (which they made and His creation) seemed alike to them." Say: "Allāh is the Creator of all things; He is the One, the Irresistible."

[Sūrah ar-Ra'd 13:16]

The Second Type: Quranic *āyāt* which are recited from the revelation that was sent down to the Messenger ﷺ. All these are proofs for the existence of the Lord ﷻ—for His perfection, His attributes, His names, and that He alone has the right to be worshiped without partners. All of them indicate that; the universal *āyāt* and the Quranic *āyāt*. The universal *āyāt* indicate their Creator, the one who brought them into existence, the one who dictates their affair.

The Quranic *āyāt* contain commands to worship Allāh, and they contain confirmation of the fact that Tawḥīd ar-Rubūbiyyah (Oneness of Lordship) and Tawḥīd al-Ulūhiyyah (Oneness of Allāh's Worship) are derived from them, as is the command to worship Allāh ﷻ. The entirety of the Qur'ān revolves around this matter, and it was revealed for the sake of this affair.

From His signs are the night and the day, and the sun and the moon. These are from the greatest of His signs ﷻ: the dark night which covers this creation and the radiant day which enlightens this creation so that the people can spread out, engaging in their occupations. The Most High said:

﴿ قُلْ أَرَأَيْتُمْ إِن جَعَلَ اللَّهُ عَلَيْكُمُ اللَّيْلَ سَرْمَدًا إِلَىٰ يَوْمِ الْقِيَامَةِ مَنْ إِلَٰهٌ غَيْرُ اللَّهِ يَأْتِيكُم بِضِيَاءٍ ۖ أَفَلَا تَسْمَعُونَ ﴿٧١﴾ قُلْ أَرَأَيْتُمْ إِن جَعَلَ اللَّهُ عَلَيْكُمُ النَّهَارَ سَرْمَدًا إِلَىٰ يَوْمِ الْقِيَامَةِ مَنْ إِلَٰهٌ غَيْرُ اللَّهِ يَأْتِيكُم بِلَيْلٍ تَسْكُنُونَ فِيهِ ۖ أَفَلَا تُبْصِرُونَ ﴿٧٢﴾ وَمِن رَّحْمَتِهِ جَعَلَ لَكُمُ اللَّيْلَ وَالنَّهَارَ لِتَسْكُنُوا فِيهِ وَلِتَبْتَغُوا مِن فَضْلِهِ وَلَعَلَّكُمْ تَشْكُرُونَ ﴿٧٣﴾ ﴾

Say (O Muḥammad ﷺ): "Tell me! If Allāh made night continuous for you till the Day of Resurrection, who is an *ilāh* (a god) besides Allāh who could bring you light? Will you not then hear?" Say (O Muḥammad ﷺ): "Tell me! If Allāh made day continuous for you till the Day of Resurrection, who is an *ilāh* (a god) besides Allāh who could bring you night wherein you rest? Will you not then see?" It is out of His mercy that He has

put for you night and day, that you may rest therein (i.e., during the night) and that you may seek of His bounty (i.e., during the day), and in order that you may be grateful.

[Sūrah al-Qaṣaṣ 28:71-73]

This is from the greatest signs of Allāh, this night and this day. The entire time does not consist of night, nor does the entire time consist of day. This is because the benefits of the servants would be suspended and they would be exhausted if the affair was like this. Allāh has made for them the night and the day following each other in succession.

Moreover, the night and the day are organized, and neither of them differs, nor do they change to the organizational structure of the other. From that which indicates the wisdom of the All-Wise ﷻ is that the actions of the servants and their concoctions will be destroyed and become mixed up, whatever they may be, and they will cease. As for the creations of Allāh ﷻ, they will not fall apart except when Allāh allows for them to fall apart.

So the night and the day run perpetually and neither of them breaks down, whereas the concoctions of the creation break down, malfunction, and expire, even if they are big and strong. How many abandoned cars, planes, and trains do you see, while they used to be strong and useful, but they expired and broke down? Do the night or the day break down? No. This is because their manufacturer is All-Capable and All-Wise ﷻ.

﴿ صُنْعَ اللَّهِ الَّذِي أَتْقَنَ كُلَّ شَيْءٍ ﴾

(It is) the work of Allāh, who perfected all things.

[Sūrah an-Naml 27:88]

THE PROOF FOR HIS LORDSHIP & DIVINITY

ORIGINAL TEXT

وَ الـدَّلِيـلُ قَوْلُـهُ تَعَـالَـى : ﴿ وَمِنْ آيَاتِهِ اللَّيْلُ وَالنَّهَارُ وَالشَّمْسُ وَالْقَمَرُ ۚ لَا تَسْجُدُوا لِلشَّمْسِ وَلَا لِلْقَمَرِ وَاسْجُدُوا لِلَّهِ الَّذِي خَلَقَهُنَّ إِن كُنتُمْ إِيَّاهُ تَعْبُدُونَ ﴾.

The proof is His, the Most High, statement:

And from among His signs are the night and the day, and the sun and the moon. Prostrate not to the sun nor to the moon, but prostrate to Allāh who created them, if you (really) worship Him.

[Sūrah Fuṣṣilat 41:37]

EXPLANATION

This is proof for His Lordship and divinity ﷻ.

﴿ وَمِنْ آيَاتِهِ اللَّيْلُ وَالنَّهَارُ وَالشَّمْسُ وَالْقَمَرُ ﴾

And from among His signs are the night and the day, and the sun and the moon.

[Sūrah Fuṣṣilat 41:37]

The sun and the moon: The sun is a great star which lights the universe, and a shining lamp. As Allāh, the Exalted, has said:

﴿ وَجَعَلْنَا سِرَاجًا وَهَّاجًا ﴾

And have made (therein) a shining lamp (the sun).

[Sūrah an-Naba' 78:13]

The moon: It is a light which lights up the night and lights the path for the people.

Also from their benefits is the well-being of the creation—its trees, fruits, and oceans. If the sun were to be obscured from the creation, the creation would be harmed and the livelihood of the people and their well-being would be damaged; likewise if the moon were to be obscured. The moon also has benefits in it for the fruits and trees, along with what it contains from (benefits) in calculating time. The Most High said:

﴿ وَالْقَمَرَ نُورًا وَقَدَّرَهُ مَنَازِلَ لِتَعْلَمُوا عَدَدَ السِّنِينَ وَالْحِسَابَ ﴾

And the moon (He made) as a light and measured out its (their) stages, that you might know the number of years and the reckoning.

[Sūrah Yūnus 10:5]

And He said:

﴿ يَسْأَلُونَكَ عَنِ الْأَهِلَّةِ ۖ قُلْ هِيَ مَوَاقِيتُ لِلنَّاسِ وَالْحَجِّ ﴾

They ask you (O Muḥammad) about the new moons. Say: "These are signs to mark fixed periods of time for mankind and for the pilgrimage."

[Sūrah al-Baqarah 2:189]

So, within the new moons is the benefit of knowing times and dates: recorded dates, dates of the *'iddah* for the women, and times of the acts of worship (fasting, Hajj, etc.)—all of them are known by calculation based upon these two lights: the sun and the moon. So solar calculations and lunar calculations contain benefits for all of the creation.

From his creations are the seven heavens. The Most High has said:

﴿ اللَّهُ الَّذِي خَلَقَ سَبْعَ سَمَاوَاتٍ وَمِنَ الْأَرْضِ مِثْلَهُنَّ ﴾

It is Allāh Who has created seven heavens, and of the earth the like thereof (i.e., seven).

[Sūrah aṭ-Ṭalaq 65:12]

He said:

﴿ الَّذِي خَلَقَ سَبْعَ سَمَاوَاتٍ طِبَاقًا ﴾

(He it is) who has created the seven heavens, one above another.

[Sūrah al-Mulk 67:3]

Meaning: One over the other—the lowest heaven, then the one after it, up to the seventh. And over all of them is the Throne of ar-Raḥmān ﷻ.

The seven earths (are from the creation), as He, the Most High, has said:

﴿ وَمِنَ الْأَرْضِ مِثْلَهُنَّ ﴾

...and of the earth the like thereof (i.e., seven).

[Sūrah aṭ-Ṭalaq 65:12]

So they are seven levels as well. Each level from the seven levels of the heavens and earths has inhabitants and life forms: that which is in the heavens from the planets, stars, and the sun and the moon; and that which is within the earth from the created beings, from the various types of animals, mountains, trees, stones, minerals, and oceans. These are from the signs of Allāh ﷻ. (They are from the) universal *āyāt* which you see and witness.

He رحمه الله said, *"And the proof is His, the Most High, statement:*

﴿ وَمِنْ آيَاتِهِ اللَّيْلُ وَالنَّهَارُ وَالشَّمْسُ وَالْقَمَرُ ۚ لَا تَسْجُدُوا لِلشَّمْسِ وَلَا لِلْقَمَرِ وَاسْجُدُوا لِلَّهِ الَّذِي خَلَقَهُنَّ إِن كُنتُمْ إِيَّاهُ تَعْبُدُونَ ﴾

"'And from among His signs are the night and the day, and the sun and the moon. Prostrate not to the sun or the moon, but prostrate to Allāh who created them, if you(really) worship Him.'"

[Sūrah Fuṣṣilat 41:37]

"From among His signs": Meaning, from the indicative signs of His Lordship, power, and His right to be worshiped over other than Him, are: the night which darkens and the day which lights the entire creation. These are from the most amazing of His signs ﷻ.

Who is He that can make the entire creation dark in one instant and then light up the entire creation in one instant? It is Allāh ﷻ. If the entire creation had gathered together for the purpose of bringing light to a place on the earth, they would only be able to light a limited space. If they were to bring all the electric machinery in the world, they would only be able to light a limited part of the earth.

As for the sun and the moon, they light up the entire earth; the night and the day follow one another in succession, and the sun and the moon likewise. The Most High has said:

﴿ لَا تَسْجُدُوا لِلشَّمْسِ وَلَا لِلْقَمَرِ وَاسْجُدُوا لِلَّهِ الَّذِي خَلَقَهُنَّ إِن كُنتُمْ إِيَّاهُ تَعْبُدُونَ ﴾

Prostrate not to the sun or the moon, but prostrate to Allāh who created them, if you (really) worship Him.

[Sūrah Fuṣṣilat 41:37]

This is invalidation of *shirk*. Do not prostrate to created things. This is because the sun and the moon are from the greatest of the created things, and the polytheists used to worship the sun and the moon and prostrate to them. From the polytheists were those who worshiped the moon and the stars, such as the people of Ibrāhīm. They built shrines for them in the images of stars, and they would worship them.

Regarding His, the Most High, statement:

﴿ لَا تَسْجُدُوا لِلشَّمْسِ ﴾

Prostrate not to the sun...

[Sūrah Fuṣṣilat 41:37]

The meaning of "prostration" (*as-sujūd,* السجود) is placing the forehead on the ground in humility to the one worshiped, and it is the greatest type of worship. Allāh's Messenger ﷺ said:

أَقْرَبُ مَا يَكُونُ الْعَبْدُ مِنْ رَبِّهِ وَ هُوَ سَاجِدٌ.

The closest a servant is to his Lord is when he is prostrating.[2]

The greatest form of worship is prostrating upon the ground. This is because you have placed your face—which is the noblest thing on you—on the ground for Allāh, in worship of Allāh and in humility before Him ﷻ. This is the true prostration, and it is not befitting that any be worshiped with it except Allāh.

As for prostrating to the sun and the moon, then this entails prostrating to a created being which does not deserve to be prostrated to. It is not permissible to prostrate to the creation. Prostration is only to be done for the Creator of the creation. As for the creation, then it is created, controlled, and managed, just as you are; so will you prostrate to an incapable, created being like yourself? This is not permissible. Where have the people's senses gone?!

Prostration is only due to the Creator ﷻ, the One who is not incapable of anything. Prostration is a right of Allāh ﷯; and it is not a right for any created being, however great and big it may be, for it is only a weak, controlled, and managed creation.

﴿لَا تَسْجُدُوا لِلشَّمْسِ وَلَا لِلْقَمَرِ وَاسْجُدُوا لِلَّهِ الَّذِي خَلَقَهُنَّ إِن كُنتُمْ إِيَّاهُ تَعْبُدُونَ﴾

Prostrate not to the sun or the moon, but prostrate to Allāh who created them, if you (really) worship Him.

[Sūrah Fuṣṣilat 41:37]

What is obligatory is that we do not worship anyone or anything except Allāh. When you prostrate to Him and you prostrate to

---

[2] Muslim reported it (#482) from the *ḥadīth* of Abū Hurayrah ﵁.

other than Him, then you are not worshipers of Allāh with the correct (manner of) worship. Rather, you are worshiping Him with *shirk*, and *shirk* corrupts worship.

ORIGINAL TEXT

وَ قَوْلُهُ تَعَالَى: ﴿ إِنَّ رَبَّكُمُ اللَّهُ الَّذِي خَلَقَ السَّمَاوَاتِ وَالْأَرْضَ فِي سِتَّةِ أَيَّامٍ ثُمَّ اسْتَوَىٰ عَلَى الْعَرْشِ يُغْشِي اللَّيْلَ النَّهَارَ يَطْلُبُهُ حَثِيثًا وَالشَّمْسَ وَالْقَمَرَ وَالنُّجُومَ مُسَخَّرَاتٍ بِأَمْرِهِ ۗ أَلَا لَهُ الْخَلْقُ وَالْأَمْرُ ۗ تَبَارَكَ اللَّهُ رَبُّ الْعَالَمِينَ ﴾.

And His, the Most High, statement:

> **Indeed, your Lord is Allāh, who created the heavens and the earth in six days, and then He *istawā'* (rose over) the Throne (really in a manner that suits His majesty). He brings the night as a cover over the day, seeking it rapidly, and (He created) the sun, the moon, and the stars subjected to His command. Surely, His is the creation and commandment. Blessed be Allāh, the Lord of the *'ālamīn* (mankind, *jinn,* and all that exists)!**
>
> *[Sūrah al-A'rāf 7:54]*

EXPLANATION

The word *inna* (indeed, إِنَّ) is a tool of emphasis, and it makes the word following it accusative. It is also a tool of oath, the oath which comes before it being latent. That which is latently left off is, "By Allāh."

﴿ إِنَّ رَبَّكُمُ ﴾

Indeed your Lord...

[Sūrah al-A'rāf 7:54]

This is what the latent oath swears to. **"Indeed your Lord..."** i.e., your Creator and the one who nurtures you with His favors.

"…is Allāh": And it is none other than Him ﷻ. Then He mentioned the evidence for that; He said:

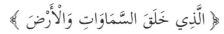

﴿ الَّذِي خَلَقَ السَّمَاوَاتِ وَالْأَرْضَ ﴾

…who created the heavens and the earth…

[Sūrah al-A'rāf 7:54]

This is the proof for the Lordship of Allāh ﷻ, that He has created the heavens and the earth and no one (besides Him) created either of them, and none aided Him ﷻ in that. Rather, He was alone in creating it.

﴿ الَّذِي خَلَقَ السَّمَاوَاتِ وَالْأَرْضَ ﴾

…who created the heavens and the earth…

[Sūrah al-A'rāf 7:54]

Has anyone from the polytheists or the atheists contradicted this and said, "Allāh did not create the heavens and the earth; the one who created it was so-and-so"? Or, "I am the one who created it"? Or, "Such-and-such idol created it"? Has anyone in the world, of old or recent times, said this, whereas this verse is recited by night and by day? None has contradicted it, nor is anyone ever able to contradict it.

﴿ فِي سِتَّةِ أَيَّامٍ ﴾

…in six days…

[Sūrah al-A'rāf 7:54]

Allāh created this amazing and magnificent creation in (only) six days, and He is able to create it in a split second. However, He created it in six days due to a wisdom which He ﷻ knows. As it relates to the six days: the first of them was Sunday and the last of them was Friday. On Friday, the creation was completed. Due to this, this day is the greatest day of the week; it is the leader of the days, the weekly Eid, and the most virtuous of days. Allāh's

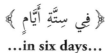

Messenger ﷺ said:

خَيْرُ يَوْمٍ طَلَعَتْ فِيهِ الشَّمْسُ يَوْمُ الْجُمَعَةِ.

The best day on which the sun has risen is Friday.[3]

This is because the creation was completed on it, and Ādam was created on this day and allowed to enter Paradise. He was expelled therefrom (on a Friday), and on it, the Hour will be established. All of this occurs on a Friday. So, it is the most virtuous of days, and it was the last of the days of creation of the heavens, the earth, and everything in them.

﴿ ثُمَّ اسْتَوَىٰ عَلَى الْعَرْشِ ﴾

... and then He *istawā'* (rose over) the Throne...

[Sūrah al-A'rāf 7:54]

"And then" is a tool of conjunction and sequence; i.e., His rising above the Throne took place after the creation of the heavens and the earth. This is because it is from the attributes of action which He does when He wills. The meaning of *al-istawā'* is "elevated and rose up."

The Throne is the ceiling of the creation. In the language, "throne" means "an elevated seat"; and it is the elevated seat which has legs, and it is carried by the angels. It is the greatest and loftiest of the created things.

Al-istawā' is an attribute from the attributes of action for Allāh, in a manner that befits His majesty. It is not like the rising of the creation above the creation. It is not due to a need for the Throne, because He is the one who makes firm the Throne and other than it.

﴿ إِنَّ اللَّهَ يُمْسِكُ السَّمَاوَاتِ وَالْأَرْضَ أَن تَزُولَا ۚ وَلَئِن
زَالَتَا إِنْ أَمْسَكَهُمَا مِنْ أَحَدٍ مِّن بَعْدِهِ ﴾

[3] Muslim reported it (#854), as did Abū Dāwūd (#1046), at-Tirmidhī (#477), and an-Nasā'ī (3/90) from the *ḥadīth* of Abū Hurayrah ﷺ.

Verily! Allāh grasps the heavens and the earth lest they move away from their places, and if they were to move away from their places, there is not one who could grasp them after Him.

[Sūrah Fāṭir 35:41]

The Throne is in need of Allāh ﷻ, because it is created, and Allāh is not in need of the Throne or other than it. However, He rose above it due to a wisdom which He knows ﷻ. *Al-istawā'* is a type of highness (*al-'ulū*); however, highness is an attribute of (Allāh's) essence.

As for *al-istawā'*, it is an attribute of action, which He does when He wills ﷻ.

﴿ يُغْشِي اللَّيْلَ النَّهَارَ ﴾

...He brings the night as a cover over the day...

[Sūrah al-A'rāf 7:54]

He covers the night with the day and He envelops the day with the night. So, you see the creation brightened, and then night covers it so that it becomes darkened; and the day covers the night so that it becomes brightened.

﴿ يَطْلُبُهُ حَثِيثًا ﴾

...seeking it rapidly...

[Sūrah al-A'rāf 7:54]

This one (night) comes directly after that (the day), without being delayed. When the night goes away, the day comes. When the day goes away, the night comes immediately afterward; one is not delayed from the other. This is from the perfection of His power ﷻ. One of them does not lag behind the other.

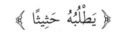

The sun is the great and well-known celestial body. The moon, likewise, is a celestial body from the celestial bodies and from the seven orbital celestial bodies. Each of them runs and orbits around the earth while the earth is firmly fixed. He made it firm (i.e., fixed and firm for the well-being of the servants), while the sun and the rest of the bodies rotate around it.

It is not as the fabricators from those who claim to have knowledge say today—they say that the sun is firmly fixed in its place while the earth rotates around it. This is the opposite of what is in the Qur'ān:

﴿ وَالشَّمْسُ تَجْرِي لِمُسْتَقَرٍّ لَّهَا ﴾

And the sun runs on its fixed course for a term (appointed).

[Sūrah Yā-Sīn 36:38]

Yet they say that the sun is firmly fixed in its place! *Yā subḥānAllāh!*

"An-nujūm" (النُّجُومَ): These are the stars.

﴿ مُسَخَّرَاتٍ بِأَمْرِهِ ﴾

...subjected to His command...

[Sūrah al-A'rāf 7:54]

(Meaning): Subjected in their orbiting and rotating perpetually, and they do not cease. This is a refutation against those who worship the sun, the moon, and the stars, since they are subjected to the command of Allāh and ordered (to do what they do). Allāh is the one who caused them to run and Allāh is the one who will cause them to stop if He so wills ﷻ. So, they are subjected and controlled, and they have nothing to do with the affair. He commands them, Glorified be He, and they run, rotate, and illuminate by way of His universal command ﷻ. This one rises and that one sets, and they follow behind each other.

"The sun" and **"the moon"** are both *manṣūb* (in the accusative case) while **"the stars"** is joined by way of a conjunction. This is because **"the heavens"** is (also) *manṣūb* since it is the object of the verb. The marking of it ("heavens") being accusative is the *kasrah* in place of the *fat'ḥah*. Then He mentioned (in the verse) the sun and the moon (both) being joined to that which is *manṣūb* by way of a conjunction. That which is joined by way of a conjunction to something *manṣūb* is, itself, *manṣūb*.

"Subjected" is *manṣūb* because it describes the state (i.e., the state of being subjected). The sign of it being *manṣūb* is the *kasrah* in the place of the *fat'ḥah*, because it is the sound feminine plural.

He said:

﴿ أَلَا لَهُ الْخَلْقُ وَالْأَمْرُ ﴾

Is not for Him the creation and commandment?

[Sūrah al-A'rāf 7:54]

"Is not" (أَلا): This is a tool of *tanbīh* (i.e., used to draw one's attention) and affirmation; i.e., it (the creation and the command) belong to Him and not to other than Him.

"The creation" (*al-khalq*, الْخَلْق): This means "bringing into existence." He is able to create when He wants to ﷻ. He creates what He wills.

"The command" (*al-amr*, الأَمْرُ): This is His command ﷻ, and it is His universal and legislative speech. His universal command is what He commands the creation with, and the creation subsequently obeys Him and responds to Him. Such as His statement:

﴿ فَقَالَ لَهَا وَلِلْأَرْضِ ائْتِيَا طَوْعًا أَوْ كَرْهًا ﴾

And He said to it and to the earth, "Come both of you, willingly or unwillingly."

[Sūrah Fuṣṣilat 41:11]

He commanded them, Glorified be He. This is the universal command with which He commanded the heavens and the earth, so that they came to be:

﴿ إِنَّمَا أَمْرُهُ إِذَا أَرَادَ شَيْئًا أَن يَقُولَ لَهُ كُن فَيَكُونُ ﴾

Verily, His command, when He intends a thing, is

only that He says to it, "Be!" and it is!

[Sūrah Yā-Sīn 36:82]

This is a universal command.

As for the legislative command, it is the revelation He sends down with which He commands His servants. He commands them to worship Him; He commands them with prayer; He commands them with *zakāh*; He commands them with treating the parents well; this is His legislative command. What falls under this are the commands and prohibitions found in the Noble Qur'ān and the Prophetic Sunnah. This is from the command of Allāh ﷻ. So, if the creation and the command belong to Him, then what remains for other than Him?

Due to this, Ibn 'Umar said, when he recited this verse: "He who has something, then let him seek it."

This verse proves the difference between the creation and the command, so it is a refutation against those who say that the Qur'ān is created. This is because the Qur'ān is from the command, and the command of Allāh is not created, because Allāh differentiated between the creation and the command. He made them two distinct things; and the Qur'ān falls into the category of the command, so it is not created. This is what Imām Aḥmad disputed against the Jahmiyyah with when they sought for him to say that the Qur'ān was created. He said:

هَلِ الْقُرآنُ مِنَ الْخَلْقِ أَوْ مِنَ الأَمْرِ؟

Is the Qur'ān from the creation or the command?

They said:

الْقُرآنُ مِنَ الأَمْرِ.

The Qur'ān is from the command.

He said:

الْأَمْرُ غَيْرُ مَخْلُوقٍ، اللهُ غَايَرَ بَيْنَهُ وَ بَيْنَ الْخَلْقِ، فَجَعَلَ الْخَلْقَ شَيْئًا وَ الْأَمْرَ شَيْئًا آخَرَ.

The command is not created. Allāh differentiated between it and the creation, and He made the creation to be one thing and the command to be another.

The command is speech. As for the creation, it is the bringing into existence and formulating of something, so there is a difference between them.

﴿ تَبَارَكَ اللَّهُ ﴾

Blessed be Allāh...

[Sūrah al-A'rāf 7:54]

Meaning: Magnified is He whose actions these are; this is His power, and this is His creation ﷻ.

"Blessed be He" (*tabārak*, تَبَارَكَ): This is a verb which is specific to Him, Glorified be He, so it is not to be applied to anyone else. *Barakah* means "an abundance and excessive amount of goodness." The *barakah* of Allāh ﷻ does not end. As for the creation, it is not to be said regarding it *"tabārak"* (i.e., "it/he has blessed such-and-such"). It is only to be said *"mubārak"* (i.e., "Allāh has placed blessing in it and made it blessed"); and all blessing is from Allāh ﷻ.

﴿ رَبُّ الْعَالَمِينَ ﴾

...the Lord of the *'ālamīn* (mankind, *jinn*, and all that exists)!

[Sūrah al-A'rāf 7:54]

As has preceded, this verse contains confirmation of Tawḥīd ar-Rubūbiyyah (Oneness of Allāh's Lordship) and Tawḥīd al-Ulūhiyyah (Oneness of Allāh's Worship/Divinity).

ORIGINAL TEXT

وَ الرَّبُّ هُوَ الْمَعْبُودُ، وَ الدَّلِيلُ قَوْلُهُ تَعَالَى: ﴿ يَا أَيُّهَا النَّاسُ اعْبُدُوا رَبَّكُمُ الَّذِي خَلَقَكُمْ وَالَّذِينَ مِن قَبْلِكُمْ لَعَلَّكُمْ تَتَّقُونَ ﴿٢١﴾ الَّذِي جَعَلَ لَكُمُ الْأَرْضَ فِرَاشًا وَالسَّمَاءَ بِنَاءً وَأَنزَلَ مِنَ السَّمَاءِ مَاءً فَأَخْرَجَ بِهِ مِنَ الثَّمَرَاتِ رِزْقًا لَّكُمْ ۖ فَلَا تَجْعَلُوا لِلَّهِ أَندَادًا وَأَنتُمْ تَعْلَمُونَ ﴿٢٢﴾ ﴾.

The Lord is al-Ma'būd (i.e., the true object of worship). The proof is the statement of the Most High:

> **O mankind! Worship your Lord (Allāh), who created you and those who were before you so that you may become *al-muttaqūn* (the pious). Who has made the earth a resting place for you, and the sky as a canopy, and sent down water (rain) from the sky and brought forth therewith fruits as a provision for you. Then do not set up rivals unto Allāh (in worship) while you know (that He alone has the right to be worshiped).**
>
> *[Sūrah al-Baqarah 2:21-22]*

EXPLANATION

His statement, *"The Lord is al-Ma'būd (i.e., the true object of worship)"*: Meaning, He is the one who deserves worship. As for other than Him, then it does not deserve worship because it is not a Lord. This is the meaning of the statement of the Shaykh رحمه الله when he said, *"The Lord is al-Ma'būd (i.e., the true object of worship)."* Meaning, He is the one who deserves worship.

Also, it is not sufficient for the person to affirm the Lordship; rather, it is a must that one affirms servitude to Allāh ﷻ and enacts it sincerely for Him. So, as long as one affirms that He is the Lord, then he is required to also affirm that He is al-Ma'būd (the true object of worship), and that none besides Him has the right to be worshiped at all.

The evidence that worship is specific for the Lord is the statement of the Most High:

﴿ يَا أَيُّهَا النَّاسُ اعْبُدُوا رَبَّكُمُ الَّذِي خَلَقَكُمْ وَالَّذِينَ مِن قَبْلِكُمْ لَعَلَّكُمْ تَتَّقُونَ ﴿٢١﴾ الَّذِي جَعَلَ لَكُمُ الْأَرْضَ فِرَاشًا وَالسَّمَاءَ بِنَاءً وَأَنزَلَ مِنَ السَّمَاءِ مَاءً فَأَخْرَجَ بِهِ مِنَ الثَّمَرَاتِ رِزْقًا لَّكُمْ ۖ فَلَا تَجْعَلُوا لِلَّهِ أَندَادًا وَأَنتُمْ تَعْلَمُونَ ﴿٢٢﴾ ﴾

O mankind! Worship your Lord (Allāh), who created you and those who were before you so that you may become *al-muttaqūn* (the pious). Who has made the earth a resting place for you, and the sky as a canopy, and sent down water (rain) from the sky and brought forth therewith fruits as a provision for you. Then do not set up rivals unto Allāh (in worship) while you know (that He alone has the right to be worshiped).

[Sūrah al-Baqarah 2:21-22]

His statement:

﴿ يَا أَيُّهَا النَّاسُ ﴾

O mankind…

[Sūrah al-Baqarah 2:21-22]

This is a summons from Allāh to all of mankind, the believers as well as the disbelievers. This is because Allāh has mentioned within this *sūrah*—Sūrah al-Baqarah—the three categories of people.

The First Category: The believers who believe in the unseen and believe in the Last Day. He has described them as being successful, in His statement:

﴿ أُولَٰئِكَ عَلَىٰ هُدًى مِّن رَّبِّهِمْ ۖ وَأُولَٰئِكَ هُمُ الْمُفْلِحُونَ ﴾

They are on (true) guidance from their Lord, and they are the successful.

[Sūrah al-Baqarah 2:5]

The Second Category: The disbelievers who outwardly display disbelief and obstinacy. The Most High has said:

﴿ إِنَّ الَّذِينَ كَفَرُوا سَوَاءٌ عَلَيْهِمْ أَأَنذَرْتَهُمْ أَمْ لَمْ تُنذِرْهُمْ لَا يُؤْمِنُونَ ﴾

Verily, those who disbelieve, it is the same to them whether you (O Muḥammad ﷺ) warn them or do not warn them; they will not believe.

[Sūrah al-Baqarah 2:6]

The Third Category: The hypocrite who is not with the disbelievers nor is he with the believers:

﴿ مُّذَبْذَبِينَ بَيْنَ ذَٰلِكَ لَا إِلَىٰ هَٰؤُلَاءِ وَلَا إِلَىٰ هَٰؤُلَاءِ ۚ وَمَن يُضْلِلِ اللَّهُ فَلَن تَجِدَ لَهُ سَبِيلًا ﴾

(They are) swaying between this and that, belonging neither to these nor to those, and he whom Allāh sends astray, you will not find for him a way (to the truth—Islām).

[Sūrah an-Nisā' 4:143]

They are believers outwardly, but they are disbelievers inwardly. These people are more evil than the disbelievers who are open with their disbelief. Due to this, Allāh revealed 10 verses regarding them, while He only revealed a few verses regarding the believers and two verses regarding the disbelievers (within Sūrah al-Baqarah).

As for the hypocrites, He began their mention from His statement:

﴿ وَمِنَ النَّاسِ مَن يَقُولُ آمَنَّا بِاللَّهِ وَبِالْيَوْمِ الْآخِرِ وَمَا هُم بِمُؤْمِنِينَآمَنَّا بِاللَّهِ وَبِالْيَوْمِ الْآخِرِ وَمَا هُم بِمُؤْمِنِينَ ﴾

And of mankind, there are some (hypocrites) who say, "We believe in Allāh and the Last Day," while in fact they believe not.

[Sūrah al-Baqarah 2:8]

Up to His statement:

﴿ يَكَادُ الْبَرْقُ يَخْطَفُ أَبْصَارَهُمْ ﴾

The lightning almost snatches away their sight...

[Sūrah al-Baqarah 2:20]

All of this (was revealed) regarding the hypocrites due to the severity of their danger and the repugnance of their actions. Then, once he had mentioned these three categories of people, He said:

﴿ يَا أَيُّهَا النَّاسُ ﴾

O mankind!

[Sūrah al-Baqarah 2:21]

This is a call to all of the categories: the believers, the disbelievers, and the hypocrites. The scholars say that the first address within the *muṣ'ḥaf* is this:

﴿ يَا أَيُّهَا النَّاسُ اعْبُدُوا رَبَّكُمْ ﴾

O mankind! Worship your Lord (Allāh)...

[Sūrah al-Baqarah 2:21]

"Worship" (اعْبُدُوا): This is a command. It means "make the worship purely for Him." Why? Because He is your Lord, and worship is not to be given to any except the Lord ﷻ. Then, He mentioned the evidence for that:

﴿ الَّذِي خَلَقَكُمْ وَالَّذِينَ مِن قَبْلِكُمْ ﴾

...He who has created you and those who were before you...

[Sūrah al-Baqarah 2:21]

Meaning: From all of the (previous) nations. Allāh ﷻ has created the angels, the *jinn*, and mankind.

﴿ لَعَلَّكُمْ تَتَّقُونَ ﴾

...so that you may become *al-muttaqūn* (pious)...

[Sūrah al-Baqarah 2:21]

Meaning: If you reflect upon this, then perhaps it will cause you to have *taqwā*—if you reflect upon the fact that He is the one who created you and created those before you. Perhaps you may have *taqwā* of Him ﷻ in worshiping Him, because nothing saves one from His punishment except obedience to Him ﷻ. Perhaps you will fear His punishment and fear the Fire, for nothing protects you from it except worshiping your Lord who has created you and created those before you.

Then He went on to derive evidence for His Lordship and servitude, in His statement:

﴿ الَّذِي جَعَلَ لَكُمُ الْأَرْضَ فِرَاشًا ﴾

Who has made the earth a resting place for you...

[Sūrah al-Baqarah 2:22]

Meaning: (He made it) widespread.

﴿ وَاللَّهُ جَعَلَ لَكُمُ الْأَرْضَ بِسَاطًا ﴾

And Allāh has made for you the earth widespread (an expanse).

[Sūrah Nūḥ 71:19]

Meaning: (He made it) expansive and (He made it) a resting place. You are able to rest therein; you sleep upon it, you build upon it, you sow upon its back, and you travel upon it in your journeys, wherever you please. So, the earth is a place of rest and repose.

﴿ وَالْأَرْضَ فَرَشْنَاهَا فَنِعْمَ الْمَاهِدُونَ ﴾

And We have spread out the earth, how excellent a spreader (thereof) are We!

[Sūrah adh-Dhāriyāt 51:48]

(This is) for your benefit.

﴿ وَالسَّمَاءَ بِنَاءً ﴾

...and the sky as a canopy...

[Sūrah al-Baqarah 2:22]

The sky is the ceiling of the earth. Within it are benefits for the servants.

﴿ وَأَنزَلَ مِنَ السَّمَاءِ مَاءً فَأَخْرَجَ بِهِ مِنَ الثَّمَرَاتِ رِزْقًا لَّكُمْ ۖ فَلَا تَجْعَلُوا لِلَّهِ أَندَادًا وَأَنتُمْ تَعْلَمُونَ ﴾

...and (He) sent down water (rain) from the sky and brought forth therewith fruits as a provision for you. Then do not set up rivals unto Allāh (in worship) while you know (that He alone has the right to be worshiped).

[Sūrah al-Baqarah 2:22]

The Different Types of Worship Allāh Has Commanded With & the Proofs for Each Type

ORIGINAL TEXT

قَالَ ابْنُ كَثِيرٍ – رَحِمَهُ اللهُ تَعَالَى: الْخَالِقُ لِهَذِهِ الْأَشْيَاءِ هُوَ الْمُسْتَحِقُّ لِلْعِبَادَةِ. وَ أَنْوَاعُ الْعِبَادَةِ الَّتِي أَمَرَ اللهُ بِهَا مِثْلُ الْإِسْلَامِ وَ الْإِيمَانِ وَ الْإِحْسَانِ.

Ibn Kathīr رحمه الله said, "The Creator of these things is the one who has the right to be worshiped." This is as it relates to the (various) types of worship with which Allāh has commanded, such as *al-islām*, *al-īmān*, and *al-iḥsān*.

------------------------------ EXPLANATION ------------------------------

When the Shaykh clarified the fact that the Lord is the (true) object of worship, he proved it by way of His, the Most High, statement:

﴿ يَا أَيُّهَا النَّاسُ اعْبُدُوا رَبَّكُمُ الَّذِي خَلَقَكُمْ وَالَّذِينَ مِن قَبْلِكُمْ لَعَلَّكُمْ تَتَّقُونَ ﴾

O mankind! Worship your Lord (Allāh), who created you and those who were before you so that you may become *al-muttaqūn* (the pious).

[Sūrah al-Baqarah 2:21]

He supported this with the statement of Ibn Kathīr ﷮ in explanation of the verse, and he went on to clarify the types of worship and the evidences for each type.

The meaning of worship in the language is "humility and submissiveness." Derived from this is *ṭarīq maʿbad* (the roadway, طريق معبد). Meaning, the road which is worn down and heavily trodden from walking upon it.

Worship is of two categories:

The First Category: Worship which is general for all of the creation. They are all servants of Allāh—the believers, the disbelievers, the evildoers, and the hypocrites; all of them are servants of Allāh. Meaning, they are under His control and (subject) to His power, and it is obligatory upon them to worship Him ﷻ. This is the worship which is general for all of the creation, the believers as well as the disbelievers from amongst them. They are all called servants of Allāh; meaning, they are His creation and are submissive to Him. None of them are outside of His grasp and authority, as the Most High has said:

﴿ إِن كُلُّ مَن فِي السَّمَاوَاتِ وَالْأَرْضِ إِلَّا آتِي الرَّحْمَٰنِ عَبْدًا ﴾

There is none in the heavens and the earth but

comes unto the Most Beneficent (Allāh) as a slave.

[Sūrah Maryam 19:93]

This includes all within the heavens and earth, the believer as well as the disbeliever. All of them will come forth on the Day of Judgment subjugated, and none of them have any share with Allāh in His dominion.

The Second Category: The servitude which is specific to the believers. As Allāh has said:

﴿ وَعِبَادُ الرَّحْمَٰنِ الَّذِينَ يَمْشُونَ عَلَى الْأَرْضِ هَوْنًا ﴾

And the slaves of the Most Beneficent (Allāh) are those who walk on the earth in humility and sedateness.

[Sūrah al-Furqān 25:63]

The Most High has said:

﴿ إِنَّ عِبَادِي لَيْسَ لَكَ عَلَيْهِمْ سُلْطَانٌ ﴾

Certainly, you shall have no authority over My slaves.

[Sūrah al-Ḥijr 15:42]

Shayṭān said:

﴿ إِلَّا عِبَادَكَ مِنْهُمُ الْمُخْلَصِينَ ﴾

"Except Your chosen (guided) slaves among them."

[Sūrah al-Ḥijr 15:40]

This is the specific servitude, and it is the servitude of obedience and drawing near to Allāh by way of *at-tawḥīd*.

The scholars differed regarding the definition of the term "worship" (العبادة) in the legislation. Meaning, their terminology differed in their defining of it, but the meaning is one and the same. From them is he who says, "Worship is the highest level of humility along with the highest level of love," as Ibn al-Qayyim said in (the poem) *An-Nūniyyah*:

وَ عِبَادَةُ الرَّحْمَنِ غَايَةُ حُبِّهِ

مَعَ ذُلِّ عَابِدِهِ هُمَا قُطْبَانِ

Worship of ar-Raḥmān is the utmost love of Him

Along with the humility of His worshiper; they are two poles.

So, he defined it as being the highest level of love along with the highest level of humility.

From them is he who says, "Worship is that which has been commanded legislatively, without cultural influence or intellectual requirements." This is because worship is *tawqīfiyyah*[4] and it is not affirmed (merely) by the intellect; it is only affirmed by the legislation. This is the correct definition.

However, the comprehensive and conclusive definition is the definition of Shaykh-ul-Islām Ibn Taymiyyah رحمه الله wherein he said:

الْعِبَادَةُ اِسْمٌ جَامِعٌ لِكُلِّ مَا يُحِبُّهُ اللهُ مِنَ الْأَقْوَالِ وَ الْأَعْمَالِ الظَّاهِرَةِ وَ الْبَاطِنَةِ.

***Al-'ibādah* is a comprehensive term for everything which Allāh loves and is pleased with, from statements and actions, both apparent and hidden.**

This is the comprehensive and conclusive definition: that worship is a term for everything Allāh has commanded with. So, doing what Allāh has commanded is obedience to Allāh, and leaving what Allāh has prohibited is obedience to Allāh.

This is worship, and its types are not restricted. Its types are many. Everything Allāh has commanded with is worship, and abandonment of what Allāh has prohibited—whether outwardly with the

---

[4] **Translator's Note:** Meaning, it only comes by way of revelation; there is no room for intellectual free-thinking in it.

limbs or inwardly with the heart—is worship. This is because worship is upon the tongue, within the heart, and upon the limbs.

It is upon the tongue, such as: *tasbīḥ*, *dhikr*, saying *lā ilāha ill-Allāh* (none has the right to be worshiped except Allāh), and pronouncing the two testimonies of faith. Every legislated statement of the tongue from the remembrance of Allāh is worship.

Likewise, that which is within the heart from the means of nearness to Allāh ﷻ is worship, such as: *al-khawf* (fear), *ar-rajā'* (hope), *al-khashyah* (awe), *ar-raghbah* (longing), *ar-rahbah* (dread), *at-tawakkul* (reliance), *al-inābah* (turning in repentance), and *al-isti'ānah* (seeking help). All of these are actions of the heart. Taking refuge with Allāh is done with the heart, as is awe of Allāh and fear of Him, longing for Him, loving Him ﷻ, having sincerity for Him, and having truthfulness in intention for Allāh ﷻ; everything within the heart, from these various types, is worship.

Likewise, worship is upon the limbs, such as: *ar-rukū'* (bowing), *as-sujūd* (prostrating), *jihād* in Allāh's path, *jihād* with one's person, and *hijrah* (emigrating); all of these are bodily acts of worship. Likewise, fasting is a bodily act of worship that manifests itself upon the limbs.

Hence, worship takes place upon the tongue, within the heart, and upon the limbs. Moreover, these acts of worship are categorized as being bodily or monetary. Bodily acts of worship are those three types which we have mentioned—they take place upon the tongue, the limbs, and within the heart. The monetary acts of worship are the likes of paying the *zakāh*, spending in the path of Allāh, and spending on *jihād*.

Allāh the Exalted has said:

﴿ وَجَاهَدُوا فِي سَبِيلِ اللَّهِ بِأَمْوَالِهِمْ وَأَنفُسِهِمْ ﴾

(And they) strove hard and fought in Allāh's cause with their wealth and their lives.

[Sūrah at-Tawbah 9:20]

He mentioned their wealth before mentioning their lives, so *jihād* with the wealth is worship.

Ḥajj is (both) from bodily worship and monetary worship. One performs the rituals: *aṭ-ṭawāf*, the *sa'ī*, the stoning of the pillars, standing at 'Arafah, spending the night at Muzdalifah; (these are) bodily acts of worship. As for spending (money) to do so, that is monetary worship, because the Ḥajj requires spending.

AL-ISLĀM, AL-ĪMĀN, AND AL-IḤSĀN & THE PROOF FOR EACH

ORIGINAL TEXT

وَ أَنْوَاعُ الْعِبَادَةِ الَّتِي أَمَرَ اللهُ بِهَا مِثْلُ الْإِسْلَامِ، وَ الْإِيمَانِ، وَ الْإِحْسَانِ.

(This goes for) all forms of worship which Allāh has commanded with, such as *al-islām*, *al-īmān*, and *al-iḥsān*.

EXPLANATION

The Shaykh رحمه الله cited examples from the perspective of illustration and not from the perspective of restriction, because they (acts of worship) are more than what he has mentioned. It is not possible to list them all within a concise treatise; however, he has mentioned examples. Shaykh-ul-Islām has a separate book titled *Al-'Ubūdiyyah* which is a book of research on worship and the various types of worship, and it is a clarification of the deviations that have occurred from the Sufis and other than them in the field of worship. It is a priceless treatise which the student of knowledge needs to read.

His statement *"such as: al-islām, al-īmān, and al-iḥsān"*: These three types are the greatest forms of worship: *al-islām*, *al-īmān*, and *al-iḥsān*. Their explanation shall come in the speech of the Shaykh رحمه الله for the second principle. He mentioned them here because they are from the types of worship.

Al-islām is by way of its five pillars: the two testimonies, the establishment of the prayer, the payment of the *zakāh*, fasting in the month of Ramaḍān, and pilgrimage to the Sacred House of Allāh. All of these are monetary and bodily acts of worship.

Likewise, *al-īmān* is by way of its six pillars, and it is from the actions of the heart. *Al-īmān* is: belief in Allāh, His angels, His Books, His messengers, the Last Day, and belief in the divine decree (its good and its evil). This is worship of the heart.

Likewise, *al-iḥsān,* and it is one pillar: that you worship Allāh as though you see Him, and even though you do not see Him, He certainly sees you. This is the highest form of worship. This is because *al-iḥsān* is the highest type of worship. These are referred to as "the levels of the religion" because together, they make up the religion. This is because, when Jibrīl questioned the Prophet ﷺ in the presence of his Companions, and the Prophet ﷺ responded to him regarding *al-islām*, *al-īmān*, and *al-iḥsān*, he said (afterwards):

هَذَا جِبْرِيلُ أَتَاكُمْ يُعَلِّمُكُمْ أَمْرَ دِينِكُمْ.

That was Jibrīl; he came to teach you your religion.[5]

He referred to these three as being the religion.

Du'ā': Its Categories & Evidence

ORIGINAL TEXT

وَ مِنْهُ الدُّعَاءُ، وَ الْخَوْفُ، وَ الرَّجَاءُ، وَ التَّوَكُّلُ، وَ الرَّغْبَةُ، وَ الرَّهْبَةُ، وَ الْخُشُوعُ، وَ الإِنَابَةُ، وَ الإِسْتِعَانَةُ، وَ الإِسْتِعَاذَةُ، وَ الذَّبْحُ، وَ النَّذْرُ، وَ غَيْرُ ذَلِكَ مِنْ أَنْوَاعِ الْعِبَادَةِ الَّتِي أَمَرَ اللهُ بِهَا، كُلُّهَا للهِ تَعَالَى.

[5] Al-Bukhārī reported it (#4777), as well as Muslim (#'s 8, 9, and 10) from the *ḥadīth* of Abū Hurayrah ﷺ.

From it is *ad-du'ā'* (supplication), *al-khawf* (reverential fear), *ar-rajā'* (hope), *at-tawakkul* (reliance), *ar-raghbah* (fervent desire), *ar-rahbah* (dread), *al-khushū'* (humility), *al-khashyah* (awe), *al-inābah* (turning in repentance), *al-isti'ānah* (seeking aid), *al-isti'ādhah* (seeking refuge), *al-istighāthah* (seeking deliverance), *adh-dhabḥ* (sacrificing), *an-nadhar* (vows), and other than that from the various types of worship which Allāh has commanded with. All of them are (exclusively) for Allāh, the Exalted.

EXPLANATION

Regarding his statement, *"From it is ad-du'ā' (supplication)"*: It means: from the types of worship are *ad-du'ā'*, etc. He began with *du'ā'* because it is the greatest form of worship.

Du'ā' is of two categories:

1) *Du'ā'* of worship

2) *Du'ā'* of request

Du'ā' of worship is praising Allāh ﷻ, as occurs in the beginning of al-Fātiḥah:

﴿ الْحَمْدُ لِلَّهِ رَبِّ الْعَالَمِينَ ۝٢ الرَّحْمَٰنِ الرَّحِيمِ ۝٣ مَالِكِ يَوْمِ الدِّينِ ۝٤ إِيَّاكَ نَعْبُدُ وَإِيَّاكَ نَسْتَعِينُ ۝٥ ﴾

All praises and thanks be to Allāh, the Lord of the *'ālamīn* (mankind, *jinn*, and all that exists). The Most Beneficent, the Most Merciful. The Only Owner (and the Only Ruling Judge) of the Day of Recompense (i.e., the Day of Resurrection). You (alone) we worship, and you (alone) we ask for help (for each and every thing).

[Sūrah al-Fātiḥah 1:2-5]

All of this is a *du'ā'* of worship.

﴿ اهْدِنَا الصِّرَاطَ الْمُسْتَقِيمَ ﴾

Guide us to the Straight Way.

[Sūrah al-Fātiḥah 1:6]

From here, to the end of the *sūrah*, is a *du'ā'* of request. *Du'ā'* of request is seeking something from Allāh ﷻ, such as seeking guidance, provision, knowledge from Allāh, and *tawfīq*.

ORIGINAL TEXT

وَ الدَّلِيلُ قَوْلُهُ تَعَالَى: ﴿ وَأَنَّ الْمَسَاجِدَ لِلَّهِ فَلَا تَدْعُوا مَعَ اللَّهِ أَحَدًا ﴾.

The proof is the statement of the Most High:

And the mosques (*masājid*) are for Allāh (alone), so invoke not anyone along with Allāh.

[Sūrah al-Jinn 72:18]

EXPLANATION

Al-masājid (الْمَسَاجِد) is an applied term, and what is intended by it is the places of *sujūd* and the spots wherein (the people) pray; and they are the most beloved places to Allāh ﷻ. There has come (in the texts) encouragement to build and prepare them. He ﷺ said:

مَنْ بَنَى مَسْجِداً لِله كَمَفْحَصِ قَطَاةٍ أَوْ أَصْغَرَ بَنَى اللهُ لَهُ بَيْتًا فِي الْجَنَّةِ.

Whoever builds a *masjid* for the sake of Allāh, the size of a sand grouse's burrow or smaller, Allāh will build for him a home in Paradise.[6]

Allāh says:

﴿ إِنَّمَا يَعْمُرُ مَسَاجِدَ اللَّهِ مَنْ آمَنَ بِاللَّهِ وَالْيَوْمِ الْآخِرِ ﴾

[6] Aḥmad reported it (4/45, #2157) from the *ḥadīth* of Ibn 'Abbās ﷺ. Ibn Mājah (#738) and Ibn Khuzaymah (#1292) also reported it from the *ḥadīth* of Jābir bin 'Abdillāh ﷺ.

The mosques of Allāh shall be maintained only by those who believe in Allāh and the Last Day.

[Sūrah at-Tawbah 9:18]

What is intended by "maintenance" is an actual maintenance and a figurative maintenance. [The actual maintenance is] maintaining them with clay (i.e., building them) so that the worshipers will be accommodated, it will shade them from the heat, and it will keep them warm from the cold. It also means maintaining them by way of worship, prayer, recitation of the Qur'ān, and the remembrance of Allāh ﷻ [and this is the figurative maintenance].

The term *masjid* is applied and intended to mean the seven body parts upon which prostration is made. They are the forehead and nose, the two hands, the two knees, and the toes of the two feet. This is because they prostrate to Allāh. The verse is inclusive of both meanings.

﴿ وَأَنَّ الْمَسَاجِدَ لِلَّهِ ﴾

And the *masājid* are for Allāh...

[Sūrah al-Jinn 72:18]

This means that the places wherein prayer is made, as well as the limbs which prostrate, are for Allāh ﷻ.

﴿ فَلَا تَدْعُوا مَعَ اللَّهِ أَحَدًا ﴾

...so invoke not anyone along with Allāh.

[Sūrah al-Jinn 72:18]

Do not make these *masājid* and places to be places of *shirk* and invocation to other than Allāh, nor should there be therein any innovations, newly invented matters, or innovated Sufi circles.

It is obligatory that the *masājid* be purified of innovations, *shirk*, and disobedience, because they are for Allāh ﷻ. There should only be within them that which pleases Allāh ﷻ. So do not call upon other than Allāh within these *masājid*, nor allow your limbs to serve other than Allāh ﷿ by way of prostration. This is because this is major *shirk*, similar to the one who prostrates to an altar or a grave, or who prostrates to an idol, for this one prostrates to other than Allāh ﷿. The point of reference is in His statement:

﴿فَلَا تَدْعُوا مَعَ اللَّهِ أَحَدًا﴾

...so invoke not anyone along with Allāh.

[Sūrah al-Jinn 72:18]

(This is) a command to have purity in supplicating to Him alone.

His statement:

﴿أَحَدًا﴾

...anyone...

[Sūrah al-Jinn 72:18]

This is general for everything which is called upon besides Allāh, whether it's an angel, a prophet, a *walī*, a tree, or a stone. It is generally applied to all who are called upon other than Allāh ﷿, for that is major *shirk*.

ORIGINAL TEXT

فَمَنْ صَرَفَ شَيْئًا مِنْهَا لِغَيْرِ اللهِ فَهُوَ مُشْرِكٌ كَافِرٌ، وَ الدَّلِيلُ
قَوْلُهُ تَعَالَى: ﴿وَمَن يَدْعُ مَعَ اللَّهِ إِلَٰهًا آخَرَ لَا بُرْهَانَ لَهُ بِهِ فَإِنَّمَا حِسَابُهُ
عِندَ رَبِّهِ ۚ إِنَّهُ لَا يُفْلِحُ الْكَافِرُونَ﴾. وَ فِي الْحَدِيثِ: ((الدُّعَاءُ مُخُّ
الْعِبَادَةِ)). وَ الدَّلِيلُ قَوْلُهُ تَعَالَى: ﴿وَقَالَ رَبُّكُمُ ادْعُونِي أَسْتَجِبْ
لَكُمْ ۚ إِنَّ الَّذِينَ يَسْتَكْبِرُونَ عَنْ عِبَادَتِي سَيَدْخُلُونَ جَهَنَّمَ دَاخِرِينَ﴾.

So, he who gives any of that to other than Allāh, then he is a *mushrik* (polytheist) and a *kāfir* (disbeliever). The proof is the statement of the Most High:

And whoever invokes (or worships) besides Allāh

any other *ilāh* (god), of whom he has no proof, then his reckoning is only with his Lord. Surely! *Al-kāfirūn* (the disbelievers in Allāh and in the oneness of Allāh, the polytheists, pagans, idolaters, etc.) will not be successful.

[Sūrah al-Mu'minūn 23:117]

And in the *ḥadīth:*

Supplication is the essence of worship.[7]

The proof is the statement of the Most High:

And your Lord said, "Invoke Me, [i.e., believe in My oneness (Islamic monotheism)] (and ask Me for anything); I will respond to your (invocation). Verily! Those who scorn My worship [i.e., do not invoke Me, and do not believe in My oneness (Islamic monotheism)], they will surely enter Hell in humiliation!"

[Sūrah Ghāfir 40:60]

EXPLANATION

"And your Lord said…": Meaning, your Lord has commanded you, saying:

﴿ ادْعُونِي أَسْتَجِبْ لَكُمْ ﴾

"Invoke Me (and ask Me for anything); I will respond to your (invocation)."

[Sūrah Ghāfir 40:60]

He commanded with invoking Him, Glorified be He, and He has promised to respond. This is from His generosity ﷻ. This is because He is Rich, (not in need) of our supplications. However, we are in

[7] At-Tirmidhī reported it (#3371) from the *ḥadīth* of Anas bin Mālik ﷺ. In its chain is Ibn Lahī'ah, and he is considered weak. At-Tirmidhī said, "This *ḥadīth* is *gharīb* though this route; we do not know of it (to come) except from the *ḥadīth* of Ibn Lahī'ah."

need of supplicating to Him ﷻ. So, He commands us with what we are in need of and with that which will rectify us; and it angers Him that we should leave off asking Him, while the created being is angered that you should ask him. Due to this, the poet said:

اللهُ يَغْضِبُ إِنْ تَرَكْتَ سُؤَالَهُ

وَ بَنِي آدَمَ حِينَ يُسْأَلُ يَغْضِبُ

Allāh is angry if you leave off asking Him;

The children of Ādam are angry when asked.

Another poet said:

فَلَوْ سُئِلَ النَّاسُ التُّرَابَ لَأَوْشَكُوا

إِذَا قِيلَ هَاتُوا أَنْ يَمَلُّوا وَ يَمْنَعُوا

If the people are asked for dirt, they are on the verge

Of becoming agitated and withholding it.

The people are of three categories:

1) He who does not supplicate to Allāh at all, for he is too arrogant to worship Allāh.

2) He who supplicates to Allāh, but he calls upon other than Him along with Him; he is a *mushrik*.

3) He who supplicates to Allāh, making the supplication purely for Him; this is the *muwaḥḥid* (true monotheist).

In the *ḥadīth*, it is mentioned that the Prophet ﷺ said:

الدُّعَاءُ مُخُّ الْعِبَادَةِ.

Supplication is the essence of worship.

In another narration:

الدُّعَاءُ هُوَ الْعِبَادَةُ.

Supplication is worship.[8]

This illustrates the magnitude of *du'ā'*, and that it is the greatest form of worship because the Messenger ﷺ said (that it is) "the essence of worship." And in another narration: "Supplication is worship." The second narration is more authentic than the narration "Supplication is the essence of worship." However, the meaning is the same.

So, this *ḥadīth*—with its two narrations—clarifies the greatness of *du'ā'* and that it is the greatest type of worship. This is similar to when he ﷺ said:

الْحَجُّ عَرَفَةٌ.

Ḥajj is 'Arafah.[9]

This means that standing at 'Arafah during Ḥajj is the greatest pillar of Ḥajj, and the meaning is not that the entire Ḥajj is 'Arafah. Rather, the standing at 'Arafah is the greatest pillar of Ḥajj. Likewise, the entirety of worship is not restricted to only *du'ā'*. However, it is the greatest of its types. Due to this, he said:

الدُّعَاءُ هُوَ الْعِبَادَةُ.

Supplication is worship.

(He said this) for the purpose of magnifying *du'ā'* and clarifying its status.

Then the Shaykh رحمه الله mentioned the proofs for the types of worship which he mentioned, and they are: *al-khawf* (reverential fear),

---

[8] Abū Dāwūd reported it (#1479), as well as at-Tirmidhī (#2969) and Ibn Mājah (#3828) from the *ḥadīth* of an-Nu'mān bin Bashīr رضي الله عنه. At-Tirmidhī said, "This is a *ḥasan ṣaḥīḥ ḥadīth*."

[9] Abū Dāwūd reported it (#1949), as did at-Tirmidhī (#889), an-Nasā'ī (#3016), and Ibn Mājah (#3015), from the *ḥadīth* of 'Abdur-Raḥmān bin Ya'mar ad-Daylī رضي الله عنه.

ar-rajā' (hope), *at-tawakkul* (reliance), *ar-raghbah* (fervent desire), *ar-rahbah* (dread), *al-khushū'* (humility), *al-khashyah* (awe), *al-inābah* (turning in repentance), *al-isti'ānah* (seeking aid), *al-isti'ādhah* (seeking refuge), *al-istighāthah* (seeking deliverance), *adh-dhabḥ* (sacrificing), *an-nadhar* (vows), and other than that from the various types of worship which Allāh has commanded with. All of them are (exclusively) for Allāh, the Exalted.

Al-Khawf (Fear): Its Types & Evidence

ORIGINAL TEXT

وَ دَلِيلُ الْخَوْفِ قَوْلُهُ تَعَالَى: ﴿ إِنَّمَا ذَٰلِكُمُ الشَّيْطَانُ يُخَوِّفُ أَوْلِيَاءَهُ فَلَا تَخَافُوهُمْ وَخَافُونِ إِن كُنتُم مُّؤْمِنِينَ ﴾.

The evidence for *al-khawf* is His, the Most High, statement:

> **It is only Shayṭān (Satan) that suggests to you the fear of his *awliyā'* [supporters and friends (polytheists, disbelievers in the oneness of Allāh and in His Messenger, Muḥammad ﷺ)], so fear them not, but fear Me, if you are (true) believers.**
>
> *[Sūrah Āli 'Imrān 3:175]*

EXPLANATION

Al-khawf is a type of worship, and it is worship of the heart. This is the case for *al-khawf*, *al-khashyah*, *ar-raghbah*, *ar-rahbah*, *ar-rajā'*, and *at-tawakkul*—each of these are worship of the heart.

Al-khawf is the expectation of that which one dislikes, and it is of two types:

1) *Khawf al-'ibādah* (fear which is worship).

2) *Khawf aṭ-ṭabī'ī* (natural fear).

The First Type: *Khawf al-'ibādah*: To give this to other than Allāh is *shirk*. This is because it means one fears other than Allāh in that which none is able to do other than Allāh. For example: fearing that someone can cause him to be ill, take his soul, or cause his child to die, as many of the ignorant people do. They fear the *jinn* (harming the) pregnancy of their wives or harming their children; they fear the magicians or one who is dead, so they do polytheistic actions in order to free themselves of this fear.

None is able to do these things except Allāh: illness, death, provision, cutting off life. None has power over these affairs except Allāh; likewise, the removal of a blessing or other than that. These matters do not occur except from Allāh ﷻ. So, if someone fears someone regarding something which none has power over except Allāh, then this is major *shirk*, because he has given a type of worship to other than Allāh.

Similarly, they fear the graves, the tombs, the *jinn*, and the *shayāṭīn*; they fear that they can touch them with evil or cause harm to descend upon them. So, they seek to draw near to these things in order to repel their harm or out of fear of them. This is major *shirk*.

He says, "I fear that if I do not sacrifice for it, then calamity will strike me, or strike my children or my wealth," or that which resembles this. As the people of Hūd said:

﴿ إِن نَّقُولُ إِلَّا اعْتَرَاكَ بَعْضُ آلِهَتِنَا بِسُوءٍ ﴾

"All that we say is that some of our gods (false deities) have seized you with evil (madness)."

[Sūrah Hūd 11:54]

They threatened him with their gods; they tried to make him frightened of their gods. He said:

﴿ إِنِّي أُشْهِدُ اللَّهَ وَاشْهَدُوا أَنِّي بَرِيءٌ مِّمَّا تُشْرِكُونَ
٥٤ مِن دُونِهِ ۖ فَكِيدُونِي جَمِيعًا ثُمَّ لَا تُنظِرُونِ ٥٥ إِنِّي
تَوَكَّلْتُ عَلَى اللَّهِ رَبِّي وَرَبِّكُم ﴾

"I call Allāh to witness and bear you witness that I am free from what you ascribe as partners in worship with Him (Allāh). So plot against me, all of you, and give me no respite. I put my trust in Allāh, my Lord and your Lord!"

[Sūrah Hūd 11:54-56]

This is the *tawḥīd* which they all opposed, them and their (false) gods.

﴿ فَكِيدُونِي جَمِيعًا ثُمَّ لَا تُنظِرُونِ ﴾

"So plot against me, all of you, and give me no respite."

[Sūrah Hūd 11:55]

Meaning: "Do not overlook me; rather, from this very moment, plot against me." They had no power over anything. Rather, Allāh gave him victory over them.

So, he who fears other than Allāh regarding that which none has power over except Allāh, then he has committed major *shirk*; and this is called *khawf al-ʿibādah.*

The *khawf* which is *shirk* is abundant amongst the people. They fear the graves or the *awliyā'*, they fear Shayṭān, they fear the *jinn*; and due to this, they give precedence to drawing near to them, and they present to them sacrifices, vows, food, and other than that—such as leaving money on their graves so that they may be safe from their evil or attain good from them—and this is the *khawf* of worship.

The Second Type: Natural fear: This is that you fear something which is clearly able to do what you fear, such as you fearing a snake, a scorpion, or the enemy. These are obvious and well-known affairs, so fearing them is not *shirk*. This is natural fear of something which is obvious and well-known. This is because you are afraid due to an obvious reason, and it is required to protect yourself from it and to beware of it. So, you take up arms; you grab a stick to kill the snake, the scorpion, and the beast of prey because these are physical matters and they contain known harm. If you fear them, this is not referred to as *shirk*; rather, it is referred to as "natural fear."

Due to this, Allāh said regarding Mūsā عليه السلام:

﴿ فَخَرَجَ مِنْهَا ﴾

So, he escaped from there…

Meaning: From the land.

﴿ خَائِفًا يَتَرَقَّبُ ﴾

…looking about in a state of fear.

[Sūrah al-Qaṣaṣ 28:21]

He was in fear from his enemies because he had killed a person from amongst them.

He عليه السلام fled to Madyan, and he was looking about and fearful that they would catch up with him; this is natural fear. However, the person knows that he must hold fast to Allāh عز وجل, take to the means which will repel the harm from him, depend upon Allāh عز وجل, and put his trust in Allāh.

The Most High said:

﴿ فَلَا تَخَافُوهُمْ وَخَافُونِ إِن كُنتُم مُّؤْمِنِينَ ﴾

So fear them not, but fear Me, if you are (true) believers.

[Sūrah Āli 'Imrān 3:175]

This verse in Sūrah Āli 'Imrān is about the story of the Prophet ﷺ and the polytheists on the day of Uḥud when the polytheists threatened them and said, "We will return to them (the Muslims) and annihilate them." So Allāh said:

﴿ إِنَّمَا ذَٰلِكُمُ الشَّيْطَانُ يُخَوِّفُ أَوْلِيَاءَهُ فَلَا تَخَافُوهُمْ وَخَافُونِ إِن كُنتُم مُّؤْمِنِينَ ﴾

It is only Shayṭān (Satan) that suggests to you the fear of his *awliyā'* [supporters and friends (polytheists, disbelievers in the oneness of Allāh and in His Messenger, Muḥammad ﷺ)], so fear them not, but fear Me, if you are (true) believers.

[Sūrah Āli 'Imrān 3:175]

Meaning: This intimidation and threat is only from Shayṭān (i.e., he tries to make you afraid of his supporters, or he tries to frighten those who yield to him from the people who are afraid of him), so he has gained mastery over them.

AR-RAJĀ' (HOPE) & ITS EVIDENCE

ORIGINAL TEXT

وَ دَلِيلُ الرَّجَاءِ قَوْلُهُ تَعَالَى: ﴿ فَمَن كَانَ يَرْجُو لِقَاءَ رَبِّهِ فَلْيَعْمَلْ عَمَلًا صَالِحًا وَلَا يُشْرِكْ بِعِبَادَةِ رَبِّهِ أَحَدًا ﴾.

And the evidence for *ar-rajā'* (hope) is the statement of the Most High:

So whoever hopes for the meeting with his Lord, let him work righteousness and associate none as a partner in the worship of his Lord.

[Sūrah al-Kahf 18:110]

EXPLANATION

Concerning His statement:

﴿ فَمَن كَانَ يَرْجُو ﴾

So whoever hopes...

[Sūrah al-Kahf 18:110]

Meaning: He is hopeful for the reward of Allāh ﷻ and seeing Him directly on the Day of Judgment. He who hopes to see Allāh directly on the Day of Judgment, then let him do righteous deeds. He must enact the means which will qualify him to attain what he seeks, which is the reward of entrance into Paradise, safety from the Fire, and looking at the Face of Allāh, because this is a requirement of it. He who enters Paradise will see Allāh ﷻ.

﴿ فَمَن كَانَ يَرْجُو لِقَاءَ رَبِّهِ فَلْيَعْمَلْ عَمَلًا صَالِحًا ﴾

So whoever hopes for the meeting with his Lord, let him work righteousness...

[Sūrah al-Kahf 18:110]

This is proof that hope alone is not sufficient. It is a must that one performs actions. As for hoping in Allāh while you do not act, then this is a negation of the means. The praiseworthy *rajā'* is the one which is accompanied by righteous action. As for the *rajā'* which is not praiseworthy, it is the *rajā'* which is not accompanied by righteous action. The righteous action is that wherein two conditions are fulfilled:

1) Sincerity for Him ﷻ

2) Following the Messenger ﷺ

The action is not righteous except if these two conditions are fulfilled: it must be sincerely for the Face of Allāh and not contain any *shirk*; and it must be correct in accordance with the Sunnah of Allāh's Messenger ﷺ, not containing any innovation. If the two conditions are fulfilled, then it is righteous. If a condition is not fulfilled, then it is a corrupt action which does not benefit the doer. The action which contains *shirk* is rejected. Likewise, the action which contains innovation is rejected. He ﷺ said:

مَنْ عَمِلَ عَمَلاً لَيْسَ عَلَيْهِ أَمْرُنَا فَهُوَ رَدٌّ.

Whoever does an action which is not from this affair of ours, then it will be rejected.

So, this verse contains hope and the fact that worship is only for Allāh ﷻ. It also contains the indication that hope is not correct unless it is accompanied by righteous action.

At-Tawakkul (Trust & Reliance) & Its Evidence

Original text

وَ دَلِيلُ التَّوَكُّلُ قَوْلُهُ تَعَالَى: ﴿ وَعَلَى اللَّهِ فَتَوَكَّلُوا إِن كُنتُم مُّؤْمِنِينَ ﴾.

The proof for *at-tawakkul* is the statement of the Most High:

And put your trust in Allāh if you are believers indeed.

[Sūrah al-Mā'idah 5:23]

Explanation

At-tawakkul means relegating and depending upon Allāh ﷻ, and relegating the affairs to Him. This is *at-tawakkul*, and it is from the greatest forms of worship. Due to this, He said:

﴿ وَعَلَى اللَّهِ فَتَوَكَّلُوا إِن كُنتُم مُّؤْمِنِينَ ﴾

And put your trust in Allāh if you are believers indeed.

[Sūrah al-Mā'idah 5:23]

He placed the preposition and the genitive noun before the doer of the action to denote restriction.

﴿ وَعَلَى اللَّهِ فَتَوَكَّلُوا ﴾

And put your trust in Allāh...

[Sūrah al-Mā'idah 5:23]

Meaning: In Him and not in other than Him. Then He said:

﴿ إِن كُنتُم مُّؤْمِنِينَ ﴾

...if you are believers indeed.

[Sūrah al-Mā'idah 5:23]

He has made trust in Allāh a condition for *al-īmān*, and indicated that the one who does not place his trust in Allāh is not a believer. *At-tawakkul* is a great act of worship; hence, the believer always puts his trust in Allāh and depends upon Allāh ﷻ.

From the names of Allāh is al-Wakīl, meaning: "He to whom the affairs of His slave are entrusted" ﷻ. So, trust is not to be placed in other than Allāh, and it is not permissible to say, "I have placed *at-tawakkul* in so-and-so." This is because *at-tawakkul* is worship, and worship is not for anyone except Allāh.

As for if you were to extend to the creation some authority (to do something for you), then this is not referred to as *at-tawakkul*. It is only referred to as *tawkīl* (entrusting). The well-known entrustment is entrusting someone to discharge a need for you. The Prophet would entrust people to deputize certain functions for him, so *at-tawkīl* is not *at-tawakkul*. *At-tawakkul* is worship, and it is not to be given except to Allāh.

It is not permissible for you to say, "I have placed my reliance upon so-and-so." You should only say, "I have entrusted so-and-so." Along with this, you entrust him and you do not put your reliance upon him—you only put your reliance upon Allāh. So, take note of the difference between the two affairs: *at-tawakkul* and *at-tawkīl*.

From the attributes of the believers is that which Allāh has mentioned in His statement:

﴿ إِنَّمَا الْمُؤْمِنُونَ الَّذِينَ إِذَا ذُكِرَ اللَّهُ وَجِلَتْ قُلُوبُهُمْ وَإِذَا تُلِيَتْ عَلَيْهِمْ آيَاتُهُ زَادَتْهُمْ إِيمَانًا وَعَلَىٰ رَبِّهِمْ يَتَوَكَّلُونَ ﴾

The believers are only those who, when Allāh is mentioned, feel a fear in their hearts, and when His verses (this Qur'ān) are recited unto them, they (i.e., the verses) increase their faith; and they put

their trust in their Lord (alone).

[Sūrah al-Anfāl 8:2]

These are the qualities of the believers. So, *at-tawakkul* is a great act of worship and it is only for Allāh ﷻ. This is because He is able to do all things; He is the owner of everything; He is the one who has the ability to actualize for you that which you seek. As for the created being, he does not have the ability to actualize for you that which you seek; so you may entrust him to discharge some affairs, but you place your reliance upon Allāh for the attainment of that thing.

Moreover, let us also know that *at-tawakkul* does not negate the fact that we must take the means (to attain what we seek). So, the Muslim combines between reliance upon Allāh and taking the necessary means, and you do not negate either of them. You enact the means which you have been commanded to enact, but you do not depend upon the means; you only depend upon Allāh. You sow that which is sowed in the earth; this is the means. However, you do not depend upon your sowing and your action. Rather, you depend upon Allāh in making that which is sowed grow and making it fruitful, and in watching over it and making it flourish. Due to this, He says:

﴿ أَفَرَأَيْتُم مَّا تَحْرُثُونَ ٦٣ أَأَنتُمْ تَزْرَعُونَهُ أَمْ نَحْنُ الزَّارِعُونَ ٦٤ ﴾

Tell Me! The seed that you sow in the ground—is it you that makes it grow, or are We the grower?

[Sūrah al-Wāqi'ah 56:63-64]

The true sower is Allāh. As for you, you have only enacted the means. Perhaps this crop will generate and grow, and perhaps it will not generate. If it does grow, then perhaps it will flourish or perhaps it will not flourish. Maybe it will be struck with scourge and be depleted.

Ar-Raghbah (Fervent Desire), ar-Rahbah (Dread), and al-Khushū' (Humility), & the Evidence for Each

ORIGINAL TEXT

وَ دَلِيلُ الرَّغْبَةِ وَ الرَّهْبَةِ وَ الْخُشُوعِ قَوْلُهُ تَعَالَى: ﴿ إِنَّهُمْ كَانُوا يُسَارِعُونَ فِي الْخَيْرَاتِ وَيَدْعُونَنَا رَغَبًا وَرَهَبًا ۖ وَكَانُوا لَنَا خَاشِعِينَ ﴾.

The evidence for *ar-raghbah*, *ar-rahbah*, and *al-khushū'* is the statement of the Most High:

Verily, they used to hasten to do good deeds, and they used to call on Us with hope and fear, and they used to humble themselves before Us.

[Sūrah al-Anbiyā' 21:90]

EXPLANATION

Ar-raghbah: This means seeking something praiseworthy. *Ar-rahbah:* This is fear from something dreadful. Allāh said:

﴿ وَإِيَّايَ فَارْهَبُونِ ﴾

...and fear none but Me.

[Sūrah al-Baqarah 2:40]

It is a type of fear. *Ar-rahbah* and *al-khawf* have the same meaning.

Al-khushū': This is a type of humility for Allāh ﷻ; it is humbleness and self-effacement before Him ﷻ. It is from the greatest stations of worship.

His statement, **"Verily, they..."** (إِنَّهُمْ): This pronoun ("they") is referring to the prophets. This is because Allāh mentions the stories of the prophets in Sūrah al-Anbiyā'. Then He said:

﴿ إِنَّهُمْ كَانُوا يُسَارِعُونَ فِي الْخَيْرَاتِ وَيَدْعُونَنَا رَغَبًا

وَرَهَبًا ۖ وَكَانُوا لَنَا خَاشِعِينَ ﴾

Verily, they used to hasten to do good deeds, and they used to call on Us with hope and fear, and they used to humble themselves before Us.

[Sūrah al-Anbiyā' 21:90]

The statement of the Most High:

﴿ كَانُوا يُسَارِعُونَ فِي الْخَيْرَاتِ ﴾

...they used to hasten to do good deeds...

[Sūrah al-Anbiyā' 21:90]

Meaning: They would race and hasten towards them. This is the description of the prophets عليهم السلام. They were not lazy or incapable. They were quick in doing good and they raced towards it.

The statement of the Most High:

﴿ وَيَدْعُونَنَا رَغَبًا ﴾

...and they used to call on Us with hope...

[Sūrah al-Anbiyā' 21:90]

Meaning: They longed for that which is with Allāh عز وجل; they longed for its attainment.

The statement of the Most High:

﴿ وَرَهَبًا ﴾

...and fear...

[Sūrah al-Anbiyā' 21:90]

Meaning: Having fear of us; so they would call upon Allāh to have mercy upon them, and they would supplicate to Him to not punish them, seize them, or chastise them. They desired the mercy of Allāh and they feared His punishment, as Allāh the Exalted has said:

﴿ أُولَٰئِكَ الَّذِينَ يَدْعُونَ يَبْتَغُونَ إِلَىٰ رَبِّهِمُ الْوَسِيلَةَ أَيُّهُمْ أَقْرَبُ وَيَرْجُونَ رَحْمَتَهُ وَيَخَافُونَ عَذَابَهُ ۚ إِنَّ عَذَابَ رَبِّكَ كَانَ مَحْذُورًا ﴾

Those whom they call upon [like 'Īsā (Jesus) son of Maryam (Mary), 'Uzayr (Ezra), angels, etc.] desire (for themselves) means of access to their Lord (Allāh), as to which of them should be the nearest; and they ['Īsā (Jesus), 'Uzayr (Ezra), angels, etc.] hope for His mercy and fear His torment. Verily, the torment of your Lord is something to be afraid of!

[Sūrah al-Isrā' 17:57]

They call upon Allāh out of fear of Him, and they also call upon Him out of hope for what is with Him. They call upon Allāh to decree good for them and to repel evil from them.

﴿ وَكَانُوا لَنَا خَاشِعِينَ ﴾

...and used to humble themselves before Us.

[Sūrah al-Anbiyā' 21:90]

Meaning: They were humble and displayed meekness for Allāh ﷻ. So, they combined these qualities: *ar-raghbah* (fervent desire), *ar-rahbah* (dread), and *al-khushū'* (humility). These were the qualities of the prophets ﷺ. These three types are from the types of worship of Allāh ﷻ.

In this is a refutation against the Sufis who say, "We do not worship Allāh out of hope for His reward nor out of fear of His punishment. We only worship Him out of love for Him." This speech is falsehood, because the prophets called upon Him out of *raghbah* (fervent desire), *rahbah* (dread), and *khushū'* (humility), and they were the most complete of the creation.

Al-Khashyah (Awe) & Its Evidence

ORIGINAL TEXT

دَلِيلُ الْخَشِيَةِ قَوْلُهُ تَعَالَى: ﴿ فَلَا تَخْشَوْهُمْ وَاخْشَوْنِ ﴾.

The proof for *al-khashyah* (awe) is the statement of the Most High:

So fear them not, but fear Me!

[Sūrah al-Baqarah 2:150]

EXPLANATION

Al-khashyah is a type of fear, and it is more specific than *al-khawf*. It is said that *al-khashyah* is *khawf* along with magnification. The Most High has said:

﴿ فَلَا تَخْشَوْهُمْ ﴾

So fear them not...

[Sūrah al-Baqarah 2:150]

Allāh ﷻ has commanded with fearing Him alone. The Most High has mentioned in the verse:

﴿ فَلَا تَخْشَوْهُمْ وَاخْشَوْنِي وَلِأُتِمَّ نِعْمَتِي عَلَيْكُمْ وَلَعَلَّكُمْ تَهْتَدُونَ ﴾

So fear them not, but fear Me! And so that I may complete My blessings on you and that you may be guided.

[Sūrah al-Baqarah 2:150]

He ﷻ commanded with having awe of Him. He said regarding those who pray:

﴿ وَالَّذِينَ هُم مِّنْ عَذَابِ رَبِّهِم مُّشْفِقُونَ ﴾

And those who fear the torment of their Lord.

[Sūrah al-Ma'ārij 70:27]

Meaning: They are terrified of it. These are the choicest of the creation; they fear Allāh ﷻ. He said regarding the angels:

﴿ يَخَافُونَ رَبَّهُم مِّن فَوْقِهِمْ وَيَفْعَلُونَ مَا يُؤْمَرُونَ ﴾

They fear their Lord above them, and they do what they are commanded.

[Sūrah an-Naḥl 16:50]

The choicest of the creation—from the angels, the messengers, the prophets, and the righteous—have the utmost level of awe, fear, and dread of Allāh ﷻ. And *rahbah* (dread), *khawf* (fear), and *khashyah* (awe) all bear the same meaning, even though some of them are more specific than others. Otherwise, they all comprise fear of Allāh. This is from the qualities of the prophets and righteous servants of Allāh; it is a great form of worship, and it is from the actions of the heart which none knows except for Allāh ﷻ.

Al-Inābah (Turning In Repentance) & Its Evidence

ORIGINAL TEXT

وَ دَلِيلُ الْإِنَابَةِ قَوْلُهُ تَعَالَى: ﴿ وَأَنِيبُوا إِلَىٰ رَبِّكُمْ وَأَسْلِمُوا لَهُ ﴾.

The proof for *al-inābah* is the statement of the Most High:

And turn in repentance to your Lord and submit to Him.

[Sūrah az-Zumar 39:54]

EXPLANATION

Al-inābah means "to return," and it bears the same meaning as *at-tawbah* (repentance). *At-tawbah* and *al-inābah* bear the same meaning. However, some of the scholars say that *al-inābah* is more specific than *at-tawbah*; meaning, (it is) more emphasized because it is *at-tawbah* along with turning to Allāh ﷻ (i.e., a specific type of *tawbah*). The person may repent, leave off the sin, not return to it, and regret it; however, his turning to Allāh may be weak. As for *al-inābah*, it is turning to Allāh ﷻ.

Due to this, He said:

﴿ وَأَنِيبُوا إِلَىٰ رَبِّكُمْ وَأَسْلِمُوا لَهُ ﴾

And turn in repentance to your Lord and submit to Him…

[Sūrah az-Zumar 39:54]

Meaning: Return to Him and turn to Him ﷻ.

﴿ مِن قَبْلِ أَن يَأْتِيَكُمُ الْعَذَابُ ثُمَّ لَا تُنصَرُونَ ﴾

…before the torment comes upon you, then you will not be helped.

[Sūrah az-Zumar 39:54]

If the destroying and overtaking punishment comes, then the repentance of the one who repents will not be accepted at that time.

﴿ إِلَّا قَوْمَ يُونُسَ لَمَّا آمَنُوا كَشَفْنَا عَنْهُمْ عَذَابَ الْخِزْيِ ﴾

…except the people of Yūnus (Jonah); when they believed, We removed from them the torment of disgrace…

[Sūrah Yūnus 10:98]

This was an exception. Otherwise, when the destructive punishment descends, then *at-tawbah* is not accepted. Due to this, He said:

﴿ مِن قَبْلِ أَن يَأْتِيَكُمُ الْعَذَابُ ثُمَّ لَا تُنصَرُونَ ﴾

…before the torment comes upon you, then you will not be helped.

[Sūrah az-Zumar 39:54]

So, *at-tawbah* and *al-inābah* both have a demarcated place and a limit; and the *tawbah* of one whose soul is leaving him or one whom death has seized will not be accepted. The *tawbah* of the one upon whom the destructive and encompassing punishment has descended, will not be accepted. Nor will *tawbah* be accepted when the sun rises from its place of setting before the Hour; *at-tawbah* will not be accepted at this time. Allāh encourages the servant to make *tawbah* and *al-inābah* before his appointed time ends:

﴿ مِن قَبْلِ أَن يَأْتِيَكُمُ الْعَذَابُ ثُمَّ لَا تُنصَرُونَ ﴾

...before the torment comes upon you, then you will not be helped.

[Sūrah az-Zumar 39:54]

The point of reference is His statement:

﴿ وَأَنِيبُوا إِلَىٰ رَبِّكُمْ ﴾

And turn in repentance to your Lord...

[Sūrah az-Zumar 39:54]

This indicates that *al-inābah* is a type of worship, because He said:

﴿ إِلَىٰ رَبِّكُم ﴾

...to your Lord...

[Sūrah az-Zumar 39:54]

This indicates that it is a type of worship.

Al-Isti'ānah (Seeking Aid) & Its Evidence

ORIGINAL TEXT

وَ دَلِيلُ الْاِسْتِعَانَةِ: ﴿ إِيَّاكَ نَعْبُدُ وَإِيَّاكَ نَسْتَعِينُ ﴾. وَ فِي الْحَدِيثِ: ((إِذَا اسْتَعَنْتَ فَاسْتَعِنْ بِاللهِ)).

The proof for *al-isti'ānah* is:

You (alone) we worship, and You (alone) we ask for

help (for each and every thing).

[Sūrah al-Fātiḥah 1:5)]

And in the *ḥadīth*:

If you seek help, then seek the help of Allāh.[10]

EXPLANATION

Al-isti'ānah means "seeking aid," and it is of two types:

1) Seeking aid in something which none is able to do except Allāh. To give this to other than Allāh is *shirk*. He who seeks aid with other than Allāh in that which none is able to do except Allāh, then he has committed *shirk*, because he has given a type of worship to other than Allāh ﷻ.

2) Seeking help in that which the creation has the ability to do. So, you seek someone's aid in constructing a wall or in carrying your luggage, or that he should assist you in some permissible action. As the Most High said:

﴿ وَتَعَاوَنُوا عَلَى الْبِرِّ وَالتَّقْوَىٰ ۖ وَلَا تَعَاوَنُوا عَلَى الْإِثْمِ وَالْعُدْوَانِ ﴾

Help you one another in *al-birr* and *at-taqwā* (virtue, righteousness, and piety); but do not help one another in sin and transgression.

[Sūrah al-Mā'idah 5:2]

So, as it relates to seeking aid in customary affairs which the people are able to do, there is no harm in this type. This is because it is from cooperation upon *al-birr* and *at-taqwā*. He ﷺ said:

وَ اللهُ فِي عَوْنِ الْعَبْدِ مَا دَامَ الْعَبْدُ فِي عَوْنِ أَخِيهِ.

Allāh supports His slave as long as the slave is supportive of his

[10] At-Tirmidhī reported it (#2516) from the *ḥadīth* of Ibn 'Abbās ﷺ.

brother.[11]

As for seeking the aid of the creation in that which none except Allāh is able to do—such as bringing forth provisions and repelling harm—then this is only for Allāh. For example: one seeking the aid of the dead, seeking the aid of the *jinn* and the devils, or seeking the aid of one who is absent while they are not able to hear you calling out their name—this is major *shirk*. [In these cases], you are seeking aid from one who is not able to aid you. Regarding the statement of the Most High:

﴿ إِيَّاكَ نَعْبُدُ وَإِيَّاكَ نَسْتَعِينُ ﴾

You (alone) we worship, and You (alone) we ask for help (for each and every thing).

[Sūrah al-Fātiḥah 1:5]

The saying, **"You (alone) we worship,"** contains mentioning the object before the doer of the action. The action **"You (alone)"** is in the place of *naṣb* (i.e., in the place of the noun that would be in the accusative case).

"We worship": This is the doer of the verb which the phrase **"You (alone)"** makes accusative. Mentioning the object before the doer of the verb denotes restriction.

So, the meaning of, **"You (alone) we worship,"** is: "We do not worship anyone other than You." So, the worship is restricted to being for Allāh عَزَّوَجَلَّ.

﴿ وَإِيَّاكَ نَسْتَعِينُ ﴾

...and you (alone) we ask for help.

[Sūrah al-Fātiḥah 1:5]

This is a restriction of the seeking of aid to Allāh عَزَّوَجَلَّ. Meaning, within the affairs which none are able to do except Allāh سُبْحَانَهُ وَتَعَالَى. In His statement:

---

[11] Muslim reported it (#2699) from the *ḥadīth* of Abū Hurayrah رَضِيَ اللَّهُ عَنْهُ.

﴿ وَإِيَّاكَ نَسْتَعِينُ ﴾

...and You (alone) we ask for help.

[Sūrah al-Fātiḥah 1:5]

There is (within this statement) a declaration that the creation is devoid of might or power, and that the person does not have any power except by Allāh, nor does he have any ability except by Allāh ﷻ. This is the epitome of worship of Allāh: when one declares himself free of *shirk* and devoid of might or power. This is the epitome of the worship of Allāh ﷻ

Al-Isti'ādhah (Seeking Refuge) & Its Evidence

ORIGINAL TEXT

وَ دَلِيلُ الْإِسْتِعَاذَةِ قَوْلُهُ تَعَالَى: ﴿ قُلْ أَعُوذُ بِرَبِّ الْفَلَقِ ﴾.

The proof for *al-isti'ādhah* is the statement of the Most High:

Say: "I seek refuge with (Allāh) the Lord of the daybreak..."

[Sūrah al-Falaq 113:1]

EXPLANATION

Al-isti'ādhah is seeking refuge with one who will protect you from the apprehensive things which you fear, so that he will repel this thing from you; this is *al-isti'ādhah*. *Al-isti'ādhah* is a type of worship. It is not permissible to seek refuge with other than Allāh ﷻ. So, he who seeks refuge with a grave, an idol, or anything other than Allāh ﷻ, then he is a *mushrik* who has committed major *shirk*.

The Most High has said:

﴿ وَأَنَّهُ كَانَ رِجَالٌ مِّنَ الْإِنسِ يَعُوذُونَ بِرِجَالٍ مِّنَ الْجِنِّ فَزَادُوهُمْ رَهَقًا ﴾

And verily, there were men among mankind who took shelter with the masculine among the *jinn*, but they (*jinn*) increased them (mankind) in sin and disbelief.

[*Sūrah al-Jinn* 72:6]

In the Days of Ignorance, when the Arabs would descend at a particular place in the land, one of them would say, "I seek refuge with the master of this valley." Meaning: the big *jinn*; he would seek refuge with him from the evil of its foolish people. So, the Prophet ﷺ said, proving the falsehood of that and clarifying what was legislated instead of it:

مَنْ نَزَلَ مَنْزِلاً فَقَالَ: أَعُوذُ بِكَلِمَاتِ اللهِ التَّامَّاتِ مِنْ شَرِّ مَا خَلَقَ. لَمْ يَضُرَّهُ شَيْىءٌ حَتَّى يَرْتَحِلَ مِنْ مَنْزِلِهِ ذَلِكَ.

When anyone lands at a place and then says, "I seek refuge in the perfect word of Allāh from the evil of what He has created," nothing will harm him until he marches from that stopping place.[12]

This is what is correct to say instead: *al-isti'ādhah* by way of the perfect words of Allāh instead of *al-isti'ādhah* with the *jinn*. The Most High has said:

﴿ قُلْ أَعُوذُ بِرَبِّ الْفَلَقِ ﴾

Say: "I seek refuge with (Allāh) the Lord of the daybreak..."

[*Sūrah al-Falaq* 113:1]

Al-falaq is the morning. The Lord of *al-falaq* is Allāh ﷻ, as is within the statement of the Most High:

﴿ فَالِقُ الْإِصْبَاحِ ﴾

(He is the) cleaver of the daybreak.

[*Sūrah al-An'ām* 6:96]

---

[12] Muslim reported it (#2708) from the *hadīth* of Khawlah bint Ḥakīm as-Salīmah ﵂.

Meaning: He is the one who makes apparent the light of the morning within the darkness of the night; who is he that has the ability to do this except Allāh?

﴿ قُلْ أَعُوذُ بِرَبِّ الْفَلَقِ ﴾

Say: "I seek refuge with (Allāh) the Lord of the daybreak..."

[Sūrah al-Falaq 113:1]

Meaning: The Lord of the morning, which He brings forth; the operating owner of it who has power over it.

﴿ مِن شَرِّ مَا خَلَقَ ﴾

...from the evil of what He has created...

[Sūrah al-Falaq 113:2]

This includes the evil of all created beings; one seeks refuge with Allāh from the evil of all created beings. This will suffice you in terms of seeking refuge; or that you seek refuge from what the people do.

﴿ وَمِن شَرِّ غَاسِقٍ إِذَا وَقَبَ ﴾

...and from the evil of the darkening (night) as it comes with its darkness...

[Sūrah al-Falaq 113:3]

Al-ghāsiq is the darkness of night. This is because the animals and the beasts of prey come out in the darkness of the night. So, you may fall into danger; thus, you seek refuge with Allāh from the evil of this darkness and that which is within it from these harmful things.

﴿ وَمِن شَرِّ النَّفَّاثَاتِ فِي الْعُقَدِ ﴾

...and from the evil of the witchcrafts when they blow in the knots...

[Sūrah al-Falaq 113:4]

This is the magicians; you seek refuge from magic and its people, because magic is a great evil.

﴿ وَمِن شَرِّ حَاسِدٍ إِذَا حَسَدَ ﴾

And from the evil of the envier when he envies.

[Sūrah al-Falaq 113:5]

Al-ḥāsid is the one who wishes for the removal of the blessing from someone else. If he sees a blessing upon someone, then he becomes enraged and he wishes for the removal of this blessing, out of envy and oppression; and refuge is sought with Allāh. It is from the greatest of the blameworthy characteristics. This is because it entails objection to (the decree of) Allāh, and harming the creation. What falls under this is the one who looks with the evil eye; the one who causes harm by his look. This is because afflicting with the evil eye is a type of envy. Hence, you seek refuge with Allāh from these evils.

This proves that *al-isti'ādhah* is an act of worship, and it is not permissible to give it to other than Allāh. You are not to seek refuge with the creation. He who seeks refuge with the created being has associated partners with Allāh عَزَّوَجَلَّ. The Prophet ﷺ said to Ibn 'Abbās رَضِيَٱللَّهُعَنْهُ:

إِذَا اسْتَعَنْتَ فَاسْتَعِنْ بِاللهِ.

If you seek help, then seek the help of Allāh.

ORIGINAL TEXT

وَ قَوْلُهُ تَعَالَى: ﴿ قُلْ أَعُوذُ بِرَبِّ النَّاسِ ﴾.

And His statement:

Say: "I seek refuge with (Allāh) the Lord of mankind..."

[Sūrah an-Nās 114:1]

EXPLANATION

Within the statement of the Most High:

﴿ قُلْ أَعُوذُ بِرَبِّ النَّاسِ ۝١ مَلِكِ النَّاسِ ۝٢ إِلَٰهِ النَّاسِ ۝٣ مِن شَرِّ الْوَسْوَاسِ الْخَنَّاسِ ۝٤ الَّذِي يُوَسْوِسُ فِي صُدُورِ النَّاسِ ۝٥ مِنَ الْجِنَّةِ وَالنَّاسِ ۝٦ ﴾

Say: "I seek refuge with (Allāh) the Lord of mankind, the King of mankind, the *Ilāh* (God) of mankind, from the evil of the whisperer (devil who whispers evil in the hearts of men) who withdraws (from his whispering in one's heart after one remembers Allāh); who whispers in the breasts of mankind, of *jinn* and men."

[Sūrah an-Nās 114:1-6]

Allāh has commanded with seeking refuge with the Lord of mankind, the King of mankind, the God of mankind. All of these are names and qualities of Allāh عَزَّوَجَلَّ. Within them are the three types of *tawḥīd*:

1) Tawḥīd ar-Rubūbiyyah (Oneness of Lordship)

2) Tawḥīd al-Ulūhiyyah (Oneness of Divinity)

3) Tawḥīd al-Asmā' waṣ-Ṣifāt (Oneness of the Names and Attributes)

Seek refuge with Allāh by way of these names and attributes. Seek refuge with Allāh from the evil of the whisperer, and that is Shayṭān. As for *al-wiswās*, it is the verbal noun derived from *waswasa, yuwas-wisu* [(وَسْوَسَ , يُوَسْوِسُ) i.e., to whisper].

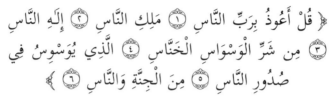

As for *al-waswās*, this is a name from the names of Shayṭān because he whispers to the person and thus deceives him; he diverts him in order to cast terror, hesitation, and confusion into his heart regarding his affairs, particularly in the matter of worship. Shayṭān whispers to the person regarding his worship until his prayer or acts of worship become mixed up. Then the affair reaches the point that he exits the prayer believing that it has been nullified; or he prays and then believes that he did not have *wuḍū'*; or he believes that he did not establish this or did not do that. He has been subjected to whispers, so he is not content with his worship. Allāh has given us a remedy for this perilous affair: by seeking refuge with Allāh from the evil of this whisperer.

Al-khannās (الْخَنَّاسِ) is that which withdraws and moves away. He whispers when you are heedless regarding the remembrance of Allāh, and he backs off (i.e., he withdraws) when you remember Allāh ﷻ. He is one who whispers when you are heedless, and he is one who withdraws when you remember Allāh.

﴿ الَّذِي يُوَسْوِسُ فِي صُدُورِ النَّاسِ ۝٥ مِنَ الْجِنَّةِ وَالنَّاسِ ۝٦ ﴾

(He) who whispers in the breasts of mankind; of *jinn* and men.

[Sūrah an-Nās 114:5-6]

It is as if the meaning—and Allāh knows best—is that there are those from the *jinn* and from mankind who whisper to the people. They come to the people and instill doubt in them. Just as there are *shayāṭīn* from the *jinn* who whisper, there are also *shayāṭīn* of mankind who whisper. So seek refuge with Allāh from the evil of the two groups.

Due to this, the Prophet ﷺ said:

مَا تَعَوَّذَ مُتَوِّذٌ بِمِثْلِهِمَا.

Refuge is not sought with anything like the two of them.[13]

Meaning: (Refuge is not sought) with anything like these two *suwar*. So it is befitting for the Muslim to recite them after the prayers,

[13] Abū Dāwūd reported it (#1463), as did an-Nasā'ī (8/253) and Aḥmad (28/530 #17297) from the *ḥadīth* of 'Uqbah bin 'Āmir ﷺ.

and to repeat them and read them when going to sleep, along with Āyatul-Kursī and Sūrah al-Ikhlāṣ.

After every prayer, one is to read Āyatul-Kursī, Sūrah al-Ikhlāṣ, and the two *suwar* of seeking refuge, and he should repeat them three times after Maghrib and after Fajr. Likewise, he is to recite them when going to sleep so that the Shayṭān will be driven away from him and not disturb his sleep and annoy him with (bad) dreams.

The point of reference from these two *suwar* is that Allāh commands with seeking refuge with Him alone. This proves that seeking refuge with other than Him—from the *jinn*, mankind, or any created being—is not permissible. This is because it is a type of worship.

AL-ISTIGHĀTHAH (SEEKING DELIVERANCE) & ITS EVIDENCE

ORIGINAL TEXT

وَ دَلِيلُ الْإِسْتِغَاثَةِ قَوْلُهُ تَعَالَى: ﴿ إِذْ تَسْتَغِيثُونَ رَبَّكُمْ فَاسْتَجَابَ لَكُمْ ﴾.

The proof for seeking deliverance is:

(Remember) when you sought help of your Lord and He answered you.

[Sūrah al-Anfāl 8:9]

EXPLANATION

Al-istighāthah is a type of worship, and it means "to seek deliverance." It is only done in dire situations. If a person falls into a dire situation, then he seeks deliverance from Allāh and safety from this dire situation.

Al-istighāthah is of two types:

1) Seeking deliverance with the created being in that from which none is able to provide deliverance except Allāh ﷻ. So, he who seeks deliverance with other than Allāh from the *jinn*, mankind, one who is not present, or the dead, he has associated partners with Allāh. To seek refuge with the dead, the absent, the devils, and the *jinn* is to associate partners with Allāh ﷻ.

2) Seeking deliverance with the created being who is present and alive, in that which he is able to do; this is permissible. Allāh said in the story of Mūsā:

﴿ فَاسْتَغَاثَهُ الَّذِي مِن شِيعَتِهِ عَلَى الَّذِي مِنْ عَدُوِّهِ ﴾

The man of his (own) party asked him for help against his foe…

[Sūrah al-Qaṣaṣ 28:15]

Adh-Dhabḥ (Sacrificing): Its Categories & Its Evidence

ORIGINAL TEXT

وَ دَلِيلُ الذَّبْحِ قَوْلُهُ تَعَالَى: ﴿ قُلْ إِنَّ صَلَاتِي وَنُسُكِي وَمَحْيَايَ وَمَمَاتِي لِلَّهِ رَبِّ الْعَالَمِينَ ﴾. وَ مِنَ السُّنَّةِ: ((لَعَنَ اللهُ مَنْ ذَبَحَ لِغَيْرِ اللهِ)).

The proof for sacrificing is the statement of the Most High:

Say (O Muḥammad ﷺ): "Verily, my *ṣalāh* (prayer), my sacrifice, my living, and my dying are for Allāh, the Lord of the *'ālamīn* (mankind, *jinn*, and all that exists).

[Sūrah al-An'ām 6:162]

And from the Sunnah:

May Allāh curse he who sacrifices for other than Allāh.[14]

[14] Muslim reported it (#1978) from the *ḥadīth* of 'Alī bin Abī Ṭālib رضي الله عنه.

EXPLANATION

Adh-dhabḥ (sacrificing) is of four categories:

The First Category: The sacrifice which is done to seek nearness to and venerate someone. It is not permissible to do this except for Allāh. This is because it is from the monetary acts of worship. So it is not permissible to sacrifice for the *jinn*, the devils, the kings, or the leaders out of veneration for them, because this is an act of worship which is only permissible for Allāh ﷻ.

Those who sacrifice for the *jinn* in order to be safe from their evil, or for the healing of the sick—as the diviners and astrologers who claim to heal do, and they say, "Sacrifice such-and-such so that your sick may be healed, and do not mention the name of Allāh upon it"—this is association of partners with Allāh, which expels one from the religion. This is what Allāh mentioned, warning from doing it for other than Allāh:

﴿ قُلْ إِنَّ صَلَاتِي وَنُسُكِي وَمَحْيَايَ وَمَمَاتِي لِلَّهِ رَبِّ الْعَالَمِينَ ﴾

Say (O Muḥammad ﷺ): "Verily, my *ṣalāh* (prayer), my sacrifice, my living, and my dying are for Allāh, the Lord of the *'ālamīn* (mankind, *jinn*, and all that exists).

[Sūrah al-An'ām 6:162]

And He said:

﴿ فَصَلِّ لِرَبِّكَ وَانْحَرْ ﴾

Therefore, turn in prayer to your Lord and sacrifice (to Him only).

[Sūrah al-Kawthar 108:2]

Meaning: Sacrifice for your Lord.

The Second Category: Sacrificing for the purpose of eating the meat. There is no harm in this because it is not sacrificing for the purpose of drawing near to or venerating anyone. It is only sacrificing due to a need and to eat from it. There is no harm in this because it is not a type of worship; (and from this) is sacrificing to sell the meat.

The Third Category: Sacrificing out of joy and happiness, on the occasion of marriage, moving into a new home, the return of one who was away, and the likes, with the gathering of relatives and sacrificing in order to display joy and happiness due to what has occurred. There is no harm in this because it does not contain veneration of anyone or seeking nearness to anyone. It is only from the perspective of happiness for something that has occurred.

The Fourth Category: Sacrificing in order to give charity from the meat to the poor, needy, and the indigent. This is considered a *sunnah* and it falls under the worship (of Allāh).

AN-NADHAR (VOWS) & ITS EVIDENCE

ORIGINAL TEXT

وَ دَلِيلُ النَّذَرِ: ﴿ يُوفُونَ بِالنَّذْرِ وَيَخَافُونَ يَوْمًا كَانَ شَرُّهُ مُسْتَطِيرًا ﴾.

The proof for *an-nadhar* (vows) is:

They (are those who) fulfill (their) vows, and they fear a Day whose evil will be wide-spreading.

[Sūrah al-Insān 76:7]

EXPLANATION

An-nadhar (vows): This is the person making binding upon himself something which is not obligatory with a legislative basis, such as one vowing that he will fast, or vowing that he will give such-and-such in charity. Then, it is binding upon him to discharge it. This is due to the statement of the Prophet ﷺ:

مَنْ نَذَرَ أَنْ يُطِيعَ اللهَ فَلْيُطِعْهُ.

The one who vows to obey Allāh should obey Him.[15]

Vowing is a type of worship which is not permissible except for Allāh. So, he who vows to a grave, an idol, or other than it has associated partners with Allāh, and he has vowed to do disobedience and *shirk*. The Prophet ﷺ said:

مَنْ نَذَرَ أَنْ يَعْصِيَ اللهَ فَلَا يَعْصِهِ.

The one who vows to disobey Allāh should not disobey Him.[16]

---

[15] Al-Bukhārī reported it (#6696, #6700) from the *ḥadīth* of ʿĀ'ishah ﷺ.

[16] Ibid.

08

The Second Principle: Knowledge of the Religion

ORIGINAL TEXT

تَعْرِيفُ الدِّينِ: اَلْأَصْلُ الثَّانِي: مَعْرِفَةُ دِينِ الْإِسْلَامِ بِالْأَدِلَّةِ.

Definition of the *Dīn*:

The Second Principle: Knowledge of the religion of al-Islām with the proofs.

EXPLANATION

When the Shaykh finished explaining the knowledge of the first principle—knowledge of Allāh ﷻ, with the evidences—he shifted to clarification of the second principle, which is: knowledge of the religion of al-Islām with the proofs. So he said, *"The Second Principle: Knowledge of the religion of al-Islām with the proofs."* Then he defined it, clarified its meaning, and mentioned its levels.

His رحمه الله statement, *"Knowledge of the religion of al-Islām"*: What is intended by *ad-dīn* (the religion) is *aṭ-ṭā'ah* (obedience). It is said "دان له" i.e., he obeyed him in what he has commanded and abandoned what he forbade.

Ad-dīn is also applied and intended to mean "reckoning," as is within His statement:

﴿ مَالِكِ يَوْمِ الدِّينِ ﴾

The Only Owner (and the Only Ruling Judge) of the Day of Reckoning (i.e., the Day of Resurrection).

[Sūrah al-Fātiḥah 1:4]

It is said "دانه" (i.e., he called him to account), as is within that which the Most High has said:

﴿ وَمَا أَدْرَاكَ مَا يَوْمُ الدِّينِ ۝١٧ ثُمَّ مَا أَدْرَاكَ مَا يَوْمُ الدِّينِ ۝١٨ ﴾

And what will make you know what the Day of Recompense is? Again, what will make you know what the Day of Recompense is?

[Sūrah al-Infiṭār 82:17-18]

Meaning, the Day of Reckoning.

﴿ يَوْمَ لَا تَمْلِكُ نَفْسٌ لِّنَفْسٍ شَيْئًا ۖ وَالْأَمْرُ يَوْمَئِذٍ لِّلَّهِ ﴾

(It will be) the Day when no person shall have power (to do) anything for another, and the decision, that Day, will be (wholly) with Allāh.

[Sūrah al-Infiṭār 82:19]

His statement *"with the evidences"*: Meaning, knowledge of the religion of al-Islām is not by way of *at-taqlīd* (blind following), nor is it by way of a person's whims. One must have proofs from the Book and the Sunnah for knowledge of the religion. As for the person who does not know his religion, then he only blindly follows the people and is an imitator of the people. This person will never know his religion, and it is suitable that when he is questioned in his grave, he will say, "Ah, ah, I don't know. I heard the people saying something, so I said it."

So it is obligatory upon the individual to know his religion with the evidences from the Book of Allāh and the Sunnah of His Messenger ﷺ; and this is not known except by studying.

ORIGINAL TEXT

وَ هُوَ الْإِسْتِسْلَامُ لَهُ بِالتَّوْحِيدِ، وَ الْإِنْقِيَادُ لَهُ بِالطَّاعَةِ، وَ الْبَرَاءَةُ مِنَ الشِّرْكِ وَ أَهْلِهِ.

And it is: To submit to Allāh in *at-tawḥīd*, to yield to Him in obedience, and to free oneself from *shirk* and its people.

EXPLANATION

"Al-Islām" is taken from "he submitted to the thing," if someone has yielded to it; i.e., "he submitted himself to be murdered," meaning he surrendered himself to be murdered. Therefore, it is said, "He submitted to the thing," if someone has yielded to it.

Hence, al-Islām is submission of one's face, aim, and intent to Him عَزَّوَجَلَّ.

﴿ وَمَنْ أَحْسَنُ دِينًا مِّمَّنْ أَسْلَمَ وَجْهَهُ لِلَّهِ وَهُوَ مُحْسِنٌ وَاتَّبَعَ مِلَّةَ إِبْرَاهِيمَ حَنِيفًا ﴾

And who can be better in religion than one who submits his face (himself) to Allāh (i.e., follows Allāh's religion of Islamic monotheism); and he is a *muḥsin* (a good-doer). And follows the religion of Ibrāhīm (Abraham) *ḥanīfa* (Islamic monotheism—to worship none but Allāh alone).

[Sūrah an-Nisā' 4:125]

﴿ بَلَىٰ مَنْ أَسْلَمَ وَجْهَهُ لِلَّهِ ﴾

Yes, but whoever submits his face (himself) to Allāh...

[Sūrah al-Baqarah 2:112]

Meaning: He makes his actions purely for Allāh, and he yields to Allāh out of his own volition and choice, and out of desire and love.

"To submit to Allāh in at-tawḥīd": This is to single out Allāh ﷻ with worship. This is the meaning of *at-tawḥīd.* So, he who worships Allāh alone, not associating anything or anyone along with Him, then he has submitted to Him.

His statement *"to submit to Allāh in at-tawḥīd"*: Meaning, in that which He has commanded you with and prohibited you from. So, you are to do what He has commanded you with, and you are to avoid what He has prohibited you from, out of obedience to Allāh ﷻ.

His statement *"and freeing oneself from shirk and its people"*: The meaning of *al-barā'ah* is cutting off [ties] and withdrawing; keeping distance from *ash-shirk* and the people of *shirk* by disbelieving in the falsehood of *shirk* and staying far away from it; and also, to believe in the obligation of having enmity for the polytheists, because they are the enemies of Allāh. So, you are not to take them as allies. You are only to take them as enemies, because they are the enemies of Allāh, His Messenger, and the religion.

You are not to love them or have allegiance for them. You are only to cut off ties with them in the religion, distance yourself from them, and disbelieve in the falsehood they are upon. Do not love them with the heart and do not aid them with statement or action, for they are the enemies of your Lord and enemies of your religion. How can you have allegiance for them while they are enemies to al-Islām?!

It is not sufficient for you to submit to Allāh and yield to Him with obedience yet you do not disassociate yourself from *shirk* and the polytheists; this is not sufficient. You are not considered Muslim until you are described with these qualities:

1) Submitting to Allāh upon *at-tawḥīd.*

2) Yielding to Him in obedience.

3) Freeing oneself from that which contradicts *at-tawḥīd* and contradicts obedience; and that is *shirk.*

4) Freeing oneself from the people of *shirk.*

By actualizing these qualities, you are a Muslim. If one of them is negated, then that makes you not a Muslim. So, by these three statements, the Shaykh has summarized the definition of al-Islām. How many are the people who do not know the meaning of al-Islām because they have not studied this thing?! If it were to be said to them, "What is al-Islām?" they would not answer with the proper response.

The Levels of the Religion

ORIGINAL TEXT

اَلْمَرْتَبَةُ الْأُولَى: اَلْإِسْلَامُ. وَ هُوَ ثَلَاثُ مَرَاتِبَ: اَلْإِسْلَامُ...

The First Level: *al-Islām*

It is of three levels:

1) *Al-islām*

EXPLANATION

The meaning of *al-marātib* is "levels," because we say, "The religion is of three levels, some of them being higher than others." The first of the levels of the religion is *al-islām*, then *al-īmān*, then *al-iḥsān*. *Al-islām* is the broadest, then *al-īmān* is more restricted than *al-islām*, and *al-iḥsān* is more restricted than *al-īmān*.

The scope of *al-islām* is broad. The hypocrites are included in it if they comply with *al-islām,* outwardly manifest it, and outwardly hold fast to it; if they pray along with the Muslims, give *zakāh*, and enact the outward actions, then they are referred to as Muslims, and the rulings of the Muslims are applied to them in the *dunyā*. They have what the Muslims have, and upon them is that which is upon the Muslims. However, in the Hereafter, they will be in the lowest depths of the Hellfire because they do not have *īmān*. They only have outward *islām*.

ORIGINAL TEXT

...وَالْإِيمَانُ، وَ الْإِحْسَانُ.

2) *Al-īmān*

3) *Al-iḥsān*

EXPLANATION

His statement *"Al-īmān"*: This is the second level, and the believers vary. From them are those who are near (to Allāh); from them are those who are righteous. Those who are near (to Allāh) are the people of the highest levels; the righteous are beneath them. From them is he who is oppressive to himself; he is the one who commits major sins which are less than *shirk*. He is the believer who is a wrongdoer, or the believer who is deficient in *īmān*. The Most High says:

﴿ ثُمَّ أَوْرَثْنَا الْكِتَابَ الَّذِينَ اصْطَفَيْنَا مِنْ عِبَادِنَا ۖ فَمِنْهُمْ ظَالِمٌ لِّنَفْسِهِ وَمِنْهُم مُّقْتَصِدٌ وَمِنْهُمْ سَابِقٌ بِالْخَيْرَاتِ بِإِذْنِ اللَّهِ ۚ ذَٰلِكَ هُوَ الْفَضْلُ الْكَبِيرُ ﴾

Then We gave the Book (the Qur'ān) for inheritance to such of Our slaves whom We chose (the followers of Muhammad ﷺ). Then of them are some who wrong their own selves, and of them are some who follow a middle course, and of them are some who are, by Allāh's leave, foremost in good deeds. That (inheritance of the Qur'ān), that is indeed a great grace.

[Sūrah Fāṭir 35:32]

His statement *"Al-iḥsān"*: This is the third level; it is *al-iḥsān*. It means that the servant does good in that which is between himself and Allāh in the worship of Allāh ﷻ. The Prophet ﷺ mentioned *al-iḥsān* and said:

الْإِحْسَانُ أَنْ تَعْبُدَ اللهَ كَأَنَّكَ تَرَاهُ، فَإِنْ لَمْ تَكُنْ تَرَاهُ فَإِنَّهُ يَرَاكَ.

Al-iḥsān **is that you worship Allāh as if you see Him; and if you cannot (worship Him as if) you see Him, then (worship Him as though) He sees you.**[1]

Meaning: You are to have certain knowledge that Allāh sees you wherever you may be.

ORIGINAL TEXT

وَ كُلُّ مَرْتَبَةٍ لَهَا أَرْكَانٌ.

Each level has pillars.

EXPLANATION

His statement, *"Each level has pillars"*: *Al-arkān* (pillars) is the plural of *rukn* (pillar). It is that which something stands upon.

The pillars of a thing are its aspects which it stands upon, and it does not stand without them. They are within the thing itself, as opposed to the conditions, which are outside of the thing; for example, the pillars of the prayer—they are outside of the prayer, before it. As for the pillars of the prayer, then they are within it, such as the opening *takbīr* and the recitation of al-Fātiḥah. If any of them are left off, then the prayer is not correct, just as if any of the pillars of a building are not present, then it will not stand or be supported.

[1] This is part of a long *ḥadīth* which al-Bukhārī reported (#50), as did Muslim (#9, #10) from the *ḥadīth* of Abū Hurayrah ﷺ.

THE PILLARS OF AL-ISLĀM

ORIGINAL TEXT

شَهَادَةُ أَنْ لَا إِلَهَ إِلَّا اللهُ وَ أَنَّ مُحَمَّداً رَسُولُ اللهِ: مَعْنَاهَا وَ دَلِيلُهَا.

فَأَرْكَانُ الْإِسْلَامِ خَمْسَةٌ: شَهَادَةُ أَنْ لَا إِلَهَ إِلَّا اللهُ، وَ أَنَّ مُحَمَّداً رَسُولُ اللهِ، وَ إِقَامُ الصَّلَاةِ، وَ إِيتَاءُ الزَّكَاةِ، وَ صَوْمُ رَمَضَانَ، وَ حَجُّ بَيْتِ اللهِ الْحَرَامِ.

The testimony that none has the right to be worshiped except Allāh and Muḥammad is the Messenger of Allāh: Its meaning and evidence.

The pillars of *al-islām* are five:

1) The testimony that none has the right to be worshiped except Allāh and that Muḥammad is the Messenger of Allāh.

2) To establish the prayer.

3) To pay the *zakāh.*

4) To fast in Ramaḍān.

5) To perform Ḥajj to the Sacred House of Allāh.

EXPLANATION

Al-islām is not established except by way of these pillars. If they are lost, then *islām* is not established; and the rest of the acts of obedience are subsidiaries of these pillars. All acts of obedience and good deeds are subsidiaries of these pillars. Due to this, Jibrīl عليه السلام asked Allāh's Messenger ﷺ, "Inform me about *al-islām.*" He said:

اَلْإِسْلَامُ أَنْ تَشْهَدَ أَنْ لَا إِلَهَ إِلَّا اللهُ، وَ أَنَّ مُحَمَّداً رَسُولُ اللهِ، وَ

تُقِيمَ الصَّلَاةَ، وَ تُؤْتِيَ الزَّكَاةَ، وَ تَصُومَ رَمَضَانَ، وَ تَحُجَّ الْبَيْتَ
إِنِ اسْتَطَعْتَ إِلَيْهِ سَبِيلاً.

***Al-islām* is that you testify that none has the right to be worshiped except Allāh and that Muḥammad is the Messenger of Allāh; and establish the prayer, pay the *zakāh*, fast in Ramaḍān, and perform Ḥajj to the House if you are able to do so.**

He explained *al-islām* to be these five pillars. However, the *ḥadīth* of Ibn 'Umar clarifies that these five are the foundations of *al-islām*. He said:

بُنِيَ الْإِسْلَامُ عَلَى خَمْسٍ.

***Al-islām* is built upon five [pillars].**[2]

Meaning: These five are not all of *al-islām*; however, they are its pillars and its foundations upon which it stands. There remains some other subsidiary legislations for these pillars.

ORIGINAL TEXT

فَدَلِيلُ الشَّهَادَةِ: ﴿ شَهِدَ اللَّهُ أَنَّهُ لَا إِلَٰهَ إِلَّا هُوَ وَالْمَلَائِكَةُ وَأُولُو الْعِلْمِ
قَائِمًا بِالْقِسْطِ ۚ لَا إِلَٰهَ إِلَّا هُوَ الْعَزِيزُ الْحَكِيمُ ﴾.

The proof for the *shahādah* is:

> **Allāh bears witness that *lā ilāha illā Huwa* (none has the right to be worshiped but He); and the angels and those having knowledge (also give this witness). (He is always) maintaining His creation in justice. *Lā ilāha illā Huwa* (none has the right to be worshiped but He), the All-Mighty, the All-Wise.**
>
> *[Sūrah Āli 'Imrān 3:18]*

[2] Al-Bukhārī reported it (#8), as did Muslim (#16) from the *ḥadīth* of Ibn 'Umar ﵄.

EXPLANATION

The statement of the Most High, **"bears witness"** (شَهِدَ): Meaning, He rules, decrees, teaches, clarifies, and makes binding. The rectification from Allāh revolves around these five meanings:

1) Ruling

2) Decreeing

3) Declaring

4) Clarifying

5) And to make binding.

So, the meaning of **"He testifies"** is that He, Glorified be He, decrees, teaches, and informs, and He makes that binding upon His slaves—that none has the right to be worshiped except Him.

Lā ilāha (لاَ إِلَـهَ) [contains] the *lā* of negation, negating everything that is worshiped other than Allāh.

Illā Huwa (إِلاَّ هُوَ) is an affirmation of worship for Allāh alone.

The meaning of *annahu lā ilāha illā Huwa* (أَنَّهُ لاَ إِلَهَ إِلاَّ هُوَ) is: there is no true object of worship except Allāh ﷻ. As for that which is worshiped besides Allāh, then worshiping it is invalid due to the statement of the Most High:

﴿ ذَٰلِكَ بِأَنَّ اللَّهَ هُوَ الْحَقُّ وَأَنَّ مَا يَدْعُونَ مِن دُونِهِ هُوَ الْبَاطِلُ وَأَنَّ اللَّهَ هُوَ الْعَلِيُّ الْكَبِيرُ ﴾

That is because Allāh, He is the truth (the only true God of all that exists, who has no partners or rivals with Him), and what they (the polytheists) invoke besides Him, it is *bāṭil* (falsehood). And verily, Allāh is the Most High, the Most Great.

[Sūrah al-Ḥajj 22:62]

He testifies to uniqueness for Himself, and He is the Most Truthful of those who speak. His testimony is the most truthful of all testimonies, because it emanates from the Wise, Well-Informed, All-Knowing. He knows everything, so it is a truthful testimony.

The angels testify that none has the right to be worshiped except Him. They are a creation which He has created for His worship. Noble angels, honorable worshipers—Allāh has created them to worship Him. They glorify Him by night and by day, and they do not become tired. He also created them to carry out His universal commands; He entrusted them to carry out what He commands with from the affairs of the universe. Every angel is entrusted with a job, and their testimony is a truthful testimony because they are possessors of knowledge, worship, and insight regarding Allāh ﷻ.

They are from the best of the creation, even though there is a difference of opinion regarding that. Is the righteous human being better than the angels or are the angels better than the righteous human being? There is a difference of opinion regarding that.

Those who possess knowledge are of two categories:

1) The angels.

2) The possessors of knowledge from the human beings.

The possessors of knowledge do not bear witness except with that which is the truth; as opposed to the ignorant, whose testimony is not to be considered. Everyone who has knowledge from the creation of Allāh testifies to Allāh's uniqueness and that none has the right to be worshiped except Him. Within this is an honoring of the people of knowledge, since Allāh has connected their testimony to His testimony and the testimony of the angels.

The testimony of the possessors of knowledge from the creation is given consideration—which proves their virtue, nobility, and status—for the greatest of that which is testified to; i.e., *at-tawḥīd*.

What is intended by **"those having knowledge"** (وَأُولُو الْعِلْمِ) are those who possess legislative knowledge. It is not, as some people say, that what is intended by "those having knowledge" is those who possess vocational or agricultural knowledge. These are not referred to as "people of knowledge" in an absolute sense. This is because their knowledge is restricted. Rather, it is said, "This person is a scholar of mathematics; this one is a scholar of engineering; this one is a scholar of medicine." It is not said about them that they are "the people of knowledge" in an absolute sense, because this is not applied except to the people of legislative knowledge.

Also, the majority of these are people of worldly knowledge, and amongst them are atheists whose knowledge, in most cases, increases them in ignorance of Allāh, delusion, and deviation, as you see today in the disbelieving nations. They are advanced in technology and agriculture, yet they are disbelievers; so how can it be said that they are the people of knowledge whom Allāh has mentioned in His statement:

﴿ وَأُولُو الْعِلْمِ ﴾

...and those having knowledge.

[Sūrah Āli 'Imrān 3:18]

This is not at all conceivable.

Likewise, His statement:

﴿ إِنَّمَا يَخْشَى اللَّهَ مِنْ عِبَادِهِ الْعُلَمَاءُ ﴾

It is only those who have knowledge among His slaves that fear Allāh.

[Sūrah Fāṭir 35:28]

What is intended by this is the scholars of the legislation who know Allāh with true knowledge, who worship Him with true worship and fear Him.

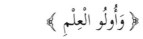

As for these people (the people of worldly knowledge), most of them do not fear Allāh. Rather, they disbelieve in Allāh, obstinately reject Him, and claim that the creation has no Lord—it is only nature that brings it into existence and controls it, as the communists believe. They deny the Lord ﷻ even though they have worldly knowledge, so how can we say that they are the people of knowledge? This is an error, for knowledge is not attributed except to its people, and it is a noble title which is not to be applied to the atheists and the disbelievers such that it is said that they are the people of knowledge!!

The angels and those who possess knowledge testify to Allāh's uniqueness. Therefore, consideration is not given to the statement of other than them from the atheists, the polytheists, and the Magians who disbelieve in Allāh ﷻ. Consideration is not given to them nor their statements, because they oppose the testimony of Allāh, the testimony of the angels, and the testimony of those who have knowledge from His creation.

﴿ قَائِمًا بِالْقِسْطِ ﴾

(He is always) maintaining His creation in justice.

[Sūrah Āli 'Imrān 3:18]

This is in the accusative case to indicate the state of the One who has testified; i.e., the state in which He is maintaining ﷻ.

Al-qisṭ (justice, القسط) means "equity." It means that Allāh ﷻ establishes equity in all things. Justice is the opposite of injustice. He has a just ruling; there does not emanate from Him except equity in all things.

﴿ لَا إِلَٰهَ إِلَّا هُوَ ﴾

***Lā ilāha illā Huwa* (none has the right to be worshiped but He)...**

[Sūrah Āli 'Imrān 3:18]

This is an emphasis for the first sentence.

﴿ الْعَزِيزُ الْحَكِيمُ ﴾

...the All-Mighty, the All-Wise.

[Sūrah Āli 'Imrān 3:18]

These are two names of Allāh ﷻ which comprise two of His attributes, and they are: might (*al-'izzah*) and wisdom (*al-ḥikmah*).

ORIGINAL TEXT

وَ مَعْنَاهَا: لَا مَعْبُودَ بِحَقٍّ إِلَّا اللهُ، ((لَا إِلَهَ)) نَافِيًا جَمِيعَ مَا يُعْبَدُ مِنْ دُونِ اللهِ، ((إِلَّا اللهُ)): مُثْبِتًا الْعِبَادَةَ لَهُ وَحْدَهُ لَا شَرِيكَ لَهُ فِي عِبَادَتِهِ كَمَا أَنَّهُ لَيْسَ لَهُ شَرِيكٌ فِي مُلْكِهِ.

Its meaning is: "None has the right to be worshiped in truth except Allāh." *Lā ilāha* (لا إله) is a negation of all that is worshiped besides Allāh. *Ill-Allāh* (إلا الله) is an affirmation of worship for Him alone, One having no partner in His worship just as He has no partner in His dominion.

EXPLANATION

His statement, *"Its meaning is: 'None has the right to be worshiped in truth except Allāh'"*: The meaning of *lā ilāha ill-Allāh* is not as the people of falsehood say, [which is] that there is no creator or provider except Allāh. This is because this is the oneness of Lordship which the polytheists affirm while they do not say *lā ilāha ill-Allāh*. Allāh says:

﴿ إِنَّهُمْ كَانُوٓا إِذَا قِيلَ لَهُمْ لَآ إِلَٰهَ إِلَّا ٱللَّهُ يَسْتَكْبِرُونَ ۝٣٥ وَيَقُولُونَ أَئِنَّا لَتَارِكُوٓا ءَالِهَتِنَا لِشَاعِرٍ مَّجْنُونٍۭ ۝٣٦ ﴾

Truly, when it was said to them, "*Lā ilāha ill-Allāh*" (none has the right to be worshiped but Allāh), they puffed themselves up with pride (i.e., denied it). And (they) said, "Are we going to abandon our *ālihah* (gods) for the sake of a mad poet?"

[Sūrah aṣ-Ṣāffāt 37:35-36]

Their statement **"our *ālihah* (gods)"** means "our objects of worship."

Their statement **"for the sake of a mad poet"** refers to the Prophet. They described him as being a poet and insane because he said to them, "Say: '*Lā ilāha ill-Allāh*,'" and he prohibited them from the worship of idols. When he said to them, "Say: '*Lā ilāha ill-Allāh*,'" they said:

﴿ أَجَعَلَ الْآلِهَةَ إِلَٰهًا وَاحِدًا ۖ إِنَّ هَٰذَا لَشَيْءٌ عُجَابٌ ﴾

"Has he made the *ālihah* (gods) (all) into one *Ilāh* (God—Allāh)? Verily, this is a curious thing!"

[Sūrah Ṣād 38:5]

They considered the gods to be many. So, this indicates that the meaning of [the testimony] is that nothing has the right to be worshiped in truth except Allāh. If its meaning were that there is no creator or provider except Allāh, then they already confirm this and they do not dispute it. If this were its meaning, then they would not have been prevented from saying *lā ilāha ill-Allāh*; because if they are asked, "Who created the heavens and the earth?" they say, "Allāh." If they are asked, "Who creates? Who is the One who provides? Who is the One who gives life and death and controls the affairs?" they say, "Allāh." They acknowledge this. So, if this were the meaning of *lā ilāha ill-Allāh*, then they would have affirmed it.

However, its meaning is that there is no true object of worship except Allāh. If you were to say, "There is no object of worship except Allāh," then this would be a big mistake. This is because all of the objects of worship are (in fact) Allāh (according to this statement); Allāh is Exalted above that. However, if you restrict them and say "in truth," then you have negated all objects of worship except Allāh ﷻ. It is a must that you say, "There is no true object of worship except Allāh," or, "There is no object of worship in truth except Allāh."

Then clarify that linguistically:

Lā ilāha (لا إله) is a negation of worship for other than Allāh.

Ill-Allāh (إلا الله) is an affirmation of worship for Allāh alone, who has no partners.

So, *lā ilāha ill-Allāh* (لا إله إلا الله) comprises a negation and an affirmation. Regarding *tawḥīd*, it is a must that one has negation and affirmation. It is not sufficient to have affirmation alone or to have negation alone. Rather, one must have negation along with affirmation. As the Most High has said:

﴿ فَمَن يَكْفُرْ بِالطَّاغُوتِ وَيُؤْمِن بِاللَّهِ ﴾

Whoever disbelieves in *ṭāghūt* and believes in Allāh…

[Sūrah al-Baqarah 2:256]

﴿ وَاعْبُدُوا اللَّهَ وَلَا تُشْرِكُوا بِهِ شَيْئًا ﴾

Worship Allāh and join none with Him in worship.

[Sūrah an-Nisā' 4:36]

So, if you were to say, "Allāh is an *ilāh* (deity)," then this is not sufficient. Al-Lāt is an *ilāh*; al-'Uzzā is an *ilāh*; Manāt is an *ilāh*; all idols are referred to as an *ilāh*.

It is a must that you say, "*Lā ilāha ill-Allāh*"; you must bring together negation and affirmation so that *tawḥīd* is actualized and *shirk* is negated.

ORIGINAL TEXT

وَ تَفْسِيرُهَا الَّذِي يُوَضِّحُهَا قَوْلُهُ تَعَالَى: ﴿ وَإِذْ قَالَ إِبْرَاهِيمُ لِأَبِيهِ وَقَوْمِهِ إِنَّنِي بَرَاءٌ مِّمَّا تَعْبُدُونَ ﴿٢٦﴾ إِلَّا الَّذِي فَطَرَنِي فَإِنَّهُ سَيَهْدِينِ ﴿٢٧﴾ وَجَعَلَهَا كَلِمَةً بَاقِيَةً فِي عَقِبِهِ لَعَلَّهُمْ يَرْجِعُونَ ﴿٢٨﴾ ﴾.

The explanation which will clarify this is His, the Most High, statement:

> **And (remember) when Ibrāhīm (Abraham) said to his father and his people, "Verily, I am innocent of what you worship; except for He (i.e., I worship none but Allāh alone) who has created me, and verily, He will guide me." And he made it [i.e., *lā ilāha ill-Allāh* (none has the right to be worshiped but Allāh alone)] a word lasting among his offspring (true monotheism), that they may turn back (i.e., to repent to Allāh or receive admonition).**
>
> *[Sūrah az-Zukhruf 43:26-28]*

EXPLANATION

The best of that which explains the Qur'ān is the Qur'ān. So, Allāh explains *lā ilāha ill-Allāh* in the Qur'ān, and that is within the statement of al-Khalīl عليه السلام in what Allāh mentioned regarding him:

﴿ إِنَّنِي بَرَاءٌ ﴾

"Verily, I am innocent..."

[Sūrah az-Zukhruf 43:26]

This is a negation; i.e., *lā ilāha*.

﴿ إِلَّا الَّذِي فَطَرَنِ ﴾

...except for He who has created me...

[Sūrah az-Zukhruf 43:27]

I.e., *ill-Allāh* (except Allāh). This is the affirmation. So, this verse is the complete explanation of *lā ilāha ill-Allāh*.

ORIGINAL TEXT

وَ قَوْلُهُ تَعَالَى: ﴿ قُلْ يَا أَهْلَ الْكِتَابِ تَعَالَوْا إِلَىٰ كَلِمَةٍ سَوَاءٍ بَيْنَنَا وَبَيْنَكُمْ أَلَّا نَعْبُدَ إِلَّا اللَّهَ وَلَا نُشْرِكَ بِهِ شَيْئًا وَلَا يَتَّخِذَ بَعْضُنَا بَعْضًا أَرْبَابًا

مِّن دُونِ اللَّهِ ۚ فَإِن تَوَلَّوْا فَقُولُوا اشْهَدُوا بِأَنَّا مُسْلِمُونَ ﴾.

And the statement of the Most High:

Say (O Muḥammad ﷺ): "O People of the Scripture (Jews and Christians): Come to a word that is just between us and you, that we worship none but Allāh, and that we associate no partners with Him, and that none of us shall take others as lords besides Allāh." Then, if they turn away, say: "Bear witness that we are Muslims."

[Sūrah Āli 'Imrān 3:64]

EXPLANATION

The statement of the Most High:

﴿ قُلْ يَا أَهْلَ الْكِتَابِ تَعَالَوْا إِلَىٰ كَلِمَةٍ سَوَاءٍ بَيْنَنَا وَبَيْنَكُمْ أَلَّا نَعْبُدَ إِلَّا اللَّهَ وَلَا نُشْرِكَ بِهِ شَيْئًا ﴾

Say (O Muḥammad ﷺ): "O People of the Scripture (Jews and Christians): Come to a word that is just between us and you, that we worship none but Allāh, and that we associate no partners with Him..."

[Sūrah Āli 'Imrān 3:64]

This verse from Sūrah Āli 'Imrān was revealed regarding the Christian delegation of Najrān who had come to the Prophet ﷺ and debated with him and questioned him; and a long discourse took place between him and them. They were Christian Arabs. At the end (of the discourse), the Prophet ﷺ sought *al-mubāhalah* (mutual cursing upon the one who is wrong) from them:

﴿ فَقُلْ تَعَالَوْا نَدْعُ أَبْنَاءَنَا وَأَبْنَاءَكُمْ وَنِسَاءَنَا وَنِسَاءَكُمْ وَأَنفُسَنَا وَأَنفُسَكُمْ ثُمَّ نَبْتَهِلْ فَنَجْعَل لَّعْنَتَ اللَّهِ عَلَى الْكَاذِبِينَ ﴾

Say (O Muḥammad ﷺ): "Come, let us call our sons and your sons, our women and your women, ourselves and yourselves—then we pray and invoke (sincerely) the curse of Allāh upon those who lie."

[Sūrah Āli 'Imrān 3:61]

When he sought *al-mubāhalah* from them, they became afraid and did not do the mutual curse with him ﷺ, and they paid the *jizyah* to him because they knew that they were upon falsehood and that he was the Messenger of Allāh ﷺ.

To mutually invoke a curse (نَبْتَهِلْ) means: "We will supplicate for the curse to be upon whoever amongst us is a liar"; and they knew that they were the liars and that, had they invoked the curse along with him, then fire would have descended upon them and burned them in their place. So they said, "No. But we will pay the *jizyah*, and we will not do the *mubāhalah* with you." So, he accepted the *jizyah* from them and he clarified to them that Allāh has commanded him with what is in this verse.

This verse contains the meaning of *lā ilāha ill-Allāh*. The statement **"that we worship none"** (أَلاَّ نَعْبُدَ) is a negation. His statement **"except Allāh"** (إِلاَّ اللّهَ) is an affirmation. This is the justice for which the heavens and the earth were established, for the heavens and the earth were established upon *tawḥīd* and justice.

We are not to associate anything as a partner along with Him; not al-Masīḥ ('Īsā), who they claim is a lord and whom they worship besides Allāh, nor other than the Masīḥ, nor Muḥammad ﷺ, nor any of the prophets, the righteous, or the *awliyā'*:

﴿ أَلَّا نَعْبُدَ إِلَّا اللَّهَ وَلَا نُشْرِكَ بِهِ شَيْئًا ﴾

"...that we worship none but Allāh, and that we associate no partners with Him..."

[Sūrah Āli 'Imrān 3:64]

﴿ وَلَا يَتَّخِذَ بَعْضُنَا بَعْضًا أَرْبَابًا مِّن دُونِ اللَّهِ ﴾

"And that none of us shall take others as lords besides Allāh."

[Sūrah Āli 'Imrān 3:64]

Meaning: As you have taken your rabbis and monks as lords besides Allāh.

﴿ اتَّخَذُوا أَحْبَارَهُمْ وَرُهْبَانَهُمْ أَرْبَابًا مِّن دُونِ اللَّهِ وَالْمَسِيحَ ابْنَ مَرْيَمَ وَمَا أُمِرُوا إِلَّا لِيَعْبُدُوا إِلَهًا وَاحِدًا ﴾

They (Jews and Christians) took their rabbis and their monks to be their lords besides Allāh (by obeying them in things which they made lawful or unlawful according to their own desires, without being ordered by Allāh), and (they also took as their lord) Messiah son of Maryam (Mary), while they (Jews and Christians) were commanded [in the Tawrāh (Torah) and the Injīl (Gospel)] to worship none but one *Ilāh* (God—Allāh).

[Sūrah at-Tawbah 9:31]

Taking the rabbis and the monks besides Allāh was clarified by the Messenger of Allāh as obeying them in making permissible that which Allāh had made impermissible, and making impermissible that which Allāh had made permissible.[3]

This is the meaning of taking lords besides Allāh. When they would make *ḥalāl* that which Allāh had made *ḥarām* and make *ḥarām* that which Allāh had made *ḥalāl,* and they (the People of the Book) obeyed them in that, then they had taken them as lords, because

---

[3] See the *ḥadīth* of 'Adiyy bin Hātim ☻, which at-Tirmidhī reported (#3095). In it is the statement of Allāh's Messenger ﷺ:

أَمَّا إِنَّهُمْ لَمْ يَكُونُوا يَعْبُدُونَهُمْ، وَ لَكِنَّهُمْ كَانُوا إِذَا أَحَلُّوا لَهُمْ شَيْئًا اسْتَحَلُّوهُ، وَ إِذَا حَرَّمُوا عَلَيْهِمْ شَيْئًا حَرَّمُوهُ.

They did not used to worship them; however, when they made something permissible for them, they deemed it to be permissible, and when they prohibited something for them, they deemed it to be impermissible.

the One who legislates and makes things permissible and impermissible is Allāh ﷻ.

﴿ فَإِن تَوَلَّوْا ﴾

Then, if they turn away…

[Sūrah Āli 'Imrān 3:64]

And they do not accept the call to *at-tawḥīd:*

﴿ فَقُولُوا اشْهَدُوا بِأَنَّا مُسْلِمُونَ ﴾

…(then) say: "Bear witness that we are Muslims."

[Sūrah Āli 'Imrān 3:64]

Call them to witness that you are monotheists and they are disbelievers. Clarify to them the falsehood of what they are upon.

So, within this verse is declaring oneself free of the religion of the polytheists and not being silent about that, and an open proclamation of the falsehood of *shirk* and a refutation of its people.

In Summary: *Lā ilāha ill-Allāh* has two pillars: negation and affirmation. So, if it is said to you, "What are the pillars of *lā ilāha ill-Allāh*?" Then say, "Negation and affirmation."

Its conditions are seven, and you will not benefit except with these conditions. Some of them (the scholars) put them in poetic form with the statement:

عِلْمٌ يَقِينٌ إِخْلَاصٌ وَ صِدْقُكَ

مَعَ مَحَبَّةٍ وَ انْقِيَادٍ وَ الْقَبُولِ لَهَا

Knowledge, certainty, purity, and your truthfulness;

Along with love, submission, and acceptance of it.

***Al-'Ilm* (Knowledge):** The opposite of it is ignorance. So, the one who says, "*Lā ilāha ill-Allāh,*" with his tongue and is ignorant of its meaning, then *lā ilāha ill-Allāh* will not benefit him.

Al-Yaqīn **(Certainty):** There should be no doubt with him; some people may know its meaning, but they may doubt it. Thus, his knowledge is not correct. He must have certainty that none has the right to be worshiped except Allāh, and that it is the truth.

Al-Ikhlāṣ **(Purity):** Its opposite is *shirk*. Some people say "*Lā ilāha ill-Allāh*" but do not abandon *shirk*, such as occurs today with the grave worshipers. *Lā ilāha ill-Allāh* will not benefit these people because one of its conditions is the abandonment of *shirk*.

Aṣ-Ṣidq **(Truthfulness):** Its opposite is lying. This is because the hypocrites say "*Lā ilāha ill-Allāh*." However, they are liars within their hearts. They do not believe in its meaning. Allāh the Exalted has said:

﴿ إِذَا جَاءَكَ الْمُنَافِقُونَ قَالُوا نَشْهَدُ إِنَّكَ لَرَسُولُ اللَّهِ ۗ وَاللَّهُ يَعْلَمُ إِنَّكَ لَرَسُولُهُ وَاللَّهُ يَشْهَدُ إِنَّ الْمُنَافِقِينَ لَكَاذِبُونَ ﴿١﴾ اتَّخَذُوا أَيْمَانَهُمْ جُنَّةً ﴾

When the hypocrites come to you (O Muḥammad ﷺ), they say, "We bear witness that you are indeed the Messenger of Allāh." Allāh knows that you are indeed His Messenger, and Allāh bears witness that the hypocrites are liars indeed. They have made their oaths a screen (for their hypocrisy).

[Sūrah al-Munāfiqūn 63:1-2]

Al-Maḥabbah **(Love):** You must be one who loves this statement and has allegiance for its people. As for the one who does not love it nor does he love its people, then it will not benefit him.

Al-Inqiyād **(Submission):** This is the opposite of turning away and abandonment. It means to submit to that which it indicates from the worship of Allāh alone, without partners, and to comply with His commands. As long as you recognize and testify that none has the right to be worshiped except Allāh, then you are required to submit to His rulings and His religion. As for you saying "*Lā ilāha ill-Allāh*" and not submitting to the rulings of Allāh and His legislation, then *lā ilāha ill-Allāh* will not benefit you.

***Al-Qabūl* (Acceptance):** Acceptance negates rejection; this is you not rejecting anything from the rights of *lā ilāha ill-Allāh* and that which it indicates. Rather, you accept everything that *lā ilāha ill-Allāh* indicates; you accept it with a correct acceptance.

An eighth condition has been added:

وَ زِيدَ ثَامِنُهَا الْكُفْرُ

بِمَا مَعَ الْإِلَهِ مِنَ الْأَشْيَاءِ قَدْ أُلِّهَا

An eighth has been added: kufr (disbelief)

In the things that have been deified along with al-Ilāh (Allāh).

Meaning: Freedom from *shirk*. One is not a monotheist until he frees himself from *shirk*.

﴿ وَإِذْ قَالَ إِبْرَاهِيمُ لِأَبِيهِ وَقَوْمِهِ إِنَّنِي بَرَاءٌ مِّمَّا تَعْبُدُونَ ﴾

And (remember) when Ibrāhīm (Abraham) said to his father and his people, "Verily, I am innocent of what you worship..."

[Sūrah az-Zukhruf 43:26]

These are the conditions of *lā ilāha ill-Allāh*; eight conditions.

ORIGINAL TEXT

وَ دَلِيلُ شَهَادَةِ أَنَّ مُحَمَّدًا رَسُولُ اللهِ قَوْلُهُ: ﴿ لَقَدْ جَاءَكُمْ رَسُولٌ مِّنْ أَنفُسِكُمْ عَزِيزٌ عَلَيْهِ مَا عَنِتُّمْ حَرِيصٌ عَلَيْكُم بِالْمُؤْمِنِينَ رَءُوفٌ رَّحِيمٌ ﴾.

The proof for the testimony that Muḥammad is the Messenger of Allāh is His statement:

Verily, there has come unto you a Messenger

(Muḥammad ﷺ) from amongst yourselves (i.e., whom you know well). It grieves him that you should receive any injury or difficulty. He (Muḥammad ﷺ) is anxious over you (to be rightly guided, to repent to Allāh, and to beg Him to pardon and forgive your sins, so that you may enter Paradise and be saved from the punishment of the Hellfire); for the believers (he ﷺ is) full of pity, kind and merciful.

[Sūrah at-Tawbah 9:128]

EXPLANATION

The first pillar of *al-islām* is made up of two things:

1) The testimony that none has the right to be worshiped except Allāh.

2) The testimony that Muḥammad is the Messenger of Allāh.

They are one pillar. The first part means purity in worship. The second part means following the Messenger ﷺ.

The proof for the testimony that Muḥammad is the Messenger of Allāh is His statement:

﴿ لَقَدْ جَاءَكُمْ رَسُولٌ مِّنْ أَنفُسِكُمْ عَزِيزٌ عَلَيْهِ مَا عَنِتُّمْ حَرِيصٌ عَلَيْكُم بِالْمُؤْمِنِينَ رَءُوفٌ رَّحِيمٌ ﴾

Verily, there has come unto you a Messenger (Muḥammad ﷺ) from amongst yourselves. It grieves him that you should receive any injury or difficulty. He (Muḥammad ﷺ) is anxious over you; for the believers (he ﷺ is) full of pity, kind and merciful.

[Sūrah at-Tawbah 9:128]

The proofs that Muḥammad is the Messenger of Allāh are many within the Book and the Sunnah, along with the miracles and miraculous deeds which indicate his messengership ﷺ.

From the Book there is this verse; the Most High says:

﴿ لَقَدْ جَاءَكُمْ رَسُولٌ مِّنْ أَنفُسِكُمْ عَزِيزٌ عَلَيْهِ مَا عَنِتُّمْ
حَرِيصٌ عَلَيْكُم بِالْمُؤْمِنِينَ رَءُوفٌ رَّحِيمٌ ﴾

Verily, there has come unto you a Messenger (Muḥammad ﷺ) from amongst yourselves. It grieves him that you should receive any injury or difficulty. He (Muḥammad ﷺ) is anxious over you; for the believers (he ﷺ is) full of pity, kind and merciful.

[Sūrah at-Tawbah 9:128]

This is a testimony from Allāh for the messengership of this Messenger ﷺ, and a clarification of his attributes.

The statement of the Most High:

﴿ لَقَدْ جَاءَكُمْ ﴾

Verily, there has come to you...

[Sūrah at-Tawbah 9:128]

The *lām* (at the beginning of the verse) is the *lām* of oath; within it is a latent oath. That which is latent from it is (the statement): "By Allāh, there has come to you..."

"Qad" (قَدْ): This is a particle of *taḥqīq* (actualization) and *ta'kīd* (emphasis) after *ta'kīd* (emphasis).

"There has come to you" (جَاءكُمْ): Meaning, "O mankind." This is an address for all of mankind, because His messengership was general for all of the two classes: mankind and the *jinn*.

"A Messenger" (رَسُولٌ): He is one to whom legislation has been revealed, and he is commanded to propagate it; (thus) he is referred to as a Messenger because he was dispatched by Allāh ﷻ.

"From amongst yourselves" (مِّنْ أَنفُسِكُمْ): Meaning, from your genus (a human being). He is not an angel. This is the *sunnah* of Allāh ﷻ: that He sends to human beings a messenger from amongst themselves so that he may clarify and converse with them, and because they recognize him.

If He had sent to them an angel, then they would not be able to converse with him because he is not from their genus. Also, they would not able to see the angel, because he is not from their genus. From the mercy of Allāh is that He sent to the people a messenger from their genus.

Rather, [he sent a messenger] from the Arabs, and from the most noble household of the Arabs in terms of lineage: Banū Hāshim, who have the most noble lineage from the Quraysh, and the Quraysh have the most noble lineage of the Arabs. So, he is the best of the best. They knew him and they knew his personality; they knew his lineage, they knew his tribe, they knew his land. If they had not known him, then how could they believe him? If he had come with other than their language, then how would they understand his speech?

﴿ عَزِيزٌ عَلَيْهِ مَا عَنِتُّمْ حَرِيصٌ عَلَيْكُم ﴾

It grieves him that you should receive any injury or difficulty...

[Sūrah at-Tawbah 9:128]

His statement **"It grieves him"** (عَزِيزٌ): Meaning, "It is difficult upon him."

His statement **"that you should receive any injury or difficulty"** (مَا عَنِتُّمْ): Meaning, "That which is difficult upon you." The meaning of العنت is "hardship and difficulty." The Messenger ﷺ finds difficult that which is a difficulty upon his *ummah*. He did not want for them any difficulty; he only wanted ease and easiness for them. Due to this, within his legislation there has come tolerance; he ﷺ said:

بُعِثْتُ بِالْحَنِيفِيَّةِ السَّمْحَةِ.

I have been sent with the tolerant *ḥanīfiyyah* (monotheism).[4]

The Most High has said:

﴿ وَمَا جَعَلَ عَلَيْكُمْ فِي الدِّينِ مِنْ حَرَجٍ ﴾

...and He has not laid upon you in religion any hardship.

[Sūrah al-Ḥajj 22:78]

He said:

﴿ مَا يُرِيدُ اللَّهُ لِيَجْعَلَ عَلَيْكُم مِّنْ حَرَجٍ ﴾

Allāh does not want to place you in difficulty.

[Sūrah al-Mā'idah 5:6]

So, his *sharī'ah* is easy, and it is compatible with the ability of the people and that which the responsible people can endure; and it does not burden them with what is beyond their scope. Due to this, the Prophet ﷺ would love ease for them, and he was never given the choice between two affairs except that he would choose the easiest of them as long as it did not entail sin. He would love to do an action, but he would leave it off out of kindness for his *ummah*.

He would abandon an action which he would love to do from the righteous actions so that it would not be a difficulty for his *ummah*; he would become happy with what made them happy and rejoice when they rejoiced. There is no doubt that the one who has this attribute would only bring good and mercy ﷺ.

"He is anxious over you" (حَرِيصٌ عَلَيْكُم): Meaning, for your guidance and your exit from darkness into light. Due to this, he would bear hardships in calling to the people, seeking their guidance and removing them from darkness into the light, to the point that Allāh said to him:

﴿ لَعَلَّكَ بَاخِعٌ نَّفْسَكَ أَلَّا يَكُونُوا مُؤْمِنِينَ ﴾

---

[4] Aḥmad reported it (36/623, #22291) from the *ḥadīth* of Abū Umāmah al-Bāhilī رضي الله عنه.

It may be that you (O Muḥammad ﷺ) are going to kill yourself with grief, that they do not become believers [in your *risālah* (messengership) and in your message of Islamic monotheism].

[Sūrah ash-Shu'arā' 26:3]

Meaning: Perhaps you will destroy yourself (over the fact that) they will not believe, due to sadness over them; so do not grieve for them. This is from the completeness of his sincerity ﷺ.

"For the believers (he ﷺ is) kind and merciful" (بِالْمُؤْمِنِينَ رَؤُوفٌ رَّحِيمٌ): *Ar-ra'ūf* is from *ar-ra'fah* (kindness); it is kindness and gentleness. *Raḥīm:* He described him with mercy, meaning he is not mean.

﴿ فَبِمَا رَحْمَةٍ مِّنَ اللَّهِ لِنتَ لَهُمْ ۖ وَلَوْ كُنتَ فَظًّا غَلِيظَ الْقَلْبِ لَانفَضُّوا مِنْ حَوْلِكَ ﴾

And by the mercy of Allāh, you dealt with them gently. And had you been severe and harsh-hearted, they would have broken away from about you.

[Sūrah Āli 'Imrān 3:159]

He ﷺ was humble and mild with the believers, lowering his wing to them and facing them with pleasantness, love, affection, and goodness. These were some of his qualities. Allāh mentioned five qualities regarding this Messenger ﷺ:

1) He is from you.

2) That which afflicts you is hard upon him.

3) He is anxious over you.

4) He is kind to the believers.

5) He is merciful.

These are five qualities of this Prophet ﷺ. He specifically mentioned the believers as it relates to his kindness and mercy, because he was stern against the polytheists and those who were obstinately rebellious. He would become angry due to the anger of Allāh ﷻ. As He said:

﴿ يَا أَيُّهَا النَّبِيُّ جَاهِدِ الْكُفَّارَ وَالْمُنَافِقِينَ وَاغْلُظْ عَلَيْهِمْ ۚ وَمَأْوَاهُمْ جَهَنَّمُ ۖ وَبِئْسَ الْمَصِيرُ ﴾

O Prophet (Muḥammad ﷺ)! Strive hard against the disbelievers and the hypocrites, and be severe against them; their abode will be Hell, and worst indeed is that destination.

[Sūrah at-Taḥrīm 66:9]

His mercy and kindness was specifically for the believers. This is also how the believers are with one another:

﴿ مُّحَمَّدٌ رَّسُولُ اللَّهِ ۚ وَالَّذِينَ مَعَهُ أَشِدَّاءُ عَلَى الْكُفَّارِ رُحَمَاءُ بَيْنَهُمْ ﴾

Muḥammad is the Messenger of Allāh, and those who are with him are severe against disbelievers and merciful among themselves.

[Sūrah al-Fat'ḥ 48:29]

These were his qualities ﷺ.

ORIGINAL TEXT

مَعْنَى شَهَادَةِ أَنَّ مُحَمَّدًا رَسُولُ اللهِ: طَاعَتُهُ فِيمَا أَمَرَ، وَ تَصْدِيقُهُ فِيمَا أَخْبَرَ، وَاجْتِنَابُ مَا عَنْهُ نَهَى وَ زَجَرَ، وَ أَلَّا يُعْبَدَ اللهُ إِلَّا بِمَا شَرَعَ.

The meaning of the testimony that Muḥammad is the Messenger of Allāh is:

1) Obeying him in what he has commanded.

2) Believing in everything that he has informed us of.

3) Avoiding what he has prohibited and disavowed.

4) Only worshiping Allāh with what he has legislated.

EXPLANATION

The testimony that Muḥammad is the Messenger of Allāh has a meaning, and it necessitates certain things; it is not merely a statement to be uttered. Its meaning is that you acknowledge with your tongue and heart that Muḥammad is Allāh's Messenger. You pronounce with your tongue and you believe in your heart that he is Allāh's Messenger ﷺ.

As for uttering it with the tongue while rejecting it with the heart, then this is the way of the hypocrites, as Allāh has informed us with His statement:

﴿ إِذَا جَاءَكَ الْمُنَافِقُونَ قَالُوا نَشْهَدُ إِنَّكَ لَرَسُولُ اللَّهِ ۗ وَاللَّهُ يَعْلَمُ إِنَّكَ لَرَسُولُهُ وَاللَّهُ يَشْهَدُ إِنَّ الْمُنَافِقِينَ لَكَاذِبُونَ ۝١ اتَّخَذُوا أَيْمَانَهُمْ جُنَّةً ﴾

When the hypocrites come to you (O Muḥammad ﷺ), they say, "We bear witness that you are indeed the Messenger of Allāh." Allāh knows that you are indeed His Messenger, and Allāh bears witness that the hypocrites are liars indeed. They have made their oaths a screen (for their hypocrisy).

[Sūrah al-Munāfiqūn 63:1-2]

"They have made their oaths": This means that their testimonies were a covering with which they covered themselves, so they are hindered from the path of Allāh. This is a proof that articulation of it with the tongue is not sufficient.

Likewise, to believe within the heart while not pronouncing it, for the one who has the ability to pronounce it, is also not sufficient.

Indeed, the polytheists know that he is Allāh's Messenger, but they obstinately reject. As the Most High has said:

﴿ قَدْ نَعْلَمُ إِنَّهُ لَيَحْزُنُكَ الَّذِي يَقُولُونَ ۖ فَإِنَّهُمْ لَا يُكَذِّبُونَكَ وَلَٰكِنَّ الظَّالِمِينَ بِآيَاتِ اللَّهِ يَجْحَدُونَ ﴾

We know indeed the grief which their words cause you (O Muḥammad ﷺ); it is not you that they deny, but it is the verses (the Qur'ān) of Allāh that the *ẓālimūn* (polytheists and wrongdoers) deny.

[Sūrah al-An'ām 6:33]

So, within their hearts they recognize the messengership and they know that he is Allāh's Messenger. However, they are prevented by arrogance and stubbornness from affirming the messengership. Likewise, *ḥasad* (envy) prevented them, just as it did the Jews and the polytheist Arabs. Abū Jahl 'Amr bin Hishām recognized and said, "We and Banū Hāshim are equal in all matters; however, they said, 'From us is Allāh's Messenger, and Allāh's Messenger is not from you.' From where would we bring a messenger? For this reason, I rejected his messengership, out of envy for Banū Hāshim."[5]

Abū Ṭālib said in his poem:

وَ لَقَدْ عَلِمْتَ بِأَنَّ دِينَ مُحَمَّدٍ

مِنْ خَيْرِ أَدْيَانِ الْبَرِيَّةِ دِيناً

لَوْ لَا الْمَلَامَةُ أَوْ حَذَارِ مَسَبَّةٍ

لَوَجَدْتَنِي سَمْحًا بِذَاكَ مُبِينًا

Indeed, I know that the religion of Muḥammad is from the best religions of the creation;

Were it not for fear of harm or apprehension of abuse,

You would have found me accepting that completely.

[5] See: *As-Sīrah an-Nabawiyyah* by Ibn Hāshim (1/251), "The Story of the Quraysh Listening to the Recitation of the Prophet ﷺ."

He recognized within his heart the messengership of Muḥammad. However, the *jāhiliyyah* concern for his people prevented him, so he did not disbelieve in the religion of 'Abdul-Muṭṭalib, which was the worship of idols. They recognized his prophethood with their hearts, so recognition with the heart that he is the Messenger of Allāh is not sufficient. Rather, one must pronounce it with his tongue.

Moreover, it is not sufficient to pronounce it with the tongue and acknowledge it within the heart. Rather, it is a must that one have a third matter, which is following (the Messenger). Allāh the Exalted says:

﴿ فَالَّذِينَ آمَنُوا بِهِ وَعَزَّرُوهُ وَنَصَرُوهُ وَاتَّبَعُوا النُّورَ الَّذِي أُنزِلَ مَعَهُ ۙ أُولَٰئِكَ هُمُ الْمُفْلِحُونَ ﴾

So, those who believe in him (Muḥammad ﷺ), honor him, help him, and follow the light (the Qur'ān) which has been sent down with him; it is they who will be successful.

[Sūrah al-A'rāf 7:157]

Even though the likes of Abū Ṭālib aided him, protected him, and knew that he was the Messenger of Allāh, he did not follow him. Therefore, he could not be a Muslim until he follows him. Due to this, the Shaykh said:

"The meaning of the testimony that Muḥammad is the Messenger of Allāh is:

1) *Obeying him in what he has commanded.*

2) *Believing in everything that he has informed us of.*

3) *Avoiding what he has prohibited and disavowed.*

4) *Only worshiping Allāh with what he has legislated."*

It is a must that one recognizes his messengership outwardly, inwardly, and in terms of belief, and it is a must that one follows him ﷺ; and that is summarized within these four statements the Shaykh has mentioned.

The First: Obeying him in what he has commanded. Allāh ﷻ says:

﴿ مَّن يُطِعِ الرَّسُولَ فَقَدْ أَطَاعَ اللَّهَ ﴾

He who obeys the Messenger (Muḥammad ﷺ) has indeed obeyed Allāh.

[Sūrah an-Nisā' 4:80]

He says:

﴿ وَمَا أَرْسَلْنَا مِن رَّسُولٍ إِلَّا لِيُطَاعَ بِإِذْنِ اللَّهِ ﴾

We sent no messenger but to be obeyed by Allāh's leave.

[Sūrah an-Nisā' 4:64]

So, He has connected obedience to the Messenger with obedience to Him ﷻ; and He has connected disobedience to the Messenger with disobedience to Him:

﴿ وَمَن يَعْصِ اللَّهَ وَرَسُولَهُ فَإِنَّ لَهُ نَارَ جَهَنَّمَ خَالِدِينَ فِيهَا أَبَدًا ﴾

And whosoever disobeys Allāh and His Messenger, then verily, for him is the Fire of Hell; he shall dwell therein forever.

[Sūrah al-Jinn 72:23]

He said:

﴿ وَإِن تُطِيعُوهُ تَهْتَدُوا ﴾

If you obey him, you shall be on the right guidance.

[Sūrah an-Nūr 24:54]

He said:

﴿ وَأَطِيعُوا الرَّسُولَ لَعَلَّكُمْ تُرْحَمُونَ ﴾

And obey the Messenger (Muḥammad ﷺ) that you may receive mercy (from Allāh).

[Sūrah an-Nūr 24:56]

So, it is a must that one obey him ﷺ. Therefore, the one who testifies that Muḥammad is the Messenger of Allāh is required to obey him in what he has commanded, due to the statement of the Most High:

﴿ وَمَا آتَاكُمُ الرَّسُولُ فَخُذُوهُ وَمَا نَهَاكُمْ عَنْهُ فَانتَهُوا ﴾

And whatsoever the Messenger (Muḥammad ﷺ) gives you, take it, and whatsoever he forbids you, abstain (from it).

[Sūrah al-Ḥashr 59:7]

And His statement:

﴿ فَلْيَحْذَرِ الَّذِينَ يُخَالِفُونَ عَنْ أَمْرِهِ أَن تُصِيبَهُمْ فِتْنَةٌ أَوْ يُصِيبَهُمْ عَذَابٌ أَلِيمٌ ﴾

And let those who oppose his (Muḥammad ﷺ) commandment (i.e., his Sunnah, legal ways, orders, acts of worship, statements, etc.) (among the sects) beware, lest some *fitnah* (disbelief, trials, afflictions, earthquakes, killing, being overpowered by a tyrant, etc.) befall them or a painful torment be inflicted on them.

[Sūrah an-Nūr 24:63]

"His commandment" refers to the command of the Messenger. So, it is a must that one obeys the Messenger ﷺ.

The Second: Believing in everything that he has informed us of. This is because the Messenger ﷺ has informed us about many affairs of the unseen. He has informed us about Allāh, the angels, and affairs of the unseen. He has informed us about affairs of the future, such as the establishment of the Hour, the signs of the Hour, Paradise, and the Fire; and he has informed us about past affairs, about the previous nations. So, it is a must that one believes in this and doesn't deny it. The Most High has said:

﴿ وَمَا يَنطِقُ عَنِ الْهَوَىٰ ۝٣ إِنْ هُوَ إِلَّا وَحْيٌ يُوحَىٰ ۝٤ ﴾

Nor does he speak of (his own) desire. It is only an inspiration that is inspired.

[Sūrah an-Najm 53:3-4]

The Messenger ﷺ does not speak with this information or these commands and prohibitions from his own self, nor does he speak with anything from his own self ﷺ; he only speaks by way of the revelation from Allāh ﷻ, so his information is true. He who does not believe in what the Messenger has informed us of is not a believer, nor is he truthful in his testimony that Muḥammad is the Messenger of Allāh. How can he testify that Muḥammad is the Messenger of Allāh while denying what he informed us of? How can he testify that Muḥammad is the Messenger of Allāh while he does not obey him in what he has commanded?!

The Third: Avoiding what he has prohibited and disavowed; this means avoiding what the Messenger ﷺ has prohibited you from. He has prohibited you from many statements, actions, and qualities. However, he has not prohibited anything except that it contains harm and evil. He does not command except with what contains good and righteousness. So, when the servant does not avoid what Allāh's Messenger ﷺ has prohibited, then he is not one who testifies to his messengership; rather, he is one who contradicts it. How can he testify that he is Allāh's Messenger, yet he does not avoid what the Messenger ﷺ has prohibited? Allāh the Exalted says:

﴿ وَمَا آتَاكُمُ الرَّسُولُ فَخُذُوهُ وَمَا نَهَاكُمْ عَنْهُ فَانتَهُوا ﴾

And whatsoever the Messenger (Muḥammad ﷺ) gives you, take it, and whatsoever he forbids you,

abstain (from it).

[Sūrah al-Ḥashr 59:7]

The Prophet ﷺ said:

فَإِذَا نَهِيتُكُمْ عَنْ شَيْءٍ فَاجْتَنِبُوهُ، وَ إِذَا أَمَرْتُكُمْ بِأَمْرٍ فَأْتُوا مِنْهُ مَا اسْتَطَعْتُمْ.

That which I have forbidden you from, stay away from it. That which I have commanded you, do as much as you are able.[6]

So, avoiding what he has prohibited is a must.

The Fourth: That Allāh is not to be worshiped except with what he has legislated. You are restricted in worship to what Allāh has legislated for his Messenger ﷺ. So, you are not to perform an act of worship which the Messenger ﷺ did not legislate. Even though your intention may be good, and even though you want the reward, this action is invalid because the Messenger ﷺ did not do it. Intention (alone) is not sufficient; rather, it is a must that one follows the Messenger.

Worship is *tawqīfiyyah,*[7] and it is not permissible to do an act of worship which Allāh's Messenger did not legislate. Allāh's Messenger said:

مَنْ عَمِلَ عَمَلاً لَيْسَ عَلَيْهِ أَمْرُنَا فَهُوَ رَدٌّ.

He who does an action which is not from this affair of ours, then it is rejected.[8]

And he said:

فَعَلَيْكُمْ بِسُنَّتِي وَ سُنَّةِ الْخُلَفَاءِ الرَّاشِدِينَ الْمَهْدِيينَ مِنْ

[6] Al-Bukhārī reported it (#7288), as did Muslim (#1337) from the *ḥadīth* of Abū Hurayrah ﷺ.

[7] **Translator's Note:** Meaning, it is only derived by way of revelation, not by intellectual free-thinking.

[8] Its reference has preceded.

بَعْدِي، تَمَسَّكُوا بِهَا وَ عَضُوا عَلَيْهَا بِالنَّواجِذِ، وَ إِيَّاكُمْ وَ مُحْدَثَاتِ الْأُمُورِ فَإِنَّ كُلَّ مَحْدَثَةٍ بِدْعَةٌ، وَ كُلَّ بِدْعَةٍ ضَلَالَةٌ.

Cling to my Sunnah and the *sunnah* of the rightly-guided and guiding *khulafā'* after me, and beware of newly invented matters. Every newly invented matter is an innovation, and every innovation is misguidance.[9]

Performing an act of worship which the Messenger of Allāh did not legislate is considered a rejected and prohibited innovation, even if so-and-so spoke with it or whoever from the people performed it; as long as it is not from what the Messenger ﷺ came with, then it is innovation and misguidance. Allāh is not to be worshiped except with what He has legislated upon the tongue of his Messenger.

The newly-invented matters and superstitions are all falsehood, and deficiency and misguidance are upon the one who brought it even if he intended good by it and wanted the reward. The due consideration is not given to the objective; due consideration is given to following (*al-ittibā'*), obedience (*aṭ-ṭā'ah*), and submission (*al-inqiyād)*. If we were free to do what we wished and to choose for ourselves what we wanted from worship, then we would have no need for the sending of the Messenger ﷺ.

However, from Allāh's mercy to us is that He did not entrust us to our intellects, nor did he entrust us to so-and-so or such-and-such from the people, because these affairs are relegated to the legislation of Allāh and His Messenger. Nothing from that will bring benefit except what is in conformity to what Allāh and His Messenger have legislated. This encompasses staying away from all acts of innovation. He who innovates anything into the religion which the Messenger ﷺ has not come with, then he has not testified that he is the Messenger of Allāh; he has not testified with a truthful testimony. This is because the one who testifies that [Muḥammad] is Allāh's Messenger with a truthful testimony is bound by what he

---

[9] Abū Dāwūd reported it (#4607), as did at-Tirmidhī (#2676), Ibn Mājah (#42, #43), and Aḥmad (28/373, #17144) from the *ḥadīth* of al-'Irbāḍ bin Sāriyah ﷺ.

has legislated, and he may not introduce anything from himself or follow anything newly-invented from those who preceded him.

This is the meaning of the testimony that Muḥammad is the Messenger of Allāh. It is not merely words to be uttered with the tongue without adherence to it, wihout actions, or without being restricted to what this Messenger has come with.

ORIGINAL TEXT ──────────────────────────

وَ دَلِيلُ الصَّلَاةِ وَ الزَّكَاةِ وَ تَفْسِيرِ التَّوْحِيدِ قَوْلُهُ تَعَالَى: ﴿ وَمَا أُمِرُوا إِلَّا لِيَعْبُدُوا اللَّهَ مُخْلِصِينَ لَهُ الدِّينَ حُنَفَاءَ وَيُقِيمُوا الصَّلَاةَ وَيُؤْتُوا الزَّكَاةَ ۚ وَذَٰلِكَ دِينُ الْقَيِّمَةِ ﴾ .

The evidence for *ṣalāh* and *zakāh*, and the explanation of *at-tawḥīd* is the statement of the Most High:

> **And they were commanded not but that they should worship Allāh, and worship none but Him alone (abstaining from ascribing partners to Him), and establish *aṣ-ṣalāh* (*iqāmah aṣ-ṣalāh*) and give *zakāh*; and that is the right religion.**
>
> [*Sūrah al-Bayyinah* 98:5]

──────────── EXPLANATION ────────────

Ṣalāh (prayer) is the second pillar of *al-islām* and *zakāh* is the third, and *zakāh* is the close companion of the prayer within the Book of Allāh. *Aṣ-ṣalāh* is a bodily action, while *zakāh* is a monetary action. Abū Bakr aṣ-Ṣiddīq said, "By Allāh! I will fight them if they differentiate between the *ṣalāh* and the *zakāh*."[10] (He said this) when people withheld the payment of the *zakāh* after the death of the Messenger . Abū Bakr fought against them and said, "By Allāh! I will fight them if they differentiate between the *ṣalāh* and the *zakāh*. By Allāh! If they withhold from me a rope"—and

---

[10] Al-Bukhārī reported it (#1400), as well as Muslim (#20).

in one narration: "a she-goat"—"which they used to pay to Allāh's Messenger, then I will fight them for it."

Zakāh is an obligatory right as it relates to money, and it is a pillar of *al-islām*; it is the close companion of the prayer within the Book of Allāh ﷻ in many verses. From them is this verse:

﴿ وَمَا أُمِرُوا إِلَّا لِيَعْبُدُوا اللَّهَ مُخْلِصِينَ لَهُ الدِّينَ حُنَفَاءَ وَيُقِيمُوا الصَّلَاةَ وَيُؤْتُوا الزَّكَاةَ ﴾

And they were commanded not but that they should worship Allāh, and worship none but Him alone (abstaining from ascribing partners to Him), and establish *aṣ-ṣalāh* (*iqāmah aṣ-ṣalāh*) and give *zakāh*.

[Sūrah al-Bayyinah 98:5]

The evidence for *at-tawḥīd* is at its beginning, in His statement:

﴿ وَمَا أُمِرُوا إِلَّا لِيَعْبُدُوا اللَّهَ مُخْلِصِينَ لَهُ الدِّينَ حُنَفَاءَ ﴾

And they were commanded not but that they should worship Allāh, and worship none but Him alone.

[Sūrah al-Bayyinah 98:5]

This is the explanation of *at-tawḥīd*: it is the worship of Allāh along with *ikhlāṣ* (purity) for Him and leaving off worship of anything besides Him. So, the religion, *at-tawḥīd*, and *al-'ibādah* bear the same meaning.

﴿ مُخْلِصِينَ لَهُ الدِّينَ حُنَفَاءَ ﴾

...and worship none but Him alone...

[Sūrah al-Bayyinah 98:5]

This means: Worship. This is the explanation of *at-tawḥīd*. It is not as the scholars of theological rhetoric say, which is that *tawḥīd* is [only] an affirmation that Allāh is the Creator, the Provider, the Giver of Life, and the Causer of Death. This is Tawḥīd ar-Rubūbiyyah (Oneness of Lordship). What is required is Tawḥīd al-Ulūhiyyah (Oneness of Worship), to which the messengers called. One does not become a Muslim unless he enacts it.

As for the one who enacts Tawḥīd ar-Rubūbiyyah only, then this person is not a Muslim, based upon the fact that the polytheists believe, state, and acknowledge this, too, but that does not enter them into al-Islām, and fighting them was not prohibited; this *tawḥīd* of theirs did not prohibit their wealth. This is because they were not monotheists, due to that which they associated with Allāh ﷻ in worship.

This is the explanation of *at-tawḥīd* from the Book of Allāh, and not from the book of so-and-so and such-and-such. The book *Al-Jawharah*[11] or the book *Al-Mawāqif*[12] or the books of the scholars of theological rhetoric—the explanation of *at-tawḥīd* is not to be taken from these books. It is only to be taken from the Book of Allāh, from the Sunnah of Allāh's Messenger ﷺ, and from the books of Ahlus-Sunnah wal-Jamā'ah, those who cling to the Book of Allāh and the Sunnah of the Messenger of Allāh ﷺ.

The evidence for the prayer is in the statement of the Most High:

﴿ وَيُقِيمُوا الصَّلَاةَ ﴾

...and establish *aṣ-ṣalāh* (*iqāmah aṣ-ṣalāh*)...

[Sūrah al-Bayyinah 98:5]

The meaning is that one performs it as Allāh has commanded, with its conditions, pillars, and requirements. As for the mere outward image of the prayer, then it is not sufficient. Due to this, He did not say "and they pray." Rather, He said **"and establish *aṣ-ṣalāh* (*iqāmah-aṣ-ṣalāh*)."** And the prayer is not established except when one does it as Allāh has commanded.

---

[11] The book *Jawharah at-Tawḥīd* is a book which affirms the methodology of the Ash'ariyyah, and it contains many oppositions to the way of Ahlus-Sunnah wal-Jamā'ah.

[12] The book *Al-Mawāqif Fī 'Ilm al-Kalām* by al-Ījī.

As for those who merely pray in a manner they choose, at whatever time they want, or without *ṭahārah* (purity) and without being at ease, nor do they perform the requirements of the prayer, then these people have not prayed. Due to this, the Prophet ﷺ said to the man who prayed badly, who was not at ease in his prayer:

ارْجِعْ فَصَلِّ، فَإِنَّكَ لَمْ تُصَلِّ.

Go back and pray, for you have not prayed.[13]

The intent is not only the outward image of the prayer, such as bowing, prostrating, and sitting; this is not the intent. Rather, the intent is that one performs it as Allāh has legislated, fulfilling all of its legislated requirements.

Then he mentioned the evidence for *zakāh* in His statement **"and give *zakāh*"**; meaning: pay the *zakāh* to those to whom it is due, those whom Allāh the Exalted mentioned in His statement:

﴿ إِنَّمَا الصَّدَقَاتُ لِلْفُقَرَاءِ وَالْمَسَاكِينِ وَالْعَامِلِينَ عَلَيْهَا وَالْمُؤَلَّفَةِ قُلُوبُهُمْ وَفِي الرِّقَابِ وَالْغَارِمِينَ وَفِي سَبِيلِ اللَّهِ وَابْنِ السَّبِيلِ ۖ فَرِيضَةً مِّنَ اللَّهِ ۗ وَاللَّهُ عَلِيمٌ حَكِيمٌ ﴾

***Aṣ-ṣadaqāt* (here it means *zakāh*) are only for the *fuqarā'* (poor), and *al-masākīn* (the poor) and those employed to collect (the funds); and to attract the hearts of those who have been inclined (towards Islām), and to free the captives, and for those in debt, and for Allāh's cause (i.e., for *mujāhidūn*—those fighting in holy wars), and for the wayfarer (a traveler who is cut off from everything); a duty imposed by Allāh. And Allāh is the All-Knower, All-Wise.**

[Sūrah at-Tawbah 9:60]

He mentioned eight categories of people, and He restricted them

---

[13] Al-Bukhārī reported it (#757), as well as Muslim (#397) from the *ḥadīth* of Abū Hurayrah ﷺ.

with the word **"only"** (إِنَّمَا). So it is not to be given to other than these eight categories. He who gives it to other than these eight categories has not paid *zakāh*, even if he spent wealth in excess of millions and billions (of dollars) and calls it *zakāh*; it is not *zakāh* until it is given to those whom Allāh has restricted it to. This is the meaning of paying *zakāh*.

Also, it must be done in its (proper) time; i.e., one pays it in its obligatory time, and he is not to be slow, delay, or be lazy in its distribution. (He does so) out of the goodness of his soul; he does not consider it to be a fine or a loss. He considers it enrichment for himself.

These three affairs are the correct religion. Religion means "system." "Correct" is a description for that which has been described and omitted; the latent phrase is "the correct system," meaning "that which is upright."

This is the evidence for *ṣalāh* and *zakāh*, and the explanation of *at-tawḥīd*.

ORIGINAL TEXT

وَ دَلِيلُ الصِّيَامِ: ﴿ يَا أَيُّهَا الَّذِينَ آمَنُوا كُتِبَ عَلَيْكُمُ الصِّيَامُ كَمَا كُتِبَ عَلَى الَّذِينَ مِن قَبْلِكُمْ لَعَلَّكُمْ تَتَّقُونَ ﴾.

The evidence for fasting is:

> **O you who believe! Observing *aṣ-ṣawm* (fasting) is prescribed for you as it was prescribed for those before you, that you may become *al-muttaqūn*.**
>
> *[Sūrah al-Baqarah 2:183]*

EXPLANATION

Fasting is only obligatory upon the Muslim. As for the disbelievers, if they were to perform it, then it would not be correct until they testify that none has the right to be worshiped except Allāh and that

Muḥammad is the Messenger of Allāh; as long as they are upon disbelief, then acts of worship will not benefit them, from fasting or other than the fast. Due to this, He addressed the believers specifically, because they are the ones who respond, they are the ones whose fasting is correct, and the fast is accepted from them.

﴿ كُتِبَ عَلَيْكُمُ الصِّيَامُ ﴾

Observing *aṣ-ṣawm* (fasting) is prescribed for you...

[Sūrah al-Baqarah 2:183]

The meaning of **"prescribed"** is "made obligatory." This is similar to the statement of the Most High:

﴿ كُتِبَ عَلَيْكُمُ الْقِتَالُ ﴾

Fighting is prescribed for you...

[Sūrah al-Baqarah 2:216]

Meaning: Fighting has been made obligatory upon you. So, the meaning of "prescription" (الكتب) in the Book of Allāh is "obligation."

﴿ كَمَا كُتِبَ عَلَى الَّذِينَ مِن قَبْلِكُمْ ﴾

...as it was prescribed for those before you...

[Sūrah al-Baqarah 2:183]

Meaning: Just as it was made obligatory upon the previous nations before you. This proves that fasting was well-known in the previous nations and in the previous legislations, and the legislation of Muḥammad ﷺ was not singled out with it.

The soul may deem the fast to be burdensome due to that which it contains from taming its desires and withholding it from lusts. Allāh ﷻ clarified that it is His *sunnah* regarding His creation, and that it was put upon all of the nations. Even in the Days of Ignorance, fasting was well-known; they would fast on the Day of 'Āshūrā'.

(Concerning His statement):

﴿ لَعَلَّكُمْ تَتَّقُونَ ﴾

...that you may become *al-muttaqūn.*

[Sūrah al-Baqarah 2:183]

This is a clarification of the wisdom behind fasting: "so that perhaps you will become pious." This is a clarification of the wisdom behind the legislation of the fast, which is that it be a means for (attaining) *taqwā*. This is because, when fasting, the individual abandons what he is accustomed to, his desires, and that which he longs for, seeking nearness to Allāh; so he acquires *taqwā*. He also breaks the desires of the soul and its urges, because Shayṭān runs through the children of Ādam like blood; so with succumbing to desires, Shayṭān gains mastery, and with abandoning desires, the blood flow weakens and Shayṭān is repelled from the Muslim. So, in fasting is the attainment of *taqwā*, which is a culmination of all good.

This is the benefit of fasting—it brings about *at-taqwā*; it causes one to have *taqwā* of Allāh and avoid the prohibited and the forbidden desires. This is because, if the person abandons permissible things out of obedience to Allāh, then he is to abandon the forbidden matters even more so. Fasting compels him to abandon the prohibited and to control his soul which inclines towards evil, and it repels Shayṭān from him and softens his heart for obedience.

Due to this, you find that the fasting person is closer to good than the one who is not fasting. You find him to be diligent upon reciting the Qur'ān and upon performing the prayer. He goes to the *masjid* early. The fast softens him for obedience and refines him.

The point of reference from the verse is His statement:

﴿ كُتِبَ عَلَيْكُمُ الصِّيَامُ ﴾

Observing *aṣ-ṣawm* (fasting) is prescribed for you...

[Sūrah al-Baqarah 2:183]

This is evidence for the obligation of fasting, and He explained it with His statement:

﴿ شَهْرُ رَمَضَانَ الَّذِي أُنزِلَ فِيهِ الْقُرْآنُ ﴾

The month of Ramaḍān in which was revealed the Qur'ān...

[Sūrah al-Baqarah 2:185]

So, His statement **"fasting has been prescribed for you"** has been explained by His statement:

﴿ فَمَن شَهِدَ مِنكُمُ الشَّهْرَ فَلْيَصُمْهُ ﴾

So, whoever of you sights (the crescent on the first night of) the month (of Ramaḍān, i.e., is present at his home), he must observe *ṣawm* (fasts) that month.

[Sūrah al-Baqarah 2:185]

ORIGINAL TEXT

وَ دَلِيلُ الْحَجِّ: ﴿ وَلِلَّهِ عَلَى النَّاسِ حِجُّ الْبَيْتِ مَنِ اسْتَطَاعَ إِلَيْهِ سَبِيلًا ۚ وَمَن كَفَرَ فَإِنَّ اللَّهَ غَنِيٌّ عَنِ الْعَالَمِينَ ﴾.

The evidence for Ḥajj is:

And Ḥajj (pilgrimage to Makkah) to the House (Ka'bah) is a duty that mankind owes to Allāh, those who can afford the expenses (for one's conveyance, provision, and residence); and whoever disbelieves [i.e., denies Ḥajj (pilgrimage to Makkah), then he is a disbeliever of Allāh], then Allāh stands not in need of any of the *'ālamīn* (mankind and *jinn*).

[Sūrah Āli 'Imrān 3:97]

EXPLANATION

The Jews claimed that they were Muslims and that they were upon the religion of Ibrāhīm, so Allāh tested them in this verse:

﴿ وَلِلَّهِ عَلَى النَّاسِ حِجُّ الْبَيْتِ مَنِ اسْتَطَاعَ إِلَيْهِ سَبِيلًا ۚ وَمَن كَفَرَ فَإِنَّ اللَّهَ غَنِيٌّ عَنِ الْعَالَمِينَ ﴾

And Ḥajj (pilgrimage to Makkah) to the House (Ka'bah) is a duty that mankind owes to Allāh, those who can afford the expenses (for one's conveyance, provision, and residence); and whoever disbelieves [i.e., denies Ḥajj (pilgrimage to Makkah), then he is a disbeliever of Allāh], then Allāh stands not in need of any of the *'ālamīn* (mankind and *jinn*).

[Sūrah Āli 'Imrān 3:97]

So, if you are Muslim, then perform Ḥajj, because Allāh made Ḥajj to the House obligatory upon the Muslims. If you do not perform Ḥajj and you refuse to perform Ḥajj, then this is proof that you are not Muslims and that you are not upon the religion of Ibrāhīm.

﴿ وَمَن كَفَرَ فَإِنَّ اللَّهَ غَنِيٌّ عَنِ الْعَالَمِينَ ﴾

And whoever disbelieves [i.e., denies Ḥajj (pilgrimage to Makkah), then he is a disbeliever of Allāh], then Allāh stands not in need of any of the *'ālamīn* (mankind and *jinn*).

[Sūrah Āli 'Imrān 3:97]

(His statement) ***"wa lillāh"*** (وَلِلَّهِ) means: This is obligatory and a right that is due to Allāh upon the people.

The linguistic meaning of Ḥajj is "objective." Legislatively, al-Ḥajj means setting one's objective on the noble Ka'bah and the sacred sites in a specified time for performing specified acts of worship, which are the rites of Ḥajj.

"Pilgrimage to the House" (حِجُّ الْبَيْتِ) means the Ka'bah and that which is around it, from the sacred sites that are subsidiary to it.

"Those who can afford the expenses" (مَنِ اسْتَطَاعَ إِلَيْهِ سَبِيلًا):

Meaning, for he who has the ability to do so. This is clarification of the condition that makes it obligatory, which is that one has the physical ability and the monetary ability. Physical ability is that one is able to walk, ride, and travel from his land to Makkah in any place on earth. This is physical (ability). Exempt from it is the one who has a chronic disability, such as the chronically ill and the decrepitly old, for they do not have the physical ability. If he has the monetary ability, then he may entrust someone to perform Ḥajj for him.

As for the monetary ability, this means paying for the ride that will take him, by mount, car, plane, or train, in accordance with every time; and one has the wealth with which he can pay for this ride which will enable him to perform Ḥajj. Also, his provisions—he should have provisions and enough to spend on the travel, round trip. And for those who are his dependents, they should have enough to suffice them until he returns to them.

So, the meaning of "provisions" is that one has what will suffice him in his journey and suffice those who are his dependents, from his children, his parents, and his wife—all those upon whom he is required to spend, he is to leave them that which will suffice them until he returns to them, after the settlement of debts (if he has any debts). This wealth is to be surplus wealth after the settlement of debts. So, when this is fulfilled, then this is the (correct) way.

الزَّادُ وَ الرَّاحِلَةِ.

Provisions and a mount.[14]

As has come within the *ḥadīth* of Ibn 'Abbās ﷺ.

He who is not able—i.e., he does not have provisions or a mount—then Ḥajj is not obligatory upon him because he is not able. The condition for the Ḥajj being obligatory is ability.

Since people come to Ḥajj from far distances—from every province

[14] At-Tirmidhī reported it (#813), as well as Ibn Mājah (2896) from the *ḥadīth* of Ibn 'Umar ﷺ; and Ibn Mājah reported it (#2897) from the *ḥadīth* of Ibn 'Abbās ﷺ.

and from every direction—and it requires subsistence, it contains difficulty and hardship, and there may occur therein dangers, then from the mercy of Allāh is that He made it (obligatory) only once in a lifetime. That which is done more than that is supererogatory. This is from the mercy of Allāh, that He did not make it obligatory upon the Muslim every year. As the Prophet ﷺ said:

إِنَّ اللهَ قَدْ فَرَضَ عَلَيكُمُ الْحَجَّ فَحَجُّوا.

Indeed, Allāh has made Ḥajj obligatory upon you; so perform Ḥajj.

Al-Aqra' bin Ḥābis ؓ said, "Every year, O Messenger of Allāh?" So the Messenger remained silent. Then he repeated the question, and the Prophet remained silent. Then he repeated the question, so the Prophet ﷺ said:

لَوْ قُلْتُ نَعَمْ لَوَجَبَتْ، وَ لَمَّا اسْتَطَعْتُمْ، الْحَجُّ مَرَّةً وَاحِدَةً فَمَا زَادَ فَهُوَ تَطَوَّعٌ.

If I had said yes, then it would have been made obligatory and you would not be able to do so. The Ḥajj is to be performed once, and what is in addition to that is optional.[15]

This is from the mercy of Allāh.

Regarding the statement of the Glorified:

﴿ وَمَن كَفَرَ فَإِنَّ اللَّهَ غَنِيٌّ عَنِ الْعَالَمِينَ ﴾

And whoever disbelieves, then Allāh stands not in need of any of the *'ālamīn* (mankind and *jinn*).

[Sūrah Āli 'Imrān 3:97]

In this is evidence that he who withholds from Ḥajj while he is able to perform it, yet he does not do it, is a disbeliever, because Allāh says, **"And whoever disbelieves..."**; i.e., whoever refuses to perform Ḥajj while he is able to perform Ḥajj, then this person is

[15] Imām Aḥmad reported it in *Al-Musnad* (4/151, #2304), as well as Abū Dāwūd (#1721) and an-Nasā'ī (5/111) from the *ḥadīth* of Ibn 'Abbās ؓ.

a disbeliever. Perhaps it could be minor disbelief. If one obstinately rejects its obligation, then this is major disbelief by consensus of the Muslims.

As for the one who acknowledges its obligation but he abandons it out of laziness, then this is minor disbelief. However, if he dies and he has wealth, then Ḥajj is to be performed for him from his wealth, because this is a debt which he owes to Allāh ﷻ.

This verse contains the obligation of Ḥajj, and it is a pillar of *al-islām*. The Messenger ﷺ clarified that it is a pillar of *al-islām* within the *ḥadīth* of Jibrīl and in the *ḥadīth* of Ibn 'Umar.

Ḥajj was made obligatory in 9 AH, according to one view. The Prophet ﷺ did not perform Ḥajj in this year. He performed Ḥajj the next year, which was 10 AH. Why is this? It is because he had sent 'Alī to announce to the people during the season:

أَلَا يَحُجُّ بَعْدَ هَذَا الْعَامِ مُشْرِكٌ، وَ لَا يَطُوفُ بِالْبَيْتِ عُرْيَانٌ.

After this year, no pagan may perform Ḥajj nor may any naked person make *ṭawāf*.[16]

So, when the pagans and the naked people were prevented from performing Ḥajj in 10 AH, the Prophet ﷺ performed the Farewell Ḥajj.

THE SECOND LEVEL: AL-ĪMĀN

ORIGINAL TEXT

تَعْرِيفُ الْإِيمَانِ:

اَلْمَرْتَبَةُ الثَّانِيَةُ: اَلْإِيمَانُ: وَ هُوَ بِضْعٌ وَ سَبْعُونَ شُعْبَةً، فَأَعْلَاهَا: قَوْلُ لَا إِلَهَ إِلَّا اللهُ، وَأَدْنَاهَا: إِمَاطَةُ الْأَذَى عَنِ الطَّرِيقِ، وَ الْحَيَاءُ

[16] Al-Bukhārī reported it (#369), as well as Muslim (#1347) from the *ḥadīth* of Abū Hurayrah ﷺ.

شُعْبَةٌ مِنَ الإِيمَانِ.

The Definition of *al-Īmān*:

The Second Level: *al-Īmān*. It is 70-some odd branches. The highest of them is the statement "*lā ilāha ill-Allāh*" (none has the right to be worshiped except Allāh); the lowest of them is to remove something harmful from the path; and *al-ḥayā'* (modesty) is a branch of *al-īmān*.

EXPLANATION

Al-īmān is more general than *al-islām*, for every *mu'min* (one who has *īmān*) is a Muslim, but not every Muslim is a *mu'min*. So, *al-īmān* is more general as it relates to itself and more specific as it relates to its people.

Al-īmān linguistically means "*at-taṣdīq*" (affirmation). The Most High said, upon the tongue of the brothers of Yūsuf:

﴿ وَمَا أَنتَ بِمُؤْمِنٍ لَّنَا ﴾

"But you will never believe us..."

[Sūrah Yūsuf 12:17]

Meaning, "You will not confirm what we say."

As for *al-īmān* in the legislation, it is that which Ahlus-Sunnah wal-Jamā'ah have explained: statement of the tongue, belief in the heart, and action with the limbs; it increases with obedience and decreases with disobedience. It is with this explanation that it is a legislative reality. This is because there are three realities: the linguistic reality, the legislative reality, and the customary reality.

The explanation of *al-īmān* with this explanation is a legislative reality. *Al-īmān* has been transitioned from the linguistic meaning to the legislative meaning.

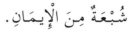

So *al-īmān* is statement with the tongue—it is a must that one articulate and acknowledge it with his tongue; and it is belief within the heart—it is a must that he be one who believes within his heart in that which he utters upon his tongue. Otherwise, it is like the *īmān* of the hypocrites:

﴿ يَقُولُونَ بِأَلْسِنَتِهِم مَّا لَيْسَ فِي قُلُوبِهِمْ ﴾

They say with their tongues what is not in their hearts.

[Sūrah al-Fat'ḥ 48:11]

Statement with the tongue and belief in the heart (alone) are not sufficient. Rather, action with the limbs is a must, as well. It is a must that one performs the obligations and avoids the prohibitions. So, he is to do acts of obedience and avoid what is forbidden. All of this is from *al-īmān*, and with this definition it is inclusive of the entire religion.

However, these acts of obedience and legislations from them are that which is a part of the reality of *al-īmān*, and from it is that which is a completer of *al-īmān*.

Īmān has pillars and branches. The Prophet ﷺ clarified them in two *aḥādīth*. He clarified the pillars of *al-īmān* in the *ḥadīth* of Jibrīl, and he clarified the branches of *īmān* in the *ḥadīth*:

اَلْإِيمَانُ بِضْعٌ وَ سَبْعُونَ شُعْبَةً.

***Al-īmān* is 70-some odd branches.**

This shall come, *inshāAllāh*. When *al-īmān* and *al-islām* are mentioned together, then each one takes on its own meaning. If only one of them is mentioned, then the other falls under it. If they are mentioned together, then *al-islām* is explained as being the apparent actions, which are the five pillars of *al-islām*. *Al-īmān* is explained as being the inward actions, which are the six pillars, and their place is in the heart. It is a must that the Muslim brings the two of them together. He must be a Muslim and a believer, establishing the pillars of *al-islām* and establishing the pillars of *al-īmān*; he must bring them together. He ﷺ said:

اَلْإِيمَانُ بِضْعٌ وَ سَبْعُونَ شُعْبَةً.

Al-īmān is 70-some odd branches.

Or he said:

اَلْإِيمَانُ بِضْعٌ وَ سِتُّونَ شُعْبَةً.

Al-īmān is 60-some odd branches.

These are two narrations.

His statement, *"branches"* (شعبة): A branch is a piece of a thing. Meaning, the pillars are 70-some odd pieces or parts.

His statement, *"the highest of them"*: Meaning, the highest of these branches is the statement *lā ilāha ill-Allāh*, for it is the head of *al-islām* and the head of *al-īmān,* and it is the first pillar; it is the entrance point of the religion.

His statement *"the lowest of them"* means: The last and the least.

His statement *"to remove something harmful from the path"* means to remove what is harmful from the path which people traverse upon. Harm means anything that harms the people, such as a thorn, a stone, garbage, or waste; anything which harms the people in their path. It is impermissible to place harmful things in the path because the path is for the pedestrians.

Harmful things hinder the pedestrians or expose them to danger, such as one parking his car in the pathway; this is harm. Pouring water from one's house into the street—this is harm. Placing trash in the pathway is harm. It is the same whether the pathway is in the city or in the valley. Placing stones, wood, or steel in the pathways of the people and (leaving) drill rigs in the pathways of the people—all of this is harm.

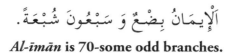

So, if the Muslim comes and removes this harmful thing and relieves the pathway of it, then this is a proof of his *īmān*. Placing harmful things in the pathway is from the branches of *kufr*, and removing harmful things from the path is a branch of *al-īmān*.

His statement, *"and al-ḥayā' (modesty, shame) is a branch of al-īmān"*: *Al-ḥayā'* is a characteristic that Allāh places within the individual which compels him to do that which will beautify and embellish him, and prevents him from that which will sully and disfigure him. *Al-ḥayā'* is that which will compel its companion upon good and keep him away from evil; this is praiseworthy. As for the *ḥayā'* which prevents its companion from doing good, seeking knowledge, and asking about that which is confusing to him, this is blameworthy, because it is [actually] timidity.

The branches of *al-īmān* are many, as you know—70-some odd branches. Imām al-Bayhaqī wrote a large book wherein he clarified the branches of *al-īmān*, and it has a summarized version which has been printed.

From the proofs of the scholars that *al-īmān* is a statement with the tongue, belief in the heart, and action of the limbs, is his ﷺ statement:

أَعْلَاهَا قَوْلُ لَا إِلَهَ إِلَّا اللهُ.

The highest of them is the statement "*Lā ilāha ill-Allāh*"...

This indicates the statement.

وَ أَدْنَاهَا إِمَاطَةُ الْأَذَى عَنِ الطَّرِيقِ.

The lowest of them is to remove something harmful from the path...

This is an action. It indicates that actions are from *al-īmān*.

وَ الْحَيَاءُ شُبْعَةٌ مِنَ الْإِيمَانِ.

And *al-ḥayā'* is a branch of *al-īmān*.

This is within the heart; *al-ḥayā'* is only within the heart. This is evidence that *al-īmān* is statement with the tongue, belief in the heart, and action with the limbs.

THE PILLARS OF AL-ĪMĀN

ORIGINAL TEXT

قَالَ: وَ أَرْكَانُهُ سِتَّةٌ: أَنْ تُؤْمِنَ بِاللهِ، وَ مَلَائِكَتِهِ، وَ كُتُبِهِ، وَ رُسُلِهِ، وَ الْيَوْمِ الْآخِرِ، وَ تُؤْمِنَ بِالْقَدَرِ خَيْرِهِ وَ شَرِّهِ.

Its pillars are six: that you believe in Allāh, his angels, his Books, his messengers, the Last Day, and that you believe in the *qadar,* its good and its evil.

EXPLANATION

Īmān is made up of pillars and branches. What is the difference between the two? The difference is that the pillars are a must; if one of them ceases, then *īmān* ceases, because a thing is not able to stand except upon its pillars. So, if a pillar of a thing is lost, then it is not actualized.

As for the branches, then they are completing elements. *Īmān* is not erased by the erasing of any of them. However, they are completing elements, either by way of obligation or by way of recommendation. So, the obligations for the completion of *al-īmān* are recommended.

If the Muslim leaves any of the obligations or he commits something which is prohibited, then his *īmān* is not erased in totality, according to Ahlus-Sunnah wal-Jamā'ah. However, its obligatory completio[n] has been erased. Therefore, he is deficient in *al-īmān* or he i[s] *fāsiq*. For example, if he were to drink intoxicants, steal, fornic[ate] or do any of the major sins—this is an individual who has [committed] something prohibited, a major sin. However, he has not disb[elieved] by way of that, nor has he exited the realm of *al-īmān*; rat[her he is] a *fāsiq,* and the prescribed punishment is mandated for [him if the] act of disobedience he committed is something that b[rings a] prescribed punishment.

Likewise, the one who leaves off an obligation, such [as one who] leaves off treating the parents with righteousness o[r ties] of kinship; these are obligations. So, the one wh[o] tory actions is defiant in his *īmān,* and he is one who is disobedient due to his abandoning of an obligation. He is disobedient either by way of abandoning the obligation or by way of doing a prohibited act. At any rate, he does not exit the realm of *al-īmān*; he is only a believer who is deficient in his *īmān.*

This is the methodology of Ahlus-Sunnah wal-Jamā'ah, as opposed to the Khawārij and the Mu'tazilah who declare *takfīr* upon the individual who commits a major sin. The Khawārij declare *takfīr* upon him and say that he has exited the religion. The Mu'tazilah exit him from the religion, but they do not say he has entered the realm of *kufr*. They only say that he is in a place between the two places, neither a believer nor a disbeliever. This is their methodology, and it is an innovated methodology which is in opposition to the evidences and in opposition to what Ahlus-Sunnah wal-Jamā'ah are upon.

The reason for that is their deficiency in the innovation of evidences, because they took the evidences dealing with the threat and they abandoned the evidences dealing with the promise, such as the statement of the Most High:

﴿ إِنَّ اللَّـهَ لَا يَغْفِرُ أَن يُشْرَكَ بِهِ وَيَغْفِرُ مَا دُونَ ذَٰلِكَ لِمَن يَشَاءُ ﴾

Verily, Allāh forgives not that partners should be set up with him in worship, but He forgives except that (anything else) to whom He pleases.

[Sūrah an-Nisā' 4:48]

This is one of the evidences dealing with the promise, indicating that the disobedient one whose disobedience has not reached the level of *shirk* and *kufr* has hope for the forgiveness of Allāh and to be turned away from the threat and the punishment. So, as it relates o the statement of the Most High:

﴿ إِلَّا بَلَاغًا مِّنَ اللَّـهِ وَرِسَالَاتِهِ ۚ وَمَن يَعْصِ اللَّـهَ وَرَسُولَهُ

﴿ فَإِنَّ لَهُ نَارَ جَهَنَّمَ خَالِدِينَ فِيهَا أَبَدًا ﴾

(Mine is) but conveyance (of the truth) from Allāh and His messages; and whosoever disobeys Allāh and His Messenger, then verily, for him is the Fire of Hell, he shall dwell therein forever.

[Sūrah al-Jinn 72:23]

Those who take to its apparent meaning have declared *takfīr* upon those who commit acts of disobedience, in an absolute manner. If they had referred it to the statement of the Most High:

﴿ إِنَّ اللَّهَ لَا يَغْفِرُ أَن يُشْرَكَ بِهِ وَيَغْفِرُ مَا دُونَ ذَٰلِكَ لِمَن يَشَاءُ ﴾

Verily, Allāh forgives not that partners should be set up with him in worship, but He forgives except that (anything else) to whom He pleases.

[Sūrah an-Nisā' 4:48]

Then the truth would have been made clear to them: he does not exit the fold of the religion, but he is threatened with the Fire. If Allāh wills, He will forgive him, and if He wills, He will punish him. Perhaps he will encounter things which expiate his sins within the *dunyā,* or face punishment in the grave which will expiate these sins. And the things which expiate are many; he may be tried with calamities and afflicted with punishments in the *dunyā* or punishment in his grave. Or it may be delayed to the Day of Judgmer when he shall be under the will of Allāh.

This is the methodology of Ahlus-Sunnah wal-Jamā'ah, anc is the difference between branches and pillars. So, he who any of the pillars has disbelieved. The one who obstinatel *at-tawḥīd* and associates partners with Allāh ﷻ, then he h lieved, because he has abandoned the first pillar. An obstinately rejects the Messenger has disbelieved, bec abandoned a pillar of *al-islām*.

He who obstinately rejects the angels has disbelieved and has exited the fold of the religion. He who disbelieves in the resurrection, or obstinately rejects Paradise and the Fire, or the Ṣirāṭ or the Mīzān, or anything from that which is affirmed from the affairs of the Hereafter, then this individual has disbelieved, because he has rejected a pillar of *al-īmān*.

Likewise, one who rejects *al-qadar* and says that the affair is unknown and the decree has not preceded from Allāh, and says that they are merely coincidental; and they say that the affairs occur by way of coincidence and there is no such thing as decree, as is said by the extremists amongst the Mu'tazilah—this individual has disbelieved, as well, because he obstinately rejects the *qadar*.

As for the one who leaves off any of the branches, then this individual is deficient in his *īmān*. Either it is a deficiency of the obligatory completion of his *īmān*, or it is a deficiency in the recommended completion of his *īmān*. However, he has not disbelieved by way of that.

And what is the evidence that *īmān* increases and decreases? As for the evidence that it increases, then it is the statement of the Most High:

﴿ إِنَّمَا الْمُؤْمِنُونَ الَّذِينَ إِذَا ذُكِرَ اللَّهُ وَجِلَتْ قُلُوبُهُمْ وَإِذَا
تُلِيَتْ عَلَيْهِمْ آيَاتُهُ زَادَتْهُمْ إِيمَانًا ﴾

The believers are only those who, when Allāh is mentioned, feel a fear in their hearts, and when His verses (this Qur'ān) are recited unto them, they (i.e., the verses) increase their faith.

[Sūrah al-Anfāl 8:2]

This indicates that *īmān* increases when listening to the Qur'ān. And the statement of the Most High:

﴿ وَإِذَا مَا أُنزِلَتْ سُورَةٌ فَمِنْهُم مَّن يَقُولُ أَيُّكُمْ زَادَتْهُ
هَٰذِهِ إِيمَانًا ۚ فَأَمَّا الَّذِينَ آمَنُوا فَزَادَتْهُمْ إِيمَانًا وَهُمْ

يَسْتَبْشِرُونَ ﴾

And whenever there comes down a *sūrah* (chapter from the Qur'ān), some of them (hypocrites) say, "Which of you has had his faith increased by it?" As for those who believe, it has increased their faith, and they rejoice.

[Sūrah at-Tawbah 9:124]

This indicates that *īmān* increases with the revelation of the Qur'ān, and with listening to it and contemplating over it. As in the statement of the Most High:

﴿ وَمَا جَعَلْنَا أَصْحَابَ النَّارِ إِلَّا مَلَائِكَةً ۙ وَمَا جَعَلْنَا
عِدَّتَهُمْ إِلَّا فِتْنَةً لِّلَّذِينَ كَفَرُوا لِيَسْتَيْقِنَ الَّذِينَ أُوتُوا
الْكِتَابَ وَيَزْدَادَ الَّذِينَ آمَنُوا إِيمَانًا ﴾

And We have set none but angels as guardians of the Fire, and We have fixed their number (19) only as a trial for the disbelievers, so that the People of the Scripture (Jews and Christians) may arrive at a certainty [that this Qur'ān is the truth, as it agrees with their Books; i.e., their number (19) is written in the Tawrāh (Torah) and the Injīl (Gospel)] and the believers may increase in faith.

[Sūrah al-Muddath'thir 74:31]

This indicates that *īmān* increases with acts of obedience and affirmation.

As for the proof of the decrease, then everything that increases likewise decreases. Everything that is subject to increase is subject to decrease. This is from one perspective. The Messenger ﷺ indicated this in his statement in an authentic narration:

ـنَّ اللهَ يَوْمَ الْقِيَامَةِ يَقُولُ: أَخْرِجُوا مَنْ كَانَ فِي قَلْبِهِ مِثْقَالُ حَبَّةٍ
ـرْدَلٍ مِنْ إِيمَانٍ...

Indeed, Allāh will say on the Day of Resurrection, "Go and take out of the Fire he whose heart has the equivalent of a mustard seed of *īmān*..."[17]

This indicates that *īmān* increases and decreases to the point that it is the weight of a mustard seed within the heart. Likewise, the saying of the Most High:

﴿ هُمْ لِلْكُفْرِ يَوْمَئِذٍ أَقْرَبُ مِنْهُمْ لِلْإِيمَانِ ﴾

They were that day nearer to disbelief than to faith...

[Sūrah Āli 'Imrān 3:167]

This indicates that *īmān* decreases until the individual is closer to *kufr*. And within his statement ﷺ:

مَنْ رَأَى مِنْكُمْ مُنْكَرًا فَلْيُغَيِّرْهُ بِيَدِهِ، فَإِنْ لَمْ يَسْتَطِعْ فَبِلِسَانِهِ، فَإِنْ لَمْ يَسْتَطِعْ فَبِقَلْبِهِ، وَ ذَلِكَ أَضْعَفُ الْإِيمَانِ.

He amongst you who sees an evil, then let him change it with his hand; if he is not able, then let him do so with his tongue; and if he is not able, then let him do so with his heart, and that is the weakest of *al-īmān*.[18]

This indicates that *īmān* weakens, meaning it decreases. So, *īmān* increases with acts of obedience and decreases with acts of disobedience.

The statement of the author *"and its pillars are six"*: Meaning, the supports upon which it stands; and it is lost by way of them being lost, or by way of one of the six pillars being lost, and they are:

The First Pillar: That you believe in Allāh. The first pillar is *īmān* in Allāh, and it comprises the three categories of *tawḥīd*: *īmān* in Allāh ﷻ, the One, the Singular, the Unique, the Self-Sufficient,

[17] Al-Bukhārī reported it (#22), as did Muslim (#184) from the *ḥadīth* of Abū Sa'īd al-Khudrī رضي الله عنه.

[18] Muslim reported it (#49) from the *ḥadīth* of Abū Sa'īd al-Khudrī رضي الله عنه.

who has no partners in His Lordship, His worship, or His names and attributes.

The Second Pillar: *Īmān* in the angels. And "angels" is the plural of "angel". And the origin of it is ملأك, and it is pronounced *malak.* And the angels are a creation of Allāh within the realm of the unseen. Allāh created them for his worship and to carry out His commands ﷻ within His kingdom.

And they are of different categories. Each category has a function with which they have been entrusted and which they establish. And they do not disobey Allāh in that which He has commanded them, and they do what they have been commanded.

So, from them is he who was instructed with the revelation, and this is Jibrīl عليه السلام; and he is the noblest of the angels. And he is the trustworthy Spirit who is mighty in his strength.

From them are those who are entrusted with carrying the Throne. Allāh says:

﴿ لَّذِينَ يَحْمِلُونَ الْعَرْشَ وَمَنْ حَوْلَهُ ﴾

Those (angels) who bear the Throne (of Allāh) and those around it...

[Sūrah Ghāfir 40:7]

And He, Exalted be He, stated:

﴿ وَالْمَلَكُ عَلَىٰ أَرْجَائِهَا ۚ وَيَحْمِلُ عَرْشَ رَبِّكَ فَوْقَهُمْ يَوْمَئِذٍ ثَمَانِيَةٌ ﴾

And the angels will be on its sides, and eight angels will, that Day, bear the Throne of your Lord above them.

[Sūrah al-Ḥāqqah 69:17]

And the Throne is the greatest of the creations of Allāh. None knows its greatness except Allāh ﷻ, and the angels carry it. This is evidence for the greatness of the angels, and the greatness of their strength and their stature. The Most High has said:

﴿ الْحَمْدُ لِلَّهِ فَاطِرِ السَّمَاوَاتِ وَالْأَرْضِ جَاعِلِ الْمَلَائِكَةِ رُسُلًا أُولِي أَجْنِحَةٍ مَّثْنَىٰ وَثُلَاثَ وَرُبَاعَ ۚ يَزِيدُ فِي الْخَلْقِ مَا يَشَاءُ ﴾

All praises and thanks be to Allāh, the (only) Originator [or the (only) Creator] of the heavens and the earth, who made the angels as messengers with wings—two or three or four. He increases in creation what He wills.

[Sūrah Fāṭir 35:1]

From them are those who have 600 wings, such as Jibrīl عليه السلام. None knows their greatness except Allāh سبحانه وتعالى. As He said:

﴿ بَلْ عِبَادٌ مُّكْرَمُونَ ﴿٢٦﴾ لَا يَسْبِقُونَهُ بِالْقَوْلِ وَهُم بِأَمْرِهِ يَعْمَلُونَ ﴿٢٧﴾ ﴾

They are but honored slaves. They speak not until He has spoken, and they act on His command.

[Sūrah al-Anbiyā' 21:26-27]

From them are those who are entrusted with land and plant life, such as Mikā'īl. From them are those entrusted with blowing the Trumpet, such as Isrāfīl, who will blow into the Trumpet and destroy everything. Allāh the Exalted has said:

﴿ وَنُفِخَ فِي الصُّورِ فَصَعِقَ مَن فِي السَّمَاوَاتِ وَمَن فِي الْأَرْضِ إِلَّا مَن شَاءَ اللَّهُ ﴾

And the Trumpet will be blown, and all who are in the heavens and all who are on the earth will swoon away, except whom Allāh wills.

[Sūrah az-Zumar 39:68]

And he will blow a second time and the souls will fly to their bodies.

﴿ ثُمَّ نُفِخَ فِيهِ أُخْرَىٰ فَإِذَا هُمْ قِيَامٌ يَنظُرُونَ ﴾

Then it will be blown a second time and behold, they will be standing, looking on (waiting).

[Sūrah az-Zumar 39:68]

The souls will fly from different generations, and it (the flying) is from the Trumpet to their bodies. They will enter their bodies and they will be given life by the permission of Allāh. Then they will walk to the plane of gathering.

From them are those who are entrusted with taking souls at the end of the appointed term, and this is the angel of death. The Most High has said:

﴿ قُلْ يَتَوَفَّاكُم مَّلَكُ الْمَوْتِ الَّذِي وُكِّلَ بِكُمْ ثُمَّ إِلَىٰ رَبِّكُمْ تُرْجَعُونَ ﴾

Say: "The angel of death, who is set over you, will take your souls; then you shall be brought to your Lord."

[Sūrah as-Sajdah 32:11]

And he has helpers with him from the angels, as Allāh has said:

﴿ تَوَفَّتْهُ رُسُلُنَا وَهُمْ لَا يُفَرِّطُونَ ﴾

Our messengers (the angel of death and his assistants) take his soul, and they never neglect their duty.

[Sūrah al-An'ām 6:61]

Meaning: Helpers for the angel of death.

From them are those who are entrusted with the contents of the wombs. The Messenger of Allāh ﷺ said:

إِنَّ أَحَدَكُمْ يُجْمَعُ خَلْقُهُ فِي بَطْنِ أُمِّهِ أَرْبَعِينَ يَوْمًا نُطْفَةً، ثُمَّ

يَكُونُ عَلَقَةً مِثْلَ ذَلِكَ، ثُمَّ يَكُونُ مُضْغَةً مِثْلَ ذَلِكَ، ثُمَّ يُرْسَلُ إِلَيْهِ الْمَلَكُ.

Indeed, the creation of one of you is gathered in the womb of his mother for a period of 40 days as a *nuṭfah* (mixed drop of male and female semen), then as an *'alaq* (a clot of blood) for a like period, then as a *muḍghah* (a lump of flesh) for a similar period; then the angel is sent to him...[19]

From them are those who are entrusted with preserving the actions of the children of Ādam. Allāh the Exalted has said:

﴿ وَإِنَّ عَلَيْكُمْ لَحَافِظِينَ ﴿١٠﴾ كِرَامًا كَاتِبِينَ ﴿١١﴾ ﴾

But verily, over you (are appointed angels in charge of mankind) to watch you; *kirāman* (honorable) *kātibīn* [writing down (your deeds)].

[Sūrah al-Infiṭār 82:10-11]

They stick by your side by night and by day. He ﷺ stated:

يَتَعَاقَبُونَ فِيكُمْ مَلَائِكَةٌ بِاللَّيْلِ وَ مَلَائِكَةٌ بِالنَّهَارِ.

Angels stay with you by night, and others stay with you by day.[20]

They gather at the Fajr prayer and at the 'Aṣr prayer, and they testify for the worshipers with Allāh ﷻ. Due to this, the Most High has said:

﴿ وَقُرْآنَ الْفَجْرِ ۖ إِنَّ قُرْآنَ الْفَجْرِ كَانَ مَشْهُودًا ﴾

And recite the Qur'ān in the early dawn (i.e., the morning prayer). Verily, the recitation of the Qur'ān in the early dawn is ever-witnessed (attended by the angels in charge of mankind of the day and the

[19] Al-Bukhārī reported it (#3208), as did Muslim (#2643) from the *ḥadīth* of 'Abdullāh bin Mas'ūd رضي الله عنه.

[20] Al-Bukhārī reported it (#555), as did Muslim (#632) from the *ḥadīth* of Abū Hurayrah رضي الله عنه.

night).

[Sūrah al-Isrā' 17:78]

Meaning: The angels attend it—the angels of night and the angels of day.

From them are those who are entrusted with guarding the children of Ādam from harm, evil, the enemy, critters, beasts of prey, snakes, and serpents as long as he remains alive. Then he has angels to safeguard him from dangers. He sleeps among beasts of prey and snakes while in the valley. So, who is the one who defends him against the snakes and the beasts of prey and critters? He has angels with him. Allāh has made them responsible for guarding him. Allāh the Exalted has said about them:

﴿لَهُ مُعَقِّبَاتٌ مِّن بَيْنِ يَدَيْهِ وَمِنْ خَلْفِهِ يَحْفَظُونَهُ مِنْ أَمْرِ اللَّهِ﴾

For each (person), there are angels in succession, before and behind him. They guard him by the command of Allāh.

[Sūrah ar-Ra'd 13:11]

Meaning: By the command of Allāh, these angels guard the children of Ādam from harms and dangers until his appointed time. When his appointed time comes, they depart from him, and there occurs that which Allāh decrees for him from death or afflictions that will result in his death.

And from them there are angels who are entrusted with carrying out the commands within the heavens and the earth. And none knows them except Allāh ﷻ.

From them are angels who seek out the circles of remembrance and attend them, as was said by Allāh's Messenger ﷺ:

مَا اجْتَمَعَ قَوْمٌ فِي بَيْتٍ مِنْ بُيُوتِ اللهِ يَتْلُونَ كِتَابَ اللهِ، وَ يَتَدَارَسُونَهُ بَيْنَهُمْ، إِلَّا نَزَلَتْ عَلَيْهِمُ السَّكِينَةُ، وَ غَشِيَتْهُمُ

الرَّحْمَةُ، وَ حَفَّتْهُمُ الْمَلَائِكَةُ.

No people gather in a house from the houses of Allāh, reciting the Book of Allāh and studying it among themselves, except that there descends upon them tranquility, mercy engulfs them, and the angels surround them.[21]

These are angels who go about the earth seeking out circles of remembrance and attending them. No one knows the angels and their various categories and descriptions except Allāh; however, we affirm and believe in what has come [about them] in the Qur'ān and authentic Prophetic *aḥādīth*. And that which has not been mentioned to us, then we withhold regarding it and we will not look into it, because this is from the knowledge of the unseen which we do not enter except by way of evidence.

Īmān in the angels is a pillar of *al-islām*. So, he who obstinately rejects the angels and says that the angels do not exist because we do not see them, then this individual is a *kāfir*, a deviant, and a *zindīq;* and refuge is sought with Allāh, because he does not believe in the unseen.

Likewise, those who misinterpret the meaning of angels such that they say the angels are only metaphorical, without physical bodies, and they are ideas which come to the individual; and if they are good ideas, then they are angels, and if they are evil ideas, they are *shayāṭīn*. This is an atheistic statement, and refuge is sought with Allāh. Unfortunately, it is in *Tafsīr al-Manār*; Muḥammad Rashīd Riḍā transmitted this from his *shaykh,* Muḥammad ʿAbduh. This is the speech of the philosophers; it is false speech. Whoever believes it is a disbeliever; however, we hope that he simply transmitted it and did not believe it. But transmitting it without commenting upon it is dangerous. And this is false speech and disbelief in the angels. We ask Allāh for safety and security.

So, an individual is not to bring anything from his intellect or his thoughts, or transmit anything from the philosophers or the

---

[21] Muslim reported it (#2699) from the *ḥadīth* of Abū Hurayrah ﷺ.

zanādiqah, for the affairs of the religion and the affairs of the unseen. He is only to depend upon the Book and the Sunnah. This is what is obligatory.

It is mentioned in *Tafsīr al-Manār* that this is transmitted from the book *Iḥyā' 'Ulūm ad-Dīn* by al-Ghazālī, and Allāh knows best. The book *Iḥyā' 'Ulūm ad-Dīn*, by al-Ghazālī, contains evils and calamities, although there is some good and benefit in it. However, it contains destructive affairs and many poisonous things, so it is a book that is mixed. Its evil is greater than its good, so it is not befitting for the beginning student or the layman to look into it except if he has knowledge and is able to distinguish between the truth and falsehood.

The angels are not metaphorical, as he says; rather, the angels have actual bodies and forms, and they can take on forms which Allāh has given them the ability to do. Due to this, Jibrīl عليه السلام would come to the Prophet ﷺ in the form of a man. Allāh gave him the ability to take on this form for the benefit of the children of Ādam, because the children of Ādam are not able to withstand seeing the angels in the [true] form Allāh created them upon.

So, they would only come to the Prophet ﷺ in the form of a man out of kindness to the children of Ādam. And the people do not see them in their original form, as they truly are, except at the time of punishment. Allāh the Exalted has said:

﴿ يَوْمَ يَرَوْنَ الْمَلَائِكَةَ لَا بُشْرَىٰ يَوْمَئِذٍ لِّلْمُجْرِمِينَ وَيَقُولُونَ حِجْرًا مَّحْجُورًا ﴾

On the day they will see the angels, no glad tidings will there be for the *mujrimūn* (criminals, disbelievers, polytheists, sinners, etc.) that day. And they (angels) will say, "All kinds of glad tidings are forbidden for you."

[Sūrah al-Furqān 25:22]

Also, at the time of death when they come to an individual, the angels of death are seen. However, in the *dunyā,* while one is still alive, he does not see them because he is not able to see them. Allāh has created them from light and has created the *shayāṭīn* from fire. As it is said in the Qur'ān, He created Ādam from dust. Allāh has power over all things.

The disbelievers believe that the angels are the daughters of Allāh. The Most High has said:

﴿ وَجَعَلُوا الْمَلَائِكَةَ الَّذِينَ هُمْ عِبَادُ الرَّحْمَٰنِ إِنَاثًا ۚ
أَشَهِدُوا خَلْقَهُمْ ۚ سَتُكْتَبُ شَهَادَتُهُمْ وَيُسْأَلُونَ ﴾

And they make the angels, who themselves are slaves to the Most Beneficent (Allāh), females. Did they witness their creation? Their evidence will be recorded, and they will be questioned!

[Sūrah az-Zukhruf 43:19]

The Third Pillar: Having *īmān* in His Books. And they are Books He has revealed to his messengers to guide the human beings. We believe that they are the speech of Allāh in truth, and we believe in those which Allāh has named and those which He has not named. Allāh has named for us from them at-Tawrāh, al-Injīl, az-Zabūr, the magnificent Qur'ān, and the scriptures of Ibrāhīm and Mūsā; therefore, we believe in them. We believe in those which Allāh has not named from amongst them. So, *īmān* in the previous Books is an *īmān* which is general. *Īmān* in the Qur'ān is an *īmān* which is detailed in all that it contains, because it is our Book and it was revealed to our Prophet, Muḥammad ﷺ.

So, he who obstinately rejects a verse or one of its letters is a disbeliever who has apostated from the religion of Islām. Likewise, whoever believes in some of the Qur'ān and disbelieves in some of it is a *kāfir*. Likewise, he who believes in some of the Books and disbelieves in some of them is also a disbeliever. And he who says, "I believe in the Qur'ān but do not believe in the Tawrāh and the Injīl," is a disbeliever. Or he who says, "I believe in the Tawrāh and the Injīl, but I do not believe in the Zabūr which Allāh sent down upon Dāwūd عليه السلام," then he is a disbeliever. Allāh has said:

﴿ وَآتَيْنَا دَاوُودَ زَبُورًا ﴾

And to Dāwūd (David) We gave the Zabūr (Psalms).

[Sūrah an-Nisā' 4:163]

Or the individual who rejects the scriptures of Ibrāhīm, then he is a disbeliever, because he has belied Allāh عز وجل and has belied his messengers; therefore, he is a disbeliever because he has obstinately rejected a pillar of *al-īmān*.

The Fourth Pillar: *Īmān* in the messengers; *īmān* in all the messengers, from the first to the last of them, those whom Allāh has named from them, and those whom He did not name—we believe in all of them and we believe that they are Allāh's messengers in truth. They came with the message and conveyed it to their nations. So, he who disbelieves in one prophet, he has disbelieved in all of the messengers, due to the statement of the Most High:

﴿ إِنَّ الَّذِينَ يَكْفُرُونَ بِاللَّهِ وَرُسُلِهِ وَيُرِيدُونَ أَن يُفَرِّقُوا بَيْنَ
اللَّهِ وَرُسُلِهِ وَيَقُولُونَ نُؤْمِنُ بِبَعْضٍ وَنَكْفُرُ بِبَعْضٍ وَيُرِيدُونَ
أَن يَتَّخِذُوا بَيْنَ ذَٰلِكَ سَبِيلًا ﴿١٥٠﴾ أُولَٰئِكَ هُمُ الْكَافِرُونَ
حَقًّا ۚ وَأَعْتَدْنَا لِلْكَافِرِينَ عَذَابًا مُّهِينًا ﴿١٥١﴾ وَالَّذِينَ آمَنُوا
بِاللَّهِ وَرُسُلِهِ وَلَمْ يُفَرِّقُوا بَيْنَ أَحَدٍ مِّنْهُمْ أُولَٰئِكَ سَوْفَ
يُؤْتِيهِمْ أُجُورَهُمْ ۗ وَكَانَ اللَّهُ غَفُورًا رَّحِيمًا ﴿١٥٢﴾ ﴾

Verily, those who disbelieve in Allāh and His messengers and wish to make distinction between Allāh and His messengers (by believing in Allāh and disbelieving in His messengers), saying, "We believe in some but reject others," and wish to adopt a way in between. They are, in truth, disbelievers. And We have prepared for the disbelievers a humiliating torment. And those who believe in Allāh and His messengers and make no distinction between

any of them (messengers), We shall give them their rewards, and Allāh is Ever Oft-Forgiving, Most Merciful.

[Sūrah an-Nisā' 4:150-152]

So, disbelief in one prophet or messenger is disbelief in all of them, due to the statement of the Most High:

﴿ كَذَّبَتْ قَوْمُ نُوحٍ الْمُرْسَلِينَ ﴾

The people of Nūḥ (Noah) belied the messengers.

[Sūrah ash-Shu'arā' 26:105]

This is in addition to the fact that they denied Nūḥ; therefore, their denial of Nūḥ became denial of the rest of the messengers. Likewise, he who disbelieves in 'Īsā and Muḥammad, such as the Jews, or he who disbelieves in Muḥammad, such as the Christians, then he has disbelieved in all of them.

It is a must that one has *īmān* in all of the messengers عليهم السلام—those whom Allāh has named from amongst them as well as those whom He has not named. And Allāh has named some of them, as is within Sūrah al-An'ām:

﴿ وَتِلْكَ حُجَّتُنَا آتَيْنَاهَا إِبْرَاهِيمَ عَلَىٰ قَوْمِهِ ۚ نَرْفَعُ دَرَجَاتٍ مَّن نَّشَاءُ ۗ إِنَّ رَبَّكَ حَكِيمٌ عَلِيمٌ ﴿٨٣﴾ وَوَهَبْنَا لَهُ إِسْحَاقَ وَيَعْقُوبَ ۚ كُلًّا هَدَيْنَا ۚ وَنُوحًا هَدَيْنَا مِن قَبْلُ ۖ وَمِن ذُرِّيَّتِهِ دَاوُودَ وَسُلَيْمَانَ وَأَيُّوبَ وَيُوسُفَ وَمُوسَىٰ وَهَارُونَ ۚ وَكَذَٰلِكَ نَجْزِي الْمُحْسِنِينَ ﴿٨٤﴾ وَزَكَرِيَّا وَيَحْيَىٰ وَعِيسَىٰ وَإِلْيَاسَ ۖ كُلٌّ مِّنَ الصَّالِحِينَ ﴿٨٥﴾ وَإِسْمَاعِيلَ وَالْيَسَعَ وَيُونُسَ وَلُوطًا ۚ وَكُلًّا فَضَّلْنَا عَلَى الْعَالَمِينَ ﴿٨٦﴾ ﴾

And that was Our proof which We gave Ibrāhīm (Abraham) against his people. We raise whom We will in degrees. Certainly, your Lord is All-Wise,

All-Knowing. And We bestowed upon him Is'ḥāq (Isaac) and Ya'qūb (Jacob), each of them We guided; and before him, We guided Nūḥ (Noah), and among his progeny Dāwūd (David), Sulaymān (Solomon), Ayyūb (Job), Yūsuf (Joseph), Mūsā (Moses), and Hārūn (Aaron). Thus do We reward the good-doers. And Zakariyyā (Zachariah), Yaḥyā (John), 'Īsā (Jesus), and Ilyās (Elias); each one of them was of the righteous. And Ismā'īl (Ishmael), al-Yasa' (Elisha), Yūnus (Jonah), and Lūṭ (Lot), and each one of them We preferred above the *'ālamīn* (mankind and *jinn*) (of their times).

[Sūrah al-An'ām 6:83-86]

He generally mentioned some of them in these verses and in other verses. So, we believe in those whom Allāh named from amongst them, and we likewise believe in those whom He has not named from amongst them.

The Fifth Pillar: *Īmān* in the Last Day. To believe in the Last Day is the fifth pillar. And what is intended by "the Last Day" is the Day of Standing. It is referred to as "the Last Day" because it is after the first day, which is the day of the *dunyā*. The *dunyā* is the first day and al-Qiyāmah is the last day. *Īmān* in the Last Day means to believe in that which is after death, the punishment of the grave and its bliss, and the questioning of the two angels in the grave. Believing in everything after the grave is from *īmān* in the Last Day.

Likewise, to believe in the resurrection, the assembling, and the gathering, as well as the recompense, the weighing of the actions, the Ṣirāṭ (the Bridge), the Mīzān (the Scale) upon which the good deeds and evil deeds will be weighed, Paradise, and the Hellfire. (Regarding) the details of what will take place on the Last Day, we believe in them in general as well as in detail, beginning from death until the time when the people of Paradise settle in Paradise and the people of the Hellfire settle in the Hellfire. We believe in everything which has been authentically narrated about this, and we do not doubt anything from it. He who doubts anything from it is a disbeliever who has apostated from the religion of al-Islām. All of this is referred to as "the Last Day" and that which it contains.

The Sixth Pillar: That you believe in *al-qadar,* its good and its evil. You must believe that whatever occurs in this universe is decreed—from good and evil, from *kufr* and *īmān*, from blessings and curses, from ease and hardship, from illness and health, from life and death—and it is not coincidence, nor is it happenstance (meaning that it is something newly initiated, having not been preceded by its decree). You must believe in all of this, that it is by the decree and preordainment of Allāh. We believe that what befalls you was not going to miss you, and what misses you was not going to befall you. And that this is by way of the decree of Allāh and its preordainment. The Most High has said:

﴿ مَا أَصَابَ مِن مُّصِيبَةٍ فِي الْأَرْضِ وَلَا فِي أَنفُسِكُمْ إِلَّا فِي كِتَابٍ مِّن قَبْلِ أَن نَّبْرَأَهَا ۚ إِنَّ ذَٰلِكَ عَلَى اللَّهِ يَسِيرٌ ﴾

No calamity befalls on the earth or in yourselves but is inscribed in the Book of Decrees (al-Lawḥ al-Maḥfūẓ), before We bring it into existence. Verily, that is easy for Allāh.

[Sūrah al-Ḥadīd 57:22]

This is *īmān* in the *qadar.*

Al-īmān in the *qadar* is comprised of four levels; he who does not believe in all of them is not a believer in the *qadar.*

The First Level: *Al-'ilm* (knowledge). It is to believe that Allāh knew everything in existence. He knew everything that would occur—that which was, that which is, and that which will never be. And Allāh knew it before it was and before it occurred. He ﷻ knew it with His foreknowledge, which He is described with always and forever. This is the level of knowledge. He who obstinately rejects this is a disbeliever.

The Second Level: The level of *al-kitābah* (writing within the

Preserved Tablet). And it means that Allāh wrote everything in the Preserved Tablet. Nothing occurs except that it was written in the Preserved Tablet. There is nothing that occurs which was not written. Due to this, the Most High has stated:

﴿مَا أَصَابَ مِن مُّصِيبَةٍ فِي الْأَرْضِ وَلَا فِي أَنفُسِكُمْ إِلَّا فِي كِتَابٍ﴾

No calamity befalls on the earth or in yourselves but is inscribed in the Book...

[Sūrah al-Ḥadīd 57:22]

Meaning: The Preserved Tablet. Allāh wrote therein the decrees of everything. The Messenger of Allāh ﷺ said:

أَوَّلُ مَا خَلَقَ اللهُ الْقَلَمَ. قَالَ اكْتُبْ، قَالَ وَ مَا أَكْتُبُ؟ قَالَ اكْتُبْ مَا هُوَ كَائِنٌ إِلَى يَوْمِ الْقِيَامَةِ.

The first thing that Allāh created was the Pen. He said, "Write." And it said, "What shall I write?" He said, "Write that which will be, all the way until the Day of Standing."[22]

He who obstinately rejects the writing and says that Allāh knew everything but He did not write it in the Preserved Tablet, then he is a disbeliever who has apostated from the religion of Islām.

The Third Level: The all-encompassing will of Allāh. And this means that Allāh, Glorified be He, wills a thing and wants it to occur. So, there is nothing which happens except that Allāh has willed it and wanted it to happen as is within the Preserved Tablet. And just as He ﷻ knew it, He wills everything to occur within its appointed time, and He wants everything to happen in the time that it happened. Nothing occurs without the will of Allāh or without His wanting it to occur. He who says that things happen without Allāh willing it to happen or wanting it to happen, then he is a disbeliever.

[22] Abū Dāwūd reported it (#4700), as did at-Tirmidhī (#2155) from the *ḥadīth* of 'Ubādah bin aṣ-Ṣāmit ﷺ.

The Fourth Level: The level of *al-khalq wal-ījād* (creation and bringing into existence). Allāh is the Creator of everything. If He wills it or wants it, then He ﷻ creates it and brings it into existence. Everything is a creation of Allāh ﷻ and is from His creation, while at the same time it is the action of the servants and that which the servants have earned.

These are the four levels which one must have *īmān* in. Otherwise the person is not a believer in *al-qadar*, the level of knowledge, writing, will, and creation and bringing into existence. One must have *īmān* in all of these. He who obstinately rejects anything from them is a disbeliever who has apostated from the religion of Islām, because he has obstinately rejected a pillar of *al-īmān,* which is to have *īmān* in *al-qadar*.

The Proof for the Pillars of al-Īmān

ORIGINAL TEXT

وَ الدَّلِيلُ عَلَى هَذِهِ الأَرْكَانِ السِّتَّةِ: قَوْلُهُ تَعَالَى: ﴿ لَّيْسَ الْبِرَّ أَن تُوَلُّوا وُجُوهَكُمْ قِبَلَ الْمَشْرِقِ وَالْمَغْرِبِ وَلَكِنَّ الْبِرَّ مَنْ آمَنَ بِاللَّهِ وَالْيَوْمِ الْآخِرِ وَالْمَلَائِكَةِ وَالْكِتَابِ وَالنَّبِيِّينَ ﴾.

The proof for the six pillars is the statement of the Most High:

> **It is not *al-birr* (piety, righteousness, and each and every act of obedience to Allāh, etc.) that you turn your faces towards east and (or) west (in prayers); but *al-birr* is (the quality of) the one who believes in Allāh, the Last Day, the angels, the Book, and the prophets.**
>
> *[Sūrah al-Baqarah 2:177]*

EXPLANATION

When the Shaykh mentioned these pillars, he mentioned their evidences from the Qur'ān and the Sunnah because anything from the affairs of the religion, worship, *'aqīdah,* and the affairs of the legislated rulings, needs to have evidence. And if there is no evidence for it, then it is not correct. When the Shaykh mentioned the six pillars of *al-īmān*, he mentioned their evidences. From the Qur'ān is His statement, Exalted be He:

﴿ لَّيْسَ الْبِرَّ أَن تُوَلُّوا وُجُوهَكُمْ ﴾

It is not piety (*al-birr*) that you turn your faces...

[Sūrah al-Baqarah 2:177]

Al-birr means to do good which will draw one closer to Allāh and cause an individual to reach Paradise. So, every action of good is from *al-birr. Al-birr* is a general term which comprises all types of good and all types of obedience. All of them fall under the term *al-birr* and the term *at-taqwā*; so, *al-birr* and *at-taqwā* are from the general terms which comprise all qualities of good.

And the statement of the Most High:

﴿ لَّيْسَ الْبِرَّ أَن تُوَلُّوا وُجُوهَكُمْ قِبَلَ الْمَشْرِقِ وَالْمَغْرِبِ ﴾

It is not *al-birr* that you turn your faces to the east or to the west...

[Sūrah al-Baqarah 2:177]

This is a refutation against the Jews who rejected the changing of the *qiblah* from Bayt al-Maqdis to the noble Ka'bah. They rejected this and obstinately rejected it while they knew that it was the truth. However, they rejected it from the perspective of obstinance, arrogance, and envy for the Prophet ﷺ and for his *ummah.*

Allāh says that it is not *al-birr* that you turn your faces to a direction without a command from Allāh. Rather, *al-birr* is the obedience of Allāh ﷻ. When He commands you with a command, it is obligatory upon you to adhere to it. This is *al-birr.* So, if He commands you to face Bayt al-Maqdis, then *al-birr* in that regard is to face Bayt al-Maqdis, because this would be obedience to Allāh عزوجل. Then if He commands you to face the Ka'bah, then *al-birr* is to face the

Ka'bah. So, *al-birr* revolves around the command of Allāh ﷻ.

You are servants. It is obligatory upon you to obey. If Allāh commands you to face a direction, then it is obligatory upon you to adhere to it. As for having fanaticism for a particular direction and saying it is incorrect to face any way other than it, then this is following desires and blind partisanship.

The true servant of Allāh revolves around Allāh's commands and he does not turn away from the commands of Allāh. Facing a direction after it has been abrogated is not considered obedience to Allāh ﷻ. Action upon what has been abrogated, and leaving off what has abrogated it, is not obedience to Allāh ﷻ. It is only obedience to desires and blind partisanship.

So, *al-birr* is connected to the obedience of Allāh. Therefore, that is the direction you face if you are true in your worship of Allāh ﷻ. As Allāh says:

﴿ لَّيْسَ الْبِرَّ أَن تُوَلُّوا وُجُوهَكُمْ قِبَلَ الْمَشْرِقِ وَالْمَغْرِبِ
وَلَٰكِنَّ الْبِرَّ مَنْ آمَنَ بِاللَّهِ ﴾

It is not *al-birr* that you turn your faces towards east and (or) west (in prayers); but *al-birr* is (the quality of) the one who believes in Allāh...

[Sūrah al-Baqarah 2:177]

ORIGINAL TEXT

وَ دَلِيلُ الْقَدَرِ قَوْلُهُ تَعَالَى: ﴿ إِنَّا كُلَّ شَيْءٍ خَلَقْنَاهُ بِقَدَرٍ ﴾.

The proof for *al-qadar* is the statement of the Most High:

Verily, We have created all things with *qadar*.

[Sūrah al-Qamar 54:49]

EXPLANATION

The proof for the sixth pillar of *al-īmān* is the statement of the Most

High:

﴿ إِنَّا كُلَّ شَيْءٍ خَلَقْنَاهُ بِقَدَرٍ ﴾

Verily, We have created all things with *qadar*.

[*Sūrah al-Qamar 54:49*]

And this means that everything Allāh has created has due proportion in His knowledge, His writing, His will, and His wanting for it to happen ﷻ. And it is not incidental or coincidental. It is none other than a command which has preceded in the knowledge of Allāh, is written in the Preserved Tablet, and has preceded in the will of Allāh and His wanting it to happen ﷻ.

The Third Level: al-Iḥsān

Original Text

تَعْرِيفُ الْإِحْسَانِ: الْمَرْتَبَةُ الثَّالِثَةُ: اَلْإِحْسَانُ، رُكْنٌ وَاحِدٌ، وَ هُوَ: أَنْ تَعْبُدَ اللهَ كَأَنَّكَ تَرَاهُ، فَإِنْ لَمْ تَكُنْ تَرَاهُ، فَإِنَّهُ يَرَاكَ.

The Definition of *al-Iḥsān*:

The third level is *al-iḥsān*; it is one pillar: that you worship Allāh as if you see Him, and even though you do not see Him, surely He sees you.

Explanation

Al-iḥsān in the Arabic language means: perfection of a thing and its completion. It is derived from *al-ḥasan*. And it is beauty, which is the opposite of ugliness. It is categorized into different types:

1) *Iḥsān* between the servant and his Lord, and this is what is intended here.

2) *Iḥsān* between the servant and the people.

3) *Iḥsān* in actions and the perfection of them. When the individual does a thing or he embarks upon an action, then it is obligatory upon him to perfect it and complete it.

The first type is *iḥsān* between the servant and his Lord. The Messenger ﷺ clarified it when Jibrīl questioned him in a gathering of the Companions, as shall come. He ﷺ said:

اَلْإِحْسَانُ أَنْ تَعْبُدَ اللهَ كَأَنَّكَ تَرَاهُ، فَإِنْ لَمْ تَكُنْ تَرَاهُ فَإِنَّهُ يَرَاهُ.

***Al-iḥsān* is that you worship Allāh as though you see Him, and even though you do not see Him, surely He sees you.**

So, *iḥsān* between the servant and his Lord is his perfection of the actions Allāh has made him responsible for, and that he does them correctly and sincerely seeking the Face of Allāh ﷻ. The action of *iḥsān* between the servant and his Lord is that which is implemented with sincerity for Allāh ﷻ and following the Messenger ﷺ.

The Prophet ﷺ clarified that *al-iḥsān* is of two levels, one of them being higher than the other:

The First Level: That you worship Allāh as if you see Him, so that your certainty and *īmān* in Allāh reaches a level as though you were looking at Allāh directly, and you have no hesitation or doubt regarding this. Rather, it is as if Allāh is in front of you ﷻ and you are looking at Him directly. He who reaches this level has reached the highest point of *al-iḥsān*.

Worshiping Allāh as though you see Him is from the perfection of certainty and sincerity; it is as if you see Allāh directly, and Allāh ﷻ is not seen in the *dunyā*. He is only seen in the Hereafter. However, you see Him with your heart until it reaches the point that it is as if you are looking at Him with your eyes. Due to that, the people of *iḥsān* are rewarded in the Hereafter with seeing Him ﷻ because they worshiped him in the *dunyā* as if they were looking at Him. So Allāh will reward them by opening for them the field (worship) by allowing them to see Him in the Home of Bliss. Allāh the Exalted has said:

﴿ لِّلَّذِينَ أَحْسَنُوا الْحُسْنَىٰ وَزِيَادَةٌ ﴾

For those who have done good is the best (reward, i.e., Paradise) and even more.

[Sūrah Yūnus 10:26]

The additional thing that they will receive is looking at the Face of Allāh. The reason for this is that they had *iḥsān* in the *dunyā*; therefore, Allāh gave them *al-ḥusnā*, which is Paradise. And they were increased by being allowed to see Allāh عَزَّوَجَلَّ.

So, you worship Allāh as though you see Him visibly, and you have love and longing for the meeting with Him ﷻ. You are delighted by obeying Him, and you are at ease with obeying Him. You long for it. This is the path of the people of *iḥsān.*

The Second Level: This is when an individual has not reached [the first] great level, so you worship Him by way of *al-marāqabah*: by knowing that Allāh sees you, He knows your state, and He knows what is in your soul. So it is not befitting for you to disobey Him and oppose His command, for He sees you and is looking at you.

This is an excellent state; however, it is less than the first. And as long as you know that Allāh is looking at you, then you will perfect your worship and complete it because [you know] Allāh sees you. And Allāh is the loftiest example. If you were in front of a created being who had status, and he gave you a command, and you discharged this command in front of him while he was looking at you, would it be befitting that you perform this action deficiently?

In summary: *Al-iḥsān* is of two levels:

1) The first level is that of the heart witnessing Allāh, and it is that you worship Allāh as though you see Him from the strength of your certainty and *īmān*; therefore, it is as if you are seeing Allāh directly.

2) The second level, which is less than the first, is that you worship Allāh while knowing that He sees you and is looking at you, so you do not disobey Him nor do you oppose His command ﷻ.

This is the level of *al-iḥsān,* and it is the highest level of the religion. He who reaches it has reached the highest level of the religion. And before it is the level of *īmān*, and before that is the level of *al-islām.*

Therefore, the religion is of three domains:

The First Domain: *Al-islām,* and this domain is broad, to the extent that even the hypocrite enters this category; it is said that he is Muslim and he is to be dealt with as the Muslims are dealt with because he has submitted outwardly, so he enters the realm of *al-islām*. And the person weak in *īmān,* who does not have from *īmān* except the equivalent of a mustard seed, also enters this category.

The Second Domain: This is more restricted than the first and more specific—it is the domain of *al-īmān*. The hypocrite, who has hypocrisy in belief, does not enter it at all. Only the people of *al-īmān* enter it, and they are of two categories: those who have complete *īmān* and those who have deficient *īmān*. So, the wrongdoing believer enters it as well as the believer who has *taqwā.*

The Third Domain: This is more restricted than the second—it is the domain of *al-iḥsān,* and it is as the Prophet ﷺ has clarified. And none enters it except the people of complete *īmān*.

The Evidence for al-Iḥsān

ORIGINAL TEXT

وَ الدَّلِيلُ قَوْلُهُ تَعَالَى: ﴿ إِنَّ اللَّهَ مَعَ الَّذِينَ اتَّقَوا وَّالَّذِينَ هُم مُّحْسِنُونَ ﴾.

وَ قَوْلُهُ تَعَالَى: ﴿ وَتَوَكَّلْ عَلَى الْعَزِيزِ الرَّحِيمِ ﴿٢١٧﴾ الَّذِي يَرَاكَ حِينَ تَقُومُ ﴿٢١٨﴾ وَتَقَلُّبَكَ فِي السَّاجِدِينَ ﴿٢١٩﴾ إِنَّهُ هُوَ السَّمِيعُ الْعَلِيمُ ﴿٢٢٠﴾ ﴾.

وَ قَوْلُهُ تَعَالَى: ﴿ وَمَا تَكُونُ فِي شَأْنٍ وَمَا تَتْلُو مِنْهُ مِن قُرْآنٍ وَلَا تَعْمَلُونَ مِنْ عَمَلٍ إِلَّا كُنَّا عَلَيْكُمْ شُهُودًا إِذْ تُفِيضُونَ فِيهِ ۚ وَمَا يَعْزُبُ عَن رَّبِّكَ مِن مِّثْقَالِ ذَرَّةٍ فِي الْأَرْضِ وَلَا فِي السَّمَاءِ وَلَا أَصْغَرَ مِن ذَٰلِكَ وَلَا أَكْبَرَ إِلَّا فِي كِتَابٍ مُّبِينٍ ﴾.

The evidence is the statement of the Most High:

> **Truly, Allāh is with those who fear Him (keep their duty unto Him), and those who are *muḥsinūn* (good-doers).**
>
> *[Sūrah an-Naḥl 16:128]*

And His statement:

> **And put your trust in the All-Mighty, the Most Merciful, who sees you (O Muḥammad ﷺ) when you stand up (alone at night for *tahajjud* prayers). And your movements among those who fall prostrate. Verily! He, only He, is the All-Hearer, the All-Knower.**
>
> *[Sūrah ash-Shu'arā' 26:217-220]*

Also, His statement:

> **You (O Muḥammad ﷺ) are not in any state, nor do you recite from Him (anything) from the Qur'ān—nor do you do any deed (good or evil), except that We are witness thereof, when you are doing it. And nothing is hidden from your Lord (so much as) the weight of an atom (or small ant) on the earth or in the heaven. Not what is less than that or what is greater than that but is (written) in a Clear Record.**
>
> *[Sūrah Yūnus 10:61]*

EXPLANATION

This is the evidence for the first level of *al-iḥsān*:

﴿ إِنَّ اللَّهَ مَعَ الَّذِينَ اتَّقَوا وَّالَّذِينَ هُم مُّحْسِنُونَ ﴾

Truly, Allāh is with those who fear Him (keep their duty unto Him), and those who are *muḥsinūn* (good-doers).

[Sūrah an-Naḥl 16:128]

This indicates that Allāh is with the people of *iḥsān*; they are those who worship Allāh as if they see Him. Indeed, Allāh is with them with a specific (type of) withness (*ma'iyyah*)—a withness of aid, strengthening, and success. His statement:

﴿ وَتَوَكَّلْ عَلَى الْعَزِيزِ الرَّحِيمِ ﴿٢١٧﴾ الَّذِي يَرَاكَ حِينَ تَقُومُ ﴿٢١٨﴾ وَتَقَلُّبَكَ فِي السَّاجِدِينَ ﴿٢١٩﴾ ﴾

And put your trust in the All-Mighty, the Most Merciful, Who sees you (O Muḥammad ﷺ) when you stand up (alone at night for *tahajjud* prayers). And your movements among those who fall prostrate.

[Sūrah ash-Shu'arā' 26:217-219]

This is evidence for the second level. This is evidence for his ﷺ statement: **"surely He sees you..."**

﴿ وَتَوَكَّلْ ﴾

Put your trust...

[Sūrah ash-Shu'arā' 26:217]

Meaning: Relegate your affairs.

﴿ عَلَى الْعَزِيزِ الرَّحِيمِ ﴾

...in the All-Mighty, the Most Merciful...

[Sūrah ash-Shu'arā' 26:217]

This is Allāh ﷻ.

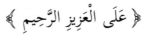

﴿ حِينَ تَقُومُ ﴾

...when you stand up...

[Sūrah ash-Shu'arā' 26:218]

Meaning: For worship and prayer.

﴿ وَتَقَلُّبَكَ فِي السَّاجِدِينَ ﴾

And your movements among those who fall prostrate.

[Sūrah ash-Shu'arā' 26:219]

He sees you when you are bowing and when you are prostrating, and in all your states of worship: standing, bowing, prostrating, He ﷻ sees you.

﴿ إِنَّهُ هُوَ السَّمِيعُ الْعَلِيمُ ﴾

Verily! He, only He, is the All-Hearer, the All-Knower.

[Sūrah ash-Shu'arā' 26:220]

He is the All-Hearer of your statements and the All-Knower of your statements.

The statement of the Most High:

﴿ وَمَا تَكُونُ فِي شَأْنٍ وَمَا تَتْلُو مِنْهُ مِن قُرْآنٍ وَلَا تَعْمَلُونَ مِنْ عَمَلٍ إِلَّا كُنَّا عَلَيْكُمْ شُهُودًا إِذْ تُفِيضُونَ فِيهِ ﴾

You (O Muḥammad ﷺ) are not in any state, nor do you recite from Him (anything) from the Qur'ān, nor do you do any deed (good or evil), except that We are witness thereof, when you are doing it.

[Sūrah Yūnus 10:61]

This is evidence for the second level.

﴿ وَمَا تَكُونُ فِي شَأْنٍ ﴾

You (O Muḥammad ﷺ) are not in any state...

[Sūrah Yūnus 10:61]

This is an address to the Messenger ﷺ; meaning, in any state of your affairs, from the affairs of worship or other than it—all of your actions and movements. You are not in any state (except that Allāh knows it).

﴿ وَمَا تَتْلُو مِنْهُ مِن قُرْآنٍ ﴾

...nor do you recite from Him (anything) from the Qur'ān...

[Sūrah Yūnus 10:61]

Meaning: From Allāh, because the Qur'ān is from Allāh. Or, the pronoun is in reference to the state, i.e., the state in which the recitation of the Qur'ān occurs.

﴿ وَلَا تَعْمَلُونَ ﴾

...nor do you do...

[Sūrah Yūnus 10:61]

This goes for the entire *ummah*; for the Messenger ﷺ and other than him.

﴿ مِنْ عَمَلٍ ﴾

...any deed...

[Sūrah Yūnus 10:61]

Meaning: Any deed, good or evil.

﴿ إِلَّا كُنَّا عَلَيْكُمْ شُهُودًا ﴾

...except that We are witness thereof...

[Sūrah Yūnus 10:61]

[Meaning]: We see you, and we are viewing you and witnessing you. This is evidence for his statement ﷺ:

...فَإِنَّهُ يَرَاكَ.

...He surely sees you.

﴿ إِذْ تُفِيضُونَ فِيهِ ﴾

...when you are doing it.

[Sūrah Yūnus 10:61]

When you are engaging in it and doing it. This lends evidence for the second level of *al-iḥsān*; He ﷻ is a witness of every doer of an action—He sees him, He knows all about him, He is viewing him, and He is not absent from him.

﴿ إِنَّ اللَّهَ لَا يَخْفَىٰ عَلَيْهِ شَيْءٌ فِي الْأَرْضِ وَلَا فِي السَّمَاءِ ﴾

Truly, nothing is hidden from Allāh, in the earth or in the heavens.

[Sūrah Āli 'Imrān 3:5]

As for the *iḥsān* between the servant and the creation, its meaning is: extending what is good to them and withholding harm from them; e.g., by feeding the hungry, clothing the naked, aiding those who need aid by way of your influence, interceding for the one who needs intercession, etc. You extend that which is good, all forms of good. You honor the guest and you honor the neighbor; there is not to emanate from you anything except good for your neighbor, and you withhold your harm from him as well. So, there is not to emanate from you any harm for him or other than him.

From the people is he who only emanates harm, and from the people there is he who emanates both harm and good, and from the people there is he who only emanates good; and [the latter type of person] is the highest of the levels. Extending good to the people and withholding harm from them is *al-iḥsān* to the people.

﴿ وَأَحْسِنُوا ۚ إِنَّ اللَّهَ يُحِبُّ الْمُحْسِنِينَ ﴾

And do good. Truly, Allāh loves *al-muḥsinūn* (the good-doers).

[Sūrah al-Baqarah 2:195]

It is even obligatory to treat the animals well by preparing for them what they need, withholding from harming them, and being kind to them. This is from *iḥsān* to the animals.

This is even the case for those who must be killed. You are not to torture them; rather, you are to kill them in a proficient manner and put them at ease. He upon whom the law of *al-qiṣāṣ* (retribution) must be applied, and he upon whom the prescribed punishment must be applied, must be dealt with in kindness. An example is not to be made of him, nor is he to be tortured or fettered. He ﷺ said:

إِنَّ اللهَ كَتَبَ الْإِحْسَانَ عَلَى كُلِّ شَيْءٍ، فَإِذَا قَتَلْتُمْ فَأَحْسِنُوا الْقِتْلَةَ، وَ إِذَا ذَبَحْتُمْ فَأَحْسِنُوا الذِّبْحَةَ.

Verily, Allāh has prescribed *iḥsān* (proficiency, perfection) in all things. So, if you kill, then kill well; and if you slaughter, then slaughter well.[23]

This is in *al-qiṣāṣ* (the law of equality or retribution) or other than that from the things which require the prescribed punishment.

If you slaughter (i.e., if you slaughter animals which are to be eaten), then perfect the slaughter. Let one of you sharpen his blade and put the animal at ease. Have *iḥsān*, even with animals. Allāh forgave the prostitute of Banū Isrā'īl due to her giving a dog a drink when she saw it panting from thirst. She gave it a drink and Allāh showed gratitude to her and forgave her of her sin;[24] and it was a great sin, the sin of prostitution (i.e., fornication). Allāh forgave her due to this action, because she treated this thirsty animal well.

---

[23] Muslim reported it (#1955) from the *ḥadīth* of Shaddād bin Aws ﷺ.

[24] See that which al-Bukhārī reported (#3467), as well as Muslim (#2245) from the *ḥadīth* of Abū Hurayrah ﷺ.

So, what about other than a dog? If you treat a thirsty Muslim well, or anyone from the children of Ādam—even a disbeliever—then Allāh will show gratitude to you for that goodness. The Most High said:

﴿ وَأَحْسِنُوا ۚ إِنَّ اللَّهَ يُحِبُّ الْمُحْسِنِينَ ﴾

And do good. Truly, Allāh loves *al-muḥsinūn* (the good-doers).

[Sūrah al-Baqarah 2:195]

The third type of *iḥsān* is the perfection of actions. You must perfect any action that you do; and do not do this so that it may said, "So-and-so is good at such-and-such." There has come within a *ḥadīth*:

إِنَّ اللهَ يُحِبُّ إِذَا عَمِلَ أَحَدُكُمْ عَمَلاً أَنْ يُتْقِنَهُ.

Indeed, Allāh loves that, if one of you does an action, he perfects it.[25]

ORIGINAL TEXT —————————————————————

وَ الدَّلِيلُ مِنَ السُّنَّةِ: حَدِيثُ جِبْرِيلَ الْمَشْهُورُ عَنْ عُمَرَ –
رَضِيَ اللهُ عَنْهُ: ((بَيْنَمَا نَحْنُ جُلُوسٌ عِنْدَ رَسُولِ اللهِ – صَلَّى
اللهُ عَلَيْهِ وَ سَلَّمَ – إِذْ طَلَعَ عَلَيْنَا رَجُلٌ شَدِيدٌ بَيَاضُ الثِّيَابِ،
شَدِيدٌ سَوَادُ الشَّعْرِ)).

The proof from the Sunnah is the well-known *ḥadīth* of Jibrīl, on the authority of 'Umar ⬡, who said:

"One day while we were sitting with the Messenger of Allāh ⬡, a man came upon us having very white clothing and very dark hair."

---

[25] Al-Bayhaqī reported it in *Shi'ab al-Īmān* (4/334, #5313, #5314) from the *ḥadīth* of 'Ā'ishah ⬡.

EXPLANATION

Speech has already preceded regarding *al-islām, al-īmān,* and *al-iḥsān* and the pillars for each level. The Shaykh رحمه الله mentioned the evidences for each level from the Qur'ān, and all of this has preceded and ended.

Then the Shaykh رحمه الله mentioned the evidence for these levels in the Sunnah of the Messenger ﷺ. So he mentioned the *ḥadīth* of Jibrīl, and that he came to the Prophet ﷺ while he was amongst his Companions. He came to them in the form of a man and sat with the Prophet ﷺ, and he questioned him about *al-islām, al-īmān,* and *al-iḥsān*. Then he asked him about the Hour and he asked him about its signs. This is what is referred to as "the *ḥadīth* of Jibrīl" or "the *ḥadīth* of 'Umar." And the *ḥadīth* has come from a number of routes of transmission from a group of the Companions, and it is an authentic *ḥadīth*.

The Shaykh رحمه الله mentioned the narration of 'Umar bin al-Khaṭṭāb[26] which comes in this *ḥadīth* with differences in the wordings of the *ḥadīth* and the other routes of transmission; however, the meaning is the same.

He said, **"One day when we were sitting with the Prophet ﷺ"**: From their way is that they used to gather with the Prophet ﷺ in the *masjid*, take knowledge from him, and listen to his answers to the questions which were put forward to him.

So, one day while they were like that, as was their way, a man entered upon them from a door. This man had extremely white clothing and extremely dark hair, meaning: Jibrīl عليه السلام took on the form of this man, and he did not come to them in his angelic form because they would not be able to see him in his angelic form.

---

[26] Muslim reported it (#8). Also, refer to *Jāmi' al-'Ulūm wal-Ḥikam* by Ibn Rajab (vol.1, p. 93) for the second *ḥadīth*.

ORIGINAL TEXT

لَا يُرَى عَلَيْهِ أَثَرُ السَّفَرِ وَ لَا يَعْرِفُهُ مِنَّا أَحَدٌ، حَتَّى جَلَسَ إِلَى النَّبِيِّ - صَلَّى اللهُ عَلَيْهِ وَ سَلَّمَ - فَأَسْنَدَ رُكْبَتَيْهِ إِلَى رُكْبَتَيْهِ، وَ وَضَعَ كَفَّيْهِ عَلَى فَخِذَيْهِ، وَ قَالَ: يَا مُحَمَّدُ أَخْبِرْنِي عَنِ الْإِسْلَامِ.

"No signs of travel were visible upon him, and none of us recognized him. He sat close to the Prophet ﷺ, connecting his knees to his knees and placing his hands upon his thighs, and he said, 'O Muḥammad, inform me about *al-islām*.'"

EXPLANATION

Regarding his statement, **"No signs of travel were visible upon him and none of us recognized him"**: Meaning, none of those present.

This is from the amazing affairs: that he did not come from traveling such that it could be said he is not from the people of Madīnah, yet they did not recognize him, so he was not from the people of that land such that they knew him. So, they were amazed at his state. He did not arrive from travel, yet he was not from the people of the land. If he had arrived from travel, the signs of travel would be apparent upon him in his clothing and his color, because the traveler has signs of travel visible upon him. Yet none of the attendees recognized him, so he was not from the people of the land. However, at the same time, he was not one who had arrived from travel. So, where did this man come from? This is what they found to be strange.

He said, **"He sat close to the Prophet ﷺ"**: Meaning, he sat in front of him in the manner of one who is learning when he sits in front of the one who is teaching him.

He said **"connecting his knees to his [the Prophet's] knees"**: Meaning, he was very close to him.

And he said **"placing his hands upon his thighs"**: Meaning, upon the thighs of the Prophet ﷺ.

And he said [that the man said], **"O Muḥammad"**: He addressed him by his name. He did not say, "O Messenger of Allāh." Perhaps he عليه السلام did this so that the Companions would think he was a Bedouin, because it was from the habits of the Bedouins that they would address the Prophet ﷺ by his name. This is how the Bedouins naturally and habitually were, and this is something which increased his strangeness and abnormality such that they did not know him.

He said, **"O Muḥammad, inform me about *al-islām*"**: Meaning, "Explain to me the meaning of *al-islām*."

ORIGINAL TEXT

قَالَ: أَنْ تَشْهَدَ أَنْ لَا إِلَهَ إِلَّا اللهُ، وَ أَنَّ مُحَمَّداً رَسُولُ اللهِ – صَلَّى اللهُ عَلَيْهِ وَ سَلَّمَ – وَ تُقِيمَ الصَّلَاةَ، وَ تُؤْتِيَ الزَّكَاةَ، وَ تَصُومَ رَمَضَانَ، وَ تَحُجَّ الْبَيْتَ إِنِ اسْتَطَعْتَ إِلَيْهِ سَبِيلاً. فَقَالَ: صَدَّقْتَ. فَعَجِبْنَا لَهُ يَسْأَلُهُ وَ يُصَدِّقُهُ.

"He [the Prophet] said, 'It is that you testify that none has the right to be worshiped except Allāh and that Muḥammad is the Messenger of Allāh; that you establish the *ṣalāh*, pay your *zakāh*, fast Ramaḍān, and make pilgrimage to the House if you have the means to do so.' So he said, 'You have spoken truthfully.' We were amazed that he questioned him yet [also] told him that he had spoken truthfully."

EXPLANATION

He ﷺ said, **"*Al–islām* is that you testify that none has the right to be worshiped except Allāh and that Muḥammad is the Messenger of Allāh; that you establish the *ṣalāh*, pay your *zakāh*, fast Ramaḍān, and make pilgrimage to the House if you have the means to do so."** The Prophet ﷺ mentioned to him the pillars of *al-islām* which are a must; if they are actualized, then *al-islām* is actualized. And that which is done beyond them from the other affairs, are affairs which complete *al-islām*.

The Messenger ﷺ sufficed with clarifying the pillars of *al-islām* because it is easier upon the student and those who hear when the response is summarized. And it is easy upon him to memorize it and understand it; if the answer were long, it would be a difficulty upon the attendees, and perhaps most of them would not understand it. This is evidence that it is befitting for the one who is asked [a question] to attempt to summarize the response, if he is able, and to suffice with what is necessary. Otherwise, *al-islām* is more than [what he mentioned]; these are just its pillars and the supports upon which it stands.

[Jibrīl] said, **"You have spoken truthfully."** This is a second thing which was amazing. So, ['Umar] said, **"We were amazed that he questioned him yet [also] told him that he had spoken truthfully."** That indicated that [the man] knew and that he was not asking the question out of ignorance. He was asking the question while he, in fact, knew the answer. The proof for this is that he said, **"You have spoken truthfully."** That indicates that he knew the answer, so why was he asking?

ORIGINAL TEXT

قَالَ: فَأَخْبِرْنِي عَنِ الإِيمَانِ. قَالَ: أَنْ تُؤْمِنَ بِاللهِ، وَ مَلَائِكَتِهِ،
وَ كُتُبِهِ، وَ رُسُلِهِ، وَ الْيَوْمِ الآخِرِ، وَ تُؤْمِنَ بِالْقَدَرِ خَيْرِهِ وَ شَرِّهِ.
قَالَ: صَدَّقْتَ.

"He said, 'Inform me about *al-īmān*,' so he ﷺ said, 'It is that you believe in Allāh, His angels, His Books, His messengers, the Last Day, and that you believe in *al-qadar*, its good and its evil.' So he said, 'You have spoken truthfully.'"

EXPLANATION

He said, **"Inform me about *al-īmān*."** So the Prophet ﷺ stated: **"It is that you believe in Allāh, His angels, His Books, His messengers, the Last Day, and that you believe in *al-qadar*, its good and its evil."**

He ﷺ mentioned to him the six pillars of *al-īmān* after he had mentioned to him the pillars of *al-islām*. When *al-islām* and *al-īmān* are mentioned together, then *al-islām* means the outward actions and *al-īmān* means the inward actions (the actions of the heart and that which it establishes from affirmation and knowledge). And it is a must that one has *al-islām* and *al-īmān* together. *Al-islām* is the outward actions and *al-īmān* is the inward actions, due to his statement ﷺ:

اَلْإِسْلَامُ عَلَانِيَّةٌ وَ الْإِيمَانُ فِي الْقَلْبِ.

***Al-islām* is apparent and *al-īmān* is within the heart.**[27]

If they are mentioned together, then each of them has a specific meaning, while if one of them is mentioned [alone], then the other is included in it. If *al-īmān* is mentioned alone, then *al-islām* is included in it, and if *al-islām* is mentioned alone, then *al-īmān* is included in it, because *al-islām* is not correct without *īmān*, and *īmān* is not correct without *islām*. It is a must that a person has both of them, so they are inseparable. Due to this, it is said that *islām* and *īmān* are from the verbs which separate if they are brought together, and are brought together if they are separated. Meaning: They each include the other because they are inseparable, and one of them cannot be separated from the other.

So, he (Jibrīl) asked him about the apparent actions and about the inward actions, and he ﷺ clarified to him the pillars of each one from *al-islām* and *al-īmān*.

[27] Aḥmad reported it (vol. 19/374, #12381) from the *ḥadīth* of Anas ؓ.

ORIGINAL TEXT

قَالَ: أَخْبِرْنِي عَنِ الْإِحْسَانِ: قَالَ: أَنْ تَعْبُدَ اللهَ كَأَنَّكَ تَرَاهُ، فَإِنْ لَمْ تَكُنْ تَرَاهُ، فَإِنَّهُ يَرَاكَ. قَالَ: فَأَخْبِرْنِي عَنِ السَّاعَةِ. قَالَ: مَا الْمَسْؤُولُ عَنْهَا بِأَعْلَمَ مِنَ السَّائِلِ.

"So he said, 'Inform me about *al-iḥsān*.' He ﷺ said, 'It is that you worship Allāh as though you see Him, and even though you do not see Him, surely He sees you.' He said, 'Inform me about the Hour.' He ﷺ said, 'The one being asked knows no more about it than the questioner.'"

EXPLANATION

[Jibrīl] said, **"Inform me about *al-iḥsān*,"** so he ﷺ said, **"It is that you worship Allāh..."** It has preceded that *al-muḥsin* is the one who worships Allāh upon *al-mushāhadah* (i.e., as if he sees Allāh) and certainty as if he sees Allāh. Or he worships Him upon *al-murāqabah* (being mindful that Allāh sees him), which means that he knows Allāh sees him, so he perfects the action. This is because Allāh is watching him. So, the *muḥsin* worships Allāh either upon *al-mushāhadah* within the heart—and this is the most complete—or upon *al-murāqabah,* and he knows that Allāh sees him in any place or in any action that he does. This is *al-iḥsān*.

[Jibrīl] said, **"You have spoken truthfully. Inform me about the Hour."** Meaning, about the establishment of the Hour—when is it? No one knows the answer to this question except Allāh ﷻ, because none knows the prescribed time for the establishment of the Hour except Allāh عز وجل.

We know that the Hour will be established, and we do not doubt this. He who doubts this is a disbeliever. We know that the Hour will be established and that it is inevitable. However, Allāh has not informed us of the time when the Hour will be established, and He has not clarified it to us. He has kept the knowledge of it to Himself. The Most High has said:

﴿ إِنَّ اللَّهَ عِندَهُ عِلْمُ السَّاعَةِ ﴾

Verily, Allāh! With Him (alone) is the knowledge of the Hour.

[Sūrah Luqmān 31:34]

The Most High has said:

﴿ يَسْأَلُونَكَ عَنِ السَّاعَةِ أَيَّانَ مُرْسَاهَا ۖ قُلْ إِنَّمَا عِلْمُهَا عِندَ رَبِّي ۖ لَا يُجَلِّيهَا لِوَقْتِهَا إِلَّا هُوَ ﴾

They ask you about the Hour (Day of Resurrection): "When will be its appointed time?" Say: "The knowledge thereof is with my Lord (alone). None can reveal its time but He."

[Sūrah al-A'rāf 7:187]

He ﷻ is the one who knows it. Likewise, The Most High has said:

﴿ وَعِندَهُ مَفَاتِحُ الْغَيْبِ لَا يَعْلَمُهَا إِلَّا هُوَ ﴾

And with Him are the keys of the *ghayb* (all that is hidden); none knows them but He.

[Sūrah al-An'ām 6:59]

And from it (the *ghayb*) is the time of the establishment of the Hour. He ﷺ said to Jibrīl, **"The one being asked knows no more about it than the questioner."**

Meaning, neither of us know when the Hour will be established. Allāh ﷻ has not allowed anyone to know this—not the angels nor the messengers, or anyone else. Rather, He has kept the knowledge of it to Himself.

ORIGINAL TEXT

قَالَ: فَأَخْبِرْنِي عَنْ أَمَارَاتِهَا: قَالَ: أَنْ تَلِدَ الْأَمَةُ رَبَّتَهَا.

"He said, 'So, inform me about its signs.' He ﷺ said, 'The slave

lady shall give birth to her master...'"

EXPLANATION

[Jibrīl] said, **"Inform me about its signs."** *Al-amārāt* is the plural of *amārah*, which means "a sign." As for *al-imārah* with a *kasrah*, then it means "leadership." He said, **"Inform me about its signs."** Meaning: the signs which indicate that its establishment is near.

Yes, the Hour has signs. Allāh ﷻ has clarified them, and there are minor signs and major signs. There are those which are intermediate; and there are signs of the approaching of the Hour, which come with the establishment of the Hour and are near to its establishment. As for the other signs, they are introductory signs.

The scholars say that the signs of the Hour fit into three categories. They are:

1) Minor and introductory signs.

2) Intermediate signs.

3) Major signs.

The minor signs and the intermediate signs have already occurred, or most of them have occurred. As for the major signs—the appearance of the Dajjāl, the descent of 'Īsā عليه السلام, the emergence of the Beast, and the emergence of Ya'jūj and Ma'jūj—these occur with the establishment of the Hour and come along with it.

So, he said, **"Inform me about its signs."** Since its signs are known, the Messenger ﷺ responded to him and said, **"The slave lady shall give birth to her master."** This is from the signs of the Hour. The slave lady is the woman who is owned, and her master is her mistress.

ORIGINAL TEXT

وَ أَنْ تَرَى الْحُفَاةَ الْعُرَاةَ الْعَالَةَ رِعَاءَ الشَّاءِ يَتَطَاوَلُونَ فِي الْبُنْيَانِ.

"'...and you shall see the barefoot, naked, destitute shepherds competing in the construction of tall buildings.'"

EXPLANATION

Some of the explainers have stated that the meaning of this—and Allāh knows best—is that, at the end of time, there shall be an abundance of concubinage, meaning an abundance of intercourse with female servants (i.e., the female servants that are owned). So, they shall give birth to daughters such that their daughter shall be free and be a master and owner of her mother. It is also said that it means that there shall be an abundance of disobedience. So, the daughter shall act as if she is a master over her mother.

He said **"and you shall see the barefoot"**: This is a second sign. He said **"barefoot"**; these are those who do not have shoes due to poverty and destitution. He said **"naked"**; these are those who do not have any clothing. He said **"destitute"**; these are the poor. He said **"shepherds"**; this is the plural of "shepherd," and they are those who herd sheep. These people, in their origin, live in the valleys, in homes which they move from place to place. At the end of time, they shall inhabit the cities and build castles and lofty emirates. This is from the signs of the Hour: that the Bedouins shall move to the cities and begin erecting buildings, competing therein and embellishing them, while this is not the norm for them. They shall become rich, refined, successful people. This is from the signs of the Hour.

As you know, the Messenger ﷺ did not speak from his own desire, and you know now how the state of the people is. The situations have changed, and the poor have become rich and cultured. The Bedouins have taken residence in the cities, and they have built and erected buildings. This is a testament to what the Messenger of Allāh ﷺ has stated.

ORIGINAL TEXT

قَالَ: فَمَضَى، فَلَبِثْتُ مَلِيًّا. فَقَالَ: يَا عُمَرُ أَتَدْرِي مَنِ السَّائِلُ؟

قُلْتُ: اللهُ وَ رَسُولُهُ أَعْلَمُ. قَالَ: هَذَا جِبْرِيلُ أَتَاكُمْ يُعَلِّمُكُمْ أَمْرَ دِينِكُمْ.

He ['Umar] said, "So, he left and we stayed there for some time. Then he ﷺ said to me, ''Umar, do you know who the questioner was?' I said, 'Allāh and His Messenger know best.' He said, 'That was Jibrīl; he came to you to teach you your religion.'"

EXPLANATION

He said, **"So, he left and we remained for some time"**: Meaning, a short while.

The Prophet ﷺ said, **"'Umar, do you know who the questioner was?"** or he said, **"Do you all know who the questioner was?"**

In another narration, it is mentioned that the Prophet ﷺ said, **"Bring him back to me."**[28] They sought after him but were not able to find him. So, he ﷺ said, **"That was Jibrīl; he came to you to teach you your religion."** Meaning: This individual who entered and asked these questions was Jibrīl عليه السلام, and he came in the form of a man, as he has been described, for the purpose of teaching the attendees the affairs of their religion by way of question and answer.

This *ḥadīth* indicates a number of great affairs:

The First Affair: The religion is classified into three levels:

1) *Al-islām*

2) *Al-īmān*

3) *Al-iḥsān*

Each level is higher than the one that comes before it; and each level has pillars—the pillars of *islām* and the pillars of *īmān*, and

[28] An-Nasā'ī reported it in *Al-Kubrā* (5/380, #5852) from the *ḥadīth* of Ibn 'Umar رضي الله عنهما. Also, Ibn Ḥibbān (#173) and ad-Dāraquṭnī (vol. 3/341, #2708) reported it from the *ḥadīth* of 'Umar bin al-Khaṭṭāb رضي الله عنه.

al-iḥsān is one pillar.

The Second Affair: It contains teaching by way of question and answer. This is an exemplary method of teaching because it draws attention, and it makes one ready to receive knowledge by him asking and preparing his mind for the answer. Then he receives the answer while he is ready for it. This is more firm.

The Third Affair: Within the *ḥadīth*, there is evidence that if one is asked about knowledge that he does not know, it is upon him to say, "Allāh and His Messenger know best." He attributes the knowledge to the one who knows it, and he does not speak with the answer while he does not know it and [is only] guessing. This is not permissible.

When the Messenger ﷺ was asked about the Hour, he said, **"The one being asked knows no more about it than the questioner."** And when he said to the Companions, **"Do you know who the questioner was?"** They did not know him, so they said, **"Allāh and His Messenger know best."** This indicates that it is not permissible to guess regarding the affairs of the legislation and the affairs of the religion because this is from placing undue burden upon oneself. However, he who has knowledge may respond, and he who does not have knowledge should say, "Allāh knows best"; and he who says, "I do not know," has answered.

Imām Mālik رحمه الله was asked 40 questions, and he responded to only six of them. For the rest of them, he said, "I don't know." So the questioner said to him, "I came from such-and-such place, and I traveled and became weary in my travel, and you say, 'I don't know'?!" Imām Mālik said, "Get on your mount and return to the land from which you came, and say, 'I asked Mālik and he said, 'I don't know.'"

It is not a defect for an individual to say, "I don't know," if he does not know an answer regarding the affairs of the legislation, even if he is a scholar. The Messenger ﷺ said, **"The one being asked knows no more about it than the questioner."** And when he

ﷺ was asked some questions about which he had not received revelation from Allāh عَزَّوَجَلَّ, then he would wait until the revelation descended from Allāh عَزَّوَجَلَّ.

Have you not read when Allāh says in the Qur'ān, for example, "They ask you about such-and-such," and "They ask you about so-and-so. Say so-and-so." For example, Allāh says:

﴿يَسْأَلُونَكَ عَنِ الْخَمْرِ وَالْمَيْسِرِ ۖ قُلْ فِيهِمَا إِثْمٌ كَبِيرٌ﴾

They ask you (O Muḥammad) concerning alcoholic drink and gambling. Say: "In them is a great sin..."

[Sūrah al-Baqarah 2:219]

And He said:

﴿يَسْأَلُونَكَ عَنِ الْأَهِلَّةِ ۖ قُلْ هِيَ مَوَاقِيتُ لِلنَّاسِ وَالْحَجِّ﴾

They ask you (O Muḥammad) about the new moons. Say: "These are signs to mark fixed periods of time for mankind and for the pilgrimage."

[Sūrah al-Baqarah 2:189]

So, the Messenger ﷺ, when he was asked about something that he did not have the answer for, would wait until the revelation had descended upon him from Allāh. Thus, it is even more incumbent on other than him to wait until he asks someone else, or until he researches the issue in the books of the people of knowledge, so that he may acquire the response.

As for being hasty, then this contains great danger, and in it is an evil manner with Allāh عَزَّوَجَلَّ, because the one who responds is responding regarding the legislation of Allāh. He says, "Allāh has made permissible such-and-such," or, "Allāh has made impermissible such-and-such," or, "He has legislated such-and-such." So the affair is very dangerous.

The Fourth Affair in the *ḥadīth* is evidence for the etiquettes of the learner. Jibrīl—the leader of the angels—sat in front of the Messenger of Allāh ﷺ and connected his knees to the knees of the Messenger ﷺ, and he placed his hands upon his thighs. He asked him with proper etiquette. This was so he could teach the people how to conduct themselves with the scholars. This is some of what the *ḥadīth* indicates.

The Fifth Affair: Clarification of some of the signs of the Hour. And he mentioned two signs; [one of them is] that the slave lady shall give birth to her master. Some of the scholars say that the meaning of "the slave lady shall give birth to her master" is that there shall be an abundance of disobedience in the last days, to the point that it will be as if the daughter is a master over her mother, commanding her, prohibiting her, and mistreating her.

09

The Third Principle: Knowledge of Our Prophet Muḥammad

ORIGINAL TEXT

إِسْمُهُ، وَ نَسَبُهُ، وَ نَشْأَتُهُ:

اَلْأَصْلُ الثَّالِثُ: مَعْرِفَةُ نَبِيِّكُمْ مُحَمَّدٍ - صَلَّى اللهُ عَلَيْهِ وَ سَلَّمَ.

His name, his lineage and his upbringing:

The Third Principle: Knowledge of our Prophet Muḥammad ﷺ.

EXPLANATION

His statement *"The Third Principle"*: Meaning, the third of the three fundamental principles, because the Shaykh رحمه الله mentioned in the beginning of the treatise that it is obligatory upon each Muslim, male and female, to have knowledge of these three principles. And they are: knowledge of Allāh, knowledge of the religion of al-Islām, and knowledge of His Prophet Muḥammad ﷺ with the evidences.

As for the first and second principles, the explanation and clarification of them, along with their evidences, has preceded. The third principle is knowledge of the Prophet Muḥammad ﷺ, because the Prophet ﷺ was the medium between Allāh and His creation in the conveyance of His religion and His message.

Therefore, is it obligatory to have knowledge of him ﷺ; otherwise, how can you follow someone whom you do not know? It is a must that you know him by way of his name, by way of the land he was born in and brought up in, and by way of the land he migrated to. You should also know the length of his lifespan ﷺ.

One should also know the categories of his lifespan ﷺ and the categories of the time frame wherein he stayed in the *dunyā;* you should know them as well as what came before prophethood and what came after it, and what came before the Hijrah and what came after it. You should know how the revelation to him ﷺ began, when the revelation began, which verse indicates his prophethood, and which verse indicates his messengership. There shall come verses which indicate his prophethood and verses which indicate his being dispatched as a messenger. It is a must that you know this, and that you know his lineage; meaning, which tribe he is from. The Arabs are of different tribes, and he was an Arab, without a doubt.

Therefore, it is a must to know these things about the Messenger ﷺ by studying the verses and the *aḥādīth* which are connected to these issues, and that you look into the *sīrah* of the Messenger ﷺ and his *da'wah* so that you may know these affairs about the Prophet you are commanded to follow and take as an example.

ORIGINAL TEXT

وَ هُوَ مُحَمَّدُ بْنُ عَبْدِ اللهِ بْنِ عَبْدِ الْمُطَّلِبِ بْنِ هَاشِمٍ، وَ هَاشِمٌ مِنْ قُرَيْشٍ، وَ قُرَيْشٌ مِنَ الْعَرَبِ، وَالْعَرَبُ مِنْ ذُرِّيَّةِ إِسْمَاعِيلَ بْنِ إِبْرَاهِيمَ الْخَلِيلِ، عَلَيْهِ وَ عَلَى نَبِيِّنَا أَفْضَلُ الصَّلَاةِ وَ السَّلَامِ.

He is Muḥammad bin 'Abdillāh bin 'Abdul-Muṭṭalib bin Hāshim, who was from the Quraysh tribe. The Quraysh are from the Arabs, and the Arabs are from the descendants of Ismā'īl, the son of Ibrāhīm al-Khalīl, upon him and upon our Prophet be the best prayers and peace.

EXPLANATION

This is his name and his lineage. His name is Muḥammad ﷺ, and he has other names besides Muḥammad. However, the most popular of his names is Muḥammad. Allāh mentioned that in the Qur'ān in a number of verses. From them:

﴿ مُّحَمَّدٌ رَّسُولُ اللَّهِ ﴾

Muḥammad is the Messenger of Allāh.

[Sūrah al-Fat'ḥ 48:29]

Likewise, His statement:

﴿ وَمَا مُحَمَّدٌ إِلَّا رَسُولٌ قَدْ خَلَتْ مِن قَبْلِهِ الرُّسُلُ ﴾

Muḥammad is no more than a messenger, and indeed (many) messengers have passed away before him.

[Sūrah Āli 'Imrān 3:144]

And His statement:

﴿ مَّا كَانَ مُحَمَّدٌ أَبَا أَحَدٍ مِّن رِّجَالِكُمْ ﴾

Muḥammad is not the father of any man among you…

[Sūrah al-Aḥzāb 33:40]

Also, His statement:

﴿ وَالَّذِينَ آمَنُوا وَعَمِلُوا الصَّالِحَاتِ وَآمَنُوا بِمَا نُزِّلَ عَلَىٰ مُحَمَّدٍ وَهُوَ الْحَقُّ مِن رَّبِّهِمْ ﴾

But those who believe and do righteous good deeds, and believe in that which is sent down to

Muḥammad, for it is the truth from their Lord.

[Sūrah Muḥammad 47:2]

So, Allāh mentioned his name as "Muḥammad" in a number of verses.

"Aḥmad" is also one of his names. Allāh mentioned it in His statement as a tiding given by al-Masīḥ ('Īsā عليه السلام) wherein He said:

﴿ وَإِذْ قَالَ عِيسَى ابْنُ مَرْيَمَ يَا بَنِي إِسْرَائِيلَ إِنِّي رَسُولُ اللَّهِ إِلَيْكُم مُّصَدِّقًا لِّمَا بَيْنَ يَدَيَّ مِنَ التَّوْرَاةِ وَمُبَشِّرًا بِرَسُولٍ يَأْتِي مِن بَعْدِي اسْمُهُ أَحْمَدُ ﴾

And (remember) when 'Īsā (Jesus), son of Maryam (Mary), said, "O Children of Israel! I am the messenger of Allāh unto you confirming the Tawrāh [(Torah) which came] before me, and giving glad tidings of a messenger to come after me, whose name shall be Aḥmad."

[Sūrah aṣ-Ṣaff 61:6]

So, he is Muḥammad and he is Aḥmad. The meaning of these names is that he is abundant in his praise ﷺ and abundant in the qualities for which he is praised.

Also from his names are: the Prophet of Mercy, and the Prophet of *al-Malḥamah*, meaning: fighting in Allāh's cause. He is also called al-Ḥāshir (the Gatherer) and al-'Āqib (the Last), for he is the one after whose sending the people are gathered, because he is the last of the messengers ﷺ. So, there is nothing after him except the establishment of the Hour. After his messengership, the Hour will be established and the people will be gathered for reward and recompense, and whoever wants to review these affairs should return to the book *Jalā' al-Afhām fiṣ-Ṣalāh was-Salām 'alā Khayr al-Anām* by Imām Ibn al-Qayyim رحمه الله.

As for his lineage: He is Muḥammad, the son of 'Abdullāh, the son of 'Abdul-Muṭṭalib, the son of Hāshim, the son of 'Abd-Manāf, the son of Quṣayy, the son of Kilāb. And he is from the tribe of the Quraysh, which is the noblest tribe, and the Quraysh are from the descendants of Ismā'īl عليه السلام.

The Arabs are of two categories, according to that which is well-known: the Arabs who are al-'Āribah (original Arabs), and they are the Qaḥṭāniyyah; and then there are the Arabs who are Musta'ribah (Arabized), and they are the 'Adnāniyyah, from the descendants of Ismā'īl عليه السلام who was the son of Ibrāhīm al-Khalīl.

They are named "the Musta'ribah" because they learned Arabic from the Arabs who are 'Āribah. When Jurhum descended in Makkah after the *hijrah* of Ismā'īl and his mother while Ismā'īl was a small boy, and when they found the water of Zamzam, they descended and requested to reside there with Hājar, and that she permit them to take from the water. Ismā'īl عليه السلام was a suckling baby at that time. Then he was cultivated, raised, and learned Arabic from the tribe of Jurhum, and they were Arabs who were 'Āribah; and he married from the tribe of Jurhum and there came from him a progeny who learned Arabic and grew up amongst the Arabs, so they became Arabs who were Musta'ribah, and they are al-'Adnāniyyah. As for the Arabs who are al-'Āribah, then they are al-Qaḥṭāniyyah, and their origin is from Yemen.

Some of the scholars say that the Arabs who are al-'Āribah are of two categories: the Arabs who have become extinct and the Arabs who still remain. The Arabs who have become extinct have died off, and they are the people of Nūḥ, 'Ād, Thamūd, and Shu'ayb. As for the Arabs who still exist, then they are divided into the Arabs who are 'Āribah and the Arabs who are Musta'ribah. They are the Arabs who still remain. And the Prophet ﷺ is from Banū Hāshim, and Hāshim is from the descendants of Ismā'īl عليه السلام.

His name is Muḥammad, the son of 'Abdullāh, the son of 'Abdul-Muṭṭalib. As for 'Abdul-Muṭṭalib, this was not his actual name; his name was Shaybah. However, he was named 'Abdul-Muṭṭalib because his uncle al-Muṭṭalib bin 'Abd-Manāf brought him with him from al-Madīnah while he was a child, from amongst his maternal uncles, Banun-Najjār. So, when the people saw him, black from the journey, they thought that he was a servant who was owned by al-Muṭṭalib, so they said "'Abdul-Muṭṭalib bin Hāshim bin 'Abd-Manāf." And 'Abd-Manāf had four children: Hāshim (who was the great-grandfather of the Messenger ﷺ), al-Muṭṭalib, 'Abd-Shams, and Nawfal.

Banū Hāshim is referred to as al-Hāshimiyūn and Banul-Muṭṭalib. They are also called al-Muṭṭalibiyūn. As for 'Abd-Shams, then from them is 'Uthmān رضي الله عنه. From them, as well, are Banū Umayyah; they are from Banū 'Abd-Shams. Nawfal, likewise, has a lineage from them: Jubayr bin Muṭ'im and Ḥakīm bin Ḥizām.

Ibrāhīm عليه السلام had Ismā'īl, who was his oldest child, and he is a forefather of the Arabs who are 'Adnāniyyah; and Is'ḥāq is the forefather of the Children of Isrā'īl. All of the prophets are from the children of Is'ḥāq, with the exception of our Prophet Muḥammad ﷺ; he is from the descendants of Ismā'īl, and he is the seal of the prophets.

As for his birth: He ﷺ was born in the Year of the Elephant. It is the year wherein Abrahah, the ruler of Yemen, was deputized by the king of Ethiopia to destroy the Ka'bah, and he came with a magnificent elephant. When he arrived at a place referred to as al-Mughammas, and there did not remain anything except that he should enter Makkah and destroy the Ka'bah, the people of Makkah fled and ascended the mountains because they had no ability to repel him.

So he wanted to go towards Makkah, but the elephant stopped and refused to stand up. Allāh had restrained it. And when he had turned to a direction other than the direction of Makkah, it stood and began walking. When he turned it around to face Makkah, it stopped and was not able to walk. Likewise, they saw a group of birds coming from the direction of the sea, carrying stones. Each bird had two stones—a stone in his beak and a stone in his claws—and they threw them so that a stone would strike a man on the top of his head and exit through his bottom, cutting him into two halves. So, Allāh destroyed them, and Allāh sent revelation regarding them while mentioning the Quraysh in Sūrah al-Fīl, wherein He said:

﴿ أَلَمْ تَرَ كَيْفَ فَعَلَ رَبُّكَ بِأَصْحَابِ الْفِيلِ ۝١ أَلَمْ يَجْعَلْ كَيْدَهُمْ فِي تَضْلِيلٍ ۝٢ وَأَرْسَلَ عَلَيْهِمْ طَيْرًا أَبَابِيلَ ۝٣ تَرْمِيهِم بِحِجَارَةٍ مِّن سِجِّيلٍ ۝٤ فَجَعَلَهُمْ كَعَصْفٍ مَّأْكُولٍ ۝٥ ﴾

Have you (O Muḥammad ﷺ) not seen how your Lord dealt with the owners of the elephant? Did He not make their plot go astray? And sent against them birds, in flocks, striking them with stones of *sijjīl* (baked clay). And made them like an empty field of stalks (of which the corn has been eaten up by cattle).

[Sūrah al-Fīl 105:1-5]

They struck them with stones from the Hellfire, and refuge is sought with Allāh. They became like straw which had been eaten by animals and then defecated out. This was the story of the elephant. So, Allāh defended His Sacred House and destroyed this tyrant.

And in this year, Muḥammad ﷺ was born. Signs appeared along with his birth: light appeared with him which caused the castles of Shām to shine; and the night of his birth, the idols shook, and the throne room of Kisrā shook and some balconies from it fell down. And the night that the Prophet ﷺ was born, there were signs of the descending of the Prophet ﷺ as a Prophet. The *jinn* and the devils were thrown into commotion on this great night.

He was born in a place referred to as a tract near the Ka'bah. He was born in Makkah, but no firm proof has been established for the exact location of the house.

ORIGINAL TEXT

وَ لَهُ مِنَ الْعُمْرِ ثَلَاثٌ وَ سِتُّونَ سَنَةً، مِنْهَا أَرْبَعُونَ قَبْلَ النُّبُوَّةِ وَ

ثَلَاثٌ وَ عِشْرُونَ نَبِيًّا وَ رَسُولاً، نُبِّئ بِاقْرَأْ.

He lived for 63 years: 40 before prophethood and 23 as a Prophet and Messenger. He was commissioned as a Prophet with (the revelation) of "*Iqra'*" ("Read!" [i.e., Sūrah al-'Alaq]).

EXPLANATION

He ﷺ was born in Makkah, and he was suckled amongst Banū Sa'd by Ḥalīmah as-Sa'diyyah. His father 'Abdullāh died while he was in the womb of his mother, then his mother died a short time after his birth. Hence, he was taken care of by Umm Ayman al-Ḥabashiyyah, whom he had inherited from his father, and he went to the care of his grandfather. Then 'Abdul-Muṭṭalib died, so he was transferred to the care of his paternal uncle, Abū Ṭālib.

He ﷺ lived for 40 years before prophethood, being well-known for trustworthiness, truthfulness, and nobility. He avoided the worship of idols and he avoided the consumption of intoxicants. He did not used to do what the people of the Pre-Islamic Days of Ignorance used to do. Rather, he used to go out to the cave of Ḥirā' and worship therein for a number of days; he would worship Allāh upon the religion of Ibrāhīm, upon *tawḥīd*.

Then, when he ﷺ had reached 40 years of age, the revelation descended upon him by way of Jibrīl عليه السلام coming to him in the cave of Ḥirā' and saying to him, "Read!" He said, "I am not one who reads." Meaning: "I do not read well." So, Jibrīl pressed him severely, then he released him and said, "Read!" He said, "I am not one who reads." Then he pressed him a second time, then he released him and said to him, "Read!" He said, "I am not one who reads." So Jibrīl said to him:

﴿ اقْرَأْ بِاسْمِ رَبِّكَ الَّذِي خَلَقَ ① خَلَقَ الْإِنسَانَ مِنْ عَلَقٍ ② ﴾

Read! In the name of your Lord, who has created (all that exists); has created man from a clot (a piece

of thick, coagulated blood).

[Sūrah al-'Alaq 96:1-2]

This was his prophethood. Allāh informed him with the revelation of *"Iqra'"* (Sūrah al-'Alaq). Meaning: He made him a Prophet. Then he went to his home, shaking from fear, because he had encountered something unknown, a frightening affair. There, he found his wife Khadījah ﵂; so she covered him and comforted him, saying to him, "No; by Allāh, Allāh will never humiliate you, for you join the ties of the womb, you honor the guests, you take care of all (people), and you take care of those who have been afflicted with calamities."

So, she prepared him and took him to her cousin Waraqah bin Nawfal; he was a man who was devoted to worship, and he used to read the previous scriptures, worshiping Allāh ﷻ by way of this. So, when [the Prophet] informed him of what he saw, he said, "This was an-Nāmūs, who descended upon Mūsā." Meaning: Jibrīl ﵇.

The Descending of the Revelation Upon Him

ORIGINAL TEXT

وَ أُرْسِلَ بِالْمُدَّثِّرِ، وَ بَلَدُهُ مَكَّةُ، وَ هَاجَرَ إِلَى الْمَدِينَةِ، بَعَثَهُ اللهُ بِالنِّذَارَةِ عَنِ الشِّرْكِ، وَ يَدْعُو إِلَى التَّوْحِيدِ، وَ الدَّلِيلُ قَوْلُهُ تَعَالَى: ﴿ يَا أَيُّهَا الْمُدَّثِّرُ ﴿١﴾ قُمْ فَأَنذِرْ ﴿٢﴾ وَرَبَّكَ فَكَبِّرْ ﴿٣﴾ وَثِيَابَكَ فَطَهِّرْ ﴿٤﴾ وَالرُّجْزَ فَاهْجُرْ ﴿٥﴾ وَلَا تَمْنُن تَسْتَكْثِرُ ﴿٦﴾ وَلِرَبِّكَ فَاصْبِرْ ﴿٧﴾ ﴾.

He was commissioned as the Messenger with the revelation of Sūrah al-Muddath'thir.

His homeland was Makkah, and he migrated to Madīnah. Allāh sent him to warn against *shirk* and to call to *tawḥīd*. The proof is the statement of Allāh the Exalted:

O you (Muḥammad ﷺ) enveloped (in garments)!

Arise and warn! And your Lord (Allāh) magnify! And your garments purify! And keep away from *ar-rujz* (the idols)! And give not a thing in order to have more (or consider not your deeds of Allāh's obedience as a favor to Allāh). And be patient for the sake of your Lord (i.e., perform your duty to Allāh)!

[Sūrah al-Muddath'thir 74:1-7]

EXPLANATION

Then the statement of Allāh, the Exalted, was revealed to him:

﴿ يَا أَيُّهَا الْمُدَّثِّرُ ۝١ قُمْ فَأَنذِرْ ۝٢ ﴾

O you (Muḥammad ﷺ) enveloped (in garments)! Arise and warn!

[Sūrah al-Muddath'thir 74:1-2]

This was the dispatching; and this is the meaning of the statement of the Shaykh wherein he said that he was commissioned as a Prophet with the revelation of *"Iqra'"* (i.e., Sūrah al-'Alaq), and he was commissioned as a Messenger with the revelation of al-Muddath'thir.

The difference between a prophet and a messenger is that the prophet is one to whom a legislation is revealed, but he is not commanded to convey it. The messenger is one to whom a revelation is revealed and he is commanded to convey it. The clarification of that is in the fact that the messenger receives legislation and a book.

So, he was commissioned as a Prophet with the revelation of *"Iqra'"*, and he was commissioned as a Messenger with the revelation of al-Muddath'thir when he was 40 years old.

Likewise were the prophets. The prophet is one who is sent with the legislation of one who came before him and the book of one who came before him; and some issues are revealed to him, as in the case of the prophets of Banū Isrā'īl after Mūsā.

The meaning of *al-muddath'thir* is "one who is covered"; he ﷺ was afflicted with fright, so he said, "Cover me, cover me." Meaning: "Wrap me up." So Allāh revealed to him:

﴿ يَا أَيُّهَا الْمُدَّثِّرُ ۝١ قُمْ فَأَنذِرْ ۝٢ وَرَبَّكَ فَكَبِّرْ ۝٣ ﴾

O you (Muḥammad ﷺ) enveloped (in garments)! Arise and warn! And your Lord (Allāh) magnify!

[Sūrah al-Muddath'thir 74:1-3]

Meaning: Magnify Him.

﴿ وَثِيَابَكَ فَطَهِّرْ ﴾

And your garments purify!

[Sūrah al-Muddath'thir 74:4]

Meaning: Purify your actions from *shirk*, for the actions are referred to as garments. Allāh the Exalted said:

﴿ وَلِبَاسُ التَّقْوَىٰ ذَٰلِكَ خَيْرٌ ﴾

And the garment of righteousness, that is better.

[Sūrah al-A'rāf 7:26]

Here He referred to *at-taqwā* as a garment. And His statement "***ar-rujz***": The meaning of *rujz* is idols.

Concerning His statement **"And keep away"**: Meaning, abandon them and stay far from them.

So, Allāh sent him [with revelation] when he was 40 years old; he remained in Makkah for 13 years calling the people to *tawḥīd* and the abandonment of worshiping idols. And there occurred disputes between him and the pagans, and they afflicted him—as well as those who believed in him and followed him—with harm. There occurred, as well, afflictions from the pagans throughout the course of the 13 years.

Three years before the Hijrah, he was taken by night to Bayt al-Maqdis, and he ascended to the heavens; and five prayers were made obligatory upon him. So, he prayed in Makkah for a period of three years; then, the Quraysh conspired to kill him and to eradicate him. So Allāh permitted him to migrate to al-Madīnah. He migrated to al-Madīnah after seeking asylum with the Anṣār in the first Pledge of al-'Aqabah and the second Pledge of al-'Aqabah. He migrated to al-Madīnah and remained there for 10 years. This makes the total length [of his prophethood] 23 years.

After prophethood came to him, he ﷺ lived for a period of 23 years: 13 in Makkah, wherein he established the call to *at-tawḥīd,* and 10 years in al-Madīnah. Then Allāh caused him to die at the beginning of his 63rd year ﷺ.

So, the period of his life as a Messenger was 23 years, and this was a blessing which Allāh ﷻ bestowed upon him. This magnificent knowledge, this *jihād*, and him remaining for this long period of 23 years was from the signs of Allāh ﷻ, and it was from the blessings of this Prophet ﷺ, the blessings of his *da'wah,* and the blessings of the revelations which were revealed to him. Before all of this, he was under the care of Allāh ﷻ. He was the one who cared for him and He was the one who protected him, helped him, and supported him such that his *da'wah* reached the east and the west; and all praises are due to Allāh, Lord of all that exists.

Concerning his statement, *"Allāh sent him to warn against shirk and to call to tawḥīd"*: This was his *da'wah* ﷺ—warning against *shirk* and calling to *tawḥīd,* and this is what is obligatory for the callers to traverse upon in their *da'wah*; they must center their *da'wah* around warning against *shirk* and calling to *tawḥīd* before everything else. Otherwise, their call will not be upon the methodology of the Messenger ﷺ.

Allāh sent the Messenger to warn against *shirk* and call to *at-tawḥīd*, so it is a must that this is established first; then, after that, one may direct attention to the other affairs. This is because affairs will not be rectified except with the existence of *at-tawḥīd.* If the person were to abandon fornication, intoxicants, and stealing, and implement every virtue from righteous actions and manners, but he did not abandon *shirk*, there would be no benefit in any of these affairs, nor would they benefit him. But if the individual were to be safe from *shirk,* and he has with him major sins that are less than *shirk,* then he has hope that Allāh will forgive him.

So, *at-tawḥīd* is the basis and the foundation, and there is no safety except by way of the existence of *at-tawḥīd* first and foremost. Due to that, it is obligatory to make it the central focus and to always give it the utmost care and concern, to call the people to it, to teach it to the people, and to clarify to them the meaning of *at-tawḥīd* and the meaning of *ash-shirk*.

It is a must that the Muslim knows this affair, actualizes it, and comprehends it himself so that he does not fall into anything from *shirk,* and so that nothing from *at-tawḥīd* should be lost. Therefore, this affair is a must, and it is a must that the *da'wah* be predicated upon this foundation.

The Length of the Da'wah in Makkah

ORIGINAL TEXT

أَخَذَ عَلَى هَذَا عَشَرَ سِنِينَ يَدْعُو إِلَى التَّوْحِيدِ...

He took to this for 10 years, calling to *at-tawḥīd*...

EXPLANATION

His statement, "*He took to this for 10 years, calling to at-tawḥīd*": This means that he took to calling the people to *at-tawḥīd* and warning them against *ash-shirk* for a period of 10 years in Makkah, and he was calling to *at-tawḥīd* and prohibiting *ash-shirk* because they used to worship idols. The wisdom in Allāh sending him to Makkah was that Makkah was the mother of all towns to which other towns returned. Allāh ﷻ says:

﴿ وَمَا كَانَ رَبُّكَ مُهْلِكَ الْقُرَىٰ حَتَّىٰ يَبْعَثَ فِي أُمِّهَا رَسُولًا ﴾

And never will your Lord destroy the towns (populations) until He sends to their mother town a messenger…

[Sūrah al-Qaṣaṣ 28:59]

And the *umm* (mother) is the point of return which is referenced. So, the origin which is returned to is the *umm*.

﴿ هُنَّ أُمُّ الْكِتَابِ ﴾

They (the verses) are the (*umm*) foundation of the Book.

[Sūrah Āli 'Imrān 3:7]

Meaning: The foundation which the unclear verses are referred to. This is the case with Makkah, may Allāh ennoble it. It is the foundation which the people of the earth return to, and the Muslims and the provinces of the earth all return to Makkah, so it is the mother of towns. Meaning: It is the point of return.

Due to this, Allāh sent his Prophet ﷺ to Makkah because it is the mother of towns, and he remained therein for a period of 13 years, prohibiting the people of Makkah from *shirk* and commanding them with *tawḥīd*, because the people of Makkah were the example for other than them. Due to this, it is obligatory that Makkah remain the home of *at-tawḥīd* and a light post for the call to Allāh until the establishment of the Hour; and that it be distant from everything which opposes that. It must be distant from *shirk*, innovations, and superstitions, because the people always look to it—what is done there spreads throughout the world. So, if what is done there is that which is good, then good shall spread. And if what is done there is the opposite of that, then evil shall spread. Therefore, it is obligatory, always and forever, to purify Makkah. Due to this, Allāh ﷻ says:

﴿ وَعَهِدْنَا إِلَىٰ إِبْرَاهِيمَ وَإِسْمَاعِيلَ أَن طَهِّرَا بَيْتِيَ لِلطَّائِفِينَ وَالْعَاكِفِينَ وَالرُّكَّعِ السُّجُودِ ﴾

And We commanded Ibrāhīm (Abraham) and Ismā'īl (Ishmael) that they should purify My House (the Ka'bah in Makkah) for those who are circumambulating it, or staying (*i'tikāf*), or bowing, or prostrating themselves (there, in prayer).

[Sūrah al-Baqarah 2:125]

So, it is obligatory to purify Makkah from everything which opposes Islām so that the religion and the *da'wah* emanates from it to the eastern and western parts of the earth. This is because Allāh sent his Prophet there and he ﷺ began his *da'wah* in it.

The Prophet ﷺ remained in Makkah for a period of 13 years. For 10 years of it, he called to *at-tawḥīd* and prohibited *ash-shirk,* and he did not command with anything other than this. He did not command with prayer, *zakāh*, fasting, or Ḥajj; rather, his *da'wah* was limited to warning against *shirk* and commanding with *tawḥīd*, saying to them: "Say, *'Lā ilāha ill-Allāh,'* and you will be successful." And they would say:

﴿ أَجَعَلَ الْآلِهَةَ إِلَٰهًا وَاحِدًا ۖ إِنَّ هَٰذَا لَشَيْءٌ عُجَابٌ ﴾

"Has he made the *ālihah* (gods) (all) into one *ilāh* (God—Allāh)? Verily, this is a curious thing!"

[Sūrah Ṣād 38:5]

AL-ISRĀ' WAL-MI'RĀJ

ORIGINAL TEXT

...وَ بَعْدَ الْعَشْرِ عُرِجَ بِهِ إِلَى السَّمَاءِ، وَ فُرِضَتْ عَلَيْهِ الصَّلَوَاتُ الْخَمْسُ، وَ صَلَّى فِي مَكَّةَ ثَلَاثَ سِنِينَ.

...and after the 10th year, he was taken up to the heavens and the five prayers were made obligatory upon him. He prayed in Makkah for a period of 13 years.

EXPLANATION

His statement "*and after the 10th year, he was taken up to the heavens*": He ﷺ remained for a period of 10 years, prohibiting *shirk*, calling to *tawḥīd,* and laying down this foundation; then, in the 11th year, he was taken by night from Masjid al-Ḥarām to Masjid al-Aqṣā. The Most High has said:

﴿ سُبْحَانَ الَّذِي أَسْرَىٰ بِعَبْدِهِ لَيْلًا مِّنَ الْمَسْجِدِ الْحَرَامِ إِلَى الْمَسْجِدِ الْأَقْصَى ﴾

Glorified (and Exalted) be He (Allāh) who took His slave (Muḥammad ﷺ) for a journey by night from al-Masjid al-Ḥarām (in Makkah) to the farthest mosque (in Jerusalem).

[Sūrah al-Isrā' 17:1]

When he ﷺ was sleeping in the home of Umm Hāni', Jibrīl عليه السلام came to him with an animal referred to as al-Burāq, which was smaller than a female mule yet bigger than a donkey, and its footsteps would be as far as the eye can see. He was made to ride upon it and was taken on its back to Bayt al-Maqdis in one night. The word *asrā* is from the word *as-sirā,* and it means "a journey that takes place at night." This is one of the things with which he ﷺ was distinguished, and it is from his miracles, upon him be prayers and peace.

He met there with the prophets in Bayt al-Maqdis, and then he ﷺ was taken up to the heavens, meaning: he ascended from Bayt al-Maqdis to the heavens in the presence of Jibrīl. And the meaning of *al-'urūj* is "ascension." So, he was taken by night from Makkah to Bayt al-Maqdis and he ascended from Bayt al-Maqdis to the heavens. Meaning, Jibrīl عليه السلام took him up and passed the inhabitants of the heavens.

Each heaven that Jibrīl sought entry to was opened for him. Then he reached the seventh heaven. Then he ascended over the heavens to the lote tree of the uppermost boundary, and there Allāh spoke to him by way of revelation with that which He willed, and He obligated upon him the five prayers. He obligated them in a day and night as 50 prayers [at first]. However, Mūsā ﵇ directed our Prophet Muḥammad ﷺ to ask his Lord to lighten it, for indeed his *ummah* would not be able to perform 50 prayers in a day and night. So, the Messenger of Allāh ﷺ continued to return to his Lord, asking Him to lighten it, until he reached five.

Allāh ﷻ said, as is within the *ḥadīth* of al-Isrā' wal-Mi'rāj:

أَمْضَيْتُ فَرِيضَتِي وَ خَفَّفْتُ عَنْ عِبَادِي، وَ أَجْزِي الْحَسَنَةَ عَشْرًا.

My decree has gone forth and I have lightened the affair for my servants, and I shall reward the good deed with 10 times its like.[1]

In the narration of Anas from Abū Dharr, He said:

هِيَ خَمْسٌ وَ هِيَ خَمْسُونَ.

It is five [prayers] yet it is 50 [in reward].[2]

Meaning: They are five prayers in terms of the action and 50 in terms of their weight upon the scale. Five prayers in a day and night which equal 50 prayers upon the scale, because the good deed equals 10 times its like, so one prayer stands in the place of 10 prayers.

Al-Isrā' is mentioned at the beginning of Sūrah Subḥān (i.e., Sūrah Banī Isrā'īl), and al-Mi'rāj is mentioned at the beginning of Sūrah an-Najm when Allāh says:

﴿ وَلَقَدْ رَآهُ نَزْلَةً أُخْرَىٰ ﴿١٣﴾ عِندَ سِدْرَةِ الْمُنتَهَىٰ ﴿١٤﴾

[1] Al-Bukhārī reported it (#3207, #3887) from the *ḥadīth* of Mālik bin Ṣa'ṣa'ah, and it is a long *ḥadīth* which contains the story of al-Mi'rāj.

[2] Al-Bukhārī reported it (#349) from the *ḥadīth* of Anas on the authority of Abū Dharr ﵁.

عِندَهَا جَنَّةُ الْمَأْوَىٰ ﴿١٥﴾ إِذْ يَغْشَى السِّدْرَةَ مَا يَغْشَىٰ
﴿١٦﴾ مَا زَاغَ الْبَصَرُ وَمَا طَغَىٰ ﴿١٧﴾ لَقَدْ رَأَىٰ مِنْ آيَاتِ رَبِّهِ
الْكُبْرَىٰ ﴿١٨﴾ ﴾

And indeed he (Muḥammad ﷺ) saw him [Jibrīl (Gabriel)] at a second descent (i.e., another time). Near Sidrah al-Muntahā [the lote tree of the utmost boundary (beyond which none can pass)]; near it is the Paradise of Abode. When that covered the lote tree which did cover it! The sight (of Prophet Muḥammad ﷺ) turned not aside (right or left), nor did it transgress beyond (the) limit (ordained for it). Indeed, he (Muḥammad ﷺ) did see, of the greatest signs, of his Lord (Allāh).

[Sūrah an-Najm 53:13-18]

This is al-Mi'rāj. Then he was taken from the heavens to Bayt al-Maqdis, and he returned to Makkah in the same night. When morning came, he informed the people of that. The believers were increased in their *īmān*; as for the disbelievers, they were increased in their evil and they rejoiced at this. They went about spreading it, saying, "How can your companion claim that he went to Bayt al-Maqdis and returned from it in one night? We ride the fastest camels to it in one month going and one month returning." They made analytical comparison between the ability of the Creator and the ability of the creation.

Al-Isrā' wal-Mi'rāj was a test from Allāh عز وجل for the people. The polytheists increased in their enmity, evil, and their belittlement of the Messenger ﷺ, whereas the believers were increased in their *īmān*. Due to this, when the polytheists said to Abū Bakr aṣ-Ṣiddīq رضي الله عنه, "Look at what your companion has said," he said, "And what has he said?" They said, "He claimed that he was taken to Bayt al-Maqdis and ascended to the heavens, and that he did this in one night."

Abū Bakr aṣ-Ṣiddīq said, "If he said it, then it is as he has said; he has spoken truthfully." They said, "How is that?" He said, "I believe him in that which is greater than that—I believe him in the fact that information from the heavens descends upon him, so how can I not believe him when he says he made a journey by night to Bayt al-Maqdis?"[3]

This was by the ability of Allāh ﷻ and not by the ability of the Messenger ﷺ. It was only by the ability of Allāh ﷻ, and this is from the miracles of this Messenger ﷺ and from the things with which he was ennobled from his Lord.

It is a must to believe that he ﷺ traveled by night and ascended with his soul and body together, fully awake and not in a dream, because some of the people say he traveled by night with his soul but his body did not leave Makkah. They say he only traveled by night and ascended with his soul—this is false speech. Rather, he traveled by night with his soul and his body, upon him be prayers and peace, and he was carried on al-Burāq. And at that time, he was fully awake and not dreaming. If it were with his soul only, or if it were a dream, then what would be the difference between it and a vision? Allāh ﷻ says:

﴿ سُبْحَانَ الَّذِي أَسْرَىٰ بِعَبْدِهِ لَيْلًا ﴾

Glorified (and Exalted) be He (Allāh) who took His slave (Muḥammad ﷺ) for a journey by night...

[Sūrah al-Isrā' 17:1]

The word *al-'abd* (servant or slave) is applied to a soul and a body together, and it is not applied to a soul by itself; it is not said that the soul by itself is an *'abd* (servant). Nor is it applied to a body by itself, that it is an *'abd* (servant). It is only applied to a soul and body together. He did not say, "Glorified be the one who took the soul of His servant by night..." Rather, He said, **"He took His servant by night..."** And the servant is a soul and body together. Allāh ﷻ is not incapable of anything. He is able to do all things.

[3] Al-Ḥākim reported it in *Al-Mustadrak* (3/60, #4407) from the *ḥadīth* of 'Ā'ishah ﷺ.

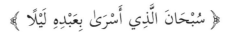

The author رحمه الله said, "*and the five prayers were made obligatory upon him; he prayed in Makkah for a period of three years*": He would pray them as two *raka'āt*. So, when the Prophet ﷺ migrated, the four *raka'āt* prayers were completed as being four, with the exception of the Fajr prayer; the recitation therein was long, so it remained as two. Maghrib prayer was also an exception, because it was three from the time that it was first obligated. This is because it is the *witr* prayer of the daytime. As for the Ẓuhr, 'Aṣr, and 'Ishā' prayers in Makkah, they were each two *raka'āt*, so when the Prophet ﷺ migrated, they were completed as four *raka'āt*.

This is as it has come in the *ḥadīth*: "The first of that which was obligated from the prayer was two *raka'āt,* so when the Prophet ﷺ migrated, the prayer of residency was completed and there remained the prayer of traveling."[4]

This is by way of consensus of the people of knowledge, that the prayer was obligated in Makkah and that the Prophet ﷺ prayed it in Makkah. However, they differ regarding whether it was obligated three years before the Hijrah; and this is the stronger view, as the Shaykh has mentioned here. It has been stated that it was obligated five years before the Hijrah. It has also been stated that it was obligated one year before the Hijrah. It has also been stated that it was obligated a year and a half before the Hijrah. However, the stronger view is that which the Shaykh has mentioned, which is that it was obligated three years before the Hijrah.

Were any of the other pillars of al-Islām obligated along with the *ṣalāh*? This is a point of contention amongst the scholars. From them are those who hold that the *zakāh* was also obligated in Makkah, and that it was only the minimum amount which makes it obligatory, the amount of the *zakāh* itself, and the people to whom the *zakāh* is due that was clarified in al-Madīnah. As for the origin of it, then it was obligated in Makkah. The proof is the statement of the Most High:

﴿وَآتُوا حَقَّهُ يَوْمَ حَصَادِهِ﴾

[4] Reported by al-Bukhārī (#350) and Muslim (#685) from the *ḥadīth* of 'Ā'ishah رضي الله عنها.

But pay the due thereof (its *zakāh*, according to Allāh's orders, 1/10th or 1/20th) on the day of its harvest…

[Sūrah al-An'ām 6:141]

What is intended by **"the due thereof"** here (in this verse) is the *zakāh,* and the entirety of this *sūrah* is Makkan.

Likewise, there is His statement:

﴿ وَالَّذِينَ فِي أَمْوَالِهِمْ حَقٌّ مَّعْلُومٌ ﴿٢٤﴾ لِّلسَّائِلِ وَالْمَحْرُومِ ﴿٢٥﴾ ﴾

And those in whose wealth there is a known right, for the beggar who asks, and for the unlucky who has lost his property and wealth (and his means of living has been straitened).

[Sūrah al-Ma'ārij 70:24-25]

This *sūrah* is also Makkan. What is intended by **"a known right"** is the *zakāh*. Therefore, its origin was obligated in Makkah; however, its details were clarified in al-Madīnah. This is one view.

The second view is that which is apparent from the speech of the Shaykh here, which is that the *zakāh* was obligated in al-Madīnah, and nothing was obligated in Makkah other than the first pillar, which is *at-tawḥīd,* and the second pillar, which is *aṣ-ṣalāh*. This is what is apparent from the speech of the Shaykh.

Hijrah to al-Madīnah

Original Text

وَ بَعْدَهَا أُمِرَ بِالْهِجْرَةِ إِلَى الْمَدِينَةِ.

After that, he was commanded to migrate to al-Madīnah.

EXPLANATION

His statement ﷺ, *"After that, he was commanded to migrate to al-Madīnah"*: When the harms of the Quraysh became severe, and they increased in their evil in hindering from the path of Allāh, their restriction of the Muslims, and their torment of the weak Muslims who did not have a group to protect them, Allāh ﷻ permitted the Muslims to migrate to Ethiopia. This was the first *hijrah*, because there was a king there who did not wrong anyone who was with him. He was a Christian, but he was just. Therefore, a large group migrated.

When the Quraysh found out about their emigration to Ethiopia, they sent a shrewd deputized duo from the Quraysh after them. One of them was 'Amr bin al-'Āṣ, and with them were guides to an-Najāshī; they said, "Indeed, these people have fled from us, and they are our relatives. We want them to return; indeed, they are evil. Do not allow them to corrupt your land..." etc.

The guides who were with them obeyed them in seeking to deceive [an-Najāshī]. However, he ﷺ called for the emigrants, and he listened to them and gave them a choice. They chose to remain in Ethiopia, so the two deputies returned to Makkah, and those who remained in Ethiopia from the emigrants stayed. Then Allāh favored an-Najāshī with embracing al-Islām, and he perfected his Islām. Therefore, when he died, the Messenger ﷺ and his Companions prayed the funeral prayer for him in absentia. In their emigration to him, there was good for him as well, for Allāh guided him to al-Islām and he entered it by way of them.

The Prophet ﷺ met the group from amongst the Anṣār at Minā during the Ḥajj season; and the Prophet ﷺ would present himself to the tribes during the Ḥajj season. He would go to the camps of the Arabs at Minā and call them to Allāh. It happened that he met a group of people from the Anṣār, and he called them to Allāh and presented to them what he had. They accepted the *da'wah* from the Messenger ﷺ and they pledged allegiance to him for al-Islām. They returned to their people after the Ḥajj season and called them to Allāh ﷻ.

So, during the next season, more people came than there were during the first season. People came from the Anṣār and pledged allegiance to the Prophet ﷺ in the second Pledge of al-'Aqabah; meaning, at the *jamrah* of al-'Aqabah. They pledged allegiance to him for al-Islām, and that they would aid him in migrating to them, and that they would protect him from that which they protected themselves and their children from.

So, after this blessed pledge, the Prophet ﷺ ordered those Muslims who were in Makkah to migrate to al-Madīnah, and they all migrated to al-Madīnah, while the Messenger and some of his Companions remained. Then Allāh gave permission for His Prophet ﷺ to migrate. Once the Quraysh found out about the emigration of the Companions to al-Madīnah, and they found out about the pledge which had taken place between him and the Anṣār, they feared that the Messenger of Allāh ﷺ would catch up with his Companions in al-Madīnah, gain strength, and subdue the Quraysh.

So on the night when the Prophet ﷺ wanted to exit for emigration, they surrounded his home and stood at the door with their weapons, intending to kill the Messenger of Allāh ﷺ. Allāh informed his Prophet ﷺ, and the Prophet ﷺ commanded 'Alī to sleep in his bed so that the pagans would see him and think that he was the Prophet ﷺ. So 'Alī ؓ slept in the bed of the Messenger of Allāh ﷺ, and he covered himself with the blanket of the Messenger of Allāh ﷺ. The pagans were waiting for his exit, thinking that he was the Messenger of Allāh ﷺ, while the Prophet ﷺ went out amongst them while they did not even know.

Allāh blinded their vision from him, and he took dirt, tossed it upon their heads, and went out amongst them. When they grew weary of searching for him after looking and investigating, they offered a reward to whoever would bring him ﷺ, dead or alive. When they gave up, the Messenger of Allāh ﷺ and his companion exited the cave, rode on their mounts, and went to al-Madīnah.

ORIGINAL TEXT

وَ الْهِجْرَةُ: الْإِنْتِقَالُ مِنْ بَلَدِ الشِّرْكِ إِلَى بَلَدِ الْإِسْلَامِ.

Al-hijrah is moving from the land of *shirk* to the land of al-Islām.

EXPLANATION

Al-hijrah, linguistically, means "the abandonment of a thing." As for *al-hijrah* in the legislation, then it is as the Shaykh has defined it: moving from the land of disbelief to the land of al-Islām. This is the legislative *hijrah*. *Hijrah* is a noble action. Allāh has linked it with *jihād* in many verses. Therefore, when the Prophet ﷺ migrated to al-Madīnah, the emigrants who were in Ethiopia came to al-Madīnah and united with their brothers in al-Madīnah, and all praise is due to Allāh; and al-Madīnah became a state for the Muslims, from the emigrants and the Anṣār. Those who had embraced Islām would come to them.

With that, Allāh legislated the remaining legislations of the religion. He obligated fasting upon His Prophet ﷺ, as well as the *zakāh* in the second year after the Hijrah, and he obligated Ḥajj upon him in the ninth year after the Hijrah, based upon the correct view. With that, the pillars of *al-islām* were completed, the first of them being the two testimonies and the last of them being Ḥajj to the Sacred House of Allāh.

The summary of this is that we know that *at-tawḥīd* is of utmost importance in calling to Allāh ﷻ and that the caller should begin with it before he begins with the *ṣalāh*, fasting, *zakāh*, or Ḥajj, because the Prophet ﷺ remained for 10 years calling to *at-tawḥīd* and prohibiting from *ash-shirk*. He did not command with *ṣalāh*, *zakāh,* Ḥajj, or fasting. These obligations were only enjoined upon him after the affirmation of *at-tawḥīd*. So, when the Prophet ﷺ would send callers, he would command them to call the people firstly to *at-tawḥīd*, as is narrated in the *ḥadīth* of Mu'ādh wherein he ﷺ said:

إِنَّكَ تَأْتِي قَوْمًا مِنْ أَهْلِ الْكِتَابِ، فَلْيَكُنْ أَوَّلَ مَا تَدْعُوهُمْ إِلَيْهِ

شَهَادَةَ أَنْ لَا إِلَهَ إِلَّا اللهُ وَ أَنْ مُحَمَّداً رَسُولُ اللهِ، فَإِنْ هُمْ أَجَابُوا لِذَلِكَ فَأَعْلِمْهُمْ أَنَّ اللهَ افْتَرَضَ عَلَيْهِمْ خَمْسَ صَلَوَاتٍ...

You're going to a people from the People of the Book, so let the first of that which you call them to be to testify that none has the right to be worshiped except Allāh and that Muḥammad is the Messenger of Allāh; and if they accept that, then teach them that Allāh has obligated upon them five prayers...[5]

This indicates that he did not command with the *ṣalāh*, *zakāh,* or fasting until after *tawḥīd* was actualized and present; and he who begins with other than *tawḥīd*, has a *da'wah* that is destined to fail, and his methodology is in opposition to the methodology of all of the messengers ﷺ. The first thing every messenger began with was *at-tawḥīd* and rectification of the belief system. This methodology is important to know for those who traverse upon this path. Today, those who seek to muddle and change this methodology have become many, and they have chosen for themselves a methodology of their own making and of other than them from the ignorant. It is necessary to return to the methodology of the Messenger ﷺ.

This is the benefit of knowing the Messenger ﷺ and his *sīrah*. And he (the author) has made that one of the three fundamental principles—that you know how he called the people and what his methodology was in calling them, so that you may traverse upon it; because he is the example, upon him be prayers and peace.

ORIGINAL TEXT

والهجرة فريضة على هذه الأمة من بلد الشرك إلى بلد الإسلام، وهي باقية إلى أن تقوم الساعة.

Hijrah is an obligation upon this *ummah* from the land of *shirk* to the land of al-Islām, and it is ongoing until the establishment of the

[5] Al-Bukhārī reported it (#1395), as did Muslim (#19) from the *ḥadīth* of Ibn 'Abbās ﷺ.

Hour.

EXPLANATION

Al-hijrah is the close companion of *jihād* in Allāh's cause, and it is an ongoing obligation which is not abrogated. It is obligatory for every Muslim who needs to perform *hijrah* to perform it. It is not permissible for a Muslim to remain in the lands of disbelief if he is not able to openly manifest his religion. It is obligatory upon him, in that case, to migrate to the lands of the Muslims. And this is an ongoing obligation, due to the statement of the Prophet ﷺ:

لَا تَنْقَطِعُ الْهِجْرَةُ حَتَّى تَنْقَطِعَ التَّوْبَةُ، وَ لَا تَنْقَطِعُ التَّوْبَةُ حَتَّى تَطْلُعَ الشَّمْسُ مِنْ مَغْرِبِهَا.

Hijrah will not be discontinued until _at-tawbah_ is discontinued, and _at-tawbah_ will not be discontinued until the sun rises from its place of setting.[6]

ORIGINAL TEXT

وَ الدَّلِيلُ قَوْلُهُ تَعَالَى: ﴿ إِنَّ الَّذِينَ تَوَفَّاهُمُ الْمَلَائِكَةُ ظَالِمِي أَنفُسِهِمْ قَالُوا فِيمَ كُنتُمْ ۖ قَالُوا كُنَّا مُسْتَضْعَفِينَ فِي الْأَرْضِ ۚ قَالُوا أَلَمْ تَكُنْ أَرْضُ اللَّهِ وَاسِعَةً فَتُهَاجِرُوا فِيهَا ۚ فَأُولَٰئِكَ مَأْوَاهُمْ جَهَنَّمُ ۖ وَسَاءَتْ مَصِيرًا ﴿٩٧﴾ إِلَّا الْمُسْتَضْعَفِينَ مِنَ الرِّجَالِ وَالنِّسَاءِ وَالْوِلْدَانِ لَا يَسْتَطِيعُونَ حِيلَةً وَلَا يَهْتَدُونَ سَبِيلًا ﴿٩٨﴾ فَأُولَٰئِكَ عَسَى اللَّهُ أَن يَعْفُوَ عَنْهُمْ ۚ وَكَانَ اللَّهُ عَفُوًّا غَفُورًا ﴿٩٩﴾ وَمَن يُهَاجِرْ فِي سَبِيلِ اللَّهِ يَجِدْ فِي الْأَرْضِ مُرَاغَمًا كَثِيرًا وَسَعَةً ۚ وَمَن يَخْرُجْ مِن بَيْتِهِ مُهَاجِرًا إِلَى اللَّهِ وَرَسُولِهِ ثُمَّ يُدْرِكْهُ الْمَوْتُ فَقَدْ وَقَعَ أَجْرُهُ عَلَى اللَّهِ ۗ وَكَانَ اللَّهُ غَفُورًا رَّحِيمًا ﴿١٠٠﴾ ﴾.

The proof is the statement of the Most High:

[6] Abū Dāwūd reported it (#3479), as did Aḥmad (28/111, #16906) from the *ḥadīth* of Mu'āwiyah bin Abī Sufyān ﷺ.

Verily! As for those whom the angels take (in death) while they are wronging themselves (as they stayed among the disbelievers even though emigration was obligatory for them), they (angels) say (to them), "In what (condition) were you?" They reply, "We were weak and oppressed on earth." They (angels) say, "Was not the earth of Allāh spacious enough for you to emigrate therein?" Such men will find their abode in Hell—what an evil destination! Except the weak ones among men, women, and children who cannot devise a plan, nor are they able to direct their way. For these, there is hope that Allāh will forgive them, and Allāh is Ever Oft-Pardoning, Oft-Forgiving. He who emigrates (from his home) in the cause of Allāh, will find on earth many dwelling places and plenty to live by. And whosoever leaves his home as an emigrant unto Allāh and His Messenger, and death overtakes him, his reward is then surely incumbent upon Allāh. And Allāh is Ever Oft-Forgiving, Most Merciful.

[Sūrah an-Nisā' 4:97-100]

EXPLANATION

These two verses contain a threat for the one who abandons *hijrah* while he is able to perform it, and his abode will be the Hellfire—what an evil place of return; however, he does not exit the fold of al-Islām. But this is from the texts of threat, and if an individual abandons *hijrah,* then he has abandoned an obligation and he has been disobedient. He has not exited al-Islām by the abandonment of *hijrah,* but there is a severe threat upon him.

Then Allāh clarified the excuse with the verse after it, the excuse which removes the obligation of *hijrah*. The Most High has said, **"Except for those who are weak from amongst men, women, and children"**: Meaning, kids. **"And they did not have the ability"**: Meaning, it is not possible for them. **"And they are not able to find a way"**: Meaning, they did not know the way to the land (i.e., al-Madīnah). This is because *hijrah* requires travel. Otherwise, a person may be destroyed by way of *hijrah* if he does not know the way.

So, they are excused by way of two matters:

1) They do not have the means.

2) They do not know the way.

Even if they have the tangible means to do so, if they do not know the way to travel nor do they have one who will guide them, then this is a valid excuse. As for the person who has the means and he knows the way, then this individual has no excuse.

ORIGINAL TEXT

وَ قَوْلُهُ تَعَالَى: ﴿ يَا عِبَادِيَ الَّذِينَ آمَنُوا إِنَّ أَرْضِي وَاسِعَةٌ فَإِيَّايَ فَاعْبُدُونِ ﴾.

قَالَ الْبَغَوِيُّ—رَحِمَهُ اللهُ تَعَالَى: ((سَبَبُ نُزُولِ هَذِهِ الْآيَةِ فِي الْمُسْلِمِينَ الَّذِينَ بِمَكَّةَ: لَمْ يُهَاجِرُوا، نَادَا هُمْ بِاسْمِ الْإِيمَانِ)).

Also, there is the statement of the Most High:

O My slaves who believe! Certainly, spacious is My earth. Therefore, worship Me (alone).

[Sūrah al-ʿAnkabūt 29:56]

Al-Baghawī ﷺ said, "The reason for the revelation of this verse was that, regarding the Muslims who were in Makkah and did not migrate, Allāh referred to them with the title of *al-īmān*."

EXPLANATION

This verse, from Sūrah al-ʿAnkabūt, contains the command to migrate, and it clarifies that the earth of Allāh is spacious. If you are in a land wherein you are not able to openly manifest your religion, then the earth of Allāh is spacious—migrate from it and do not remain in this evil place. Rather, leave it to go to this spacious earth of Allāh, for Allāh has made His earth spacious.

The evidence for *al-hijrah* from the Sunnah is his ﷺ statement:

لَا تَنْقَطِعُ الْهِجْرَةُ حَتَّى تَنْقَطِعَ التَّوْبَةُ، وَ لَا تَنْقَطِعُ التَّوْبَةُ حَتَّى تَطْلُعَ الشَّمْسُ مِنْ مَغْرِبِهَا.

***Hijrah* will not be discontinued until *at-tawbah* is discontinued, and *at-tawbah* will not be discontinued until the sun rises from its place of setting.**

As for his statement ﷺ:

لَا هِجْرَةَ بَعْدَ الْفَتْحِ.

There is no *hijrah* after the conquest.[7]

That which is apparent from this *ḥadīth* is that *hijrah* ended after the conquest of Makkah, and some of the people find a contradiction between this *ḥadīth* and his statement ﷺ:

لَا تَنْقَطِعُ الْهِجْرَةُ حَتَّى تَنْقَطِعَ التَّوْبَةُ، وَ لَا تَنْقَطِعُ التَّوْبَةُ حَتَّى تَطْلُعَ الشَّمْسُ مِنْ مَغْرِبِهَا.

***Hijrah* is not discontinued until *at-tawbah* is discontinued, and *at-tawbah* is not discontinued until the sun rises from its place of setting.**

However, the people of knowledge have responded regarding this *ḥadīth*, saying that the intended meaning of the statement, **"There is no *hijrah* after the conquest,"** is that there is no *hijrah* from Makkah, because it became *dār al-Islām* after the conquest.

(Some) think that the *hijrah* is ongoing from Makkah after the conquest, so they intend to achieve the reward of *hijrah*. As for

[7] Al-Bukhārī reported it (#2783), as well as Muslim (#1353, #75) before *ḥadīth* #1764 from the *ḥadīth* of Ibn 'Abbās ﷺ. And Muslim reported it, as well, from the *ḥadīth* of 'Ā'ishah ﷺ (#1874).

hijrah from the land of disbelief, then it is ongoing until the establishment of the Hour, and the proof is the aforementioned verses and the aforementioned Prophetic *aḥādīth*. This is the response to this doubt.

Settling in al-Madīnah, the Revelation of the Remaining Legislations, & the Completion of the Religion

ORIGINAL TEXT

فَلَمَّا اسْتَقَرَّ فِي الْمَدِينَةِ أُمِرَ بِبَقِيَّةِ شَرَائِعِ الْإِسْلَامِ مِثْلَ الزَّكَاةِ ، وَ الصَّوْمِ، وَ الْحَجِّ، وَ الْأَذَانِ، وَ الْجِهَادِ، وَ الْأَمْرِ بِالْمَعْرُوفِ، وَ النَّهْيِ عَنِ الْمُنْكَرِ، وَ غَيْرِ ذَلِكَ مِنْ شَرَائِعِ الْإِسْلَامِ. أَخَذَ عَلَى هَذَا عَشْرَ سِنِينَ، ثُمَّ تُوفِيَ - صَلَوَاتُ اللهِ وَ سَلَامُهُ عَلَيْهِ – وَ دِينُهُ بَاقٍ، وَ هَذَا دِينُهُ لَا خَيْرَ إِلَّا دَلَّ الْأُمَّةَ عَلَيْهِ وَ لَا شَرَّ إِلَّا حَذَّرَ مِنْهُ، وَ الْخَيْرُ الَّذِي دَلَّهَا عَلَيْهَا: التَّوْحِيدُ وَ جَمِيعُ مَا يُحِبُّهُ اللهُ وَ يَرْضَاهُ، وَ الشَّرُّ الَّذِي حَذَرَ هَا مِنْهُ: الشِّرْكُ وَ جَمِيعُ مَا يَكْرَهُهُ اللهُ وَ يَأْبَاهُ. بَعَثَهُ اللهُ إِلَى النَّاسِ كَافَّةً، وَ افْتَرَضَ طَاعَتَهُ عَلَى جَمِيعِ الثَّقَلَيْنِ - الْجِنِّ وَ الْإِنْسِ، وَ الدَّلِيلُ قَوْلُهُ تَعَالَى: ﴿ قُلْ يَا أَيُّهَا النَّاسُ إِنِّي رَسُولُ اللَّهِ إِلَيْكُمْ جَمِيعًا ﴾.

When he had settled in al-Madīnah, he was commanded with the remaining legislations of al-Islām, such as *az-zakāh*, fasting, Ḥajj, *jihād*, the *adhān*, enjoining the good, forbidding the evil, and other than that from the legislations of al-Islām. He took to this for a period of 10 years, after which he passed away, may the prayers and peace of Allāh be upon him. His religion remains, and this is his religion. There is no good except that he guided the *ummah* to it, and there is no evil except that he warned the *ummah* against it. The good that he guided the *ummah* to is *at-tawḥīd* and everything Allāh loves and is pleased with. The evil that he warned against was *ash-shirk* and everything Allāh hates and is displeased with. Allāh sent him to all of mankind, and Allāh made obedience to him obligatory upon the two classes (i.e., the *jinn* and mankind). The proof is the statement of the Most High:

Say (O Muḥammad ﷺ): "O mankind! Verily, I am sent to you all as the Messenger of Allāh."

[Sūrah al-A'rāf 7:158]

EXPLANATION

This is the clarification of what has preceded: that the legislation was revealed in stages until it was complete—and all praise is due to Allāh—before the death of the Prophet ﷺ. Allāh sent down to him:

﴿ الْيَوْمَ أَكْمَلْتُ لَكُمْ دِينَكُمْ وَأَتْمَمْتُ عَلَيْكُمْ نِعْمَتِي وَرَضِيتُ لَكُمُ الْإِسْلَامَ دِينًا ﴾

This day, I have perfected your religion for you, completed My favor upon you, and have chosen for you Islām as your religion.

[Sūrah al-Mā'idah 5:3]

A short time after the revelation of this verse, the Prophet ﷺ died, and his religion remains until the establishment of the Hour.

ORIGINAL TEXT

وَ كَمَّلَ اللهُ بِهِ الدِّينَ، وَ الدَّلِيلُ قَوْلُهُ تَعَالَى: ﴿ الْيَوْمَ أَكْمَلْتُ لَكُمْ دِينَكُمْ وَأَتْمَمْتُ عَلَيْكُمْ نِعْمَتِي وَرَضِيتُ لَكُمُ الْإِسْلَامَ دِينًا ﴾.

Allāh completed the religion by way of him. The proof for this is the statement of the Most High:

This day, I have perfected your religion for you, completed My favor upon you, and have chosen for you Islām as your religion.

[Sūrah al-Mā'idah 5:3]

EXPLANATION

He ﷺ did not die except after Allāh had completed, by way of him, the religion and perfected, by way of him, the favor; and He sent down to him the statement of the Most High:

﴿ الْيَوْمَ أَكْمَلْتُ لَكُمْ دِينَكُمْ وَأَتْمَمْتُ عَلَيْكُمْ نِعْمَتِي وَرَضِيتُ لَكُمُ الْإِسْلَامَ دِينًا ﴾

This day, I have perfected your religion for you, completed My favor upon you, and have chosen for you Islām as your religion.

[Sūrah al-Mā'idah 5:3]

This verse was revealed to Allāh's Messenger ﷺ while he was standing at 'Arafah during the Farewell Pilgrimage on Friday. He lived thereafter for a short while, and then he moved on to the highest companionship. He left his *ummah* upon a clear path; its night is like its day. No one deviates from it except one who is destroyed.

Within this verse is a testament from Allāh ﷻ to the completion of this religion and its comprehensiveness for the benefit of the servants. (It is) also a remedy for their issues and their problems until the establishment of the Hour. It is that which will rectify every time and place, such that they do not need after it another legislation, or another book to be sent down, or another messenger to be sent after the Messenger ﷺ.

So, no issue arises nor does any calamity descend, up until the Day of Standing, except that its remedy and the ruling concerning it lies within the legislation of Muḥammad ﷺ. However, the issue is relative to he who is proficient in derivation and extracting evidence regarding the rulings and issues.

So, when the people of knowledge are abundant and the people of *ijtihād*—in whom the conditions of *ijtihād* are fulfilled—(are present), then indeed this legislation is complete and it contains a solution to all problems. Deficiency only occurs from us due to our shortcomings in knowledge and our lack of comprehension of what

Allāh ﷻ has revealed. Or (it occurs) from desires, by there being desires which divert people from the truth. Otherwise, this *dīn* rectifies, and it is comprehensive and complete. Allāh has enriched the Islamic nation by way of it until the time when the Hour is established, if they act upon it truthfully and return to it in their affairs. The Most High has said:

﴿ فَإِن تَنَازَعْتُمْ فِي شَيْءٍ فَرُدُّوهُ إِلَى اللَّهِ وَالرَّسُولِ ﴾

(And) if you differ in anything amongst yourselves, refer it to Allāh and His Messenger.

[Sūrah an-Nisā' 4:59]

"Refer it to Allāh" means to refer it to the Book of Allāh, and **"refer to the Messenger,"** after his death, means to refer it to his Sunnah. The Most High has said:

﴿ وَمَا اخْتَلَفْتُمْ فِيهِ مِن شَيْءٍ فَحُكْمُهُ إِلَى اللَّهِ ﴾

And in whatsoever you differ, the decision thereof is with Allāh (He is the Ruling Judge).

[Sūrah ash-Shūrā 42:10]

This verse contains a refutation against those who accuse the Islamic legislation of containing shortcomings or deficiencies, such as the atheists and *zanādiqah*, or the semi-students whose intellects fall short in comprehending the intricacies of this legislation, so they attribute deficiencies to the legislation while not realizing that the deficiency is in their own selves. So, in this verse is a refutation against the one who accuses the legislation of having deficiencies and of not sufficing for the needs and benefits of the servants until the Hour is established.

Or they say that it is specific to ancient times; many of the ignorant people, if it is said to them, "This is the legislative ruling," then they say, "This was during the time of the Messenger, in the previous era. As for now, situations have changed and the affairs have altered, and the rulings of the legislation were for people who passed and the problems of old." This is what they say, and this is disbelief in

Allāh ﷻ and denial of the statement of the Most High:

﴿ الْيَوْمَ أَكْمَلْتُ لَكُمْ دِينَكُمْ وَأَتْمَمْتُ عَلَيْكُمْ نِعْمَتِي وَرَضِيتُ لَكُمُ الْإِسْلَامَ دِينًا ﴾

This day, I have perfected your religion for you, completed My favor upon you, and have chosen for you Islām as your religion.

[Sūrah al-Mā'idah 5:3]

Allāh completed the religion for this *ummah* up until the Hour is established—for every time, for every place, and for every group of people. In this verse is a refutation, as well, against the people of innovation who innovate acts of worship from themselves and ascribe it to the religion, while they do not have evidence for it from the Book of Allāh and the Sunnah of His Messenger ﷺ. They have only innovated it because they deem it to be good, or due to their blind following of those who deem it to be good from the people of superstition and the people who follow desires and lusts. Therefore, they invent acts of worship in the religion, acts for which Allāh has sent down no authority.

The Prophet ﷺ said:

مَنْ أَحْدَثَ فِي أَمْرِنَا هَذَا مَا لَيْسَ مِنْهُ فَهُوَ رَدٌّ.

Whoever invents into this affair of ours that which is not from it, shall have it rejected.

And he ﷺ said:

وَ إِيَّاكُمْ وَ مُحْدَثَاتِ الْأُمُورِ، فَإِنَّ كُلَّ مُحْدَثَةٍ بِدْعَةٌ، وَ كُلَّ بِدْعَةٍ ضَلَالَةٌ.

Beware of newly invented matters, for every newly invented matter is an innovation and every innovation is misguidance.

Therefore, the one who innovates acts of worship for which there is no proof from the Book of Allāh or the Sunnah of the Messenger of Allāh, then he has accused this religion of being incomplete; he wants to complete the religion from himself, and he does not acknowledge Allāh's completion of it. So, whatever was not from the religion during the time of the Prophet ﷺ, then indeed it is not from the religion after him. This is a refutation against these groups.

The group who says that Islām is not suitable for every time; or those who innovate innovations and newly invented matters for which there is no proof from the Book of Allāh and the Sunnah of His Messenger, yet they attribute it to the religion—within this verse is a refutation against them, because the religion has been completed by Allāh ﷻ. There is no room for addition into it nor is there any deficiency. And there is no room for doubting and confusion, believing that it is not suitable for the people of later times.

Allāh has said, **"This day, I have perfected for you your religion."** This is the speech of Allāh, and He is the most truthful of those who speak.

The Most High has said, **"And I have completed upon you My favor and I am pleased for you with Islām as your religion."**

This is the last of what was revealed to the Prophet ﷺ, and it is a testament from the Lord of all that exists to the fact that this religion has been completed, and it is comprehensive and suitable for every time and place. His statement, Glorified be He, is an address to this *ummah*—from the first of it to the last of it—and it is not an address to the first group only. Rather, it is an address to the entire *ummah* up until the Hour is established.

As for the consensus, then the *ummah* is united upon the fact that he ﷺ has died, and no one disagrees with this except the people of superstition who say that the Messenger did not die, and they negate death from the Messenger ﷺ. This is rejected speech; it is speech which is clearly rejected. It is refuted by way of sensory perception as well as the reality of what occurs. Indeed, the Messenger ﷺ passed away amongst his Companions. He ﷺ was washed, shrouded, prayed over, and buried. Are these actions done while an individual is still alive? He ﷺ was dealt with in the manner in which the dead are dealt with: being washed, shrouded, prayed over, then buried within his grave ﷺ.

This is the *sunnah* of Allāh عَزَّوَجَلَّ as it relates to His creation. Then where are the messengers that came before him? His *sunnah* is the *sunnah* of the messengers who passed away before him, and they all died. He was one of them, and therefore he also died. This is by way of the consensus of Ahlus-Sunnah wal-Jamā'ah, and no one opposes this except the people of superstition who falsely attach themselves to the Messenger ﷺ and seek deliverance from him as opposed to Allāh, and they say that he is alive.

ORIGINAL TEXT

وَ الدَّلِيلُ عَلَى مَوْتِهِ (صَلَّى اللهُ عَلَيْهِ وَ سَلَّمَ) قَوْلُهُ تَعَالَى: ﴿ إِنَّكَ مَيِّتٌ وَإِنَّهُم مَّيِّتُونَ ۝٣٠ ثُمَّ إِنَّكُمْ يَوْمَ الْقِيَامَةِ عِندَ رَبِّكُمْ تَخْتَصِمُونَ ۝٣١ ﴾.

The proof that he has died ﷺ is the statement of the Most High:

Verily, you (O Muḥammad ﷺ) will die and verily, they (too) will die. Then, on the Day of Resurrection, you will be disputing before your Lord.

[Sūrah az-Zumar 39:30-31]

EXPLANATION

When Allāh had completed by way of him the religion and perfected by way of him the favor, the Prophet ﷺ passed away, as is the *sunnah* of Allāh تَعَالَى regarding His creation. As Allāh says:

﴿ كُلُّ نَفْسٍ ذَائِقَةُ الْمَوْتِ ﴾

Everyone shall taste death.

[Sūrah Āli 'Imrān 3:185]

The prophets and messengers fall under the generality (of this statement): "Everyone shall taste death." So, the Prophet ﷺ died, and he made the transition from this *dunyā* to his Lord عَزَّوَجَلَّ. This is affirmed by way of the text, the consensus, and the analytical comparison.

As for the text, then there is the statement of the Most High:

﴿ إِنَّكَ مَيِّتٌ وَإِنَّهُم مَّيِّتُونَ ﴾

Verily, you (O Muḥammad ﷺ) will die and verily, they (too) will die.

[Sūrah az-Zumar 39:30]

This is information from Allāh to His Messenger ﷺ, [telling him] that he shall die. Allāh said, **"Verily, you will die,"** meaning: you will pass away. The one who passes away is referred to as *mayyit*. As for the one who passes away by way of an action, then he is called *maytun*, due to the statement of the Most High:

﴿ أَوَمَن كَانَ مَيْتًا فَأَحْيَيْنَاهُ ﴾

Is he who was dead (without faith by ignorance and disbelief) and We gave him life…

[Sūrah al-An'ām 6:122]

Al-mayyit is the one whose soul has departed from his body. As for *al-maytun*, he is the one who shall die in the future.

10

Conclusion: Īmān in the Resurrection

ORIGINAL TEXT

وَ النَّاسُ إِذَا مَاتُوا يُبْعَثُونَ، وَ الدَّلِيلُ قَوْلُهُ: ﴿ مِنْهَا خَلَقْنَاكُمْ وَفِيهَا نُعِيدُكُمْ وَمِنْهَا نُخْرِجُكُمْ تَارَةً أُخْرَىٰ ﴾.

When the people die, they shall be resurrected. The proof is the statement:

Thereof (the earth) We created you, and into it We shall return you, and from it We shall bring you out once again.

[Sūrah Ṭā-Hā 20:55]

EXPLANATION

Here, the author moved on to another principle, which is: believing in the resurrection. Meaning, what is intended is not death only. We, as well as everyone else—even the disbelievers, the atheists, and the heretics—know that death is inevitable. No one rejects death, because it is a thing that is known. However, the issue lies with the resurrection after death. This is the point of contention between the believers and the disbelievers: resurrection after death. And it is the return to the bodies which have decayed, become dirt, and have separated within the earth. They shall return and reestablish themselves just as they were, because the One who was able to give them life the first time is able to return them. Then the souls shall be breathed into them, and they will move and travel from their graves to the gathering place. This is due to the statement of the Most High:

﴿ يَوْمَ يَخْرُجُونَ مِنَ الْأَجْدَاثِ سِرَاعًا كَأَنَّهُمْ إِلَىٰ نُصُبٍ يُوفِضُونَ ﴾

The Day when they will come out of the graves quickly, as if racing to a goal...

[Sūrah al-Ma'ārij 70:43]

Also, the Most High has stated:

﴿ خُشَّعًا أَبْصَارُهُمْ يَخْرُجُونَ مِنَ الْأَجْدَاثِ كَأَنَّهُمْ جَرَادٌ مُّنتَشِرٌ ۝٧ مُّهْطِعِينَ إِلَى الدَّاعِ ﴾

They will come forth, with humbled eyes from (their) graves as if they were locusts spread abroad, hastening towards the caller.

[Sūrah al-Qamar 54:7-8]

No one shall lag behind. This resurrection is true, and there is no doubt in it. Whoever denies this is a disbeliever in Allāh ﷻ. *Īmān* in the resurrection is one of the six pillars of *al-īmān*, concerning which the Prophet ﷺ said:

أَنْ تُؤْمِنَ بِاللهِ وَ مَلَائِكَتِهِ وَ كُتُبِهِ وَ رُسُلِهِ وَ الْيَوْمِ الْآخِرِ وَ تُؤْمِنَ بِالْقَدَرِ خَيْرِهِ وَ شَرِّهِ.

It is that you believe in Allāh, His angels, His Books, His messengers, the Last Day, and that you believe in *al-qadar*, its good and its evil.

So, he who does not believe in the resurrection and the Last Day is a disbeliever in Allāh ﷻ. Even if he testifies that none has the right to be worshiped except Allāh and that Muḥammad is the Messenger of Allāh, and even if he prays, fasts, performs pilgrimage, pays *zakāh*, and does other acts of obedience—if he rejects the resurrection or if he doubts it, then he is a disbeliever in Allāh ﷻ.

The proofs for the resurrection are many; from them is the statement of the Most High, **"From it We have created you,"** meaning: the earth. (This was) when Allāh created Ādam عليه السلام, the father of humanity.

Then He said, **"and you shall return to it"**: Meaning, after death, within your graves.

And He said, **"and from it We shall bring you out a second time"**: This is the resurrection. This verse consists of the beginning and the return, as Allāh says:

﴿ مِنْهَا خَلَقْنَاكُمْ وَفِيهَا نُعِيدُكُمْ وَمِنْهَا نُخْرِجُكُمْ تَارَةً أُخْرَىٰ ﴾

Thereof (the earth) We created you, and into it We shall return you, and from it We shall bring you out once again.

[Sūrah Ṭā-Hā 20:55]

ORIGINAL TEXT

وَ قَوْلُهُ تَعَالَى: ﴿ وَاللَّهُ أَنبَتَكُم مِّنَ الْأَرْضِ نَبَاتًا ۝١٧ ثُمَّ يُعِيدُكُمْ فِيهَا وَيُخْرِجُكُمْ إِخْرَاجًا ۝١٨ ﴾.

Also, the statement of the Most High:

And Allāh has brought you forth from the (dust of) earth. Afterwards, He will return you into it (the earth), and bring you forth (again).

[Sūrah Nūḥ 71:17-18]

EXPLANATION

So, He says, **"And Allāh has brought you forth from the dust of the earth"**: This was when He created Ādam عليه السلام from it.

And He said, **"then He shall return you to it"**: Meaning, with death in the graves.

And He said, **"and He shall bring you forth again"**: This is the resurrection.

They shall come out of the graves and walk to the gathering place. The Most High has said:

﴿قَالَ فِيهَا تَحْيَوْنَ وَفِيهَا تَمُوتُونَ وَمِنْهَا تُخْرَجُونَ﴾

He said, "Therein you shall live, and therein you shall die, and from it you shall be brought out (i.e., resurrected)."

[Sūrah al-A'rāf 7:25]

Meaning, you were alive upon its surface, and in it you die, and from it you come out for the resurrection on the Day of Standing.

These are proofs from the Qur'ān for the resurrection. Also, there is intellectual evidence from the Qur'ān itself, and it is the fact that the One who is able to begin the creation is likewise able to repeat it, and even more so.

The Most High has said:

﴿وَهُوَ الَّذِي يَبْدَأُ الْخَلْقَ ثُمَّ يُعِيدُهُ وَهُوَ أَهْوَنُ عَلَيْهِ ۚ وَلَهُ الْمَثَلُ الْأَعْلَىٰ فِي السَّمَاوَاتِ وَالْأَرْضِ ۚ وَهُوَ الْعَزِيزُ الْحَكِيمُ﴾

And He it is who originates the creation, then will repeat it, and this is easier for Him. His is the highest description in the heavens and in the earth.

And He is the Almighty, the All-Wise.

[Sūrah ar-Rūm 30:27]

He who has the ability to bring mankind into existence from a state of nothingness has the ability to bring them back after death, even more so. This is evidence which is heard and comprehended by way of the intellect.

From the evidences for the resurrection is that which happens to the earth from the life of vegetation. You see the earth dead, having no vegetation, barren. Then Allāh ﷻ sends rain down upon it, so vegetation begins to grow while it was previously dead stubble.

Likewise, the bodies within the earth were buried in the earth. Allāh will send down upon them rain, so the bodies will grow and become whole; then the souls shall be breathed into them. So, you see how the earth was dry and arid but then it comes to life with the vegetation which grows from it. Allāh ﷻ is the one who gives life to the earth after its death, as Allāh says:

﴿ وَمِنْ آيَاتِهِ أَنَّكَ تَرَى الْأَرْضَ خَاشِعَةً فَإِذَا أَنزَلْنَا عَلَيْهَا الْمَاءَ اهْتَزَّتْ وَرَبَتْ ۚ إِنَّ الَّذِي أَحْيَاهَا لَمُحْيِي الْمَوْتَىٰ ۚ إِنَّهُ عَلَىٰ كُلِّ شَيْءٍ قَدِيرٌ ﴾

And among His signs (in this) is that you see the earth barren, but when We send down water (rain) to it, it is stirred to life and growth (of vegetation). Verily, He who gives it life, surely, (He) is able to give life to the dead (on the Day of Resurrection). Indeed! He is able to do all things.

[Sūrah Fuṣṣilat 41:39]

So, the One who has the ability to give life to the earth after its death is able to give life to the bodies after their death; this is because both will be alive after death.

From the evidences for the resurrection, as well, is that if there were no resurrection, then this would necessitate that the creation of mankind would be in vain. It would be such that they would live their lives, from them being the obedient who has *taqwā* and is a believer in Allāh and His messengers, and from them being the disbeliever who is an atheist, a *zindīq*, an oppressor, an arrogant individual, and one who is disobedient; (this would necessitate that) all of them would live their lives and then die without this believer attaining anything from his reward, or that this disbeliever, *zindīq*, atheist, and transgressing tyrant against the people would not attain his due punishment.

Does it befit Allāh that he should leave the people like this, without rewarding the people of *īmān* for their *īmān*, the people of *iḥsān* for their *iḥsān*, and the people of crime and disbelief for their crime and disbelief? This is not befitting of the wisdom of Allāh ﷻ. Due to this, He said:

﴿ وَلِلَّهِ مَا فِي السَّمَاوَاتِ وَمَا فِي الْأَرْضِ لِيَجْزِيَ الَّذِينَ أَسَاءُوا بِمَا عَمِلُوا وَيَجْزِيَ الَّذِينَ أَحْسَنُوا بِالْحُسْنَى ﴾

And to Allāh belongs all that is in the heavens and all that is in the earth, that He may requite those who do evil with that which they have done (i.e., punish them in Hell), and reward those who do good, with what is best (i.e., Paradise).

[Sūrah an-Najm 53:31]

This does not take place except on the Day of Standing. Likewise, there is His statement, Glorified be He:

﴿ أَمْ حَسِبَ الَّذِينَ اجْتَرَحُوا السَّيِّئَاتِ أَن نَّجْعَلَهُمْ كَالَّذِينَ آمَنُوا وَعَمِلُوا الصَّالِحَاتِ سَوَاءً مَّحْيَاهُمْ وَمَمَاتُهُمْ ۚ سَاءَ مَا يَحْكُمُونَ ﴾

Or do those who earn evil deeds think that We shall hold them equal with those who believe and do righteous good deeds, in their present life and after

their death? Worst is the judgment that they make.

[Sūrah al-Jāthiyah 45:21]

He ﷻ has said:

﴿ أَمْ نَجْعَلُ الَّذِينَ آمَنُوا وَعَمِلُوا الصَّالِحَاتِ كَالْمُفْسِدِينَ فِي الْأَرْضِ أَمْ نَجْعَلُ الْمُتَّقِينَ كَالْفُجَّارِ ﴾

Shall We treat those who believe and do righteous good deeds, as *mufsidūn* (those who associate partners in worship with Allāh and commit crimes) on earth? Or shall We treat the *muttaqūn* (pious) as the *fujjār* (criminals, disbelievers, wicked, etc.)?

[Sūrah Ṣād 38:28]

He ﷻ has also said:

﴿ أَفَحَسِبْتُمْ أَنَّمَا خَلَقْنَاكُمْ عَبَثًا وَأَنَّكُمْ إِلَيْنَا لَا تُرْجَعُونَ ﴾

Did you think that We had created you in play (without any purpose), and that you would not be brought back to Us?

[Sūrah al-Mu'minūn 23:115]

He has also stated:

﴿ أَيَحْسَبُ الْإِنسَانُ أَن يُتْرَكَ سُدًى ﴿٣٦﴾ أَلَمْ يَكُ نُطْفَةً مِّن مَّنِيٍّ يُمْنَىٰ ﴿٣٧﴾ ثُمَّ كَانَ عَلَقَةً فَخَلَقَ فَسَوَّىٰ ﴿٣٨﴾ فَجَعَلَ مِنْهُ الزَّوْجَيْنِ الذَّكَرَ وَالْأُنثَىٰ ﴿٣٩﴾ أَلَيْسَ ذَٰلِكَ بِقَادِرٍ عَلَىٰ أَن يُحْيِيَ الْمَوْتَىٰ ﴿٤٠﴾ ﴾

Does man think that he will be left *suda* [neglected without being punished or rewarded]? Was he not a *nuṭfah* (mixed male and female discharge of semen) poured forth? Then he became an *'alaqah* (a clot); then (Allāh) shaped and fashioned (him) in due proportion. And made him in two sexes, male and

female. Is not He (Allāh who does that) able to give life to the dead?

[Sūrah al-Qiyāmah 75:36-40]

He has refuted the disbeliever who says:

﴿ مَن يُحْيِي الْعِظَامَ وَهِيَ رَمِيمٌ ﴾

"Who will give life to these bones when they have rotted away and become dust?"

[Sūrah Yā-Sīn 36:78]

(Doing so) by way of His statement:

﴿ قُلْ يُحْيِيهَا الَّذِي أَنشَأَهَا أَوَّلَ مَرَّةٍ ۖ وَهُوَ بِكُلِّ خَلْقٍ عَلِيمٌ ﴿٧٩﴾ الَّذِي جَعَلَ لَكُم مِّنَ الشَّجَرِ الْأَخْضَرِ نَارًا فَإِذَا أَنتُم مِّنْهُ تُوقِدُونَ ﴿٨٠﴾ ﴾

Say (O Muḥammad ﷺ): "He will give life to them Who created them for the first time! And He is the All-Knower of every creation!" He, who produces for you fire out of the green tree, when behold! You kindle therewith.

[Sūrah Yā-Sīn 36:79-80]

The One who is able to bring out fire which burns from a fresh green tree, is He not able to give life to the dead?

From the evidences for the resurrection is: using as evidence the creation of the heavens and the earth. The One who created these tremendously huge and awesome created things is fully able to restore man to life, because the one who is able to do something tremendous will be able to do something less tremendous, even more so.

The Most High has said:

﴿ أَوَلَيْسَ الَّذِي خَلَقَ السَّمَاوَاتِ وَالْأَرْضَ بِقَادِرٍ عَلَىٰ أَن

يَخْلُقَ مِثْلَهُم ۚ بَلَىٰ وَهُوَ الْخَلَّاقُ الْعَلِيمُ ﴾

Is not He, who created the heavens and the earth, able to create the like of them? Yes, indeed! He is the All-Knowing Supreme Creator.

[Sūrah Yā-Sīn 36:81]

The Most High has said:

﴿ لَخَلْقُ السَّمَاوَاتِ وَالْأَرْضِ أَكْبَرُ مِنْ خَلْقِ النَّاسِ وَلَٰكِنَّ أَكْثَرَ النَّاسِ لَا يَعْلَمُونَ ﴾

The creation of the heavens and the earth is indeed greater than the creation of mankind, yet most of mankind knows not.

[Sūrah Ghāfir 40:57]

These are evidences for the resurrection, which affirm that Allāh ﷻ shall resurrect those who are within the graves, and He shall reward each doer of an action for his action. If it was good, then his reward shall be good, and if it was evil, then his reward shall be evil. So, let the disbeliever disbelieve and let the wicked doer do wicked things; likewise, the *zindīq* and the atheist, for indeed there is, before him, the resurrection, the gathering, the reward, and the recompense.

As for the believer who has *taqwā*, worships Allāh, and draws near to Allāh, then indeed his action shall not be lost. Indeed, there is a promise which Allāh shall fulfill regarding his action. He shall multiply the reward for him, and He will give him that which he cannot even imagine.

The Reckoning & the Scale

ORIGINAL TEXT

وَ بَعْدَ الْبَعْثِ مُحَاسَبُونَ وَ مُجْزَوْنَ بِأَعْمَالِهِمْ، وَ الدَّلِيلُ قَوْلُهُ تَعَالَى: ﴿ وَلِلَّهِ مَا فِي السَّمَاوَاتِ وَمَا فِي الْأَرْضِ لِيَجْزِيَ الَّذِينَ أَسَاءُوا

بِمَا عَمِلُوا وَيَجْزِيَ الَّذِينَ أَحْسَنُوا بِالْحُسْنَى ﴾.

After the resurrection, they shall be reckoned and rewarded for their actions. The proof is the statement of the Most High:

> **And to Allāh belongs all that is in the heavens and all that is in the earth, that He may requite those who do evil with what they have done (i.e., punish them in Hell), and reward those who do good, with what is best.**
>
> *[Sūrah an-Najm 53:31]*

EXPLANATION

From that which will take place on the Day of Standing is the reckoning and the Scales. "The reckoning" bears the meaning of debating with the people of disobedience. Therefore, the Muslims are of different categories on the Day of Standing:

The First Category: From them are those who will not be reckoned. They will enter Paradise without reckoning or punishment, as it has been narrated in the *ḥadīth* regarding the 70,000 people who shall enter Paradise without any reckoning or punishment.[1]

The Second Category: From the people are those who shall have an easy reckoning, and this refers to the presentation (of their books) only. They will not be reckoned by way of debate; they are only reckoned by way of the presentation (of their books). This is also from the good things. The Most High has stated:

﴿ فَأَمَّا مَنْ أُوتِيَ كِتَابَهُ بِيَمِينِهِ ۝٧ فَسَوْفَ يُحَاسَبُ حِسَابًا يَسِيرًا ۝٨ وَيَنقَلِبُ إِلَىٰ أَهْلِهِ مَسْرُورًا ۝٩ ﴾

Then, as for him who will be given his record in his right hand, He surely will receive an easy reckon-

[1] Al-Bukhārī reported it (#5705), as did Muslim (#218) from the *ḥadīth* of 'Imrān bin Ḥusayn ﷺ.

ing, and will return to his family in joy!

[Sūrah al-Inshiqāq 84:7-9]

The Third Category: Those who will be reckoned by way of debate. And this one is in danger due to the statement of the Prophet ﷺ:

مَنْ نُوقِشَ الْحِسَابَ عُذِّبَ.

Whoever is debated regarding the reckoning shall be punished.[2]

As for the disbelievers, then the scholars have differed regarding them, as to whether or not they will be reckoned. From the scholars, there is he who says that the disbelievers shall not be reckoned because they have no good deeds; they shall only be taken to the Fire. This is because they do not have any good. And from the scholars, there is he who says that they shall be reckoned with a reckoning of affirmation; meaning, as it relates to their actions, their disbelief, and their atheism. Then they shall be taken to the Fire.

Regarding the Scale: it is the tool by which the actions of the servants are weighed. The good deeds shall be placed on one side of the Scale and the evil deeds shall be placed on the other side of the Scale. The Most High has stated:

﴿ فَمَن ثَقُلَتْ مَوَازِينُهُ فَأُولَٰئِكَ هُمُ الْمُفْلِحُونَ ﴿١٠٢﴾ وَمَنْ خَفَّتْ مَوَازِينُهُ فَأُولَٰئِكَ الَّذِينَ خَسِرُوا أَنفُسَهُمْ فِي جَهَنَّمَ خَالِدُونَ ﴿١٠٣﴾ ﴾

Then, those whose scales (of good deeds) are heavy—these, they are the successful. And those whose scales (of good deeds) are light, they are those who lose their own selves; in Hell will they abide.

[Sūrah al-Mu'minūn 23:102-103]

So, if the evil deeds are heavy, then the individual shall be in a state

[2] Al-Bukhārī reported it (#103), as did Muslim (#2876) from the *ḥadīth* of 'Ā'ishah ﷺ.

of loss. And if the good deeds are heavy, then the individual shall be successful. This Scale is the scale of actions.

Likewise, he who is given his book in his right hand, then his reckoning shall be light; and he who is given his book in his left hand, then his reckoning shall be difficult, and he will see great terrors and perils. He who reflects upon the evils on the Day of Standing, the reckoning, and the gathering—then these are affairs which are terrifying if we think about them.

ORIGINAL TEXT

وَ مَنْ كَذَّبَ بِالْبَعْثِ كَفَرَ، وَ الدَّلِيلُ قَوْلُهُ تَعَالَى: ﴿ قُلْ بَلَىٰ وَرَبِّي لَتُبْعَثُنَّ ثُمَّ لَتُنَبَّؤُنَّ بِمَا عَمِلْتُمْ ۚ وَذَٰلِكَ عَلَى اللَّهِ يَسِيرٌ ﴾.

He who denies the resurrection has disbelieved. The proof is the statement of the Most High:

> **The disbelievers pretend that they will never be resurrected (for the Account). Say (O Muḥammad ﷺ): "Yes! By my Lord, you will certainly be resurrected; then you will be informed of (and recompensed for) what you did, and that is easy for Allāh."**
>
> *[Sūrah at-Taghābun 64:7]*

EXPLANATION

He stated, *"He who denies the resurrection has disbelieved"*: This is because he has obstinately rejected a pillar of *al-īmān*. This is also because he has denied Allāh, His messengers, and His Books. This is because Allāh ﷻ, the messengers, and the Books have all informed us about the resurrection, so he who rejects it is a disbeliever. The proof is the statement of the Most High: **"those who disbelieve claim"**; and "to claim" means "denial." He said, **"that they shall not be resurrected."**

Therefore, this verse proves that rejection of the resurrection is disbelief. They say that there is no resurrection after death. The polytheists and the worshipers of idols, during the time of the Prophet ﷺ, used to debate against the resurrection, as Allāh says:

﴿ أَإِذَا كُنَّا عِظَامًا نَّخِرَةً ۝١١ قَالُوا تِلْكَ إِذًا كَرَّةٌ خَاسِرَةٌ ۝١٢ ﴾

"Even after we are crumbled bones?" They say, "It would, in that case, be a return with loss!"

[Sūrah an-Nāzi'āt 79:11-12]

They said:

﴿ مَن يُحْيِي الْعِظَامَ وَهِيَ رَمِيمٌ ﴾

"Who will give life to these bones when they have rotted away and become dust?"

[Sūrah Yā-Sīn 36:78]

From their arguments is that they said:

﴿ أَيَعِدُكُمْ أَنَّكُمْ إِذَا مِتُّمْ وَكُنتُمْ تُرَابًا وَعِظَامًا أَنَّكُم مُّخْرَجُونَ ﴾

"Does he promise you that when you have died and have become dust and bones, you shall come out alive (resurrected)?"

[Sūrah al-Mu'minūn 23:35]

There are other statements of the disbelievers from the previous nations and the polytheists during the time of the Prophet ﷺ. So, he who denies the resurrection, then he has joined these disbelievers, and no one denies the resurrection except a disbeliever. Allāh ﷻ has commanded His Prophet ﷺ to swear by Him regarding the resurrection, wherein He said, **"Say: 'Yes! By my Lord'"**; this is an oath. He said:

﴿ لَتُبْعَثُنَّ ثُمَّ لَتُنَبَّؤُنَّ بِمَا عَمِلْتُمْ ﴾

"...you will certainly be resurrected, then you will

be informed of (and recompensed for) what you did..."

[Sūrah at-Taghābun 64:7]

This is one of three verses wherein Allāh commanded His Prophet to swear an oath regarding the resurrection.

The first verse is in Sūrah Yūnus:

﴿ وَيَسْتَنبِئُونَكَ أَحَقٌّ هُوَ ۖ قُلْ إِي وَرَبِّي إِنَّهُ لَحَقٌّ ۖ وَمَا أَنتُم بِمُعْجِزِينَ ﴾

And they ask you (O Muḥammad ﷺ) to inform them (saying): "Is it true (i.e., the torment and the establishment of the Hour—the Day of Resurrection)?" Say: "Yes! By my Lord! It is the very truth! And you cannot escape from it!"

[Sūrah Yūnus 10:53]

The second is in Sūrah Saba':

﴿ وَقَالَ الَّذِينَ كَفَرُوا لَا تَأْتِينَا السَّاعَةُ ۖ قُلْ بَلَىٰ وَرَبِّي لَتَأْتِيَنَّكُمْ عَالِمِ الْغَيْبِ ۖ لَا يَعْزُبُ عَنْهُ مِثْقَالُ ذَرَّةٍ فِي السَّمَاوَاتِ وَلَا فِي الْأَرْضِ وَلَا أَصْغَرُ مِن ذَٰلِكَ وَلَا أَكْبَرُ إِلَّا فِي كِتَابٍ مُّبِينٍ ﴿٣﴾ لِّيَجْزِيَ الَّذِينَ آمَنُوا وَعَمِلُوا الصَّالِحَاتِ ۚ أُولَٰئِكَ لَهُم مَّغْفِرَةٌ وَرِزْقٌ كَرِيمٌ ﴿٤﴾ ﴾

Those who disbelieve say, "The Hour will not come to us." Say: "Yes, by my Lord, it will come to you." (Allāh, He is) the All-Knower of the unseen; not even the weight of an atom (or a small ant) or less than that or greater, escapes from His knowledge in the heavens or in the earth, but it is in a Clear Book. That He may recompense those who believe and do righteous good deeds. Those, theirs is forgiveness

and *rizq karīm* (generous provision, i.e., Paradise).

[Sūrah Saba' 34:3-4]

The third verse is the one we are covering now, in Sūrah at-Taghābun:

﴿ زَعَمَ الَّذِينَ كَفَرُوا أَن لَّن يُبْعَثُوا ۚ قُلْ بَلَىٰ وَرَبِّي لَتُبْعَثُنَّ ثُمَّ لَتُنَبَّؤُنَّ بِمَا عَمِلْتُمْ ۚ وَذَٰلِكَ عَلَى اللَّهِ يَسِيرٌ ﴾

The disbelievers pretend that they will never be resurrected (for the Account). Say (O Muḥammad ﷺ): "Yes! By my Lord, you will certainly be resurrected, then you will be informed of (and recompensed for) what you did, and that is easy for Allāh."

[Sūrah at-Taghābun 64:7]

The wisdom behind the resurrection is to reward the servants for their actions.

The statement of the Most High, **"and you shall be informed"**: This means that you shall be informed regarding your actions and you shall be rewarded for them.

Īmān in the Messengers

ORIGINAL TEXT

وَ أَرْسَلَ اللهُ جَمِيعَ الرُّسُلِ مُبَشِّرِينَ وَ مُنْذِرِينَ، وَ الدَّلِيلُ قَوْلُهُ تَعَالَى: ﴿ رُّسُلًا مُّبَشِّرِينَ وَمُنذِرِينَ لِئَلَّا يَكُونَ لِلنَّاسِ عَلَى اللَّهِ حُجَّةٌ بَعْدَ الرُّسُلِ ۚ وَكَانَ اللَّهُ عَزِيزًا حَكِيمًا ﴾.

Allāh sent all of the messengers as bearers of glad tidings and as warners. The proof is the statement of the Most High:

Messengers as bearers of good news as well as of warning, so that mankind should have no plea

against Allāh after the messengers. And Allāh is Ever All-Powerful, All-Wise.

[Sūrah an-Nisā' 4:165]

EXPLANATION

Īmān in the messengers is one of the six pillars of *īmān*. The Prophet ﷺ said, "*Īmān* is that you believe in Allāh, His angels, His Books, His messengers…" Therefore, *īmān* in the messengers is one of the pillars of faith, so it is a must that one believes in all of the messengers, from the first of them to the last of them. He who obstinately rejects one messenger from amongst them, then he is disbeliever in all of them. As the Most High has said:

﴿ إِنَّ الَّذِينَ يَكْفُرُونَ بِاللَّهِ وَرُسُلِهِ وَيُرِيدُونَ أَن يُفَرِّقُوا بَيْنَ اللَّهِ وَرُسُلِهِ وَيَقُولُونَ نُؤْمِنُ بِبَعْضٍ وَنَكْفُرُ بِبَعْضٍ وَيُرِيدُونَ أَن يَتَّخِذُوا بَيْنَ ذَٰلِكَ سَبِيلًا ﴿١٥٠﴾ أُولَٰئِكَ هُمُ الْكَافِرُونَ حَقًّا ۚ وَأَعْتَدْنَا لِلْكَافِرِينَ عَذَابًا مُّهِينًا ﴿١٥١﴾ ﴾

Verily, those who disbelieve in Allāh and His messengers and wish to make distinction between Allāh and His messengers (by believing in Allāh and disbelieving in His messengers), saying, "We believe in some but reject others," and wish to adopt a way in between—they are in truth disbelievers. And We have prepared for the disbelievers a humiliating torment.

[Sūrah an-Nisā' 4:150-151]

Hence, it is necessary to have *īmān* in all of the messengers, from the first of them to the last of them, those whom Allāh has named in His Book and those whom He has not named. Indeed, the messengers are many. Due to this, it has been narrated in the *ḥadīth* that their number was:

مِائَةُ أَلْفٍ وَ أَرْبَعَةُ وَ عِشْرُونَ أَلْفًا، الرُّسُلُ مِنْ ذَلِكَ ثَلَاثُمِائَةٍ وَ

خَمْسَةَ عَشَرَ جَمًّا غَفِيرًا.

124,000; the messengers from amongst them were 315, which is a very large number.[3]

Allāh has named many of the messengers within His Book. There are also those He has not named. It is obligatory upon us to believe in all of them, from the first of them to the last of them.

ORIGINAL TEXT

وَ أَوَّلُهُمْ: نُوحٌ -عَلَيْهِ السَّلَامُ- وَ آخِرُهُمْ: مُحَمَّدٌ -صَلَّى اللهُ عَلَيْهِ وَ سَلَّمَ- وَ الدَّلِيلُ عَلَى أَنَّ أَوَّلَهُمْ نُوحٌ -عَلَيْهِ السَّلَامُ قَوْلُهُ تَعَالَى: ﴿ إِنَّا أَوْحَيْنَا إِلَيْكَ كَمَا أَوْحَيْنَا إِلَىٰ نُوحٍ وَالنَّبِيِّينَ مِن بَعْدِهِ ﴾.

The first of them was Nūḥ ﷺ and the last of them was Muḥammad ﷺ. The evidence that the first of them was Nūḥ ﷺ is the statement of the Most High:

> **Verily, We have inspired you (O Muḥammad ﷺ) as We inspired Nūḥ (Noah) and the prophets after him.**
>
> *[Sūrah an-Nisā' 4:163]*

EXPLANATION

The proof that the first of them was Nūḥ is the statement of the Most High: **"Verily, We have inspired you..."** This is an address to Muḥammad ﷺ. He said:

﴿ كَمَا أَوْحَيْنَا إِلَىٰ نُوحٍ وَالنَّبِيِّينَ مِن بَعْدِهِ ۚ وَأَوْحَيْنَا إِلَىٰ إِبْرَاهِيمَ وَإِسْمَاعِيلَ وَإِسْحَاقَ وَيَعْقُوبَ وَالْأَسْبَاطِ وَعِيسَىٰ وَأَيُّوبَ وَيُونُسَ وَهَارُونَ وَسُلَيْمَانَ ۚ وَآتَيْنَا دَاوُودَ زَبُورًا ﴾

[3] Aḥmad reported it in *Al-Musnad* (36/617-619, #22287) from the *ḥadīth* of Abū Umāmah al-Bāhilī ﷺ.

...as We inspired Nūḥ (Noah) and the prophets after him. We (also) inspired Ibrāhīm (Abraham), Ismā'īl (Ishmael), Is'ḥāq (Isaac), Ya'qūb (Jacob), and al-Asbāṭ [the twelve sons of Ya'qūb (Jacob)], 'Īsā (Jesus), Ayyūb (Job), Yūnus (Jonah), Hārūn (Aaron), and Sulaymān (Solomon); and to Dāwūd (David) We gave the Zabūr (Psalms).

[Sūrah an-Nisā' 4:163]

Here, in this verse, Allāh mentioned a number of their names. Likewise, He mentioned a number of their names in these verses of Sūrah al-An'ām:

﴿ وَوَهَبْنَا لَهُۥٓ إِسْحَٰقَ وَيَعْقُوبَ ۚ كُلًّا هَدَيْنَا ۚ وَنُوحًا هَدَيْنَا مِن قَبْلُ ۖ وَمِن ذُرِّيَّتِهِۦ دَاوُۥدَ وَسُلَيْمَٰنَ وَأَيُّوبَ وَيُوسُفَ وَمُوسَىٰ وَهَٰرُونَ ۚ وَكَذَٰلِكَ نَجْزِى ٱلْمُحْسِنِينَ ﴿٨٤﴾ وَزَكَرِيَّا وَيَحْيَىٰ وَعِيسَىٰ وَإِلْيَاسَ ۖ كُلٌّ مِّنَ ٱلصَّٰلِحِينَ ﴿٨٥﴾ وَإِسْمَٰعِيلَ وَٱلْيَسَعَ وَيُونُسَ وَلُوطًا ۚ وَكُلًّا فَضَّلْنَا عَلَى ٱلْعَٰلَمِينَ ﴿٨٦﴾ ﴾

And We bestowed upon him Is'ḥāq (Isaac) and Ya'qūb (Jacob), each of them We guided, and before him, We guided Nūḥ (Noah), and among his progeny Dāwūd (David), Sulaymān (Solomon), Ayyūb (Job), Yūsuf (Joseph), Mūsā (Moses), and Hārūn (Aaron). Thus do We reward the good doers. And Zakariyyā (Zachariah), Yaḥyā (John), 'Īsā (Jesus), and Ilyās (Elias)—each one of them was of the righteous. And Ismā'īl (Ishmael), al-Yasa' (Elisha), Yūnus (Jonah), and Lūṭ (Lot), and each one of them We preferred above the *'ālamīn* (mankind and *jinn*) (of their times).

[Sūrah al-An'ām 6:84-86]

So, the first of them was Nūḥ عليه السلام. The evidence is the statement of the Most High: **"and the prophets after him."** Allāh sent him to his people when they went to extremes regarding the righteous people, after the people had been upon the religion of *tawḥīd* since the time of Ādam for up to 10 generations after.

When the people of Nūḥ came, there were amongst them righteous men; and when these righteous men passed away, the people were extremely sad. Shayṭān took advantage of this opportunity and said to them, "Make images of these righteous men and erect them in your gatherings so that, whenever you look at these images, you will be reminded of their state and their activity in worship."

So, they made images of these dead people and erected them in their gathering places. They were not worshiped at the beginning of the affair due to the presence of scholars who clarified to the people *at-tawḥīd* and rejected *ash-shirk*. When the scholars passed away and the first group of people had vanished, there came a later group while the scholars were dead. Shayṭān came to them and said to them, "Indeed, your forefathers did not erect these images except to worship them, and the rain would descend by way of them."

He beautified for them the worship of these righteous men, and they worshiped them instead of Allāh. From this, *shirk* appeared on the earth. Therefore, Allāh sent His prophet Nūḥ عليه السلام to call them to Allāh عز وجل and return them to *at-tawḥīd*, which was the religion of their father Ādam عليه السلام. However, they refused and were arrogant. Allāh said:

﴿ وَقَالُوا لَا تَذَرُنَّ آلِهَتَكُمْ وَلَا تَذَرُنَّ وَدًّا وَلَا سُوَاعًا وَلَا يَغُوثَ وَيَعُوقَ وَنَسْرًا ﴾

And they have said, "You shall not leave your gods, nor shall you leave Wadd, nor Suwā', nor Yaghūth, nor Ya'ūq, nor Nasr."

[Sūrah Nūḥ 71:23]

Ibn 'Abbās said, "These were the names of righteous men. They made images and erected them in their places, so the affair took them to the point where they worshiped them."

So, when Nūḥ ﷺ came to them and prohibited them from worshiping [the idols], and he commanded them with the worship of Allāh, they said, "Do not leave your gods and do not obey Nūḥ, and continue in your disbelief, transgression, and rejection." This was the first occurrence of *shirk* on the earth, and the reason for it was images. Due to that, the Prophet ﷺ said:

إِنَّ أَشَدَّ النَّاسِ عَذَابًا يَوْمَ الْقِيَامَةِ الْمُصَوِّرُونَ.

The most severely punished from amongst the people with Allāh on the Day of Judgment are the picture makers.[4]

And he ﷺ said:

إِنَّ الَّذِينَ يَصْنَعُونَ هَذِهِ الصُّوَرَ يُعَذَّبُونَ يَوْمَ الْقِيَامَةِ يُقَالُ لَهُمْ أَحْيُوا مَا خَلَقْتُمْ.

Indeed, those who make these images shall be punished on the Day of Standing, and it will be said to them, "Give life to that which you have created."[5]

They will be commanded to breathe a soul into these images, from the perspective of their inability to do so and as a means of punishment for them; and refuge is sought with Allāh. This is because image making is a means to *ash-shirk,* as occurred with the people of Nūḥ.

So, the first of the messengers was Nūḥ; as for the last of the messengers and their seal, he is Muḥammad ﷺ. The Most High has said:

﴿ مَّا كَانَ مُحَمَّدٌ أَبَا أَحَدٍ مِّن رِّجَالِكُمْ وَلَٰكِن رَّسُولَ اللَّهِ وَخَاتَمَ النَّبِيِّينَ ﴾

Muḥammad is not the father of any man among

[4] Reported by al-Bukhārī (#5950) and Muslim (#2109) from the *ḥadīth* of 'Abdullāh bin Mas'ūd ﷺ.

[5] Al-Bukhārī reported it (#5951), as well as Muslim (#2108) from the *ḥadīth* of 'Abdullāh bin 'Umar ﷺ.

you, but he is the Messenger of Allāh and the last (end) of the prophets.

[Sūrah al-Aḥzāb 33:40]

And he ﷺ said:

وَ أَنَا خَاتِمُ النَّبِيِّينَ، لَا نَبِيَّ بَعْدِي.

I am the seal of the prophets; there is no prophet after me.[6]

By way of him ﷺ, the heavenly messages were sealed; therefore, there will be no prophet sent after him until the establishment of the Hour. However, his legislation remains until the Hour is established and his religion remains until the Hour is established, as has preceded. So he who claims prophethood after Muḥammad ﷺ, then he is a disbeliever, and whoever believes him (this false prophet) is a disbeliever. This is because there is no prophet after him ﷺ.

A large number of people claimed prophethood after him, and Allāh humiliated them and exposed their lies. From the last of them, according to what we know, is al-Qādiyānī, Ghulām Aḥmad al-Qādiyānī al-Hindī, who at first claimed knowledge and worship, then he claimed that he was ʿĪsā bin Maryam, then he claimed prophethood. Now he has followers who are called the Qādiyāniyyah.

The Muslims have declared them to be disbelievers, and they oppose them and consider them to be a disbelieving sect which is outside the fold of Islām. And they are rejected and ostracized—and for Allāh is all praise—from the lands of the Muslims. They have some activity; however, their activity is weak.

In summary: There is no prophet after the Messenger of Allāh ﷺ. He who claims prophethood after him is a liar, as he ﷺ has said:

لَا تَقُومُ السَّاعَةُ حَتَّى يَبْعَثَ دَجَّالُونَ كَذَّابُونَ، قَرِيبًا مِنْ ثَلَاثِينَ،

[6] Abū Dāwūd reported it (#4252), as did at-Tirmidhī (#2219) from the *ḥadīth* of Thawbān ﷺ.

كُلُّهُمْ يَزْعَمُ أَنَّهُ رَسُولُ اللهِ.

The Hour will not be established until there appear approximately 30 liars, all of them claiming that he is the messenger of Allāh.[7]

ORIGINAL TEXT

وَ كُلُّ أُمَّةٍ بَعَثَ اللهُ إِلَيْهِمْ رَسُولاً مِنْ نُوحٍ إِلَى مُحَمَّدٍ يَأْمُرُهُمْ بِعِبَادَةِ اللهِ وَحْدَهُ وَ يَنْهَاهُمْ عَنْ عِبَادَةِ الطَّاغُوتِ، وَ الدَّلِيلُ قَوْلُهُ تَعَالَى: ﴿وَلَقَدْ بَعَثْنَا فِي كُلِّ أُمَّةٍ رَّسُولًا أَنِ اعْبُدُوا اللَّهَ وَاجْتَنِبُوا الطَّاغُوتَ﴾.

Allāh sent a messenger to every nation, from Nūḥ to Muḥammad, commanding them with the worship of Allāh alone and prohibiting them from worshiping *aṭ-ṭāghūt*. The proof is the statement of the Most High:

> **And verily, We have sent among every *ummah* (community, nation) a messenger (proclaiming): "Worship Allāh (alone), and avoid (or keep away from) *ṭāghūt*."**
>
> *[Sūrah an-Naḥl 16:36]*

EXPLANATION

Those who claim prophethood are many; however, Allāh exposes their affair, removes their covering, and clarifies their deception to the people. He who believes them is a disbeliever, because he has denied Allāh, His Messenger ﷺ, and the consensus of the Muslims regarding the sealing of prophethood by way of Muḥammad ﷺ.

His statement, **"Allāh sent to every nation a messenger"**: This means that Allāh sent to every nation a messenger from amongst the people, in order to establish the proof against them so that they would not be able to say, "There did not come to us a bringer of

[7] Al-Bukhārī reported it (#3609), as did Muslim (#2923).

glad tidings nor a warner." And due to the statement of the Most High:

﴿ وَمَا كُنَّا مُعَذِّبِينَ حَتَّىٰ نَبْعَثَ رَسُولًا ﴾

And We never punish until We have sent a messenger (to give warning).

[Sūrah al-Isrā' 17:15]

Hence, Allāh sent a messenger to every nation from the previous nations. As the Most High has said:

﴿ وَإِن مِّنْ أُمَّةٍ إِلَّا خَلَا فِيهَا نَذِيرٌ ﴾

And there never was a nation but a warner had passed among them.

[Sūrah Fāṭir 35:24]

However, it is obligatory that we know what the *da'wah* of the messengers was. The *da'wah* of all the messengers, from the first of them to the last of them, was a call to *at-tawḥīd*, due to the statement of the Most High:

﴿ وَلَقَدْ بَعَثْنَا فِي كُلِّ أُمَّةٍ رَّسُولًا أَنِ اعْبُدُوا اللَّهَ وَاجْتَنِبُوا الطَّاغُوتَ ﴾

And verily, We have sent among every *ummah* (community, nation) a messenger (proclaiming): "Worship Allāh (alone), and avoid (or keep away from) *ṭāghūt*."

[Sūrah an-Naḥl 16:36]

Everything which is worshiped other than Allāh is *ṭāghūt*, as shall come in the explanation of the various types of *ṭāghūt*. From the types is he who is worshiped besides Allāh while being pleased with that, as shall come.

So, the meaning of the statement of the Most High, **"and avoid (or keep away from) *ṭāghūt*,"** is to avoid the worship of idols, false deities, graves, and mausoleums. These are all *ṭāghūt*. This noble verse indicates that the call of all the messengers was the establishment of *at-tawḥīd*, from the first of them to the last of them. As Allāh ﷻ has stated:

﴿ وَمَا أَرْسَلْنَا مِن قَبْلِكَ مِن رَّسُولٍ إِلَّا نُوحِي إِلَيْهِ أَنَّهُ لَا إِلَٰهَ إِلَّا أَنَا فَاعْبُدُونِ ﴾

And We did not send any messenger before you (O Muḥammad ﷺ) but We inspired him (saying): *Lā ilāha illā Ana* [none has the right to be worshiped but I (Allāh)], so worship Me (alone and none else).

[Sūrah al-Anbiyā' 21:25]

Also, there is His statement:

﴿ يُنَزِّلُ الْمَلَائِكَةَ بِالرُّوحِ مِنْ أَمْرِهِ عَلَىٰ مَن يَشَاءُ مِنْ عِبَادِهِ أَنْ أَنذِرُوا أَنَّهُ لَا إِلَٰهَ إِلَّا أَنَا فَاتَّقُونِ ﴾

He sends down the angels with inspiration of His command to whom of His slaves He pleases, (saying): "Warn mankind that *lā ilāha illā Ana* (none has the right to be worshiped but I), so fear Me."

[Sūrah an-Naḥl 16:2]

So, all of the messengers called to *at-tawḥīd,* the singling out of Allāh ﷻ with worship, and the prohibition of *shirk*. This is the call of the messengers. After *tawḥīd* comes the other legislations, from the *ḥalāl* and the *ḥarām*. The details of the legislations vary with the different nations and the need of the nations for them.

Allāh abrogated from [the legislations] that which He wills. Then, all of it was abrogated by way of the legislations of al-Islām—the *ḥalāl* and the *ḥarām*, the rulings, the acts of worship, and the commands and the prohibitions. As for the foundation, then it is *at-tawḥīd*. There is no difference in this [between the messengers] nor is it ever abrogated. This is one religion. The religion of all of the messengers, from the first of them to the last of them, was one.

As Allāh, the Most High, has stated:

﴿ لِكُلٍّ جَعَلْنَا مِنكُمْ شِرْعَةً وَمِنْهَاجًا ﴾

To each among you, We have prescribed a law and a clear way.

[Sūrah al-Mā'idah 5:48]

The religion of *at-tawḥīd* is to worship Allāh as He has legislated, in every time. So, if this legislation is abrogated, then the authority transfers to the one that is abrogating. He who persists and remains upon what has been abrogated and abandons what has abrogated it, then he is a disbeliever in Allāh ﷻ. This is because the religion which has been abrogated is no longer a religion after its abrogation. It was only a religion before it was abrogated. Therefore, when it is abrogated, it is no longer a religion. The religion is that which has abrogated it.

Due to this, the legislation of al-Islām has abrogated what came before it from the previous legislations. So, he who remains upon Judaism or Christianity after the sending of Muḥammad ﷺ, then he is a disbeliever. This is because he has acted upon a religion which was abrogated and whose time has ended.

Disbelief in aṭ-Ṭāghūt & Belief in Allāh

ORIGINAL TEXT

وَافْتَرَضَ اللهُ عَلَى جَمِيعِ الْعِبَادِ الْكُفْرَ بِالطَّاغُوتِ وَ الْإِيمَانَ بِاللهِ.

Allāh has made obligatory upon all of the servants disbelief in *aṭ-ṭāghūt* and *īmān* in Allāh.

EXPLANATION

The Shaykh رحمه الله stated, *"Allāh has made obligatory upon all of the servants disbelief in aṭ-ṭāghūt and īmān in Allāh."* Then he mentioned the definition of *aṭ-ṭāghūt*.

Aṭ-ṭāghūt has been mentioned by Allāh ﷻ in many verses. From them is the statement of the Most High, in Sūrah al-Baqarah:

﴿ لَا إِكْرَاهَ فِي الدِّينِ ۖ قَد تَّبَيَّنَ الرُّشْدُ مِنَ الْغَيِّ ۚ فَمَن يَكْفُرْ بِالطَّاغُوتِ وَيُؤْمِن بِاللَّهِ فَقَدِ اسْتَمْسَكَ بِالْعُرْوَةِ الْوُثْقَىٰ لَا انفِصَامَ لَهَا ۗ وَاللَّهُ سَمِيعٌ عَلِيمٌ ﴿٢٥٦﴾ اللَّهُ وَلِيُّ الَّذِينَ آمَنُوا يُخْرِجُهُم مِّنَ الظُّلُمَاتِ إِلَى النُّورِ ۖ وَالَّذِينَ كَفَرُوا أَوْلِيَاؤُهُمُ الطَّاغُوتُ يُخْرِجُونَهُم مِّنَ النُّورِ إِلَى الظُّلُمَاتِ ۗ أُولَٰئِكَ أَصْحَابُ النَّارِ ۖ هُمْ فِيهَا خَالِدُونَ ﴿٢٥٧﴾ ﴾

There is no compulsion in religion. Verily, the Right Path has become distinct from the wrong path. Whoever disbelieves in *ṭāghūt* and believes in Allāh, then he has grasped the most trustworthy handhold that will never break. And Allāh is All-Hearer, All-Knower. Allāh is the Walī (Protector or Guardian) of those who believe. He brings them out from darkness into light. But as for those who disbelieve, their *awliyā'* (supporters and helpers) are *ṭāghūt* (false deities and false leaders, etc.); they bring them out from light into darkness. Those are the dwellers of the Fire, and they will abide therein forever.

[Sūrah al-Baqarah 2:256-257]

Likewise, in Sūrah an-Nisā', there is the statement of the Most High:

﴿ أَلَمْ تَرَ إِلَى الَّذِينَ أُوتُوا نَصِيبًا مِّنَ الْكِتَابِ يُؤْمِنُونَ بِالْجِبْتِ وَالطَّاغُوتِ وَيَقُولُونَ لِلَّذِينَ كَفَرُوا هَٰؤُلَاءِ أَهْدَىٰ مِنَ الَّذِينَ آمَنُوا سَبِيلًا ﴾

Have you not seen those who were given a portion of the scripture? They believe in *jibt* and *ṭāghūt* (false deities) and say to the disbelievers that they are better guided regarding the way than the believers.

[Sūrah an-Nisā' 4:51]

This verse was revealed concerning the Jews. He, Exalted be He, has stated concerning the hypocrites:

﴿ أَلَمْ تَرَ إِلَى الَّذِينَ يَزْعُمُونَ أَنَّهُمْ آمَنُوا بِمَا أُنزِلَ إِلَيْكَ وَمَا أُنزِلَ مِن قَبْلِكَ يُرِيدُونَ أَن يَتَحَاكَمُوا إِلَى الطَّاغُوتِ وَقَدْ أُمِرُوا أَن يَكْفُرُوا بِهِ ﴾

Have you seen those (hypocrites) who claim that they believe in what has been sent down to you, and what was sent down before you, and they wish to go for judgment (in their disputes) to the *ṭāghūt* (false judges, etc.) while they have been ordered to reject them.

[Sūrah an-Nisā' 4:60]

In Sūrah an-Naḥl, Allāh ﷻ says:

﴿ وَلَقَدْ بَعَثْنَا فِي كُلِّ أُمَّةٍ رَّسُولًا أَنِ اعْبُدُوا اللَّهَ وَاجْتَنِبُوا الطَّاغُوتَ ﴾

And verily, We have sent among every *ummah* (community, nation) a messenger (proclaiming): "Worship Allāh (alone), and avoid (or keep away from) *ṭāghūt*."

[Sūrah an-Naḥl 16:36]

Aṭ-ṭāghūt is derived from the word *aṭ-ṭughyān*, and it means "going beyond the bounds." It is said, "The water has gone beyond the bounds" when it rises above its tide. Allāh the Exalted said:

﴿ إِنَّا لَمَّا طَغَى الْمَاءُ حَمَلْنَاكُمْ فِي الْجَارِيَةِ ﴾

Verily! When the water rose beyond its limits (Nūḥ's flood), We carried you (mankind) in the floating ship.

[*Sūrah al-Ḥāqqah 69:11*]

ORIGINAL TEXT ————————————————————————

قَالَ ابْنُ الْقَيِّمِ: مَعْنَى الطَّاغُوتِ: مَا تَجَاوَزَ بِهِ الْعَبْدُ حَدَّهُ مِنْ مَعْبُودٍ، أَوْ مَتْبُوعٍ، أَوْ مُطَاعٍ.

Ibn al-Qayyim has said, "The meaning of *aṭ-ṭāghūt* is that regarding which the servant goes beyond the bounds, from what is worshiped, followed, or obeyed."

———————————————————— EXPLANATION ————————————————————

As for the meaning of *aṭ-ṭāghūt* in the legislation, it is as Ibn al-Qayyim ﷭ has mentioned, and the Shaykh has transmitted that from him here. *Aṭ-ṭāghūt* is that regarding which the servant goes beyond the bounds. The servant has a boundary; this is because he is a servant. Allāh sets boundaries for him, and it is obligatory upon him to stop at these boundaries. If he transgresses them, he becomes a *ṭāghūt*. So, he who transgresses the boundaries of Allāh—which He has set for His servants and commanded them not to transgress and not to approach—then he is a *ṭāghūt*. Therefore, if one disobeys Allāh and transgresses and infringes upon His bounds, then he is referred to as *ṭāghūt* because he has infringed and transgressed the limits of Allāh.

Regarding his statement *"that regarding which the servant goes beyond the bounds, from what is worshiped, followed, or obeyed"*: This is a comprehensive definition of *aṭ-ṭāghūt*, because Allāh ﷻ has commanded with worshiping Him alone and associating none as a partner with Him. And He has commanded with following the Messenger ﷺ, and He has commanded with obedience to Him and obedience to His Messenger in that which he makes *ḥalāl* and *ḥarām*. So, he who transgresses this command is a *ṭāghūt*. He who transgresses the limit of worship—which Allāh has obligated, specified Himself with, and negated from other than Him—so that he worships Allāh along with other than him, then he is a *ṭāghūt.*

The *mushrik* is a *ṭāghūt* because he has transgressed the boundaries in worship, and he worships other than Allāh along with Him, and he has given worship to other than the One to whom it is due.

Likewise, he who is worshiped and is pleased with that; one who the people worship, and he enjoys this and directs them to this thing, then he is a *ṭāghūt.* For example: Fir'awn, Nimrod, and the *mashāyikh* of the extreme Sufi paths, whose followers worship them while they are pleased with that. Or they call the people to this; meaning, to worship them, as shall come. Then this (person) is a *ṭāghūt* in worship.

The statement *"or followed"*: Allāh ﷻ has commanded all of the creation to follow Muḥammad ﷺ. Therefore, it is not permissible for anyone to follow other than him. He who follows other than the Messenger ﷺ and claims that this is permissible, then he is a *ṭāghūt.* This is because he has followed other than the Messenger ﷺ, whose following has been commanded. So, following is specific to the Messenger. As for other than him, from the scholars and the callers, then these are followed (only) if they follow the path of the Messenger ﷺ. The one who is followed is the Messenger ﷺ. As for these, then they are only conveyors of the truth and whatever they are in conformity with from the following of the Messenger ﷺ. For that wherein they oppose the Messenger ﷺ, then following them is not permissible in that.

The example of this is the *mashāyikh* of the Sufi paths. Their mureeds and servants follow them in other than the obedience of the Messenger ﷺ. Rather, they say, "We are in no need of the Messenger ﷺ. We take from that which the Messenger ﷺ has taken from, and we take from Allāh directly. The Messenger ﷺ took from Allāh by way of a medium, and the medium was Jibrīl. We take from Allāh directly." And they say, "You narrate your religion from one who is dead, and we narrate our religion from Allāh ﷻ."

This is because they claim that their *shuyūkh* contact Allāh and take from Allāh directly. The limit with them has reached this (level of) transgression, and refuge is sought with Allāh. This is their path. There is no doubt that these people are heads of the *ṭāghūt*, and refuge is sought with Allāh. This is because there is no path to Allāh ﷻ except by way of following His Messenger ﷺ. The Most High has stated:

﴿ قُلْ إِن كُنتُمْ تُحِبُّونَ اللَّهَ فَاتَّبِعُونِي يُحْبِبْكُمُ اللَّهُ وَيَغْفِرْ لَكُمْ ذُنُوبَكُمْ ۗ وَاللَّهُ غَفُورٌ رَّحِيمٌ ﴿٣١﴾ قُلْ أَطِيعُوا اللَّهَ وَالرَّسُولَ ۖ فَإِن تَوَلَّوْا فَإِنَّ اللَّهَ لَا يُحِبُّ الْكَافِرِينَ ﴿٣٢﴾ ﴾

Say (O Muḥammad ﷺ to mankind): "If you (really) love Allāh, then follow me (i.e., accept Islamic monotheism, follow the Qur'ān and the Sunnah), Allāh will love you and forgive you of your sins. And Allāh is Oft-Forgiving, Most Merciful." Say (O Muḥammad ﷺ): "Obey Allāh and the Messenger (Muḥammad ﷺ)." But if they turn away, then Allāh does not like the disbelievers.

[Sūrah Āli 'Imrān 3:31-32]

So, the one who follows other than the Messenger is considered a *ṭāghūt*.

Likewise, the one who calls to following himself and says to the people, "I come to you with a command directly from Allāh," then this is the greatest of the *ṭāghūt* in the world, and refuge is sought with Allāh.

His statement *"or obeyed"*: Obedience is only for Allāh and for His Messenger in that which He has made *ḥalāl* or *ḥarām*. The Most High has said:

﴿ يَا أَيُّهَا الَّذِينَ آمَنُوا أَطِيعُوا اللَّهَ وَأَطِيعُوا الرَّسُولَ وَأُولِي الْأَمْرِ مِنكُمْ ۖ فَإِن تَنَازَعْتُمْ فِي شَيْءٍ فَرُدُّوهُ إِلَى اللَّهِ

وَالرَّسُولِ إِن كُنتُمْ تُؤْمِنُونَ بِاللَّهِ وَالْيَوْمِ الْآخِرِ ۚ ذَٰلِكَ خَيْرٌ وَأَحْسَنُ تَأْوِيلًا ﴾

O you who believe! Obey Allāh and obey the Messenger (Muḥammad ﷺ), and those of you (Muslims) who are in authority. (And) if you differ in anything amongst yourselves, refer it to Allāh and His Messenger, if you believe in Allāh and in the Last Day. That is better and more suitable for final determination.

[Sūrah an-Nisā' 4:59]

So, what is *ḥalāl* is that which Allāh has made *ḥalāl*, and what is *ḥarām* is that which Allāh has made *ḥarām*. It is not for anyone to share with Allāh in making things *ḥalāl* and *ḥarām*. Due to that, Allāh has ruled that whoever makes something *ḥalāl* or *ḥarām* or obeys the one who does that, then he is a *mushrik*. Allāh ﷻ has said:

﴿ فَكُلُوا مِمَّا ذُكِرَ اسْمُ اللَّهِ عَلَيْهِ إِن كُنتُم بِآيَاتِهِ مُؤْمِنِينَ ﴿١١٨﴾ وَمَا لَكُمْ أَلَّا تَأْكُلُوا مِمَّا ذُكِرَ اسْمُ اللَّهِ عَلَيْهِ وَقَدْ فَصَّلَ لَكُم مَّا حَرَّمَ عَلَيْكُمْ إِلَّا مَا اضْطُرِرْتُمْ إِلَيْهِ ۗ وَإِنَّ كَثِيرًا لَّيُضِلُّونَ بِأَهْوَائِهِم بِغَيْرِ عِلْمٍ ۗ إِنَّ رَبَّكَ هُوَ أَعْلَمُ بِالْمُعْتَدِينَ ﴿١١٩﴾ وَذَرُوا ظَاهِرَ الْإِثْمِ وَبَاطِنَهُ ۚ إِنَّ الَّذِينَ يَكْسِبُونَ الْإِثْمَ سَيُجْزَوْنَ بِمَا كَانُوا يَقْتَرِفُونَ ﴿١٢٠﴾ وَلَا تَأْكُلُوا مِمَّا لَمْ يُذْكَرِ اسْمُ اللَّهِ عَلَيْهِ وَإِنَّهُ لَفِسْقٌ ۗ وَإِنَّ الشَّيَاطِينَ لَيُوحُونَ إِلَىٰ أَوْلِيَائِهِمْ لِيُجَادِلُوكُمْ ۖ وَإِنْ أَطَعْتُمُوهُمْ إِنَّكُمْ لَمُشْرِكُونَ ﴿١٢١﴾ ﴾

So eat of that (meat) on which Allāh's name has been pronounced (while slaughtering the animal), if you are believers in His *āyāt* (proofs, evidences, verses, lessons, signs, revelations, etc.). And why

should you not eat of that (meat) on which Allāh's name has been pronounced (at the time of slaughtering the animal), while He has explained to you in detail what is forbidden to you, except under compulsion of necessity? And surely many do lead (mankind) astray by their own desires through lack of knowledge. Certainly, your Lord knows best the transgressors. Leave (O mankind, all kinds of) sin, open and secret. Verily, those who commit sin will get due recompense for that which they used to commit. Eat not (O believers) of that (meat) on which Allāh's name has not been pronounced (at the time of the slaughtering of the animal); for sure it is *fisq* (a sin and disobedience of Allāh). And certainly, the *shayāṭin* (devils) do inspire their friends (from mankind) to dispute with you, and if you obey them, then you would indeed be *mushrikūn* (polytheists).

[Sūrah al-An'ām 6:118-121]

This is because the people of Jāhiliyyah said that *al-maytah* is *ḥalāl* because Allāh is the one who has slaughtered it. Therefore, it (according to them) has more right to be *ḥalāl* than what you have slaughtered and sacrificed, for Allāh has said, **"Do not eat except that which is sacrificed legislatively, and He has made *al-maytah* *ḥarām* for you."**

These people say *al-maytah* is *ḥalāl*. [They say] it has more right to be permissible than that which is sacrificed, because the sacrifice is slaughtered by people. As for the *maytah,* then Allāh is the one who has slaughtered it (according to them). Due to this, Allāh has refuted the polytheist and said:

﴿ وَلَا تَأْكُلُوا مِمَّا لَمْ يُذْكَرِ اسْمُ اللَّهِ عَلَيْهِ وَإِنَّهُ لَفِسْقٌ ﴾

Eat not (O believers) of that (meat) on which Allāh's name has not been pronounced (at the time of the slaughtering of the animal); for sure it is *fisq* (a sin

and disobedience of Allāh).

[Sūrah al-An'ām 6:121]

Meaning, it is going outside of the realm of obedience to Allāh, Glorified be He. And He said thereafter:

﴿ وَإِنَّ الشَّيَاطِينَ لَيُوحُونَ إِلَىٰ أَوْلِيَائِهِمْ لِيُجَادِلُوكُمْ ﴾

And certainly, the *shayāṭin* (devils) do inspire their friends (from mankind) to dispute with you.

[Sūrah al-An'ām 6:121]

They say, "*Al-maytah* is slaughtered by Allāh; and that which is sacrificed, then you yourselves have slaughtered it. So, how can you deem *ḥalāl* that which you have slaughtered, and you do not deem *ḥalāl* that which Allāh has slaughtered?" This is a false argument.

Then the Most High says:

﴿ وَإِنْ أَطَعْتُمُوهُمْ إِنَّكُمْ لَمُشْرِكُونَ ﴾

And if you obey them, then you would indeed be *mushrikūn* (polytheists).

[Sūrah al-An'ām 6:121]

This is from *shirk* in obedience, because making *ḥalāl* and *ḥarām* is a right that is exclusively for Allāh. Therefore, it is not permissible for anyone to make something *ḥalāl* or *ḥarām* from himself, or to obey one who makes something *ḥalāl* or *ḥarām* from himself. Whoever does that, then he is *ṭāghūt*; and the one who obeys the *ṭāghūt* that has made something *ḥalāl* or *ḥarām* in opposition to Allāh, then this is the meaning of His statement **"or obeyed"**—meaning, obeyed in making *ḥalāl* and *ḥarām*. This is because making *ḥalāl* and *ḥarām* is a right that is exclusively for Allāh ﷻ. And the Messenger ﷺ conveys from his Lord that which He has made *ḥalāl* and *ḥarām*.

The Types of Ṭāghūt

ORIGINAL TEXT

وَ الطَّوَاغِيتُ كَثِيرُونَ، وَ رُءُوسُهُمْ خَمْسَةٌ: إِبْلِيسُ لَعَنَهُ اللهُ، وَ مَنْ عُبِدَ وَ هُوَ رَاضٍ...

The *ṭāghūt* are many, and their heads are five. They are:

1) Iblīs, may Allāh curse him.

2) He who is worshiped and is pleased with that.

EXPLANATION

His statement, *"The ṭāghūt are many, and their heads are five"*: The *ṭāghūt* that this definition is applied to is everything that is worshiped, followed, or obeyed; and they are many. However, their heads are five—meaning, the greatest forms of them are five.

The first is Iblīs, may Allāh curse him. Meaning, may Allāh repel him and distance him from His mercy. This is because he withheld from prostrating to Ādam, he disobeyed Allāh, and he was arrogant. He said:

﴿ قَالَ أَنَا خَيْرٌ مِّنْهُ ۖ خَلَقْتَنِي مِن نَّارٍ وَخَلَقْتَهُ مِن طِينٍ ﴾

He (Iblīs) said, "I am better than him. You created me from fire, and You created him from clay."

[Sūrah Ṣād 38:76]

He disobeyed the command of Allāh and was arrogant. Therefore, Allāh cursed him, repelled him, and distanced him from His mercy; thus, He named him Iblīs. It is said that this is because he despaired from the mercy of Allāh; meaning, he has no hope for the mercy of Allāh. The one who despairs has no hope for a thing. Therefore, Iblīs, may Allāh curse him, is the head of the *ṭāghūt*. This is because he is the one who commands with worship of other than Allāh. He is the one who commands the following of other than the Messenger ﷺ, and he is the one who commands the obedience of other than Allāh in making things *ḥalāl* and *ḥarām*. Therefore, Iblīs is the origin of evil and he is the head of the *ṭāghūt*.

Secondly is he who is worshiped while being pleased. Meaning, he is pleased that the people worship him; he is *ṭāghūt*.

As for he who is worshiped while he is not pleased with that, then he does not fall under this heading. This is because 'Īsā عليه السلام is worshiped besides Allāh, but he is not pleased with that. Likewise, his mother and 'Uzayr, the *awliyā'*, and the righteous people from the worshipers of Allāh are not pleased with that. Rather, they reject that and they wage war against doing it. So, if he is worshiped while he is not pleased with that, then he is not referred to as *ṭāghūt*.

Due to this, when Allāh revealed His statement:

﴿ إِنَّكُمْ وَمَا تَعْبُدُونَ مِن دُونِ اللَّهِ حَصَبُ جَهَنَّمَ أَنتُمْ لَهَا وَارِدُونَ ﴾

Certainly! You (disbelievers) and that which you are worshiping now besides Allāh, are (but) fuel for Hell! (Surely), you will enter it.

[Sūrah al-Anbiyā' 21:98]

The pagans rejoiced, saying, "We worship the Messiah, and we worship this and we worship that, so they will be with us in the Fire." So Allāh, the Most High, revealed:

﴿ إِنَّ الَّذِينَ سَبَقَتْ لَهُم مِّنَّا الْحُسْنَىٰ أُولَٰئِكَ عَنْهَا مُبْعَدُونَ ﴿١٠١﴾ لَا يَسْمَعُونَ حَسِيسَهَا ۖ وَهُمْ فِي مَا اشْتَهَتْ أَنفُسُهُمْ خَالِدُونَ ﴿١٠٢﴾ ﴾

Verily, those for whom the good has preceded from Us, they will be removed far therefrom (Hell) [e.g., 'Īsā (Jesus), son of Maryam (Mary), 'Uzayr (Ezra), etc.]. They shall not hear the slightest sound of it (Hell), while they abide in that which their own

selves desire.

[Sūrah al-Anbiyā' 21:101-102]

In another verse, they said:

﴿ وَقَالُوٓا۟ ءَأَٰلِهَتُنَا خَيْرٌ أَمْ هُوَ ﴾

And say, "Are our *ālihah* (gods) better or is he?"

[Sūrah az-Zukhruf 43:58]

They were referring to 'Īsā عليه السلام. Then Allāh said:

﴿ مَا ضَرَبُوهُ لَكَ إِلَّا جَدَلًۢا ۚ بَلْ هُمْ قَوْمٌ خَصِمُونَ ۝٥٨ إِنْ هُوَ إِلَّا عَبْدٌ أَنْعَمْنَا عَلَيْهِ وَجَعَلْنَٰهُ مَثَلًا لِّبَنِىٓ إِسْرَٰٓءِيلَ ۝٥٩ ﴾

They quoted not the above example except for argument. Nay! But they are a quarrelsome people. He ['Īsā (Jesus)] was not more than a slave. We granted Our favor to him, and We made him an example to the Children of Israel.

[Sūrah az-Zukhruf 43:58-59]

Therefore, he is a servant of Allāh, and he is not pleased to be worshiped instead of Allāh. Rather, Allāh sent him to reject that, as he said:

﴿ مَا قُلْتُ لَهُمْ إِلَّا مَآ أَمَرْتَنِى بِهِۦٓ أَنِ ٱعْبُدُوا۟ ٱللَّهَ رَبِّى وَرَبَّكُمْ ﴾

"Never did I say to them aught except what You (Allāh) did command me to say, 'Worship Allāh, my Lord and your Lord.'"

[Sūrah al-Mā'idah 5:117]

Therefore, the one who is worshiped while he is not pleased with that does not fall under this threat and he is not *ṭāghūt*, because he rejects that. This is because the *ṭāghūt* is the one who is pleased that he is worshiped beside Allāh ﷻ.

ORIGINAL TEXT

...وَ مَنْ دَعَا النَّاسَ إِلَى عِبَادَةِ نَفْسِهِ...

3) The one who calls people to the worship of himself.

EXPLANATION

The third is the one who calls people to the worship of himself, such as the heads of the pagans who call the people to worship themselves, like Fir'awn. He said:

﴿ فَقَالَ أَنَا رَبُّكُمُ الْأَعْلَىٰ ﴾

Saying, "I am your lord, most high."

[Sūrah an-Nāzi'āt 79:24]

Also, like Nimrod and the extreme Sufis who call the people to worship them, to the point that they advise them to worship them after they die. So one of them would say, "When your affairs become difficult, then come to my grave." Meaning, "When you are not able to take care of your affairs, then come to my grave. And do not be hindered by a small amount of dirt (i.e., the distance you travel)." So they would advise the people to come to their graves and promise them that they would take care of their needs. Therefore, he who calls the people to the worship of himself, whether dead or alive, is from the heads of the *ṭāghūt*.

Likewise, he who calls the people to the worship of other than himself is from the *ṭāghūt*. These are the callers to *shirk*. These are the *ṭāghūt*. Those who beautify *shirk* for the people and call it by other than its name, and they say that this is from the perspective of *at-tawassul* (seeking a means of approach to Allāh), or that this is from seeking intercession, and they are many—indeed, these are the *ṭāghūt*, because they call to *shirk*. They call to the worship of other than Allāh, they call it by other than its name, and they beautify it for the people by way of doubts and adorned speech. These are, in fact, the *ṭāghūt*. Callers to *shirk* are *aṭ-ṭāghūt*. And anyone who is worshiped other than Allāh while being pleased with that, who calls the people to the worship of himself, or who calls the people to the worship of other than Allāh, then he is from the *ṭāghūt*. Rather, he is from the heads of the *ṭāghūt*, and we ask Allāh for safety.

ORIGINAL TEXT

...وَ مَنْ ادَّعَى شَيْئًا مِنَ الْغَيْبِ...

4) He who claims to have knowledge of the unseen.

EXPLANATION

The fourth is the one who claims to have knowledge of the unseen; and the magicians are included in this, as are the astrologists, fortune-tellers, soothsayers, and all those who claim to have knowledge of the unseen. And they say to the people, "Such-and-such shall happen to you." And, "You shall acquire happiness." Or, "Some difficulty shall come to you." Or, "You will be successful in marriage." Or, "You shall not be successful." These people are claiming to have knowledge of the unseen, while the unseen is not known except by Allāh ﷻ. Allāh, the Most High, has stated:

﴿ قُل لَّا يَعْلَمُ مَن فِي السَّمَاوَاتِ وَالْأَرْضِ الْغَيْبَ إِلَّا اللَّهُ ﴾

Say: "None in the heavens and the earth knows the *ghayb* (unseen) except Allāh."

[Sūrah an-Naml 27:65]

The Most High has said:

﴿ عَالِمُ الْغَيْبِ فَلَا يُظْهِرُ عَلَىٰ غَيْبِهِ أَحَدًا ﴿٢٦﴾ إِلَّا مَنِ ارْتَضَىٰ مِن رَّسُولٍ ﴾

"(He alone is) the All-Knower of the *ghayb* (unseen), and He reveals to none His *ghayb* (unseen)." Except

to a messenger (from mankind) whom He has chosen.

[Sūrah al-Jinn 72:26-27]

The Most High has said:

﴿ وَعِندَهُۥ مَفَاتِحُ ٱلْغَيْبِ لَا يَعْلَمُهَآ إِلَّا هُوَ ۚ وَيَعْلَمُ مَا فِى ٱلْبَرِّ وَٱلْبَحْرِ ۚ وَمَا تَسْقُطُ مِن وَرَقَةٍ إِلَّا يَعْلَمُهَا وَلَا حَبَّةٍ فِى ظُلُمَـٰتِ ٱلْأَرْضِ وَلَا رَطْبٍ وَلَا يَابِسٍ إِلَّا فِى كِتَـٰبٍ مُّبِينٍ ﴾

And with Him are the keys of the *ghayb* (all that is hidden), none knows them but He. And He knows whatever there is in (or on) the earth and in the sea; not a leaf falls, but He knows it. There is not a grain in the darkness of the earth nor anything fresh or dry, but is written in a Clear Record.

[Sūrah al-An'ām 6:59]

His statement, **"none knows them but He,"** is a restriction. Therefore, none knows the unseen except Allāh or the one whom Allāh reveals something from the unseen to, from His messengers, in order to bring about a benefit to humanity and as a miracle for the messenger. However, none knows the unseen by virtue of himself; he only knows the unseen by way of Allāh teaching it to him. Therefore, none knows the unseen but Allāh. He who claims knowledge of the unseen is claiming to be a sharer with Allāh in that which is specific to Him, Glorified be He; therefore, he is a *mushrik*, he is a *ṭāghūt*, and he is a disbeliever. This is the greatest of the types of apostasy from al-Islām.

ORIGINAL TEXT

...وَ مَنْ حَكَمَ بِغَيْرِ مَا أَنْزَلَ اللهُ.

5) He who rules by other than what Allāh has sent down.

EXPLANATION

Fifth is the one who rules by other than what Allāh has sent down. The proof is the statement of the Most High:

﴿ يُرِيدُونَ أَن يَتَحَاكَمُوا إِلَى الطَّاغُوتِ ﴾

They wish to go for judgment (in their disputes) to the *ṭāghūt* (false judges, etc.).

[Sūrah an-Nisā' 4:60]

The one who rules by other than what Allāh has sent down, deeming this to be permissible, then he is a *ṭāghūt*. The one who says that it is permissible to rule by way of the [worldly] laws, or by the policies of the time of Jāhiliyyah, or by the policies of the tribes and the Bedouins; and they leave off the legislation, saying that this is *ḥalāl* or that it is the equivalent to what Allāh has sent down; or if he says this is better than what Allāh has sent down or equivalent to what Allāh has sent down; or he says that it is permissible only, not saying that it is equal or better, but saying that it is *ḥalāl* and permissible—then this one is considered to be a *ṭāghūt*.

This is by way of the text of the Qur'ān, for the Most High has stated:

﴿ يُرِيدُونَ أَن يَتَحَاكَمُوا إِلَى الطَّاغُوتِ ﴾

They wish to go for judgment (in their disputes) to the *ṭāghūt* (false judges, etc.)

[Sūrah an-Nisā' 4:60]

Therefore, He has named them *aṭ-ṭāghūt* because they have transgressed the limit. As for the one who rules by other than what Allāh has sent down while he affirms that what Allāh has sent down is obligatory to follow, and that it is the truth and it is not falsehood, and that what he is ruling by is falsehood—then this individual is considered to be one who has disbelieved with minor *kufr*, which does not expel one from the religion. However, he is in great danger and upon a path that may lead him to the *kufr* that expels one from the religion, if he is negligent regarding this matter.

As for the one who unintentionally rules by other than what Allāh sent down—rather, by way of *ijtihād* (deductive reasoning), and he is from the people qualified to make *ijtihād* from the jurists, and he makes *ijtihād* but he was not correct regarding the ruling of Allāh and he erred in his *ijtihād*—then this one will be forgiven.

The Prophet ﷺ said:

إِذَا حَكَمَ الْحَاكِمُ، فَاجْتَهَدَ، ثُمَّ أَصَابَ، فَلَهُ أَجْرَانِ، وَ إِنْ حَكَمَ وَاجْتَهَدَ، فَأَخْطَأَ، فَلَهُ أَجْرٌ.

When the judge rules and makes *ijtihād* and is correct, then he receives two rewards. If he makes *ijtihād* and errs, then he receives one reward.[8]

This is because he did not intentionally err. He desired the truth and he desired to conform to the ruling of Allāh ﷻ; however, he did not conform to it. He is to be excused [for his error] and rewarded. However, it is not permissible to follow him in his error. It is not permissible for us to follow him upon his error.

Based upon this, the *ijtihād* of the jurists in which they erred, or the *ijtihād* of the judges in the courts—if they make *ijtihād* and exert their effort in seeking to arrive at the truth, but they did not arrive at it, then their errors are forgiven.

ORIGINAL TEXT

وَ الدَّلِيلُ قَوْلُهُ تَعَالَى: ﴿ لَا إِكْرَاهَ فِي الدِّينِ ۖ قَد تَّبَيَّنَ الرُّشْدُ مِنَ الْغَيِّ ۚ فَمَن يَكْفُرْ بِالطَّاغُوتِ وَيُؤْمِن بِاللَّهِ فَقَدِ اسْتَمْسَكَ بِالْعُرْوَةِ الْوُثْقَىٰ لَا انفِصَامَ لَهَا ۗ وَاللَّهُ سَمِيعٌ عَلِيمٌ ﴾.

The evidence is the statement of the Most High:

There is no compulsion in religion. Verily, the Right

[8] Al-Bukhārī reported it (#7352), as did Muslim (#1716) from the *ḥadīth* of 'Amr bin al-'Āṣ ﷺ.

Path has become distinct from the wrong path. Whoever disbelieves in *ṭāghūt* and believes in Allāh, then he has grasped the most trustworthy handhold that will never break. And Allāh is All-Hearer, All-Knower.

[Sūrah al-Baqarah 2:256]

EXPLANATION

Allāh ﷾ has stated:

﴿لَا إِكْرَاهَ فِي الدِّينِ ۖ قَد تَّبَيَّنَ الرُّشْدُ مِنَ الْغَيِّ ۚ فَمَن يَكْفُرْ بِالطَّاغُوتِ وَيُؤْمِن بِاللَّهِ فَقَدِ اسْتَمْسَكَ بِالْعُرْوَةِ الْوُثْقَىٰ لَا انفِصَامَ لَهَا ۗ وَاللَّهُ سَمِيعٌ عَلِيمٌ﴾

There is no compulsion in religion. Verily, the Right Path has become distinct from the wrong path. Whoever disbelieves in *ṭāghūt* and believes in Allāh, then he has grasped the most trustworthy handhold that will never break. And Allāh is All-Hearer, All-Knower.

[Sūrah al-Baqarah 2:256]

Regarding His statement, **"There is no compulsion in religion"**: The meaning is that an individual is not forced to enter al-Islām. This is because entrance into Islām must be by way of conviction and belief within the heart, and no one is compelled to enter it. The hearts are not controlled except by Allāh ﷾. No one is compelled to enter Islām because we do not have power over the hearts. Only Allāh ﷾ has power over them and controls them. However, we call to Islām and we incite the people towards it. We strive in the cause of Allāh against those who disbelieve, in order to spread Islām, to extend the opportunity to he who wishes to embrace Islām, and in order to subdue the enemies of Allāh. As for guidance, then it is in the Hand of Allāh ﷾. No one is compelled to believe and to enter Islām. These things only return to Him.

Then, the Most High said, **"the Right Path has become distinct**

from the wrong path": Hence, Islām—and for Allāh is all praise—contains nothing that one would detest. Rather, all of it is beloved and desirable.

Disbelief and *shirk* are completely evil and undesirable. The two have become clearly distinguished from one another. Guidance and the truth have become distinct from misguidance, which is falsehood. The person has an intellect, and he has intelligence by which he can weigh the truth and falsehood. Therefore, his intellect—if it is pure and upright—shall guide him away from desires and hindrances in the path. His sound intellect shall guide him to the acceptance of the truth without compulsion.

This is one statement regarding the verse. The second statement is that this verse was revealed regarding the People of the Book, and that the People of the Book are not compelled to enter Islām. Rather, if they want to remain upon their religion, then they may do so with the condition that they pay the *jizyah* to the Muslims and that they are humiliated. As for other than them from the disbelievers, then nothing is accepted from them except Islām or death because they do not have a religion, and idolatry is a false religion.

The third statement is that this verse has been abrogated by way of the verses of *jihād*. [It is said that] this verse was revealed at the beginning of the affair, before *jihād* was legislated; then *jihād* was legislated and this verse was abrogated.

However, the first statement is the one that is correct: the verse is not abrogated, and the religion does not enter the hearts by way of compulsion. It only enters by way of choice. However, he who does not accept the religion is dealt with with what is suitable for him, from killing or acceptance of the *jizyah*, from that which Allāh has legislated regarding him.

Allāh says, **"Whoever disbelieves in *aṭ-ṭāghūt* and believes in Allāh"**: What is intended by *aṭ-ṭāghūt* here is all forms of *aṭ-ṭāghūt:* in worship, following, or obedience. This is because the word *ṭāghūt* here is general. Therefore, He mentioned disbelieving in *ṭāghūt* before mentioning *īmān* in Allāh, because *īmān* in Allāh does not benefit except after disbelieving in *aṭ-ṭāghūt*. So, he who believes in Allāh and does not disbelieve in *aṭ-ṭāghūt*, his *īmān* will not benefit him. Hence, the one who says that he is a believer, who prays, fasts, pays *zakāh*, makes Ḥajj, and does acts of obedience, but he does not free himself from *shirk* nor from the polytheists, and he says, "I have nothing against them," then this individual is not considered a Muslim, because he has not disbelieved in *aṭ-ṭāghūt*.

Therefore, it is necessary to disbelieve in *aṭ-ṭāghūt*; this means to reject *aṭ-ṭāghūt*, to believe that it is false, and to distance oneself from it and its people. This is a must. Therefore, *īmān* is not correct except after disbelief in *aṭ-ṭāghūt*.

In another verse, Allāh says:

﴿ وَلَقَدْ بَعَثْنَا فِي كُلِّ أُمَّةٍ رَّسُولًا أَنِ اعْبُدُوا اللَّهَ وَاجْتَنِبُوا الطَّاغُوتَ ﴾

And verily, We have sent among every *ummah* (community, nation) a messenger (proclaiming): "Worship Allāh (alone), and avoid (or keep away from) *ṭāghūt*."

[Sūrah an-Naḥl 16:36]

So, the worship of Allāh is not correct except by way of avoiding *aṭ-ṭāghūt*. Two opposites do not unite. *Īmān* and *kufr* do not unite within the heart. *Īmān* and major *kufr* do not unite within the heart. As for minor *kufr*, then perhaps it may unite with *īmān*.

ORIGINAL TEXT

وَ هَذَا هُوَ مَعْنَى لَا إِلَهَ إِلَّا اللهُ، وَ فِي الْحَدِيثِ: ((رَأْسُ الْأَمْرِ الْإِسْلَامُ، وَ عُمُودُهُ الصَّلَاةُ، وَ ذُرْوَةُ سَنَامِهِ الْجِهَادُ فِي سَبِيلِ اللهِ.))

This is the meaning of *lā ilāha ill-Allāh* (none has the right to be worshiped except Allāh). And in the *ḥadīth* it says:

The head of the matter is al-Islām; its supporting pillar is the prayer, and its apex is *jihād* in the path of Allāh.[9]

EXPLANATION

The Shaykh has said, "*This is the meaning of lā ilāha ill-Allāh*": Meaning, disbelief in *aṭ-ṭāghūt* and belief in Allāh. Islām is to submit to Allāh in *at-tawḥīd*, to yield to Him in obedience, and to separate oneself from *shirk* and its people. This is the head of the affair of the religion. The two testimonies are the head of al-Islām and they are the origin of al-Islām. Therefore, an individual does not enter Islām unless he brings the two testimonies in statement, knowledge, action, and belief. An individual is not Muslim except by way of that.

The religion resembles a body that has a head, supporting legs, and a highest point. So, if the head is cut or there is no head for it, then it will not remain alive. Likewise, without *at-tawḥīd*, the religion will not remain, because it is the head; if it is cut or it discontinues, then life discontinues or the body will be corrupted.

The supporting pillar upon which it stands is the prayer. Without the supporting pillar, Islām will not stand, similar to a house made of fur or a tent. If there is no support for it to stand upon, then it will not stand, for a house will not stand except by way of supports. Therefore, if the supports are lost, then the house will not stand. Similarly, if the prayer is lost, then Islām will not stand.

Due to that, the scholars say that whoever abandons the prayer out of laziness has disbelieved—based on the correct statement—even if he acknowledges its obligation. This is because there is no benefit in acknowledging the obligation while not applying it and acting upon it. There is no benefit in that. Due to that, the verifiers from the people of knowledge ruled with disbelief upon the one who

---

[9] At-Tirmidhī reported it (#2616), as did an-Nasā'ī in *Al-Kubrā* (10/214-215, #11330) from the *ḥadīth* of Mu'ādh bin Jabal 📛.

abandons the prayer intentionally, even if he affirms its obligation. As for the one who rejects its obligation, then he is a disbeliever based on the consensus of the Muslims.

His statement, **"and its apex is *jihād* in the path of Allāh"**: The apex of the affair—meaning, the religion—is *jihād* in the path of Allāh, for *jihād* is a proof of the strength of al-Islām. When *jihād* is present in the path of Allāh, then this is a proof of the strength of al-Islām. This is because *jihād* is only by way of strength in *īmān* as well as tangible strength.

Therefore, the Prophet ﷺ (in this *ḥadīth*) mentioned three things for the religion: a head, a supporting pillar, and a highest point. With the absence of the head, there is no foundation present for the religion, for the one who does not actualize the head (which is *at-tawḥīd*) does not have a religion. In addition, the one who does not pray, then his religion will not stand, even if he testifies that none has the right to be worshiped except Allāh and Muḥammad is the Messenger of Allāh; he is in need of a supporting pillar upon which the religion will stand, and it is not present except by way of the prayer. Moreover, if *jihād* is lost, then the strength of Islām is lost and Islām will become weak, and the Muslims shall become weak; there is no strength for Islām and the Muslims except by way of *jihād* in the path of Allāh ﷻ. Therefore, it is a sign of strength, and it being lost is a sign of weakness.

This is the meaning of the Messenger ﷺ striking a similitude for these three affairs of the religion: the head, the supporting pillar, and the highest point. Just like how, if the camel has a hump, that indicates it is strong, and if it does not have a hump, then this indicates that it is slow and weak. Similarly, the Muslims today are weak within the earth. Due to this, it has been narrated in the *ḥadīth*:

إِذَا تَبَايَعْتُمْ بِالْعِينَةِ وَ أَخَذْتُمْ أَذْنَابَ الْبَقَرِ وَ رَضِيتُمْ بِالزَّرْعِ وَ تَرَكْتُمُ الْجِهَادَ سَلَّطَ اللهُ عَلَيْكُمْ ذُلاًّ لَا يَنْزِعُهُ حَتَّى تَرْجِعُوا إِلَى دِينِكُمْ.

If you deal in *ribā* and you hold to the tails of cows and abandon *jihād,* then Allāh will cause humility to overtake you and will not remove it from you until you return to your religion.[10]

Therefore, the abandonment of *jihād* is humiliation and weakness for the Muslims, and its presence is evidence of strength and influence; this is similar to the apex of animals, and Allāh knows best.

May prayers and peace be upon our Prophet Muḥammad.

This concludes the explanation of this blessed book, *The Three Fundamental Principles.*

[10] Abū Dāwūd reported it (#3462) from the *ḥadīth* of Ibn 'Umar ﷺ.